My Work Is That of Conservation

environmental history and the american south

My Work Is That of Conservation

AN ENVIRONMENTAL BIOGRAPHY OF

GEORGE WASHINGTON CARVER

Mark D. Hersey

The University of Georgia Press | Athens and London

A Sarah Mills Hodge Fund Publication
This publication is made possible in part through a grant from
the Hodge Foundation in memory of its founder, Sarah Mills
Hodge, who devoted her life to the relief and education of
African Americans in Savannah, Georgia.

Set in 10.5/13.5 Adobe Caslon Pro by BookComp, Inc.

Printed digitally in the United States of America

Library of Congress Cataloging-in-Publication Data
Hersey, Mark D.
  My work is that of conservation : an environmental biography
of George Washington Carver / Mark D. Hersey.
      p. cm. — (Environmental history and the American South)
  Includes bibilographical references.
  ISBN-13: 978-0-8203-3088-4 (hardcover : alk. paper)
  ISBN-10: 0-8203-3088-4 (hardcover : alk. paper)
  ISBN-13: 978-0-8203-3870-5 (pbk. : alk. paper)
  ISBN-10: 0-8203-3870-2 (pbk. : alk. paper)
   1. Carver, George Washington, 1864?-1943. 2. Carver,
George Washington, 1864?-1943—Political and social views.
3. Agriculturists—United States—Biography. 4. African
American agriculturists—Biography. 5. African American
scientists—Biography. 6. Conservationists—Southern States—
Biography. 7. Agricultural conservation—Black Belt (Ala. and
Miss.)—History. 8. African American farmers—Black Belt
(Ala. and Miss.)—History. 9. Environmental protection—Black
Belt (Ala. and Miss.)—History. 10. Black Belt (Ala. and
Miss.)—Environmental conditions. I. Title.
  S417.C3H47 2011
  630.92—dc22
  [B]   2010043987

British Library Cataloging-in-Publication Data available

To Laurie

CONTENTS

FOREWORD

Few prominent figures in U.S. history have become quite so two-dimensional as George Washington Carver. Once "the most widely recognized and admired black man in America," acclaimed for his scientific and technological expertise and lauded as a model of African American achievement, Carver today is relegated to children's textbooks and inspirational literature. I know this to be true, for while I have never covered Carver in either my U.S. history or my environmental history course, and while none of the college-level textbooks weighing down my shelves have Carver in their indexes, I helped my older son, *on two different occasions* during his elementary school career, complete class projects on Carver. It is as if the legacy of Carver has been imprisoned in the countless shoebox dioramas that continue to dramatize his 105 ways of preparing the peanut.

Serious historians have a hard time knowing what to make of Carver. For a while he served as a contributionist hero, proof-in-the-flesh that racist theories of black inferiority could not withstand close scrutiny. For much of the twentieth century, many saw Carver, as *Time* magazine referred to him in 1941 (in reference to his skill as a painter as well as his other capabilities and achievements), as a "Black Leonardo." But such contributionist heroes are less useful to a nation transformed by the modern civil rights movement—except, perhaps, to children in elementary school. Thus, we are left with Carver the "Peanut Man," whose apparent chief claim to fame was his advocacy for the lowly goober—not only as a nitrogen-fixing alternative to the destructiveness of southern cotton culture but also as a source, like Henry Ford's beloved soybean, of all sorts of useful chemurgical by-products. And as we have come to understand more fully the pathologies that ate away at the southern agricultural economy in the late nineteenth and early twentieth centuries, it has become only too easy to depict Carver's enthusiasm for the peanut as the functional equivalent of Michael Dukakis's infamous suggestion in the heat of the 1988 Iowa caucus that the crisis of the family farm might be solved by planting Belgian endive.

And yet, as Mark Hersey makes clear in this powerful new study, much has been lost in the marginalization of Carver. Hersey's chief claim—and it is at once a compelling and subtle one—is that we need to take Carver seriously as a central figure in the American environmental tradition. "My work is that of conservation," Carver maintained late in his life, insisting that his advocacy for the South's African American farmers was of a piece with the broader conservation movement of the first half of the twentieth century. What did Carver mean by that, and how did his work and thought fit within that movement? To answer those questions, Hersey argues, we need to understand the fullness of Carver's life.

Hersey's environmental biography of Carver has several striking elements. First, Hersey portrays George Washington Carver the native midwesterner who, as a child and young adult, was quick to find wonder in the natural world. Although Carver frequently felt the sting of racial discrimination and witnessed racial violence, he grew up in a largely white world that offered him pockets of freedom. In the early 1890s he found himself at the Iowa Agricultural College (IAC) in Ames (now Iowa State University), where he completed undergraduate and master's degrees in agricultural science and worked with several leaders in the field. Indeed, it was at IAC that Carver, under the tutelage of botanist Louis Pammel, became both an accomplished naturalist and a trained practitioner of the new science of ecology. The rich scientific milieu of Ames put Carver at the center of one of the most important environmental developments of the late nineteenth century—the rise of the applied ecological and agricultural sciences and the growth of both governmental and university interest in research to serve the nation's farmers. One wonders what might have become of Carver if he had stayed in the Midwest and found a place in the agricultural research establishment developing there.

But he didn't. When Carver stepped off of a train in Macon County, Alabama, in 1896—just a year after his new boss, Booker T. Washington, delivered his "Atlanta Compromise" address and at the same moment that de jure segregation was taking hold on the South—he entered a foreign world, and Hersey gives us a full environmental rendering of the place that Carver would call home for the next half century. Macon County was at the very heart of the Black Belt, a region dominated by plantation production of cotton and worked by a largely African American labor force suffering under the various degrading iterations of tenancy. Unlike the Midwest, where science and technology were already being applied to agriculture in transformative ways, the plantation South seemed retrograde—poor tenants farmed small plots with mules and crude tools as they struggled to stay out of debt in a system stacked against them. And the land—galled and gullied and exhausted from the ordeal—provided supporting evidence that these circumstances were neither just nor sustainable.

The myth of Carver, to a certain degree, is that he brought science, invention, and diversification to the Black Belt by offering a blueprint for how farmers might escape the stranglehold of cotton. But Hersey suggests the truth was subtler. In his rendering, Carver's chief innovation was his attempt to bring a practical ecological approach to the problems of the region's African American farmers— to suggest that they might improve themselves and the lands they worked not only by leaving cotton behind but also by looking to the resources of local landscapes to restore fertility and rejuvenate their lands. Study the natural world, Carver implored the region's black farmers, to find answers not only to the land's decline but also to their own empowerment. Carver, in other words, was quick to appreciate the strong connections between land use and poverty, and he came to believe that environmental improvement might bring economic and social improvement as well.

While Hersey readily admits that Carver's approach had shortcomings, he nonetheless shows Carver's prescriptions for agricultural reform to have been quietly subversive. More than that, he gives us a figure who over several decades consciously adapted the tools of agricultural and ecological science to the problems of Black Belt tenants and smallholders. Carver may not have led a frontal assault on the Jim Crow power structure in Macon County, but he did adapt the tools he brought with him from Ames to the local conditions in some fascinating ways. Indeed, to a large degree Carver's environmental vision emerged when his formal training collided with the denuded landscapes and impoverished farmers of Macon County. By giving us this portrait of Carver as an African American agrarian conservationist, Hersey challenges readers not only to rethink their understanding of what constituted the conservation movement but also to recognize that Carver was an important forebear of what we would today call ecological or sustainable agriculture.

My Work Is That of Conservation does not treat Carver as an environmental hero; Hersey is not interested in replacing one two-dimensional hagiography with another. But it does ask its readers to recognize Carver's deep affection for and connection with the natural world, an affinity that Carver often talked about in religious terms. Indeed, Hersey rightly suggests that we cannot fully fathom Carver's environmental vision or the work of agricultural conservation that defined his later life without understanding Carver as a religious person who, during an era when secular science and fundamentalist Christianity seemed in constant tension, creatively reconciled his commitment to the scientific study of nature with his Christian faith. Moreover, Hersey provides an uncommonly careful assessment of what Carver did and did not accomplish as an agricultural scientist, a vital exercise, given the mythos that guides so much the current popular appreciation of Carver's historical importance. Hersey is frank in his recognition that Carver's scientific accomplishments have been overblown, but in correcting that misapprehension he gives us a different Carver to study and admire.

Carver's life and accomplishments at Tuskegee, according to Hersey, were inescapably shaped by the larger reality that the South's African Americans often experienced their second-class citizenship as an environmental predicament. It is perhaps no mistake that the postwar civil rights movement, whose great success contributed to Carver's slow fade from prominence, proceeded with force only when so many of those connections between African Americans and the land—connections that were at once rich and confining—were severed. That, of course, is another story, and one that still awaits adequate historical treatment. What Mark Hersey gives us in this full and fair rendering of George Washington Carver's life and work is the portrait of a man who struggled creatively to resolve that environmental predicament. It is a story that will redefine our sense of Carver's importance.

Paul S. Sutter

ACKNOWLEDGMENTS

This book owes its origins to a conversation I had with Donald Worster nearly a decade ago following his return from a trip that took him through Tuskegee, Alabama. Then a rudderless graduate student at the University of Kansas still contemplating a number of ill-conceived dissertation topics, I had the great fortune to have an adviser who could steer me in productive directions, and it was Don who first pointed me toward Carver. As the germ of an idea became a dissertation and then a book, I racked up an enormous debt of gratitude to a long list of individuals. Much of the credit for the book's merits belongs to them; the fault for any shortcomings rests entirely with me.

In Lawrence, Don's incisive questions and suggestions were supplemented by those of a number of fine scholars, most especially Ken Armitage, Karl Brooks, Paul Kelton, Bruce Mactavish, and Jeff Moran. My collegial and talented peers in the graduate program collectively served as a sounding board for the project as it developed. Among those who merit special note for helping to clarify my argument and writing are Kevin Armitage, Lisa Brady, Robb Campbell, Brian Drake, John Egan, Henry Fortunato, Jerry Frank, John Grigg, Maril Hazlett, Shen Hou, and John McCool.

The generosity of Randy and Terri Mullis in providing a place for me to stay in Alabama enabled me to carry out longer research forays than would otherwise have been possible. The same might be said of Rich Megraw, who not only encouraged me to go to graduate school while I was an undergraduate at the University of Alabama, but put me up when I was researching in Tuscaloosa. James Pritchard and Dianne Debinski welcomed me into their home and fed me while I was in Ames, setting a standard for scholarly hospitality that I can only hope to emulate in the coming years.

I also owe heartfelt thanks to two first-rate scholars whose work on Carver provided a foundation for mine and whose support has facilitated this project enormously: Linda McMurry Edwards and Gray Kremer provided feedback on the manuscript at various stages and saved me from some embarrassing errors. If this book can stand proudly on the shelf next to theirs, it is a success indeed. A third Carver scholar, John Ferrell, also gave me valuable assistance, both in breaking ground on Carver's environmental thought and in offering his comments on portions of the manuscript.

Dana Chandler, Cynthia Wilson, and the late Sandra Peck from Tuskegee's archives granted me liberal access to Carver materials. Likewise, Curtis Gregory of the National Park Service was more than generous in providing me with materials, and Michele Christian, collections archivist at Iowa State's Parks Library in Ames, went above and beyond in helping me gather documents. The Robert L. Greaves, Ambrose Saricks, and Arthur and Judith McClure families all provided financial backing for the research that went into this project, as did the State Historical Society of Iowa.

A handful of scholars went out of their way to assist me. Foremost among these is Mart Stewart, who read portions of the dissertation, suggested sources, met with me at conferences, and encouraged me to ask difficult questions about the South's environmental history. In the last of these efforts he was joined by Tim Silver, a model scholar in the field. While I was writing the dissertation, Dianne Glave provided important suggestions about the ways in which Carver offers insights into African American environmental thought. Kimberly Smith did the same for the book manuscript and helped me reframe the work in some important ways. Ryan Schumacher, a superb editor, generously commented on the entire manuscript.

I am particularly fortunate to have colleagues at Mississippi State whose research interests overlap with mine. Among them, Alan Marcus provided comments on portions of the manuscript and Jim Giesen was a frequent sounding-board. I am equally lucky to have exceptional editors working with me at the University of Georgia Press. Andrew Berzanskis, Derek Krissof, and John Joerschke have helped to walk me through the publishing process. Mindy Conner, whom the press wisely trusted with the copyediting, sharpened the writing and kindly indulged my frequent questions. But I chose the press in no small measure because it afforded me the opportunity to work with Paul Sutter, an exemplary scholar who rewarded my choice by proving to be everything I thought he would be as a series editor.

John Beeler at the University of Alabama and Peter Wallenstein at Virginia Tech offered encouragement at vital times. My parents, Rich and Rose, instilled in me a love of learning and inadvertently fostered my appreciation of things agricultural by frequently taking me to the Catskills, where I grew curious about the abandoned farmland I encountered there. My brothers, Brian and Eric, patiently tolerated discursions about Carver on many occasions, as did my in-laws: Gil and Linda, Kelly and Joe, Lance and Katie, Devon, and Elna. If they didn't always understand what I was doing, their support remained unflagging. While the late Dan Bradley will not see this book in print, it would not have been completed had I not known him. My children, Jenna and Andrew, arrived after most of the research for this book was finished, but their presence has given it a new, more profound meaning.

My wife, Laurie, helped with this book in too many ways to be enumerated. This book is dedicated to her: my love, my friend, my editor, and my true companion in life's myriad adventures.

Mark Hersey
Gilboa, New York
May 2010

Parts of this book appeared previously in different form as "Hints and Suggestions to Farmers: George Washington Carver and Rural Conservation in the South," *Environmental History* 11 (April 2006): 239–68. Reprinted with permission of Oxford University Press.

Parts of chapter 6 appeared previously in different form as "'Their Plows Singing beneath the Sandy Loam': African American Agriculture in the Late-Nineteenth-Century South," in *African Americans in the Nineteenth Century: People and Perspectives*, ed. Dixie Ray Haggard. Copyright 2010 by ABC-CLIO, LLC. All rights reserved. Reproduced with permission of ABC-CLIO, LLC, Santa Barbara, California.

Parts of chapter 6 appeared previously in different form as "The Transformation of George Washington Carver's Environmental Vision, 1896–1918," in *Land and Power: Sustainable Agriculture and African Americans*, ed. Jeffrey Jordan, Edward Pennick, Walter A. Hill, and Robert Zabawa, 57–76 (SARE, 2009).

My Work Is That of Conservation

Macon County, Alabama, 1896

In the autumn of 1896 George Washington Carver stepped down from a train in Macon County, Alabama. As the only African American then holding an advanced degree in agricultural science, he arrived in the Deep South with a head full of knowledge and a deeply held conviction that God had chosen him to be of service to his people. A native midwesterner, Carver could hardly have been less prepared for the social, economic, and ecological realities he encountered in Alabama. Arriving as he did in October, he must have seen African American tenant families wearily picking cotton in dozens of scarred and denuded fields as the train stretched its way across Alabama. The gentle fields of Iowa would have seemed very far away.

Standing on that platform, Carver did not know that Macon County would be his home for the remainder of his life, let alone that during his last years he would become the most widely recognized and admired black man in America. He would not have considered himself a chemist, and having never worked with peanuts, he could not have imagined how completely he would one day be identified with them. But Carver felt sure he understood the eroded and exhausted fields surrounding him. He was, after all, an agriculturist by training and would spend the better part of his life thinking about how people ought to interact with the natural world, especially through agriculture. Indeed, as he discovered that several of the tenets of conventional scientific agriculture proved impracticable for most African American farmers in the region, he would adapt them to the circumstances, and in so doing become a prophet of sustainable agriculture.

During his first two decades at Tuskegee, in fact, Carver waged a campaign to persuade impoverished black farmers to adopt a modified version of scientific agriculture that promised both to help them gain economic independence and to revitalize the land itself—the two goals, he believed, were intertwined. He encouraged rural African Americans to defend themselves against the economic and political vicissitudes they faced by turning to the natural world. By learning to abhor waste and to appreciate the "mutual relationship of the animal, mineral and vegetable kingdoms," farmers could satisfy many of their needs and wants with things they encountered every day but either overlooked or neglected.[1] For a number of reasons, Carver's campaign ultimately failed to lift African American farmers out of their desperate poverty and restore the vitality of southern soils, but it shaped his thinking in profound ways and helped foment one of the early twentieth century's most distinctive conservation ethics.

Carver, however, is not remembered as a conservationist. He is instead the Peanut Man, a caricature so shrouded in mythology that talking about his real accomplishments proves difficult. Like Thomas Jefferson, Carver is something of a sphinx.[2] Few Americans have been held up as a hero by both the United Daughters of the Confederacy and the National Association for the Advancement of Colored People, by Christian fundamentalists and advocates of gay rights, by supporters of industrial agriculture and environmentalists. In the years since his death, postage stamps and commemorative coins bearing his image have been distributed; dozens of buildings—especially schools—have been named in his honor; his birthplace has been set aside as a national monument; a nuclear submarine has been christened in his honor; and a U.S. Department of Agriculture building has been dedicated in his name.

Carver thus left a rather disjointed legacy. In popular culture he remains the Peanut Man. A staple of elementary and junior high school social-studies classes and the subject of manifold children's, juvenile, and religious hagiographies, he is celebrated for helping to overthrow King Cotton by convincing southerners to plant peanuts and developing peanut products to create a market for them. Popular television shows from *Saturday Night Live* to *Seinfeld* to *American Dad* have run episodes in which Carver figures prominently. Musical artists from children's entertainers to Stevie Wonder have crafted songs about him.[3] And every February, as America celebrates Black History Month, television networks roll out paeans to Carver and advertisers manipulate his reputation to push their products.[4] In February 2006, for instance, Southwest Airlines' in-flight magazine, *Spirit*, carried a tribute to Carver that drew a tenuous link between the famous scientist and the airline (peanuts are "the official snack of Southwest Airlines"). "Although best known for his work with the humble peanut, George Washington Carver spent years revolutionizing the farming industry," the magazine claimed. "His agricultural genius not only salvaged the economy of the South during the early 1900s, but secured his place in history as one of the most influential botanists of all time." A remarkable assertion, to be sure, but unfortunately not one grounded in fact.[5]

Indeed, *Spirit*'s tribute speaks as much to the divide between academic historians and the public as to Carver's enduring popularity. To be sure, scholars have paid scant attention to him since the 1970s, when they debunked his reputation as a scientist and recast him as an Uncle Tom for his relative silence on racial injustice.[6] In 1981 Linda O. McMurry rectified this depiction to a considerable extent in her excellent and balanced biography, *George Washington Carver: Scientist and Symbol*, the first book-length, scholarly treatment of the man. The publication of Gary Kremer's *George Washington Carver: In His Own Words* (1987), an edited collection of Carver's writings and the only other scholarly book on Carver to date notwithstanding, historians have seemingly been of the opinion that McMurry's biography put an end to the matter.[7] Most apparently agree with the conclusion Pulitzer Prize–winning historian David Herbert Donald reached in his otherwise favorable review of the biography: Carver is "no longer part of our usable past."[8]

Such a conclusion is shortsighted for many reasons, most especially because these critiques of Carver were directed more at the myths surrounding him than at his actual achievements. The mythical Carver was the Peanut Man, a cultural icon whose scientific contributions were emphasized and inflated, obscuring the legitimate reasons for his place in modern American history.[9] As Linda McMurry first pointed out, it is one of the great ironies of Carver's life that his undeserved fame as a "creative chemist" obscured the work for which he rightly merits continued attention.

Perhaps it was inevitable that a capitalist nation would judge Carver's agricultural vision on the basis of its industrial and economic merits. Scientists are generally evaluated by their contributions to knowledge (theoretical science) or their commercial innovations (applied science). Carver's list of such accomplishments is small indeed. Ironically, if he had pursued his PhD in botany when he had the opportunity to do so at the turn of the twentieth century, historians might have left his reputation as a scientist intact; it is unlikely, however, that anyone reading this today would have heard of him. Few Americans can name any mycologists. The name George Washington Carver would likely have lingered in comparative anonymity, like that of his mentor, Louis Pammel, or Howard biologist Ernest Just.[10]

The real Carver thought in farseeing, if sometimes contradictory, ways about the relationship between people and nature. I am hardly the first person to recognize this fact. McMurry asserted that "the philosophy of Carver became relevant" only after the birth of the modern environmental movement, when people began "to accept what Carver tried to say—that only short-term success can come to any system that ignores the whole, that man cannot subvert and destroy the environment without destroying himself."[11] McMurry's biography focuses on Carver's significance as a scientist and a racial symbol, however, and devotes little space to the actual substance of his environmental work. Only in the conclusion did she suggest that Carver might be considered something of an environmental visionary.

More recently, Carver has attracted increasing attention from those concerned with environmental issues. John Ferrell's *Fruits of Creation: A Look at Global Sustainability as Seen through the Eyes of George Washington Carver*, published in 1995 by the Christian Society of the Green Cross, assembles a wide array of Carver's quotations in linking him to the modern environmental movement. Less than a decade ago, the National Park Service commissioned a study of Carver carried out by Peter Duncan Burchard that resulted in a publication titled *George Washington Carver: For His Time and Ours*.[12] An even more impressive collection of quotations than Ferrell's, this study links Carver to myriad contemporary issues, environmental and otherwise. And yet there remains a yawning historiographical gap calling for a study that examines Carver's work along conservation lines and places it within the historical context of its time. That is what this book seeks to do.

This is an examination of Carver's conservation *work*, a word deliberately chosen but not narrowly construed. Too often the histories of conservation and environmentalism are histories of ideas that emphasize the intellectual frameworks of leaders rather than the work of those who made up the movement. This is perhaps nowhere more evident than in accounts of conservation's emergence as a politically influential movement during Carver's lifetime. The fight over whether or not to construct a dam in Yosemite's Hetch Hetchy Valley that pitted John Muir and his "preservationist" ideas against Gifford Pinchot and his "conservationist" ideas, for example, was undeniably important, but it has attracted disproportionate attention. The consensus view that, above all, conservation saw the triumph of a technocratic and bureaucratic elite to oversee the rational consumption of natural resources has marginalized the work of those who do not fit neatly into that paradigm.[13] Among other things, the perception of conservation as principally an intellectual movement has marginalized those who supported the movement's agrarian impulses and others whose appreciation of the natural world was rooted in a working landscape rather than wilderness. As a consequence, Carver—a famous figure who made no effort to conceal his conservationist leanings—has been more or less neglected both by historians of late nineteenth- and early twentieth-century conservation and by those involved in the environmental movement.

Carver's work was rooted in ideas, of course: ideas about the interdependence of the natural world, ideas about how impoverished African American farmers could overcome the obstacles facing them, and ideas about the ways in which God revealed himself through nature. But it was no less rooted in his upbringing; his scholarly training; his experiences (both serendipitous and otherwise); and the larger social, political, scientific, and ecological contexts in which he labored. Indeed, Carver merits a place in discussions of the conservation movement not because he articulated an original and profound environmental philosophy, but because he was the most important and influential African American conservationist of his day and because his work highlights a neglected aspect of the larger movement.

Carver's Progressive Era campaign on behalf of impoverished black farmers lies at the center of this work, but the study neither begins nor ends there. The experiences of Carver's youth and his formal training at the Iowa Agricultural College provided the foundation from which he would launch that campaign. And he did not abandon his environmental ideals when his campaign came to a close during World War I. On the contrary, those ideals continued to shape his career. Carver's deep religious sensibilities, which blended Christianity with a profound veneration of the natural world that bordered on mysticism, shaped his work as well. Indeed, many of his writings and speeches, especially those from his later years, contain paeans to nature and warnings about violating its limits that would do justice to the environmental movement's more celebrated heroes. Thus, in looking back over his career, an elderly Carver would insist that the entirety of his life's work might be categorized under the heading of conservation—a phrase borrowed to title this book.

Almost necessarily, then, this is a biography, albeit perhaps an unconventional one. It does not purport to be comprehensive or to offer a definitive account of Carver's life, and it is not intended to scuttle McMurry's study of Carver's significance as a scientist and symbol. Instead it traces, assesses, and contextualizes the development and transformation of Carver's environmental vision, the ways his life came to embody a neglected aspect of American conservation, and how his conservation work came to be forgotten. Aspects of Carver's life that do not address those issues are marginalized here.

Moreover, Carver's work is unintelligible outside the context of the landscape that most shaped it. Macon County, of which Tuskegee is the seat, lies in the Black Belt of Alabama, where, to paraphrase Louis XIV, the crop-lien system supported agriculture in much the same way a noose supports a condemned man.[14] Since the depleted fields of Macon County's working landscape were in large measure a relic of this system, its agroecosystems bore the marks of political and social relationships. Consequently, Carver's attempts to facilitate the economic independence of black tenants necessarily entailed a delicate navigation of the region's social and political institutions.

The natural environment of Macon County—shaped as it was by human hands—mattered to Carver. It was not merely a backdrop to his career. It was the world in which he took daily nature walks to commune with the Great Creator; its agroecosystems were the ones he spent countless hours pondering; and it served as the testing ground for the grand campaign that he hoped would sweep through the South. A sketch of his work provided to the USDA in 1902 noted that his efforts had been felt largely within twenty miles of Tuskegee, and though he believed that what was "true of Macon County is true of the adjoining counties, and is more or less true of the entire South," most of his bulletins dealt specifically with Macon County.[15] Thus, Carver was thinking of profoundly local landscapes even if he hoped the solutions he developed could be applied to the rest of the Cotton Belt. The environmental history of Macon County is thus an essential component of this study. Indeed, the county's streams, forests, soils, and cotton fields shaped Carver's agricultural and environmental thought no less than his years at the Iowa Agricultural College did.

In that sense this is also a work of southern environmental history. Because Carver arrived in Macon County in 1896 (the same year the U.S. Supreme Court handed down its decision in *Plessy v. Ferguson*, sanctioning segregation under the doctrine "separate but equal") and died during World War II (when African Americans were leaving the southern countryside in unprecedented numbers), his career at Tuskegee and his efforts to improve the lives of impoverished farmers offer a unique lens through which to view the tenant landscapes of the Jim Crow South.

The region's racial politics and prevailing economic structures—both of which favored the tenants' white landlords—ultimately undercut Carver's ability to persuade the poorest black farmers that the natural world provided them with sufficient advantages to facilitate their economic independence. But standing on that railroad platform in the autumn of 1896, taking in the sights and smells and sounds that would become so familiar to him, he saw a world he was confident he could remake. And if the ensuing years would disabuse him of his youthful optimism, they would reward him with a perceptive and nuanced environmental vision, a remarkably relevant one that suggests Carver remains very much a part of our usable past.

CHAPTER 1

Were It Not for His Dusky Skin

Some people develop an appreciation for nature late in life. George Washington Carver was not one of them. He had no mountaintop epiphany, no camping-and-tramping moment of clarity, no sudden awakening at the sight of a cotton field on the boll at sunset. His profound and abiding connection to the natural world was instead rooted and nurtured in his childhood. What is known about that childhood, however, has been pieced together from a decidedly fragmentary record: a small handful of documents along with the reminiscences of Carver himself and those of a few "old-timers" who had known him in his childhood and youth. The documents occasionally contradict one another, and many of the reminiscences are of dubious authenticity because they reflect clear influences of the mythology that came to surround Carver in his later years. As a consequence, the broad outline of Carver's first twenty-five years or so is clear enough, but the details tend to be murky. Among the details now irrevocably lost is the precise date—for that matter, the precise year—on which Carver entered this world.[1]

In his first autobiographical sketch, written shortly after he began his life's work at Tuskegee Institute in Alabama, Carver claimed that he "was about two weeks old when the war closed." This is consistent with a similar sketch he penned in the early 1920s in which he wrote that he had been born "about the close of the great Civil War." Later in his life Carver would tell biographers he had been born in 1864, and this became the generally accepted year of his birth.[2] After dedicating the George Washington Carver National Monument in the 1950s, however, the National Park Service launched an investigation of Carver's childhood. "To their pointed frustration," the park historians "were unable to tap one significant source not then ... available to researchers."[3] Nevertheless, they concluded that Carver had actually been born in 1860 because the 1870 census indicated that Carver was ten years old when his family was counted. The park historians found it "inconceivable" that George's foster father "could have been so grossly in error on this point."[4] Indeed, it does seem unlikely that Moses Carver could have so badly misjudged the age of a child whom he had raised since infancy.

That opinion held sway for about two decades, until another park historian pointed out that Carver was hardly likely to have been five years off in the assessment of his own age, especially as the 1880 census listed him as a fifteen-year-old boy.[5] Perhaps, as the park historian suggested, "Moses Carver was not present at the time of the 1870 enumeration ... or ... the 1870 enumerator might have set down the record incorrectly."[6] By 1981, when Linda O. McMurry published the first biography of Carver that documents its sources, she could comfortably assert that "it seems likely that he was born in the spring of 1865."[7] But that date, if accurate, would demolish a significant feature of the Carver myth—that he was born a slave—because the Missouri legislature voted to abolish slavery on January 11, 1865. Whatever the date of his birth, Carver came into this world on a farm in southwestern Missouri, the child of a woman named Mary, who either belonged or had recently belonged to a white man named Moses Carver.

Born in Ohio in 1812, Moses Carver had migrated first to Illinois, where he married Susan Blue in 1834, before heading to the frontier in 1838. He settled near a diamond-shaped grove of trees in Newton County, in southwestern Missouri, that would lend its name to the community that grew up around it.[8] When Marion Township, in which Diamond Grove was situated, was formally organized in 1843, Moses Carver, as one of its first settlers, was in a position to file a claim for some of the best land in the area. Over the ensuing decade he added to his holdings, and by 1853 he owned some 240 acres of well-watered land. By 1860, 100 of those acres were in cultivation.

At various times he grew Indian corn, wheat, oats, Irish potatoes, hay, flax, and rye. In addition, he cultivated an orchard, kept enough bees to produce two hundred pounds of honey a year, and tended fifty-four head of stock, primarily horses, sheep, hogs, and cattle.[9] According to the census of that year, Moses Carver was worth roughly $7,000, with the farm itself valued at $3,000 and his personal property at another $3,964.[10] He was a reasonably prosperous man for the area, but hardly a wealthy one.

Moses and Susan Carver did not have any children of their own, but took in the three children of Moses' older brother George following his death in 1839. No doubt George's daughter assisted Susan around the house while the two boys helped Moses work the farm. By the mid-1850s, however, the children were grown and the Carvers could no longer depend on their help. Though the accounts of those who knew Moses Carver universally report him to have been opposed to slavery, he purchased a slave, a thirteen-year-old girl named Mary, for $700 in 1855. Four years later she gave birth to a son, George's older brother, Jim.[11] Thus, by 1860 Moses Carver owned two of the seventeen slaves in Marion Township.[12]

Newton County lay south of the bitter raids that characterized Bleeding Kansas and far to the west of the Civil War's major battlefields. It was only one county removed from the Confederate state of Arkansas, however, and its western border adjoined Indian Territory, which was also slave territory. Caught between antislavery Kansas to the northwest and Arkansas to the south, southwestern Missouri was contested terrain throughout the Civil War, both physically and philosophically. Confederate and Union forces fought numerous skirmishes in the county, which was occupied at different times by troops from both sides. Predictably, the general tumult of the area led unprincipled opportunists to embrace crime when they could make it pay. Moses Carver, as a slave-owning Unionist, could expect quarter from neither Confederate nor Union sympathizers, and as one of the more prosperous men in the community he made an attractive target. His property was raided at least three times during the war. In 1863 would-be thieves reportedly suspended him by his thumbs from a tree and burned his feet with hot coals in an effort to induce him to reveal where he had hidden his money.[13]

This provides the backdrop for perhaps the most romanticized aspect of Carver's childhood: the kidnapping of George and his mother.[14] The details are difficult to confirm, but as the war was winding down—or perhaps shortly after its close when guerrilla activities were not uncommon in the area—Mary and George were kidnapped from the Carvers' farm and taken to Arkansas. Moses Carver commissioned John Bentley, a Union scout stationed in nearby Neosho, to retrieve them, supposedly promising him $300 and a racehorse for his efforts. Bentley returned with George but without Mary, who may have died in the interim. The most common telling of the story has Bentley declining the $300 because he had proven unable to return Mary, but accepting the racehorse in payment for his services.

Though hagiographers later made dramatic use of the episode, the most immediate effect of the kidnapping was that Carver never knew his mother. Since his father, a slave from a nearby farm, died in an accident around the same time—"while hauling wood to town on an oxwagon," Carver later wrote—the only parents Carver remembered were Moses and Susan Carver.[15] By all indications, they were good providers and loving foster parents to George and Jim.

Even apart from raising two black children, the Carvers were an anomaly in the neighborhood, in large measure because Moses was something of an eccentric. Among other things, as McMurry pointed out, he had "an uncanny rapport with animals" and rejected organized religion.[16] But Moses was hardworking and thrifty as well, characteristics that endeared him to his neighbors and were reflected in the farm itself. Indeed, the Carver farm would serve as an implicit model for George when he undertook his campaign to improve the lives of the South's impoverished black farmers. In addition to the one hundred acres put in cultivation each year, the Carver farm had a barn large enough to house twenty-five or thirty horses and milk cows; a stock shed and pens for other cattle, sheep, and hogs; a smokehouse that doubled as a summer kitchen; and, given its orchard of more than five hundred trees, likely a cider house as well. The presence of the large barn—a nineteenth-century symbol of prosperity—carried a number of implications, the most important being that Moses Carver almost certainly collected and composted the manure of his horses and cattle in the manner of high-minded agriculturists of the time. In that regard, his farm was rather unusual on the frontier. Agricultural reformers of the day (most of whom lived in states along the East Coast) decried the frontier as a place of wanton waste cultivated by people prone to exhaust the soil before pushing farther west.[17] The fact that he kept bees suggests that Moses incorporated clover into a larger crop rotation, not only to provide flowers for his bees but as a graze for his cattle and as a means of bolstering the fertility of his fields by returning nitrogen to the soil.

The cultivated fields alone did not provide the entirety of the Carvers' sustenance, of course. The eighty acres of woodlands and sixty of "unimproved" prairie on the Carver place sheltered geese, turkeys, ducks, quail, deer, and other game animals as well as blackberries, huckleberries, nuts, and wild grapes. While the Carver family doubtless purchased some goods— staples such as sugar—the farm was more or less self-sufficient. And Moses endeavored to keep it that way, fostering a keen distaste for waste of any kind despite the abundance of natural resources at his disposal—a distaste that the youngest of his adopted children would internalize and carry with him for the remainder of his life.[18] Indeed, much of the inspiration for the message George would later preach from Tuskegee harkened back to the high-minded husbandry of the nineteenth century. What lay in the future for young George notwithstanding, the Carvers lived modestly, and like many an American folk hero, George spent the formative years of his childhood in what amounted to a log cabin.

In contrast to Jim, who was strong and hardy, George was frail and sickly, suffering from whooping cough and frequent bouts of what doctors diagnosed as croup, though McMurry pointed out that George's "stunted growth and apparently impaired vocal chords suggest instead tubercular or pneumococcal infection."[19] The effects of his childhood sickness lingered throughout Carver's life; his voice was abnormally high and he regularly suffered from chest congestion and voice loss.[20] While George's duties during his time with the Carvers would have been reasonably light even had he been healthy, his recurring illnesses generally exempted him from field labor, though he helped Susan around the house. With fewer responsibilities than his older brother, George had the freedom to roam the fields and woods of the farm to satisfy his curiosity and search for "floral beauties" and rocks.[21] Thus began a lifelong obsession with collecting biological and geological specimens, initially as an amateur naturalist and later as a trained scientist.

"I literally lived in the woods," Carver wrote in 1922. "I wanted to know every strange stone, flower, insect, bird, or beast."[22] The young naturalist collected so many "specimens" that Susan began requiring him to empty his pockets before he entered the house. In the woods nearby, he kept a small garden of wildflowers. "Strange to say," he later noted, "all sorts of vegetation succeed [sic] to thrive under my touch until I was styled the plant doctor, and plants from all over the county would be brought to me for treatment."[23] Whether or not local farmers actually brought their plants to Carver for treatment, Carver displayed an undeniable affinity for plants from an early age. Indeed, he remembered specific flowers many years later. Writing to the granddaughter of Moses Carver's brother in 1929, for instance, he took pains to ask if "the spring [was] still full of blue flag, water cress and calamus."[24]

Those who knew Carver as a child invariably remembered him as an unusually curious, observant, and intelligent boy, and he was doubtless aware of his intellectual gifts. The Carvers taught him to read, and he learned much about the natural world by observation, but both state law and the community's social norms limited his opportunities for a formal education. Under the Missouri constitution as rewritten in 1865, townships with twenty or more African Americans between the ages of five and twenty were required to open a school for them. Blacks were not legally forbidden to enroll in public schools for whites in the other townships, though pressure from whites could certainly discourage it. By 1875, however, segregation had become state policy. Whether George and Jim ever attended the public school that met at the local Locust Grove Church is not known, but by 1876 they would not have been permitted to do so.[25] As George's "parents" and playmates had heretofore been white, his exclusion from the school may well have been the first time that race was an issue for him. It would not, of course, be the last.

For a few months in 1876 and 1877 the Carvers hired Steven L. Slane to tutor the boys.[26] In 1877, however, George persuaded Moses and Susan to allow him to spend his weekdays in Neosho, a small town eight miles south of the Carvers' farm, so that he could attend an African American school. Though he would return on weekends in 1877, his departure for Neosho marked the end of his permanent residence at the Carver farm. His first twelve or so years had on the whole been pleasant ones. Even in later years he would look back fondly on his time there, writing to Moses' great-niece, "How I would love to get with your father and talk over old times at home, indeed you really are my home folks."[27] As he set out in search of an education denied to him in his own community because of the color of his skin, he must have been keenly—even painfully—aware that prevailing racial mores not only circumscribed his opportunities to put his intellect to use but also threatened his happiness and security.

It is tempting to look for harbingers of Carver's future success in his formative years in Diamond Grove. To be sure, many of his biographers have looked for and found such indicators. But portents are found in novels more often than life, and but for some serendipity down the road, Carver might have been lost to history. The formative years, however, are so-called with good reason, and the adolescent boy who walked toward Neosho already had many of the qualities of the man he would become. He possessed a love of nature, especially plants, and a desire to commune with it in solitude. Through his daily work at Susan's side he had learned traditionally feminine skills such as sewing, cooking, needlework, and laundering that would help him earn a living as he pursued his education, and would stay with him as hobbies in the form of his "fancy work" for the remainder of his life. Moses had imparted fewer skills than values to George: independence of thought, frugality of living, and above all abhorrence of waste. And his careful management of the farm had provided an object lesson to George in the benefits of convertible agriculture and diversified farming.[28]

In Neosho, Carver spent his weekdays (and often weekends) in the home of Andrew and Mariah Watkins, an African American couple who boarded him in exchange for his help with chores. Mariah was a midwife whose skill and hard work had won her the respect of the white community.[29] In contrast to the Carvers, the Watkinses were deeply religious, and Carver attended Neosho's African Methodist Episcopal church with them on the weekends when he did not return to the Carvers' farm. Andrew and Mariah expected much of George, requiring him, for instance, to come home and work during recess, but by all indications he never begrudged the work. He appears to have accepted the fact that he would have to work for his education and seems to have viewed the chores in which he assisted Mariah as an opportunity to hone the skills he first learned from Susan.

Public schooling for African Americans in Missouri was woefully underfunded. Teachers received lower salaries, school terms were shorter, and funds were very limited relative to those for white schools. In fact, the state could boast only one black public high school. This situation was compounded by the shortage of qualified teachers, as educated whites generally eschewed positions at black schools, and few African Americans, only a decade removed from slavery, had the necessary education. Consequently, most black schools, including the one in Neosho, could not offer much beyond basic literacy and math skills. The teacher at Neosho knew little more than Carver, and though he stuck it out for a year, Carver soon grew disillusioned.[30] His time there, he later recalled, "simply sharpened my apetite [sic] for more knowledge."[31]

When the opportunity arose for him to join a family moving westward into Kansas, Carver jumped at the chance. His departure may have been sudden inasmuch as he apparently did not consult the Carvers prior to leaving. The first they learned of the move was a letter telling them that he "was cooking for a wealthy family in Ft Scott Kans. for my board, cloths [*sic*] and school privileges."[32]

Carver was hardly the only black emigrant in Kansas in the late 1870s. As Reconstruction ended in the South, many ex-slaves looked toward the Sunflower State, which had refused to accept a proslavery government in the 1850s and had produced radical abolitionist John Brown. Kansas became a kind of Canaan in the minds of many black southerners, a Promised Land where the soil had been "washed by the blood of humanitarians for the cause of freedom," as one African American from Louisiana wrote to Kansas governor John P. St. John in 1879.[33] The state's black population rose from 627 in 1860 to 43,000 by 1880, with nearly 60 percent of the emigrants arriving during the 1870s.[34]

Kansas was somewhat ambivalent about welcoming its new citizens. In 1876, for instance, the *New York Times* published an anonymous letter from Topeka expressing concern over the arrival of "penniless and aimless" blacks. "Kansas is not altogether happy over this unexpected acquisition," the writer asserted, "and, like the individual with the elephant on his hands, doesn't exactly know what to do with it."[35] White Kansans were proud of their opposition to slavery and had pretensions of upholding the ideals that had resulted in the abolition of slavery, but they were not, by and large, comfortable with the idea that African Americans were their equals. Even so, African Americans had a great deal more freedom in Kansas than they had in the South. In the early 1880s, for instance, black newspapers exchanged barbs with their white counterparts, African Americans and whites danced together in Nicodemus (the most prominent and successful all-black settlement in the state), and there were even scattered reports of interracial marriage. In many regards, however, the state mirrored national trends in moving from a period of racial fluidity following the Civil War to a period of racial hardening at the close of the nineteenth century. By 1888 Nicodemus' paper felt obliged to assure whites who might attend the town's July 4 celebration that they would "be treated white," which is to say with deference.[36]

Though racial hardening was still a decade away when Carver arrived in Fort Scott, the recent influx of black emigrants had already heightened racial tensions in Kansas. This was especially true in Fort Scott, which had been on the proslavery side of the Bleeding Kansas conflict and remained adamantly antiblack. The precise date when Carver arrived there is not known, but in March 1879 he witnessed a savage lynching in which an "immense crowd of people numbering fully 1,000" dragged a young man accused of molesting a white girl from jail, hanged him from a lamppost, and burned his corpse in a "fire of dry goods boxes and coal oil."[37] The event left an indelible impression on Carver. "As young as I was," he recalled near the end of his life, "the horror haunted me and does even now."[38]

Carver fled Fort Scott immediately. His exact path is a bit hazy. He may or may not have returned to the Carver farm in Diamond Grove for the summer, but by the end of 1879 he had moved into the home of Ben and Lucy Seymour in Olathe, Kansas. Much as Andrew and Mariah Watkins had done in Neosho, the Seymours served as surrogate black parents for him. The skills he had learned from Susan Carver and polished under the tutelage of Mariah Watkins enabled him to find "employment just as a girl," he later noted, and for about a year he attended school and did odd jobs in Olathe—taking in laundry, polishing shoes, and cooking for a white family.[39] "It was during this time," his biographer Basil Miller contended, "that George gave himself without reserve to the Master, accepting Him as his personal Redeemer."[40] Whether or not the Seymours were as important a religious influence as Miller argued, by the time Carver was in Olathe he had clearly adopted a faith that would prove—as Miller's assertion suggests—an integral part of the mythology that came to surround him in later years.

When the Seymours moved to Minneapolis, Kansas, Carver moved briefly to nearby Paola. At the time of the 1880 census—the one that listed his age as fifteen—he was living there with the family of Richard Moore and may have been running a laundry. His stay in Paola was short, however, and in the summer of 1880 he joined the Seymours in Minneapolis.[41] He attended the high school there, made friends among the white students, joined the Presbyterian church to which the Seymours belonged—a denomination with which he would at least nominally remain affiliated for the remainder of his life—and borrowed money to start his own laundry business. Like the Watkinses, the Seymours were well respected in the white community for their piety and work ethic, and this respect was extended to Carver. He ate at the homes of his white friends and received whites' business when he opened his laundry—"got all I could do," he remembered in 1922.[42] The doctor for whom Lucy Seymour worked as a nurse was impressed with Carver's intellect and loaned him books, which Carver devoured. And it was in Minneapolis that Carver added the middle initial "W." to his name, to avoid having his mail directed to another George Carver in the town. (Carver never claimed that the W stood for Washington, and always signed his correspondence simply "George W. Carver.")

At the end of 1884 Carver sold the property he had bought to establish his laundry and moved to Kansas City with a white friend, Chester Rarig, stopping first in Diamond Grove to visit the Carvers.[43] (His brother Jim had died of smallpox in Seneca, Missouri, the previous year, leaving Carver without any blood relatives.) In Kansas City he bought a typewriter and took a job as a clerk at the Union Depot. The racial mores of the city, however, proved less accommodating than those of Minneapolis, where many of the people knew and respected him. On entering a restaurant for breakfast one morning with Rarig, Carver was informed that he was not welcome in the establishment. Carver enjoined his friend to stay and went in search of his own breakfast. According to one account that cited Rarig as a source, Carver never saw his friend again.[44] Whether or not that was the case, Carver's stay in Kansas City was brief. Keen to continue his education, he applied by post for admission and was accepted to Highland College, a Presbyterian school for Native Americans in northeastern Kansas.

When Carver arrived in Highland, Kansas, in 1885, he met with profound disappointment. Highland College did not accept African Americans, and he was turned away at the door. Deeply discouraged, Carver would wait five years before attempting to enroll in college again, and then only at the urging of close friends. In the short term, however, he found himself scrambling for work in Highland. He found it, at least in part, in the employ of the John Beeler family. Some sketchy evidence suggests that Carver also worked as a tenant farmer or farm laborer outside the town.[45] Whether or not that was the case, it is clear that during the year he stayed in Highland he grew close with the Beeler family; indeed, they were the first white family to befriend him since the Carvers. The Beelers played a significant role in the Arkansas Valley Town Company, a speculative homesteading endeavor in Ness County in western Kansas. They were actively recruiting emigrants from Doniphan County, in which Highland was located, and their efforts persuaded a number of young men from the county to head west to try their hand at homesteading; Carver was among them.[46]

When Carver arrived in Ness County late in August 1886, the Atchison, Topeka and Santa Fe Railroad was extending its CK&W line westward across Kansas, but the line did not reach the county until late December.[47] The aptly named Beelerville was thus a quintessential frontier community on the western plains marked by the boosterism and rugged individualism peculiar to such settlements.[48] Carver bought a relinquishment on a quarter section of land roughly a mile south of Beelerville and filed on it in October.[49] As he had arrived after the growing season, he sought wage labor to tide him over the winter, ultimately finding it with George H. Steeley, whose property lay three-quarters of a mile southwest of Carver's. Steeley employed Carver to help him construct outbuildings and generally assist him around the house, and Carver spent his first winter on Steeley's place.

When spring came, Carver began work on his own property. He completed a sod house on April 18, 1887, and moved in two days later, furnishing it with a cookstove, a bed, a cupboard, chairs, a table, and laundering equipment.[50] He next set to work on his land, breaking seventeen acres and putting ten of them in cultivation. In his proof of settlement the following year he listed corn, rice corn (a sorghum), and garden vegetables as his crops. Like many of his late nineteenth-century peers, he began planting trees as well. When he "proved up" on his land in June 1888, he claimed to have planted eight hundred "forest trees" (valued at $200) and fifty fruit trees, primarily mulberries, plums, and apricots (valued at $25).[51] He may also have owned a few hens, though he did not claim any "domestic animals and livestock" in his proof of settlement.[52] He valued his sod house at $50, his work in breaking the land at $50, and the shrubbery he had planted at $10, and (mistakenly) reached a total worth for his property of $325.[53]

Carver's farm was not situated on the best agricultural land in the state. In 1942 a former neighbor of Carver's told the *Kansas City Times*, "I remember that quarter well. The land was not very good."[54] Though he dug for a well, Carver never hit water. In fact, the nearest well was on the Steeley place. For that matter, Carver's timing in settling on the western plains could hardly have been worse. The first years of the 1880s had been unusually wet for the region, but land west of the 100th meridian (which in Kansas lies just to the east of Carver's homestead) receives inadequate rainfall to ensure regular crops in most years, and droughts are not uncommon. The lush fields of western Kansas today reflect drought-resistant crops and center-pivot irrigation that taps into the Ogallala Aquifer. Carver arrived toward the beginning of a drought cycle that lasted into the early 1890s.

Many emigrants abandoned their homesteads during those drought years, some attaching signs to their wagons as they left the state reading: "In God we trusted, in Kansas we busted."

Drought was not Carver's only problem. The winters from 1885–86 through 1887–88 brought the worst blizzards in America's history. Among those Carver witnessed was the School Children's Blizzard of January 1888, so called because it struck across the Great Plains as school was letting out. Many children lost their way in the blowing snow and never made it home.[55] More than two hundred people died in that blizzard, which reached from Texas to Canada.

But as McMurry pointed out, the "grimness of the frontier" was not without its rewards. Everyone shared the hardships, which "created a spirit of communal help and friendship among settlers that sometimes partially erased racial barriers."[56] By all indications, Carver was well liked in Ness County. Steeley, who was probably Carver's closest friend, loaned him farm implements (Carver owned only a spade, a hoe, and a corn planter).[57] Carver continued to work for his friend even after he had settled into his soddy, and Steeley permitted Carver to keep a greenhouse of sorts on his property where visitors were surprised to find flowers blooming all year.

Steeley was not alone in thinking highly of Carver. Although he had few black neighbors, Carver did serve as a witness for Bird Gee, "a colored citizen of Eden township" (and former resident of Doniphan County) in March 1888 when Gee offered proof of settlement on his homestead. A short sketch of Carver, whom the editors found "by reason of his color and opportunities to be a somewhat remarkable character," followed notice of Gee's proof of settlement in the *Ness County News*. The sketch, which amounts to the first biographical work about Carver, took particular note of Carver's scientific knowledge. After his attempt to enroll in Highland College "was defeated by a rebel element of the community," the paper reported, "he improved every opportunity for private study, which extended to many of the sciences." Carver's "knowledge of geology, botany and kindred sciences" not only marked "him as a man of more than ordinary ability" but was evident in his "collection of about five hundred plants in a conservatory adjoining the residence of his employer [Steeley], besides having a large geological collection in and around the place," a clear indication that Carver's interests as an amateur naturalist had not waned since his childhood in Missouri. The sketch concluded by noting that Carver "is a pleasant and intelligent man to talk with, and were it not for his dusky skin—no fault of his—he might occupy a different sphere, to which his abilities would otherwise entitle him."[58]

While Carver's abilities as a naturalist and his skin color set him apart from his neighbors, he was an eager participant in community activities. He played his accordion and sang at social events; the local literary society elected him assistant editor; and he had the first "art teacher" of his experience, a black homesteader named Clara C. Duncan who had taught at Talladega College in Alabama.[59] Under her tutelage he began to refine his "brushwork" and may well have decided to pursue a career in art. Some sketchy evidence suggests that he did odd jobs in the community, and despite the drought he seems to have made a fair living.[60] There is little to indicate that he was unhappy or unwelcome in Ness County. John F. Beeler, Bolivar Beeler, Elmer E. Beeler, and Steeley testified on Carver's behalf when he offered proof of settlement in June 1888, and all acknowledged seeing Carver regularly and believed that he intended to stay on his land.[61]

He did not stay in Ness County, of course. Shortly after he made his final proof he "drifted . . . to Winterset" in Madison County, Iowa.[62] It is possible that he originally planned to return. In June 1888 he borrowed $300, $100 more than he needed to cover the $1.25 per acre he was required to pay under the Homestead Act of 1862 to secure title to his land. With his remaining money he headed east for the more fertile soils of Iowa but continued to make payments on his mortgage through at least 1891.[63] By that year, however, he had had an epiphany of sorts and had decided that God was directing him to help "his people."

In 1890 Carver was working as the head cook in Winterset's St. Nicholas Hotel. He "had been there but a very few days," he later recalled, when his singing during a church service caught the attention of the choir director, Helen Milholland.[64] Her husband, Dr. John Milholland, invited Carver to dinner, and thus began one of the most important friendships of Carver's life. The white Milhollands opened their home to Carver, who shared their deep Christian faith. All three were profoundly influenced by the Social Gospel, a broad movement within Christianity (especially Protestantism) that emphasized the use of Christian principles such as love and charity to solve societal problems.[65] By the turn of the century the movement was influencing the direction of American theology and providing a foundation for the Progressive movement that blossomed in the early twentieth century. Their letters reflect their commitment to this applied Christianity. Writing to Dr. Milholland in 1928, for instance, Carver decried "the money mad, self centered age" in which they were living, but took solace in the fact that there "are . . . a number of outstanding characters who believe and live the Gold Rule Way of living, which is the Jesus way of life."[66]

Undoubtedly, the Milhollands' interest in Carver was at least in part an effort to be charitable to a less fortunate "brother in Christ." Carver acknowledged as much when he wrote to their daughter following Mrs. Milholland's death: "I know their crowns [John Milholland had already died] are full of stars of the first magnitude for what they did for me alone. I rise up and call them blessed."[67] As Carver's oblique reference to their quasi-parental role implies, the affection between the three was no less genuine for that. Each evening he dutifully recited to them what he had done that day.[68] When he needed to borrow money to open a laundry, the Milhollands loaned it to him. Perhaps most significant, the Milhollands encouraged him to give college another try, even steering him to one: Simpson, a Methodist college a few miles up the road in Indianola.[69]

Carver was roughly twenty-five years old when he enrolled in Simpson College in September 1890. He was not the first African American to matriculate at Simpson, though his one black predecessor had graduated well before Carver set foot on campus. That is not to say that his being black did not present obstacles. There were no dormitories for men, so male students were expected to board in local homes. His race made this considerably more difficult, and the president of the college had to arrange for Carver to live for a time in "an old abandoned shack not too far from the campus."[70] Even so, Simpson was "an ideal place for Carver to resume his quest for an education," McMurry noted, because it had already been integrated and its "religious affiliation provided an environment in which Carver's faith and piety would win respect."[71]

Though he was the only black student at Simpson, Carver eagerly participated in a variety of campus activities. His fellow students accepted him as a peer, including him in less formal events (like baseball games), bringing him their laundry when word got out that he was taking in washing to support himself, and secretly furnishing his apartment (and denying it when he asked them). "I often came home," he later recalled, "and found 25 cents or 50 cents under my door. I would not have the slightest idea who put it there."[72] Even the female students treated Carver as their peer, calling him George rather than Mr. Carver—in the absence of authority figures. A female classmate remembered that the instructors were "very anxious for we girls not to do anything that wasn't just the right thing for girls to do in regard to a young colored man," so when their instructors were around, the girls called him Mr. Carver.[73] "The people are very very kind to me here," he wrote Mrs. Milholland, "and the students are wonderfully good." Indeed, his experience at Simpson confirmed his faith. "I am learning," he concluded his letter, "to trust and realise the blessed results from trusting in Him every day."[74] His fellow students' inclusion of him touched Carver deeply; he would later poignantly note, "They made me believe I was a real human being."[75]

Classified as a "preparatory student," Carver took courses in grammar, arithmetic, essays, and etymology his first semester, and added voice and piano to those in the spring. By all indications Carver was a talented musician. He boasted in a letter to Mrs. Milholland that he could reach a high D when singing and had good enough range to sing three octaves below to boot.[76] His real passion, however, was painting. Accepted first on a trial basis, his abilities won him permission to enroll formally in the art class of Miss Etta M. Budd during the winter term. His connection with her proved fortunate. Through Budd he met Mrs. W. Arthur Liston, a white woman who served as yet another mother figure to Carver and secured a place for him to board at a friend's house and possibly a job at her husband's bookstore.[77] Carver often studied at the Listons' house, and he and Mrs. Liston exchanged gardening and painting tips. Indeed, the two grew so close that for the remainder of her life she signed her correspondence to him "Your Mother."[78] Though Mrs. Liston would prove an important ally for Carver in Iowa, Miss Budd had an even more significant influence on Carver, as it was through her prompting that a long-term vision for his life began to coalesce.

By the end of Carver's first semester, Miss Budd, who was three or four years older than Carver, had recognized his considerable talents as a painter. Although her doubts regarding his artistic abilities had been removed, she still feared that an African American man could not make a serious career as an artist given the racial climate of the time, regardless of his abilities. Carver's affinity for plants led her to suggest that he enroll at the Iowa Agricultural College in Ames, where her father, noted horticulturist Joseph Lancaster Budd, was a professor. The chance to pursue a career as a scientific agriculturist appealed to Carver, the more so as his Social Gospel leanings inclined him toward a life of service, but he wanted to continue as an artist and remain at Simpson College. By 1891, however, he was certain that God was leading him to study scientific agriculture and that his Christian duty lay in sharing that knowledge with his black brethren in the South. "The more my ideas develop," he wrote to the Milhollands in August that year, "the more beautiful and grand seems the plan that I have laid out to pursue, or rather the one God has destined for me."[79] He convinced himself that his mission would be temporary, and, viewing it as an act of martyrdom, laid down his brushes to pursue a career as an agriculturist.[80]

CHAPTER 2

The Earnest Student of Nature

When Carver arrived in Ames in 1891, the Iowa Agricultural College was emerging from a low point in the uneven growth that marked its early years. Its origins date to March 1858, when the Iowa legislature created a state agricultural college. The following year the state purchased nearly 650 acres near Ames, and by 1861 the first building had been erected. In 1862 the state legislature voted to endorse the Morrill Act, which had been passed by Congress that year to fund land-grant colleges designed to encourage the teaching of "such branches of learning as related to agriculture and mechanic arts, in such manner as the legislatures of the states may respectively prescribe."[1] The Civil War and its aftermath interrupted the school's development, however, and the first students did not enroll in the college until 1869.

Without precedents to follow, land-grant colleges such as the IAC (as its students affectionately called it) struggled to adopt a coherent vision for their future and to secure legitimacy among the farmers they were ostensibly founded to serve. As they were subject to legislative oversight and many politicians were skeptical of their value, they were often forced to make do with less rather than more. The IAC was more fortunate than most in being able to hire three particularly qualified and influential agriculture professors in its first full decade in operation. The first to come on board was Charles Edwin Bessey, who joined the faculty in 1870 as the head of horticulture, botany, and zoology. A former student of Asa Gray at Harvard, Bessey would rank among the most prominent botanists of his generation, leading the push to legitimate botany as a laboratory science and later playing a vital role in shaping the young field of ecology.[2]

Bessey relinquished his position as head of horticulture in 1877 (though he retained his other titles) when the second of the three influential professors arrived, Etta Budd's father, Joseph L. Budd. A New York native, Budd had been educated at Union College in Schenectady. He moved to Iowa in 1862 and, with a shortage of jobs available for horticulturists, operated a nursery prior to his appointment at the IAC. Though Budd is not as well remembered as Bessey, he was among the most respected horticulturists of his time, particularly in the field of hybridization. Indeed, in some ways Budd embodied the scientific zeitgeist of the second half of the nineteenth century in America and its push toward improving plants by introducing new species, selectively breeding them, and altering their distribution.[3] Indicative of Budd's reputation is the fact that in 1882 the U.S. State Department supported his effort to introduce new species of apple trees from Russia that might thrive on the Great Plains or be crossbred to do so. The endeavor ultimately yielded little fruit, largely because the participating nurseries mismanaged the specimens and kept poor records.[4] Its failure notwithstanding, the endeavor itself conferred a certain level of status on the young IAC.

Two years after Budd arrived in Ames, a third significant agricultural professor was added when Seaman A. Knapp, an important figure in Iowa's agricultural press, was appointed to head the Department of Practical and Experimental Agriculture, a position he took up in 1880. Knapp would go on to serve as the single most important figure in establishing the USDA's extension service, but in the 1880s he proved no less influential in shaping the IAC's agricultural curriculum.

Even with well-qualified teachers the school faced substantial hurdles. State legislators, like most of the farmers who elected them, had little use for scientific agriculture and could see no reason to allocate tax dollars to experimental work they deemed impractical. (Farmers then—as today—tended to judge practicality on the basis of increased profits rather than "enlightened" methods of cultivation.) Though Knapp asked for $5,000 per annum, he never received more than $750 a year to operate an experiment station at the school.[5]

Frustrated by this lack of funding from the state, he and Bessey drafted a speech outlining a plan to get national funding for state agricultural experiment stations. Knapp delivered the speech before the Iowa State Breeders Association, which amounted to a "who's who" of Iowa's influential agricultural voices. The speech was a success, and Iowa representative Cyrus C. Carpenter introduced a modified version of it as a bill in Congress.[6] The bill precipitated a national debate between systematists, who opposed funding experiment stations for agricultural colleges, and scientific agriculturists that lasted until Missouri representative William Hatch and Mississippi senator James Z. George managed to guide the bill through Congress in November 1886. The Hatch Act allocated $15,000 a year to each state for an experiment station to be run in connection with its land-grant college. Its passage marked a significant moment for land-grant colleges and for American agriculture generally. Historian Alan Marcus noted that such funding "was an admission not merely that agricultural scientists had something to offer agriculture but also that the future success of American farming depended to some extent on the scientists' determinations and inquiries."[7] By the time President Grover Cleveland signed the bill into law in March 1887, however, Knapp had left the IAC.

While Congress was debating the merits of funding agricultural experiment stations, political factionalism in Iowa was creating a good deal of turbulence for the Iowa Agricultural College. Debates over the proper aims of the state's land-grant school prompted political meddling and led the board of trustees to demote the college's first president, Adonijah Welch, to a professorial position in 1883—a demotion he discovered when he returned from a leave of absence in Europe, where he had been investigating agricultural schools abroad. If presidents pro-tem are included, over the next eight years the IAC ran through six presidents. The board of trustees chose Knapp to be the second permanent president of the school, and he served as president in 1883 and 1884 before returning to the agricultural department. "Few professors of agriculture in the country had wrought more in five years for their departments than had Knapp," noted his biographer, Joseph C. Bailey. "Yet his rewards had scarcely been commensurate with his work."[8] He took a leave of absence from the school in 1886 and joined a business venture in Louisiana, formally tendering his resignation in 1887.

Coupled with the defection of Bessey, who had accepted a more lucrative offer from the University of Nebraska in August 1884, Knapp's departure contributed to the college's instability and the deterioration of the IAC's agricultural department over the second half of the decade.[9] With two of the three men who had placed the department on solid footing gone, criticism of the college mounted, ironically encouraging more political interference.

Among the more vocal critics of the school was "Uncle" Henry Wallace, arguably Iowa's most influential agricultural voice. In talks before the state agricultural society and Stock Breeders Association, as well as in his newspaper, the *Iowa Homestead*, Wallace began taking the school to task for emphasizing the scientific components of the students' education over the practical ones. The school was "nominally an agricultural college," Wallace noted, but "very little agriculture was taught" there. The lone exception was Professor Budd's "quite strong" horticulture program.[10]

Wallace, of course, was not the only one disillusioned with the direction the IAC was taking, and in 1890 Budd went down to Winterset to inform Uncle Henry that if he wanted a position as head of the school's agricultural department, he could almost certainly have it. Wallace was probably not the shoo-in Budd thought he would be. Though he wielded a good deal of influence in the state, Wallace had developed powerful enemies by 1890, largely because of his opposition to the politicization of the Farmers' Alliance just as the Populist movement was gaining momentum.[11]

Consequently, Wallace approached his friend James Wilson, who agreed to take the position if it were offered but refused to campaign for it. Knowing that "some of the Alliance committee were ready to oppose anything [he] wanted," Wallace had to angle carefully to secure the position for his friend. He later boasted of his success in duping his rivals at the meeting of the Alliance's Agricultural College Committee (of which Wallace was a member) that was to determine the candidate whom the organization would support for the position. When someone brought up Wilson's name, Wallace recalled, "I opposed him. . . . Those who differed with me evidently figured that I was fishing for the place myself and became quite vehement in their advocacy of Mr. Wilson." After several weak protests, Wallace declared that he "would not stand against the opinion of the rest," and conceded that Wilson should be offered the position.[12]

Wilson took up his duties as the director of the agricultural department and the experiment station in 1891, the same year Carver began his studies at Ames. As fate would have it, then, Carver's arrival coincided with the return of stability at the college. William M. Beardshear, who was recruited to the IAC from his position as a superintendent of the Des Moines public schools, enjoyed extraordinary public support as the school's president from the time of his arrival in 1891 until his death in 1902.[13] With a more stable atmosphere, Wilson at its head, and $15,000 in Hatch funds for the experiment station, the agricultural department blossomed and the IAC returned to its former position as one of the leading agricultural institutions in the nation.

Carver was the first black student admitted to the college, and according to at least one contemporary, "the only colored boy . . . in Ames."[14] Although his enrollment apparently met with little opposition, perhaps because Professor Budd carried enough clout to smooth the process, Carver's initial reception in Ames was rather cold.[15] Finding a place to board proved as awkward as it had in Indianola. As at Simpson, students lodged in the homes of local residents, who tapped the student rents as a source of extra revenue, fostering close connections to the school as a consequence. But Ames residents had had little contact with African Americans, and Carver's race represented a substantial hurdle among those who would ordinarily put up an IAC student. Louis Hermann Pammel, the school's botany professor, recalled that he tried to find a room for Carver, even enlisting the help of Wilson, "or rather Mrs. Wilson." The people they contacted "liked Mr. Carver well enough but owing to the fact that he was a colored boy they all said they would not like to have him in the house."[16] Consequently, Pammel got Wilson's permission to allow Carver to stay in an empty office in North Hall in exchange for Carver's taking up the janitorial duties for the building.[17]

The first months were tough for Carver. As the school terms ran from late February through mid-June and from mid-July through mid-November, he had been there several months when he noted in a letter to the Milhollands in August, "I as yet do not like it as well here as I do at S [Simpson] . . . but the Lord helping me I will do the best I can." Nonetheless, convinced that he was pursuing the "beautiful and grand . . . plan . . . God has destined for me," he was determined to stick it out. "Let us pray," he enjoined them, "that the Lord will completely guide us in all things, and that we may gladly be led by him."[18]

Although his affection for Simpson remained—he returned during the winter break of his first year at the IAC to enroll in another of Miss Budd's art classes—he eventually developed a fondness for his new school. In time Carver's relationship with his white peers in Ames grew as rich as it had been with those in Indianola.[19] He threw himself into campus activities, joining the Welsh Eclectic Society (an all-male debating club), the German Club, the Art Club, and the Agricultural Society. He also served as the trainer, or "rubber," for the IAC's football team, a title that derived from his obligation to massage cramped and sore muscles.[20] He picked up odd jobs to help support himself: cutting wood for professors and tending their gardens, cleaning houses, and taking care of the school's greenhouse and science laboratories.[21] He offered music lessons to his fellow students and continued painting in his free time. In short, apart from gathering wild plants and mushrooms to supplement his diet, making some of his own clothes, and recycling other students' castoffs (stub pencils, for example), he led a normal college life for the time.[22]

A telling indication of his acceptance came at the end of Carver's sophomore year. His talents as an artist were well respected, and his peers encouraged him to enter some of his artwork in the Cedar Rapids Art Exhibition at the end of that year. Lacking the funds for the trip (and perhaps self-conscious of his work), he declined to go. On the day after Christmas 1892, however, Carver got in a wagon with a number of his friends, ostensibly to go to Professor Budd's house. He was instead escorted downtown, where Professor Pammel bought him a suit and Professor Wilson handed him a train ticket to Cedar Rapids. Four of Carver's paintings were entered in the exhibit, and one—his best known, *Yucca and Cactus*—was among those selected to represent Iowa's artists at the 1893 World's Fair in Chicago, where it won honorable mention.[23]

Carver's most significant relationships, however, were forged not with his fellow students but with his professors. As an undergraduate he evidently spent a good deal of time with Professor Budd and his family. Carver reported that Etta Budd's "interest in me never waned" while he was in Ames, and other contemporaries recalled him being a frequent guest at the Budds' house.[24] Indeed, it seems likely that Budd suggested the topic and worked with Carver on his BSA thesis, a horticultural study that referenced experiments carried out in the school's orchard, which Budd oversaw.[25] In the end, however, Carver's training was probably more influenced by three other professors: Henry C. Wallace, James Wilson, and Louis Pammel.

Henry Cantwell Wallace—Harry, as Uncle Henry's eldest son was known to his friends—had first entered the Iowa Agricultural College in

1885. Unable to decide on a course of study or career, he left school at the end of 1886 and took over one of his father's three farms.[26] The following year he married, and a year later he and his wife had their first child, the third of Iowa's famous Henry Wallaces, Henry A. Wallace. Though the 1880s were difficult years for farmers, Harry did reasonably well. In 1891, however, Wilson, a close family friend, persuaded Harry to finish his degree. Consequently, in February 1892 (Carver's second year in Ames) Harry returned to school. He finished his remaining coursework in a single year and was offered a position as a faculty member in the agriculture department beginning in 1893. Thus, he was first Carver's peer and then one of his professors.

Carver would later remember that Wallace was "a born teacher [who] . . . enthused and inspired me."[27] He credited Wallace with being "a master of soils . . . [who] set me thinking along lines practically unknown at the time, but which are now found to be almost, if not quite, as important as the exploding of the theory of spontaneous generation."[28] Unfortunately, Carver never clarified what those lines of thinking were. It is clear, however, that Wallace played an influential role in shaping Carver's thinking in the field of scientific agriculture.

The two men developed a close friendship, not surprising given that they shared similar interests and were roughly the same age. Secretary of Agriculture Henry A. Wallace, Harry's son, later recalled that Carver "was a good friend of my father's at the Iowa State College" and remembered hearing his "parents talk about George Carver's future . . . as if it were their own."[29] Carver was a frequent guest in the Wallaces' home, and he often took young Henry A. along with him on his daily nature walks. "Because of his friendship with my father," the younger Wallace wrote, "and perhaps his interest in children George Carver often took me with him on his botany expeditions, and it was he who first introduced me to the mysteries of plant fertilization." The secretary of agriculture and future vice president fondly reminisced, "He seemed to have great sympathy with me." Indeed, a biographer of the Henry Wallaces described Carver as "the closest friend to [Henry A.] outside of his own family in early youth." Henry A. later credited Carver for sparking his interest in botany and for serving as the inspiration for a philosophy he dubbed "the genetic basis of democracy," which Wallace employed to criticize the policies of Nazi Germany in the years leading up to World War II.[30]

Henry C. Wallace played as significant a role in shaping Carver's political thinking, especially in terms of confirming and clarifying Carver's agrarian values, as he did in influencing Carver's thinking in the field of scientific agriculture. Like his father, Harry Wallace was an unapologetic supporter of scientific farming, but principally for the benefits it promised farmers rather than those it held for industry in the form of increased agricultural production. Years later, as secretary of agriculture under Warren G. Harding, he would conclude that his initial optimism had proven naïve, indicting a federal policy "enacted presumably in aid of agriculture" that had really aimed "to increase production instead of to insure a fair reward for the farmer's labor or a fair return on his capital."[31] But in the 1890s, Wallace was still confident that scientific agriculture portended not only more productive farms but more contented and better-rewarded farmers as well. Carver, too, would place tremendous faith in scientific agriculture, though he would lose faith in its inevitable benefits well before Wallace did. He would later contend that increasing agricultural production without making farmers' "consumption . . . commensurate with it" amounted to "a bad case of agricultural economics," undeniably a reflection of Wallace's sentiments.[32]

To be sure, Wallace was an unabashed agrarian, arguing that the "farmers' part in making and maintaining the Nation is not confined to the production of material things" and suggesting that "the farmer has always been the national stabilizer."[33] He recognized the need for reform, but hoped it would occur within the existing political system rather than through radical measures. Thus, like his father, he was sympathetic to the complaints of farmers in the 1880s and early 1890s but refused to support the creation of a Populist Party.

The motto of *Wallace's Farmer*, an agricultural newspaper Wallace and his father launched after he left the IAC, is a concise synopsis of Wallace's agricultural vision: Good Farming, Clear Thinking, Right Living. In an editorial published four days before his death in February 1916, Uncle Henry "interpreted the word 'farm' as meaning 'the farmer and his family as well'" and held "that the marketing of crops was as important as production." By "clear thinking" Wallace meant embracing scientific cultivation. After all, he concluded, a farmer "must understand his soil, and the laws of nature operating therein. . . . He must understand the plants which he grows, and the livestock which convert the plants to meat." And by "right living" he meant embracing a Judeo-Christian moral ethic. "Whatever views we may have on minor matters, whether Christians or not," he argued, "we all accept the ancient writings called the Scriptures as the foundation and source of the civilization of America." Moral concerns were in the Wallaces' view as important as economic ones; indeed, they were part and parcel of them. Right living, so their logic went, grew out of clear thinking, and without clear thinking, good farming was impossible.[34] In time Carver would develop a distinctive agricultural vision of his own, but that vision would reflect enough of the Wallaces' views to indicate that, if nothing else, his friend and professor helped to confirm his agrarian inclinations.

Though Wallace proved a loyal friend to Carver, he made enemies as adeptly as he did friends. This proved his undoing at the IAC when the bickering between Wallace and the chemist at the school's experiment station became embarrassingly public, forcing the college to fire both men along with two other faculty members who had become embroiled in the dispute.[35] Wallace's dismissal, however, hardly cost Carver his only ally.

Indeed, if anything, Carver was more influenced by James Wilson, who as a good friend of Uncle Henry doubtless also confirmed and shaped Carver's agrarian values. Easily the best known of the IAC's faculty members, Wilson had been born in Scotland in 1835. His family emigrated to the United States in 1851 and settled in Connecticut. Like Budd and Knapp, Wilson was caught up in the mid-nineteenth-century wave of settlers moving from the Northeast to the Midwest in search of better farmland. He settled in Tama County, Iowa, in 1861 and married a year later. His success as a farmer along with his considerable abilities as a speaker led to his election to the Iowa House of Representatives in 1868, where he led the fight for livestock fencing laws and was influential enough to be elected Speaker in 1872.[36]

In 1872 Wilson was elected as a Republican to the U.S. House of Representatives. Dubbed "Tama Jim" to distinguish him from Iowa senator James "Fairfield Jim" Wilson, he struck up what would become a lifelong friendship there with an aspiring congressman named William McKinley.[37] Though the precise details are a bit shadowy—accounts vary—in a subsequent bid for reelection Wilson garnered only a twenty-three-vote majority, and the Democrats contested his seat and forced him out. He returned to Congress in 1883, though only for a single term.[38] Wilson remained an influential figure in Iowa's agricultural press during these years and consequently cast a large shadow when he took over the IAC's agricultural department in 1891.[39]

Wilson was by all accounts a warm man, and Carver developed as close a personal relationship with him during his time in Ames as he did with any of his professors. Wilson clearly reciprocated Carver's affection. In a letter of recommendation for Carver, he wrote, "I have been more intimate with Mr. Carver than with any other student on campus. . . . We have nobody to take his place and I would never part with a student with so much regret as George Carver."[40] The crux of their friendship rested in their shared faith. During Carver's first year in Ames, he had lamented to the Milhollands that "the helpful means of Christian growth [was] not so good" at the IAC as it had been at Simpson.[41] In Wilson's Bible study group Carver found more than just a "helpful means" for his spiritual growth; he also found a friendship that would serve as a fount of encouragement in later years.

Writing to Carver at Tuskegee in 1911, Wilson recalled their shared efforts "to turn young men [at the IAC] from agnosticism, which was too prevalent at the institution at the time," and praised Carver's religious leadership there. The four-page letter, written at a stressful time for both men (Wilson, as secretary of agriculture, was attempting to navigate a dispute between Secretary of the Interior Richard Ballinger and his own department's chief forester, Gifford Pinchot; and Carver was fighting a losing battle with Booker T. Washington at Tuskegee Institute in Alabama), cheerfully reminisced about their religious collaboration. "I have told many of my intimates," Wilson confided to Carver, "how when students began to come in at the beginning of a new term, Carver and I would sit down and plan how to get boys who were Christians to go down to the depot and meet them, . . . help them get registered, help them get rooms, and . . . get them into prayer meetings, etc." Indeed, "before Mr. Carver and I left the institution," he had told his friends, "there had been quite a reformation brought about."[42]

In contrast to Harry Wallace, Wilson had no training in scientific agriculture. His appointment to head the department was based on his success as a practical farmer and his considerable political clout, useful for obtaining funding from the legislature. Nevertheless, he spent a good deal of time contemplating agricultural education. Because, like the Wallaces, he believed that scientific agriculture promised to keep farmers on their farms, he came to believe that the United States had "passed the stage where a common school education, with higher mathematics, philosophy and literature . . . will best fit a man for doing everything the world wants done."

This was "particularly true of agriculture," Wilson thought, because the "soil may be made poorer by bad handling." Although most agricultural problems were entirely preventable, they required "the study of the physics and chemistry of soils, their origin and composition."[43] The problem, as Wilson saw it, was that "the advancement being made in agriculture [was] in research rather than pedagogy," owing primarily to a "want of instructors in agricultural education."[44]

While no direct trail links Wilson's educational views with Carver's, Wilson's influence is clear. Carver would go on to give numerous lectures at teachers' conferences throughout the South advocating an increased emphasis on agricultural education. Shortly after he took the position at Tuskegee, Carver was asked to sit on the editorial board of the *Nature Study Review*, the primary vehicle for a movement that sought to ground elementary education in the outdoors and encouraged activities such as gardening in schools. Significantly, this emphasis on a practical education fit neatly with the philosophy of Booker T. Washington and Tuskegee Institute. Writing to Washington in 1896, Carver professed his beliefs that Tuskegee's "line of education is the key to unlock the golden door of freedom to our people" and that Washington had "the correct solution to the 'race problem.'"[45] That faculty members at a land-grant college would advocate increased emphasis on agricultural and practical education is not surprising, but it was certainly a departure for a man who initially entered college as an art student—even if he had become convinced that God intended him to pursue a practical education for the sake of "his people." Consequently, it seems likely that Wilson (and to a lesser extent Carver's other professors) affirmed his thinking about both the practicality of an agricultural education and the need to expand its emphasis in rural schools.

Although Henry C. Wallace and James Wilson influenced Carver's thinking in his years at the Iowa Agricultural College, it was Carver's graduate adviser, Louis Pammel, who most shaped his training. Carver readily admitted as much, acknowledging in a letter to Pammel in 1918, "I certainly consider it an honor to have been a pupil of yours, and as I have said to you a few times and to others many times, you influenced my life possibly more than anyone else."[46]

In many ways Pammel and Carver were kindred souls. Pammel, the second child of Prussian immigrants, was born on a Wisconsin farm in 1862. Like Carver, he demonstrated an affinity for the natural world from an early age, recalling identifying and "making friends" with animals as a favorite hobby.[47] Though nominally Lutheran, his parents did not attend church, and so like Carver he spent his most formative years in a relatively areligious home. He enrolled in the University of Wisconsin in 1881, the same year William Trelease, a recent graduate of Cornell University, arrived in Madison to teach botany. Trelease sparked Pammel's interest in the subject and became his most important adviser. "What I have done in botany," he would write to Trelease, "I owe to you."[48] Pammel graduated with honors in 1885, and his senior thesis, "On the Structure of the Testa of Several Leguminous Seeds," was published the following year in the prestigious *Bulletin of the Torrey Botanical Club*.[49]

Although Pammel wanted to pursue a career in botany, opportunities in that field were few, so he moved to Chicago and went to work at a seed company. Deciding that his botanical knowledge would be put to better use in medicine, he applied and was accepted to Hahnemann Medical College, where he began classes in October 1885. A month into his medical studies, however, he received a letter from Harvard botanist William Gilson Farlow offering him a job as an assistant on the recommendation of Trelease. The latter had left Wisconsin during Pammel's senior year to study for his PhD under Asa Gray at Harvard. Pammel jumped at Farlow's offer. He moved to Boston shortly after Thanksgiving and spent several months at Harvard working with Farlow (and to a lesser extent Gray).

In the spring of 1886, Trelease, who had been appointed to the Gray professorship at the Shaw School of Botany in St. Louis (a position that included the charge of Missouri's Botanical Gardens), offered Pammel a position as his assistant.[50] As part of his new job Pammel led personal tours of the botanical gardens for important visitors, in the process meeting some of the leading lights of his field—men such as Alfred Russell Wallace, one of Charles Darwin's most vigorous defenders and a co-discoverer of evolution through natural selection.

Pammel was doubtless well connected, having impressed some of America's leading botanists, but he did not begin to make a name for himself until 1888. He spent the summer of that year in Texas studying cotton rot. The paper he would ultimately publish describing the results of his study demolished the conventional understanding that worms caused the rot. Pammel discovered that "a fungus mycelium" was responsible, and further noted that "the fungus was not *Ozonium auricomas* as Dr. Farlow . . . [had] advised him to call it, but . . . was probably a Pyrenomycete."[51] This discovery, coupled with his connections, thrust Pammel into relative prominence, and he would go on to publish several hundred scientific articles over the course of his career.[52]

He returned from Texas to St. Louis in the fall of 1888 and seemed reasonably content there with his mentor, wife, and first child. At the end of that year, however, the botanist who had replaced Bessey at the IAC resigned his position to accept a similar one at Rutgers, and Trelease encouraged Pammel to apply. He was not the candidate William Chamberlain, the IAC's president, initially favored, but he was easily the most qualified applicant, and Chamberlain reluctantly agreed to hire him. Thus, Carver arrived at the beginning of Pammel's third year in Ames.

Carver spent a good deal of time at Pammel's home—even more, perhaps, than he did at the homes of Wallace, Wilson, and Budd. Writing one of the Pammels' daughters to express his sympathy for her mother's passing in the 1930s, Carver expressed the grief he shared with the family. "I am sure all you children can appreciate my feeling," he scribbled, "as your home at Ames was my home, and your Sainted mother and father never tired of doing lovely things for me."[53] Pammel's legacy to Carver lay not primarily in their friendship, however—though both valued it highly—but rather in Carver's scientific training, particularly in his exposure to the ideas that were then coalescing into the nascent field of ecology.

Although Charles Darwin laid the foundation for the science of ecology in the mid-nineteenth century, modern ecology did not begin to come into its own until the 1890s.[54] In part this is due to the fact that in America, at least, the natural sciences were not especially well funded. Botany was still in its infancy, and many of its branches—phylogeny, cytology, mycology, and plant pathology—were just beginning to develop. This is evident in the fact that the Botanical Society of America was not established until 1894, with Trelease as its first president.[55] As botany was widely linked to agriculture (even Darwin had offered practical advice to farmers based on the principle that cross-fertilization was superior to self-fertilization), the passage of the Hatch Act rectified the lack of funding to some degree and contributed to botany's rapid growth in the 1890s.[56]

European botanists had made rather more progress than Americans over the course of the late nineteenth century. While the influence of Gray, Farlow, Bessey, William J. Beal, and a few other American botanists was felt across the Atlantic, European scientists such as Herman Mueller, Fritz Mueller, Frederico Delpino, Johan Severin Axell, Anton Kerner von Marilaun, Ernst Haeckel, Oscar Drude, Eugenius Warming, and Andreas

Schimper pioneered most of the innovations in the field. The last four have attracted particular attention among historians who have studied ecology's history. Haeckel, Darwin's leading proponent in Germany, first used the term "œcology" in 1866 to refer to "the science of the relations of living organisms to the external world, their habitat, energies, parasites, etc."[57] But it was Warming, Drude, and Schimper who led the push toward modern ecology in Europe.[58] In his classic history of ecological ideas, *Nature's Economy*, Donald Worster argued that the most influential of these "was Eugenius Warming, a Danish professor who produced the key synthesis that forced the scientific world to take note at last of the new field of ecology."[59] Warming's synthesis, later translated into English as *The Oecology of Plants*, was published in 1895, only two years after ecologists held their first international meeting at the International Botanical Congress in Madison, Wisconsin, in 1893.

It is significant that the first international gathering of ecologists came at a botanical conference. Early on, botanists viewed ecology as a branch of botany, much like mycology or cytology. "It is a well known fact," Pammel asserted in a 1903 textbook titled *Ecology*, "that the plant is dependent on its surroundings." The study "of these life relations," Pammel continued, "is a branch of physiological botany known as ecology." As such, the study of ecology "should not precede structure or elementary principles of vegetable physiology."[60] Carver's mentor was hardly alone in considering ecology a branch of botany. As late as 1936, Walter P. Taylor pointed out in the journal *Ecology* that "according to a student of plants, ecology is perhaps very little more than a branch of botany."[61] Ecology soon gained traction in entomology, zoology, and forestry, however, prompting a debate among scientists as to its status: Was it "a scientific field or a point of view"?[62] But if the field had yet to coalesce while Carver was at the Iowa Agricultural College (the Ecological Society of America was not organized until 1915) ecology's central tenet was already clear: organisms and their environment are interdependent, or as Taylor later put it, "Nature . . . is not an accidental collocation of independent and unrelated objects, but is normally an organized and functioning whole."[63]

Pammel was in the vanguard of botanists attracted to the emerging field. Indeed, he published a book titled *Flower Ecology* (the first book in English with the term "ecology" in its title) no later than 1893, well before Warming published *The Oecology of Plants*. This suggests that the development of the science was less linear than renowned ecologist Paul B. Sears allowed when he contended that Americans were introduced to ecology only "when the works of Warming and Schimper made their way across the Atlantic."[64] Regardless, by the turn of the century the vital center of the nascent science rested in midwestern universities—especially the University of Nebraska, where a number of Bessey's students pioneered the field, and the University of Chicago, where Henry C. Cowles trained many of the most influential ecologists of the early twentieth century.[65] The Iowa Agricultural College, which was renamed Iowa State College in the late 1890s, did not contribute as much to the young field, but its botanist was certainly part of this movement.

Several things about Pammel's ecological interests merit particular notice with regard to the formal training Carver received under him. Perhaps most notable to contemporary students of ecology is his interest in what today are known as invasive species. Pammel had first developed an interest in weeds while studying with Trelease, and his interest in the subject never faltered. Noting that people are an integral part of the environment in which they live and work, Pammel gave some space to what might be termed "working landscapes" in his 1903 textbook. Pointing to railroads, irrigation ditches, and other "roadways," Pammel noted that "weeds in their migration have followed well defined lines of travel."[66] Though he recognized that such plant dispersal had been going on for a very long time—"There is no doubt that the Crusaders brought back many weeds from western Asia into Europe"—he expressed concern at its quickening pace in the early twentieth century, in the United States and elsewhere in the world.[67]

Pammel's concern over invasive species was chiefly agricultural, and in this regard he was hardly alone. By the middle of the 1890s scientists were recognizing that the push to introduce new species into North America had resulted in some serious problems, epitomized in the proliferation of pests that threatened either agriculture (e.g., the boll weevil, the San Jose scale, wheat rust, and the Russian thistle) or desirable native species (e.g., the trees assailed by the gypsy moth). This realization, compounded by economic concerns sparked by the Panic of 1893, had led to widespread calls to pass legislation requiring farmers to check the spread of such species through various means. Most of these efforts were carried out at the state level, but the passage of the Lacey Act (1900), which gave the USDA regulatory authority over the deliberate introduction of exotic species, indicates that the concern was national.[68]

For his part, Pammel supported such legislation but considered it inadequate. He later poked fun at the attempt to regulate the spread of harmful invasive species by law as an effort "to remove by legislation some of the injurious weeds, expecting, of course, that the law would be obeyed and the weeds would soon be eliminated."[69] He was not alone in being skeptical that such legislation would by itself solve the problems. In an address to the American Association for the Advancement of Science delivered in the midst of the economic downturn that followed the Panic of 1893, for instance, the renowned horticulturist Liberty Hyde Bailey argued that Russian thistle and other pests filled gaps caused by the environmental disturbances inherent in agriculture and that only an understanding of individual weeds and their place in the environment would ultimately rectify the issue. The solution was to educate farmers; there was no getting around the fact that "laws cannot correct a vacancy in nature."[70] Pammel viewed the spread of "injurious weeds" as an inherently botanical problem that botanists could best address by developing what he termed "crop ecology."[71] To be sure, he had yet to articulate all of these ideas while Carver was his student, but his research was already tacking in that direction. Indeed, Pammel belonged to a sizable cadre of botanists—including notable figures such as Joseph C. Arthur, John Weaver, and Frederick Clements—who stressed the inherently agricultural applications of the nascent science of ecology.[72]

Thus, Pammel was in lockstep with the main currents of Progressive Era botany in viewing ecology as a practical science and education as an integral part of the solution to the crisis in agriculture. Recognizing the interdependence of plants and the environments in which they live was an important aspect of that education. After discussing the coevolution of bees and flowers in his textbook, for example, Pammel noted that farmers' common complaint that they "do not generally obtain a profitable agricultural harvest of red clover seed from the first crop of clover" stemmed from the fact "there are not enough bumble bees to pollinate the flowers."[73] Writing in 1914, Pammel contended that "a large number of botanical subjects need elucidation . . . especially crop ecology. What crops can be grown together to give the maximum returns for the money invested? It is the business of the ecologist to determine these crop relations."[74] Six years later, Barrington Moore, the first editor of *Ecology*, agreed with Pammel, writing in the journal's inaugural issue, "All agricultural research, except breeding, is ecology. To garner successful harvests it is necessary to know the relation of the cultivated plant to its environment."[75] Indeed, ecologists conceived of their field as a utilitarian science until the 1920s, when tensions over the credibility of ecology as a theoretical science caused a rift in the field that ultimately obscured the early connections between agriculture and ecology.[76] Though conservation and ecology are often conflated, it was not until the last decade of Carver's life that Sears, Taylor, Aldo Leopold, and others would find in ecology the undergirding philosophy of what would develop into the modern environmental movement.[77]

This is not to say that Pammel and his fellow ecologists were not concerned with conservation or were indifferent to the natural world they studied. On the contrary, Pammel marveled at the complex workings of Nature (always with a capital N). Discussing the coevolution of insects and flowers, for instance, he quoted Kerner to the effect that if "casual observation" of "flowers and their insect visitors" resulted in "aesthetic pleasure" and the production of "works of art, it may be imagined how great must be the incentive to scientific study supplied by a deeper insight into these phenomena."[78] By the 1920s Pammel was arguably the leader of Iowa's conservation movement, lamenting the fact that "many most interesting places have been destroyed because . . . people lacked interest in the things out of doors."[79] In 1921 he would introduce resolutions at the annual meeting of the Ecological Society of America recommending that the society formally declare that the deliberate introduction of nonnative species into national parks ought to be proscribed. The resolutions, which were unanimously endorsed, exemplify one of the ways in which Pammel believed legislation could aid the fight against invasive species that threatened to outcompete native ones.[80]

The foundational principles of ecology as Pammel presented them resonated with Carver, who had been a keen observer of the natural world since his childhood in Missouri, and whose religious sensibilities led him to see in nature the hand of a beneficent creator. Many of the terms that would come to be associated with ecology had yet to be coined at the time Pammel exposed Carver to the ideas that would undergird it. The term "ecosystem," for instance, was introduced in 1935 by British ecologist Arthur Tansley less than a decade before Carver's death (and in part, at least, as a repudiation of the school of ecology that had held sway among scholars for most of Carver's career). The science of ecology, of course, is no more static than the ecosystems it studies. But if Carver did not always use the vocabulary familiar to students of ecology today, he certainly embraced concepts they would recognize. After he left Iowa for Alabama, for instance, he habitually emphasized the need for farmers to appreciate the "mutual relationship of the animal, mineral and vegetable kingdoms, and how utterly impossible it is for one to exist in a highly organized state without the other."[81]

Considering Carver's deep religious faith, it is worth noting his acceptance of a field grounded in evolutionary science. Like Pammel (who had become active in the Episcopal church as an undergraduate), Liberty Hyde Bailey, Asa Gray, and many of their peers in the scientific community who were both devoutly religious and ardent advocates of science, Carver was not at all conflicted.[82] So far as Carver was concerned, science was truth; Christianity was truth as well, and the law of noncontradiction forbade conflict between them. He would not understand the bitter feud between fundamentalists and scientists that emerged in the wake of the Scopes Monkey Trial. In a letter to Mrs. Milholland written in the 1930s, for instance, Carver wrote, "My dear, dear friend if we could only learn that science is only *truth*, how it would quiet the turbulent waters in many instances. You and I wonder why humanity gropes . . . so over things that are so clear to me."[83] To be sure, in its early years ecology reflected "a self-consciously Christian social reform spirit," as Eugene Cittadino put it, in step with the values of the Progressive Era in which it emerged. Inasmuch as scientific inquiry is carried out within a cultural context, the early ecological models' focus "on communities of organisms that behaved as goal directed, integrated units in equilibrium with their natural environments" is not surprising.[84] If anything, Carver's introduction to ecology reinforced his faith and Social Gospel leanings.

There was more to Carver's education, of course, than the principles of ecology. In most regards his coursework was typical of agricultural college curricula for the period. During his first year he took only one agriculturally specific course—livestock—although his botany, entomology, and horticulture classes doubtless had an agricultural tilt to them. His sophomore year saw a heightened emphasis on the sciences, with more botany and horticulture classes as well as chemistry, zoology, and a general course in agriculture. By his junior year the bulk of his coursework listed decidedly in the direction of specific agricultural disciplines and included bacteriology, agricultural chemistry, principles of heredity, dairying, and vegetable pathology. His senior year was similar to his junior one; if anything the courses were even more topical as he took classes in the bacteriology of milk, farm drainage, seeds and grasses, and animal and vegetable nutrition.[85]

Carver compiled a very strong academic record at the college, earning less than a 3.0 out of a possible 4.0 in only one of his classes (algebra, during his first year). His lowest grades came in math, his highest in botany and horticulture. In the latter classes as well as the more specific courses that Pammel would have taught, such as vegetable pathology, Carver never earned less than a 3.9. This success, along with his connections with Budd, Wallace, Wilson, and Pammel (who was elected president of the Iowa Academy of Science in 1893), earned Carver invitations to speak around the state. One of his addresses, delivered before the Iowa State Horticultural Society after his junior year, was carried in the organization's yearly report and became his first publication.

The talk, titled "Grafting the Cacti," reflected Pammel's influence and indicated that the environmental vision Carver would espouse for the remainder of his life was well on its way to coalescing. Defending what he believed to be an unappreciated plant—"Those who have given [cacti] little or no thought," he began, "are apt to judge too harshly concerning their merits and demerits"—he argued that "nature does not expend its forces upon waste material, but that each created thing is an indispensable factor in the great whole, and one in which no other factor will fit exactly as well." His logic here is unquestionably ecological but was in step with his time inasmuch as he turned it toward a decidedly utilitarian end. Since "the cacti is one of these factors," he continued, "their widest range of usefulness [is] yet locked up within them waiting for the kindly hand of man . . . to wave his magic wand over them that they may show forth their long hidden usefulness."[86] In later years Carver's fame hinged on his ability to find uses for neglected plants, but the salient point here is that he viewed the natural world through an anthropocentric, even utilitarian, lens. Applied science was not in opposition to nature but, as his reference to "the kindly hand of man" suggests, in harmony with it. His later writings would clarify his anthropocentric view to some extent. He never suggested that nature existed only for human use, let alone for wanton consumption or abuse, and he insisted that human use was always to be carried out with the supposition that waste was anathema.

Carver's BSA thesis likewise reflected his belief in a harmony between scientists and the natural world they explored. Titled "Plants as Modified by Man," it grew out of research in hybridization, a relatively new branch of botany and horticulture that was rapidly expanding (and drawing criticism from those who believed that scientists were meddling with natural processes that ought to be left alone). "The casual observer regards us as usurping more privileges than belong to us," Carver contended of scientists who worked in the field (singling out Luther Burbank), but just "as the Chemist takes original elements or compounds, breaks up their combination or combines them into various proportions to suit his purpose, so we are to do the same without violating the laws of nature in the least." In the work being done on the genetic modification of plants, man was "simply nature's agent or employee to assist her in her work."[87]

He did sound a few notes of caution regarding hybridization research, pointing out, for instance, that "nature refuses to indulge man only so far on his modifications of both plants and animals as we find hybrids in either case as a rule are sterile." More troubling, breeding plants for economic purposes such as farming could prove counterproductive inasmuch as doing so favored one characteristic over another. Nature would allow such meddling, Carver noted, "but at the expense of some other function of the plant." He viewed the manipulation of plant breeding to purify stocks or create flowers or fruits of "abnormal" size as "a violation to nature's laws and hence must be done at the expense of vitality." And yet, he concluded, after tracing experiments done in the IAC's orchard, "why should not the horticulturist know just how to build up size, flower, vigor and hardiness in his fruits and shrubs?"[88]

Carver's thesis capped his career as an undergraduate. On November 13, 1894, he formally graduated from the school's course in agriculture. He did not graduate with honors, as only one student from each division could do so; the agricultural award that year went to Carver's friend Charles D. Reed.[89] Even so, Carver had sufficiently impressed his instructors that they suggested he pursue an advanced degree at the college and offered him a position as an assistant botanist at the school's experiment station. "The Lord is wonderfully blessing me and has for these many years," he wrote the Milhollands a month before graduating. "I have been elected assistant station bottanist [sic]. I intend to take a post graduate course here, which will take two years," he informed them before adding that he hoped "in the meantime" to "take a course at the Chicago Academy of Arts and the Moody institute."[90] Apparently Carver had won the favor of the community by the time of his graduation, as he was no longer living in an office but was boarding, along with two other men, in the home of Eliza Owens, a widow who worked as a professor of domestic economy at the school. Though the 1895 state census listed his age as twenty-seven, he was probably closer to thirty when he began his graduate studies.[91]

"Gifted with an intense love of nature," the school's 1895 yearbook noted of Carver, "he is an artist of the most delicate touch and is also an earnest conscentious [sic] Christian worker."[92] Though he was technically a faculty member, he continued to eat with the undergraduates and continued his connection with the college's Art Club. Having been the first African American undergraduate at the school, he became the first black graduate student and the first African American to instruct students there, teaching in the bacteriology laboratory and leading classes in systematic botany.[93] But his work increasingly shifted toward helping Pammel, who oversaw the bulk of Carver's graduate study. Pammel later recalled that Carver "was much interested in collecting fungi" and proved to be "the best collector I ever had in the department or have ever known."[94]

In his first year as a graduate student, Carver jointly published two articles with his mentor, both in the field of mycology—the branch of botany dealing with fungi—where Pammel had already distinguished himself. The first was a refutation of a study done by a scientist at the USDA that challenged some of Pammel's earlier findings relative to the effectiveness of the most commonly applied fungicide of the era, a copper sulphate–based concoction known popularly as Bordeaux mixture. The second amounted to a list of parasitic fungi found in Ames that year "for the purpose of making comparison" in subsequent years.[95]

Carver also collaborated with F. C. Stewart, one of Pammel's former students and a mycologist at the New York State Experiment Station. Their joint article traced a particular rust associated with red cedars that in its immature form attacked fruit trees but was noticeably absent from Iowa despite controlled attempts to introduce it for study. He wrote three of his own works as well, two of which were published as experiment station bulletins. The first was a typical bulletin that offered practical advice for selecting and raising ferns in Iowa.[96] The second, which dealt with "window gardens," he wrote at the request of Wilson, who in his capacity as station director had felt compelled to produce something on the topic as a consequence of the "increasing interest shown by the ladies of our state in Floriculture." Carver enjoined the bulletin's readers to "become acquainted with [their] plants," to study their "habits in a state of nature and . . . in fact [to] find out all you can about them and give to each plant as nearly as possible its natural environment."[97] The third work, titled "Plant Environment" and delivered as a paper at the annual meeting of the Iowa State Horticultural Society, had a similar bent, offering a "few simple illustrations to teach us that much of our success in orchard, field and garden will depend on the closeness with which we stick to nature's laws in the way of giving to each plant its proper environment."[98]

By 1895, a year in which Carver secured funding from the state horticultural society for research on cross-breeding and was tabbed as a judge for the state fair by the Iowa State Agricultural Society, his reputation clearly was growing.[99] It had, in fact, begun to reach beyond the state's borders, as evidenced in November of that year when Alcorn Agricultural and Mechanical College, an African American institution in the Mississippi Delta, wrote President Beardshear to offer Carver a faculty position at the school. Pointing out that Carver was "universally liked by faculty and students," Beardshear replied, "We would not care to have him change unless he can better himself." The unsolicited offer piqued Carver's interest and flattered him to boot. The letters of recommendation he furnished for the position were predictably strong. Budd claimed that the IAC wanted to keep him and pointed out that Carver "will get next year as good a salary as you offer." Pammel's acknowledged "great confidence in Mr. Carver's ability. This has been backed up by having him reappointed assistant with an increase in salary. I believe," Pammel asserted, "Mr. Carver has a great future before him." Wilson's letter, however, was perhaps the most glowing. In "cross-fertilization . . . and the propagation of plants, he is by all means the ablest student we have here. Except the respect owe [sic] the professors, I would say he is fully abreast of them and exceeds in special lines in which he has a taste." Indeed, Wilson maintained, the school would find it "difficult, in fact impossible, to fill his place. These are warm words," Wilson concluded with the sort of resounding endorsement of which graduate students dream, "such as I have never before spoken in favor of any young man leaving our institution, but they are all deserved."[100]

While Carver was mulling over Alcorn's offer in the spring of 1896, Booker T. Washington, the president of the best-known black school in the country, was despairing of finding an African American candidate qualified to head Tuskegee Institute's new agricultural department. Easily the leading black voice of his time, Washington had burst onto the national scene less than a year earlier with an address at the Atlanta Exposition in which he laid out the quintessential expression of accommodationism, professing that African Americans were willing to tolerate social segregation in return for economic opportunity. When Washington learned of Carver in late March, he wrote to offer him a position as the head of Tuskegee's nascent agricultural school.

"I have just returned from a lecture tour and found your letter waiting for me," Carver wrote Washington on April 3. For Carver, who had left his beloved art classes at Simpson in the hope of pursuing just such an opportunity, an offer to work at the school headed by the most famous African American figure in the nation could hardly have been more welcome. Downplaying his enthusiasm, however, Carver informed Washington that he intended to finish his master's degree in the fall and that "until then I hardly think I desire to make a change, although I expect to take up work among my people and have known of and appreciated the great work you are doing." He indicated his interest in the position only in the note's postscript: "Should you think further upon this matter I can furnish you with all the recommendations you will care to look over."[101] Two days later, Carver thought better of his initial letter and penned a second to Washington. "Of course I should prefer to stay here until the fall," he wrote, "but should I get a satisfactory position I might be induced to leave before."[102] A week later he wrote again to Washington, telling him that "it has always been the one great ideal of my life to be of the greatest good to the greatest number of 'my people' possible, and it is to this end I have been preparing myself for these many years." He informed Tuskegee's president that he intended "to give a more definite answer" in his next communiqué.[103]

After reading Carver's letters, Washington practically begged the young scientist to take the position at Tuskegee. Explaining that he had secured the funding for an agricultural department at the school from the John F. Slater Fund, he acknowledged that the fund's board of trustees had suggested that he hire a white man for the position because "there was no colored man in the country fitted for such work." His discovery of Carver had made it possible for him to retain an all-black faculty. Should Tuskegee fail to "secure" Carver, "we should be forced perhaps to put in a white man." Hinting to Carver that the Tuskegee position presented an opportunity superior to Alcorn's offer, Washington promised that the new school would "certainly be the best equipped and only distinct agricultural school in the South for the benefit of colored people." He offered Carver a salary of one thousand dollars a year, a sum he confessed "may not seem a large salary." His real appeal was to Carver's moral conscience. Tuskegee had "made a policy of trying to get teachers who come not only for the money but also for their deep interest in the race." Linking Carver's decision to the future of Tuskegee's agricultural program, Washington suggested that the remainder of the money they needed for an agricultural building might be raised "much faster" if Carver decided to come. "If the terms I have named are not satisfactory," Washington at last conceded, revealing his desperation, "we shall be willing to do anything in reason that will enable you to decide in favor of coming to Tuskegee."[104]

Predictably, Carver was "very much pleased with the spirit" of Washington's letter. He informed Tuskegee's president that one of his professors "told me today they would raise my wages here if I would stay," but added that he had "been looking for some time at Tuskegee with favor" and that "the financial feature" of Tuskegee's offer was "at present satisfactory." Requesting that Washington let him know specifically what he would be expected to teach and broaching the idea of bringing "my collections and cabinets with me for use"—implicitly asking for a place to put them—Carver finally notified Washington that if "the course of study is not something out of my range I will accept the offer." He concluded by noting, "I shall await an answer with a considerable degree of anxiety."[105]

When Carver still had not heard from Washington a week later, he wrote an urgent note begging acknowledgment of his previous letter. As fate would have it, Carver's note and the reply he awaited crossed in the mail. The matter was settled by the end of the first week of May 1896. Carver would finish his degree in the fall and go to Tuskegee immediately afterward. "Providence permitting," he wrote Washington, I will be there in Nov[ember]."[106] The plan Etta Budd had inspired was coming to fruition. Washington's offer confirmed Carver's belief that God had destined the plan for him. He was to be a missionary to the impoverished black farmers of the South, bringing them a gospel of scientific agriculture that promised a better life. "I . . . shall be glad to cooperate with you in doing all I can through Christ who strengtheneth me to better the condition of our people," he wrote Washington in mid-May. And with a martyr's resolve, he finished the preparations for his mission.

By early October Carver had finished his graduate work, and on Monday, October 5, fully a month ahead of schedule, he left the Midwest for the first time in his life. At his sendoff, his friends and professors presented him with "a microscope with case complete" to take with him to Tuskegee. The sentiment of his peers at the time of his departure was the antithesis of the cool greeting he had received on his arrival. "We know of no one who failed to be won to friendship by his genial disposition," the *Iowa Agricultural College Student* asserted, "and we are not guilty of meaningless praise when we wish him God Speed."[107] After his arrival in Alabama, Carver wrote a public thank-you note to his "dear IAC Friends." "This evening," he wistfully began, "as I sit at my writing desk, many miles from you, in the sunny south-land, I wish I could make you feel how thankful I am for the beautiful and useful presents you so kindly gave me." Embracing the rhetoric of a martyr, Carver continued, "You who have no such problems to face as I have here can scarcely appreciate their usefulness to me."[108] To be sure, Carver had much to be thankful for as he began his work in the heart of the Deep South. His conviction that Providence had ordained him for the task of turning agricultural science to the "uplift" of benighted ex-slaves and their children, however, would be tested almost from his very arrival at Tuskegee.

CHAPTER 3

The Ruthless Hand of Mr. Carenot

Despite his thorough scientific training, Carver was unprepared in some significant ways for the world he encountered when he stepped down from the train in Macon County, Alabama. As a native of the Midwest, Carver found himself in unfamiliar social, political, and ecological terrain. Understanding that terrain is essential to understanding Carver's environmental vision, for his efforts to reform the prevailing agricultural landscape are unintelligible considered outside the agroecological context of Alabama's Black Belt—along with the socioeconomic and political world that shaped it. Furthermore, this was the world in which he went for daily nature walks, collected mycological specimens, plowed, planted, and communed with "the Great Creator." It was the world he needed to understand if he was to fulfill the plan he believed God had ordained for his life, a world full of secrets for him to reveal to his people.

Macon County, Alabama, of which Tuskegee is the seat, was a relatively new world in its own right. Less than one hundred years earlier it had been situated in territory belonging to the largest and arguably most feared group of southeastern Indians; indeed, it lay in the very heart of Creek country.[1] Although Creek towns were concentrated along the Coosa, Tallapoosa, and Chattahoochee rivers in eastern Alabama and western Georgia, the Creeks

claimed sovereignty over a substantially larger area. At the time of naturalist William Bartram's expedition in the 1770s, Creek country amounted to
some 62,130 square miles stretching from the Tombigbee River in the west,
where it bordered Choctaw and Chickasaw territories in what today is eastern Mississippi and western Alabama, to the Oconee River in present-day
east-central Georgia in the east. To the south the Creeks' territory blended
with that of their close allies, the Seminoles, along the Gulf Coast; to the
north their territorial claims ended in Cherokee country along the Tennessee River.

In the very middle of Creek country—along the Upper Trading Path
connecting Tuckabatchee, the most important town of the Upper Creek,
with Coweta, its counterpart among the Lower Creek along the Chattahoochee—lay the area that would become Macon County. Located along
the fall line, an ecotone marking the convergence of the longleaf pine forest
of Alabama's coastal plain and the mixed southern forest of the piedmont,
Macon County held the southeasternmost settlements of the Upper Creek.
As the Creeks generally built their towns along the alluvial terraces of the
three main rivers, it is not surprising that the towns of Autosee, Tallas-
see, and a small portion of Tuckabatchee were on the Tallapoosa, along
what would later be Macon County's western border. Smaller towns such
as Chattuckchufaula (on Uphapee Creek in what would become Macon
County) and satellite settlements (distinguished by their lack of ceremo-
nial centers) occupied sites on secondary and tertiary streams. In general,
however, the area from which Macon County was carved was sparsely
populated, and the impressive and diverse landscape of "savannahs, groves,
cane swamps and open pine forests, watered by innumerable rivulets and
brooks" that Bartram described was more often crossed and hunted on than
lived in.[2]

At the fall line, the Tallapoosa River and Macon County's numerous
streams break into waterfalls, then widen and slow down, and so are more
prone to flooding. That factor provided a significant incentive for the Creek
to live at or above the fall line. The location was prudent for reasons other
than flood avoidance as well. The waters just below the falls and the shoals
above them contained abundant fish. Anthropologist Robbie Ethridge
pointed out that "even today the freshwater ecosystems of the southeastern United States contain the greatest variety of freshwater fish in North
America, and they are famous for their diversity of mollusks."[3] Macon
County was particularly blessed in terms of fishing. Benjamin Hawkins,

the U.S. Creek Indian agent from 1796 to 1816, reckoned Uphapee Creek to be "the most valuable creek known here for fish in the spring and summer," listing "sturgeon, trout, perch, rock, [and] red horse [red drum]" as being among them.[4] The shoals above the falls provided a nearly ideal environment for waterfowl and proved especially conducive to the growth of moss naturally rich in salt that attracted game, especially deer.

The wetlands along many of the waterways at the fall line offered an ideal habitat for many plants and animals, from river cane to berries, from birds to black bears. Depending on their purpose for being in Creek country, white observers either feared the swamps or saw possibilities in them. Those merely passing through the area avoided the swamps, and when forced to cross them often refused to dismount for fear of stepping on a "serpent" or "viper."[5] To be sure, Alabama's swamps are home to a number of venomous snakes—copperheads, cottonmouth moccasins, and coral snakes. Even a few alligators ventured as far north as Macon County. Whites who hoped to develop Creek country along the lines of the rest of the nation, however, saw potential farmland. Hawkins, for instance, described a wetland near the Creek town of Cooloome as "a rich swamp . . . which, when reclaimed, must be valuable for corn or rice, and could easily be drained."[6] Indeed, the canebrakes along rivers and creeks—swampy places where bamboo-like river cane had proliferated—were already well known as markers of unusually rich soil.[7]

The fall line also represents a transitional ecological zone, and thus marks changes not only in the waterways themselves but in the flora and fauna of the region. To the north lay the mixed forests of the southern uplands. As its name implies, the southeastern mixed forest contained large numbers and varieties of both coniferous and deciduous trees; its undergrowth proved equally diverse. Certain hardwood trees, such as the American chestnut, could be ten feet in diameter and so tall that the trunk did not branch until forty feet or more above the ground, with branches reaching fifty feet on either side of the trunk. In some years, the mast from the chestnut, oak, and hickory trees could be measured in inches. "To keep within the bounds of truth and reality, in describing the magnitude and grandeur of these trees," Bartram wrote, "I fear, fail of credibility."[8]

To the south of the fall line lay Bartram's "open pine forests" of the coastal plain, which though interspersed with other species were dominated by longleaf pines. The trunks of the pines often extended seventy or eighty feet above the forest floor, and when the wind blew, the branches whistled, sang, or whispered. In Creek country the pines were widely spaced, leaving wire-grass as the dominant ground cover. Other grasses grew there as well, as did some three thousand species of wildflowers. Given the region's substantial rainfall, the predilection of its waterways to flood, and the general flatness of the coastal plain, swamps were more prevalent below the fall line.

Where the two regions converged along the fall line, their biotas over-lapped, producing an extraordinarily diverse assembly of plant and animal resources. In large measure this biodiversity was the driving force behind the location of the vast majority of Creeks' towns within the transitional zone between the longleaf pine forest and southeastern mixed forest. The towns of Macon County were no exception.

In addition to the advantages provided by the diverse biota, the transition zone along the fall line had one more significant feature peculiar to its environment: the savannah-like plains of the Black Belt, a name that describes a distinctive geology and soil rather than the demographic pre-ponderance of African Americans as a result of the plantation culture that would thrive there. From Macon County, which sits on its eastern edge, the Black Belt curves along the fall line west and north into northeastern Mississippi, following the ancient shoreline of a sea that lapped the hills rolling up toward the Appalachians during the Cenozoic Era. Over millions of years, plates of drifting microscopic algae settled on the bottom and formed limestone subsoil known today as Selma Chalk. In what amounted to a geological perfect storm, large pockets of this limestone remained near the surface after the sea receded. Because the limestone was impermeable, plant nutrients collected near the surface, creating an organically rich and responsive topsoil with few equals in the South, albeit a comparatively difficult one to work as it was a rather sticky clay.[9]

The fact that the soils were shallow—generally less than a foot deep—and alkaline rather than acidic (in marked contrast to most southern soils) made them less than ideal for longleaf pine but ideally adapted to prairie bunchgrasses and wildflowers. The result was a series of smallish prairies dotted across the landscape that eighteenth-century white observers referred to as "savannahs," "plains," or "meadows." Bartram, for instance, noted "expansive, illumined grassy plains" paralleling the Tallapoosa. The "upper stratum or vegetable mould of these plains is perfectly black, soapy and rich . . . [and] lies on a deep bed of white, testaceous, limestone rocks, which in some places resemble chalk."[10] Bartram's description of the soil explains why the region would subsequently be dubbed the "Black Belt," though in recent years scientists have often called it the "Black Prairie" in order to avoid confusion with the demographic Black Belt.

Bartram described glades of trees from the surrounding forests "project[ing] into the plains on either side, dividing them into many vast fields."[11] The British naturalist Philip Henry Gosse likewise observed these fields during his brief stay in the region in 1838. Each, he noted, was surrounded by woods "on every side like an abrupt wall" and ranged in size from a few acres to a square mile.[12] While the Creeks did not farm the prairies because the clay soil was too difficult to work—rich alluvial soil was as readily available, easier to cultivate, and plenty responsive—the Black Belt prairies provided rich browse and graze for white-tailed deer and other game animals. White observers, however, noted the agricultural potential of the organically rich soil and the ease with which the prairies might be brought into cultivation because little was needed in the way of clearing. As a further inducement to future white settlers, the limestone subsoil had dissolved away over millions of years, creating in essence a funnel that brought Alabama's major rivers through the region: the Tombigbee from the northwest, and the Alabama, formed from the confluence of the Coosa and Tallapoosa rivers about thirty miles west of Macon County, from the east. In an era in which water transportation was paramount, this was no small matter, and it made the region even more desirable to would-be settlers.

With its mild climate, high annual rainfall, long growing season, and Black Belt soils, Macon County was thus—to borrow a phrase Carl Ortwin Sauer applied to the entirety of the territory belonging to the southeastern Indians—"an especially favored country for extensive agriculture."[13] The county's Creek residents could indeed boast, as Carver would later assert of the South as a whole, of having "natural advantages of which [they] may justly feel proud."[14]

Of course, Creek country was not an Eden entirely unstressed by its human population. The Creeks manipulated the environment both for their sustenance and for economic and political leverage against colonial powers and later the United States. Their growing dependence on European manufactures over the course of the eighteenth century prevented Creeks living along the major trading paths from moving away when their fields became less responsive, and so by the time of the American Revolution there were localized soil crises.[15] The introduction of livestock led Creeks to be of one mind with European Americans in pushing for the extirpation of predators such as wolves and cougars. Even in the absence of predators, however, white-tailed deer had been pushed to the brink of extinction by the explosion of the deerskin trade in the wake of the Yamasee War (1715).[16] Considering the extraordinary reproductive capabilities of the white-tailed deer, their relative scarcity by the dawn of the nineteenth century provides a clear example of large-scale environmental transformation prior to white settlement.[17]

The decline in the deer population coincided with another event that would bode ill for the Creeks. Eli Whitney's cotton gin, patented in 1793, facilitated the extraction of seeds from the bolls of short-staple cotton. That in turn made growing cotton away from the coast (where the more finicky Sea Island cotton was already a highly profitably raised crop) a lucrative endeavor, the more so since it coincided with an international boom in the demand for cotton as a less expensive alternative to woolen, silk, and linen textiles. White Americans, especially Georgians, turned their eyes inland toward Creek country and saw something they had not seen before—a compelling reason to expropriate it (to borrow a phrase from Chief Justice Earl Warren) with all deliberate speed. During the height of the deerskin trade, Creek hunters had been a vital part of the global economy. By the 1790s, however, as Ethridge pointed out, "the Creeks as well as all of the southern interior Indian societies found themselves not only unnecessary to the American economy, but in fact . . . impediments to it."[18]

The Creeks' struggle to keep their land stretched out over decades, but by 1826 they had been forced to cede their claims to all but 5 million acres in eastern Alabama.[19] Macon County, which remained part of this diminished Creek territory, saw its population boom, leaping from about 1,500 in 1800 to roughly 6,000 in the wake of the 1826 treaty.[20] Where there had been four towns there were now fifteen, among them the town of Tuskegee along Calebee Creek, situated not far from where the federal road connecting New Orleans with Washington, D.C., crossed the creek and began to follow its south bank toward the Tallapoosa River. Its location along the federal road made Tuskegee a reasonably important trading town, and Creeks there (and elsewhere along the road) hocked wares to migrating settlers, stage passengers, and postal carriers and provided shelter when rains washed out the road or wagons broke down.[21]

Even though it was still legally occupied by the Creeks, Macon County was formally incorporated in 1832 and completely surveyed and mapped by early the following year. Predictably, the county's chief business was land speculation. Bystanders and victims by turn in the speculative rush, the Creeks began making plans to emigrate west. When in the spring of 1836 armed conflict broke out as small bands of Creeks launched "a reprisal against the land speculators" who sought to take advantage of them, white settlers feared that the scattered attacks would result in a full-fledged uprising.[22] Some counseled caution, such as the editors of the *Montgomery Advertiser* in neighboring Montgomery County, which "deprecate[d] the conduct of those who are continually sounding the cry of danger when there is none to be apprehended." But their words were drowned out by the shouts of those who wanted the Creeks gone forever, and the governors of Alabama and Georgia appealed to the federal government to intervene and crush the Indian "uprising."[23]

In June 1836 a U.S. Army contingent under General Thomas Jesup arrived in the white town of Tuskegee, a speculative endeavor a couple of miles north of "Indian Tuskegee" to which the federal road had been rerouted. By the end of the month, Jesup considered the Creek War concluded. On August 17 he issued orders for the removal of 2,700 Creeks, and on September 2 the forced exodus began. The following February, whites raided the remaining Creek communities, burning and plundering Creek landholdings. The Creeks fled the county and were escorted by the army to Mobile and from there to the West.

Despite the environmental changes that had attended the previous half-century, at the time of Creek removal Macon County still looked more like the environment through which Bartram had passed in 1775 than the one Carver would encounter in 1896. Mrs. Basil Hall, for instance, marveled in 1828 that the forest was sufficiently open to permit horses to pull a carriage through "the very heart of it." Her husband, Captain Basil Hall, acknowledged that the region was marked by "very pretty woods." Six years later, G. W. Featherstonaugh passed through the county and commented on the "pleasantly running" streams and their banks "covered with laurels, live oaks and other evergreens," and noted that "wild grass was growing everywhere in profusion." Other travelers commented on the clarity of the water, the beauty of the wildflowers, and the general aesthetic appeal of the place. Europeans in particular were fulsome in their praise of the region's beauty.[24] To be sure, the landscape itself was changing: white-tailed deer were virtually gone; wolves and river cane were fading fast; fences surrounded the now-abandoned Creek fields; and cattle and hogs foraged in the woods. The changes wrought by the Creeks' successors, however, would far outstrip these.

Indeed, the newcomers would push back the forest, strip the soil of its humus, and turn the region's signature waterways brown with silt. Those ecological changes did not occur overnight. For some time following Creek removal and the failure of two speculative endeavors along the Tallapoosa, white Tuskegee remained the only inhabited town in Macon County.[25] Settlers had begun farming along the county's two main roads and along the rich bottomlands of its streams, but the real business there was still land speculation. Eighty-seven percent of the land forcibly appropriated from the Creeks was bought by individuals (or land companies) whose purchases in the county met a minimum standard of 2,000 acres. One company, Watson, Walker, Harris, et al., for example, purchased some 477,000 acres in the late 1830s and early 1840s, and realized a nearly 100 percent profit in selling the land, primarily to planters emigrating from South Carolina and Georgia.[26]

Typical of the men investing in the county was T. S. Woodward, who is remembered as the founder of Tuskegee. Woodward had first seen the area in 1813 and 1814 as a soldier under Andrew Jackson, and had passed through it again in 1818 on his way to fight the Seminoles in Florida. Following the county's incorporation in 1832, Woodward had organized and laid out white Tuskegee, and then had begun buying Indian allotments. Relatives of his won the contract to regrade the federal road through the county, and rerouted it through white Tuskegee. His own company, Woodward, Strange, Harris, Jones, et al., purchased more than 46,000 acres in the county, and he was a silent partner with his brother-in-law, J. C. Watson, in Watson, Walker, Harris, et al. By the end of the 1830s Woodward had speculated on some of the choicest land in the county, including a three-square-mile block along the county's main thoroughfare.[27]

Although some 142,000 acres—slightly less than a quarter of the county's land—were open to public purchase at auction, speculators had no difficulty unloading their property. By 1840 the county was booming. Tuskegee, with a population of three hundred, remained the largest town, but others, including Union Springs and Auburn, had been established and were growing quickly. Within a few years many of the speculators, including Woodward, had sold the last of their land and moved on. Woodward, like his counterparts, had profited handsomely, as is indicated by the $20,000 dowry he left to a slave daughter he freed on his death. At the end of the 1840s, a debating society could meet in Tuskegee to discuss whether or not the government was justified in appropriating Indian lands without so much as a hint of irony.[28]

By virtue of sheer numbers, the county's new residents placed an increased strain on its environment. The Creek population of the county had never exceeded 6,000, even at its densest, but the 1840 census counted more than 11,000 people living in the county. The forest was pushed back continually as white settlers and their slaves moved in. The Creeks had cleared land almost exclusively in the floodplain, where the forest was in various stages of succession. Not so with their white successors, who cleared the old-growth forest along the ridges as well. In a recently cleared section of the west-central portion of the county, one contemporary counted some 320 rings on the stump of a felled tree.[29]

By 1850 the population of Macon County had peaked at 26,898 people. The fact that 15,612 of them were slaves indicates the degree to which its residents were engaged in commercial agriculture. A decade earlier the population of the county had been nearly evenly divided between slaves and free. To be sure, some large slaveholders had settled in the county by 1840 and more were moving in, but much of the land was still held by independent white farmers, many of whom were essentially squatters. Over the course of the 1840s, however, the planters had consolidated their landholdings and political power, and by 1850 the solidification of a plantation culture in Macon County was very nearly complete.[30]

Only about one-third of the 1,273 farming households that the 1850 census reported living in the county owned no slaves. And of these 420 non-slave-owning households, only 224—slightly more than one-half—owned the land they worked. Thus, fewer than 20 percent of the farmers in the county could be considered yeomen, and most of their holdings were relegated to marginal soils of the rolling ridges in the northeastern portion of the county. By contrast, 444 farming households owned between one and nine slaves, with the average small slaveholder owning five; only 82 households owned a single slave. Virtually all of these 444 households owned their own land, and they farmed, on average, an area twice as large as their non-slave-holding counterparts but were eight times wealthier. These small slaveholders, who often pooled their slaves' labor at harvest and other busy times, were still considered small farmers inasmuch as they devoted most of their attention to the production of subsistence rather than cash crops.[31]

The real power—political, economic, and social—rested with the plantation owners who controlled the 409 farming households with ten or more slaves. They owned roughly 80 percent of the slaves and a large majority of the land in the county. A quick survey of some statistics from the 1850 census confirms their economic dominance. Non-slave-holding households had an average landholding wealth of $445; the average small slaveholder, $1,113. The county's 275 small plantations (those with at least ten but fewer than twenty-five slaves) had an average landholding wealth of $2,550. The average land wealth of the one hundred medium-sized plantations (with more than twenty-five but fewer than fifty slaves) amounted to $5,854; the thirty large plantations (of between fifty and one hundred slaves) could claim average landholdings of $8,912; and the four largest plantations (of more than one hundred slaves) had an average landholding wealth of $15,650, better than fourteen times that of the households owning fewer than ten slaves. When slave wealth was factored in, even the small plantation owners controlled three times the wealth of their small slaveholding counterparts, and the largest plantations had an average wealth nearly eight times that of the small plantations.[32]

Though the specific figures differed, what was true of Macon County in 1850 was true of other Black Belt counties as well. Macon County was not exceptional among them in having slaveholders constitute roughly two-thirds of its households, or in the fact that one-third of its farming households were considered plantations. As in other Black Belt counties, the planters held a monopoly on the best lands, including the rich Black Belt soil, and virtually all the political power. In many ways, then, the foundation for the world Carver encountered had been laid by 1850 with the emergence of a plantation culture in which a few people dominated the political, economic, and social community, and African Americans worked the fields.

The planters' wealth and power was directly related to their production of the crop Alabamians held most dear: cotton. Historian Weymouth T. Jordan noted that plantation owners produced almost all of the cotton grown in the state and "made a ritual of their homage to cotton." They cultivated other crops as well, of course. The collapse of the boom market that had helped fuel the rise of cotton production—which more than tripled in the state during the 1830s—fostered a good bit of crop diversification in the early 1840s. Even so, cotton remained the principal source of the state's wealth, and perhaps more important, it retained an elevated place in planters' hearts—and nowhere more so than in the Black Belt, where, as Jordan succinctly and elegantly phrased it, "Alleluias were showered on agriculture; hosannas were reserved for cotton."[33]

As of 1850 Alabama led the nation in cotton production, and a decided majority of its cotton bales found their way down the state's rivers to Mobile, which was second only to New Orleans as a cotton port. A British visitor caught the spirit of Mobile in the 1850s, aptly describing it as "a pleasant cotton city of some 30,000 inhabitants—where people live in cotton houses and ride in cotton carriages. They buy cotton, sell cotton, think cotton, eat cotton, drink cotton, and dream cotton. They marry cotton wives, and unto them are born cotton children." Cotton was "the great staple, the sum and substance of Alabama."[34] The relocation of the state capital from Tuscaloosa to Montgomery, the chief trading hub of the Black Belt, in 1846 was one telling indication of how deeply Alabamians valued the cotton plantations of the Black Belt. By 1850, then, the political geography of the state reflected the overwhelming importance of cotton: its locus of power resided in the Black Belt, and cotton shipping was the chief business of the state's largest city.

The natural environment of Alabama bore the imprint of cotton no less than did the state's politics and culture. Macon County planters produced the nation's leading export in much the same way, and with the same sort of pride, as planters elsewhere. Winters generally found the slaves clearing new land, generally in the same way the Creek inhabitants had done before them: girdling trees and returning a few years later to burn the deadfalls, debris, and stumps. In addition to preparing what Macon County planter James M. Torbert called "newground," slaves cleared ditches; slaughtered livestock; burned "stubbleground" where the previous year's crops had been; planted spring wheat, oats, and potatoes; and hauled manure to the fields so that no time would be wasted when temperatures warmed sufficiently to plant corn.[35]

As spring arrived—typically in late February or early March in Macon County—corn was planted, followed quickly by garden crops. In 1856, for example, Torbert followed his corn with radishes, watermelons, squash, and peas. By April planters focused on getting their cotton in the ground, though if time allowed after the crops were in, slaves might return to "deadening" pines and clearing plots where girdled trees had already died.[36] May, June, and early July were typically spent chopping cotton and pulling grass to prevent it from choking out the cotton before it could be laid by (cultivated for the last time). July and August were spent harvesting grains, and by September the cotton was ripening and all hands were sent to the fields for picking. Shortly after the last of the cotton had been picked (and generally before all of it had been ginned), it was time to begin the process once again.

Torbert ran a medium-sized plantation near Society Hill in the eastern portion of the county, and his operation was typical of the place and time. In 1856 Torbert planted 165 acres in cotton and reaped 29 bales weighing an average of 586 pounds. Smaller plantations generally produced less than that; larger ones produced considerably more. His 120 acres of corn produced a scant 1,100 bushels of poor quality ("too much wet weather then too much dry," he noted in his journal). In addition he harvested 37 acres of oats and 12 of wheat, gathered 41 bushels of peas, and slaughtered 23 hogs (averaging slightly over 170 pounds) and "2 beefs."[37] The following year he put in 5 additional acres of corn and 10 of cotton. By 1860 he had 195 acres in cotton, 155 acres in corn, 20 acres in wheat, 40 in oats, and 7 in potatoes.[38] Thus, while he grew more cotton than any other single crop, other crops made up more in the aggregate.

Torbert's interest in raising cotton led him to protect the plantation community's investment in slaves. By comparison to many of his neighbors, Torbert treated his slaves relatively well—permitting them, for example, to plant 6 acres of their own cotton, which he later ginned and sold with his own, returning the profits to the adults—but he did not share the abolitionists' sentiment that African Americans could ever be his equals. Motivated partly by practical concerns and partly by cultural mores, he patrolled the local roads with his fellow planters to watch for runaways and verify slave passes. This was by no means an effective way to monitor the movements of slaves, however, because a secondary network of footpaths connected the slave quarters of neighboring plantations. Slaves could move almost unnoticed along the paths when they wanted to visit nearby family members. These footpaths would be expanded in the wake of the Civil War and would serve, in the words of sociologist Charles S. Johnson, "as the threads of neighborliness" in the county's black community well into the twentieth century: the law of unintended consequences at work in shaping the landscape Carver would encounter.[39]

Although agriculture was not the only economic engine for the county—Torbert, for instance, opened a sawmill in 1857—it was the plantation agriculture of Macon County that most altered and degraded its ecosystems. There is no evidence that planters were willfully "butchering the soil," but intent is no fair measure of outcome. Even by the 1840s soil exhaustion was becoming an increasing problem, especially in the poorer soil of the county's uplands. This was largely due to the county's (and state's) second-largest crop, corn. (Cotton does not place especially large demands on the soil.) The county's single greatest agricultural problem was erosion, however, and cotton cultivation was the single biggest contributor to it. Where plows rip into the earth to expose and loosen the tilth, the vulnerability of soil to erosion increases exponentially.[40] And in Macon County, where the forest was being pushed back over rolling land and few planters (or small farmers) were employing conservation measures, the rich humus of the topsoil was washed year after year into the county's numerous creeks and streams, turning them brown with silt and carrying away the land's very fertility. To be sure, the rich clay soils of the flatter Black Belt prairies eroded less easily, and so accounted for comparatively little of the silt muddying the waterways, especially in the antebellum years. But the shallow prairie soils were not immune to erosion, which posed perhaps a greater threat to them because once the limestone subsoil had been exposed, the fields could not be salvaged.

The planters sought to counteract the declining fertility by spreading fertilizer over their fields, most notably Peruvian guano (though by the late 1850s some planters, including Torbert, had turned to cottonseed as a fertilizer).[41] But whatever benefits such fertilizers might have had were more than undercut (at least in the long run) by the damage caused by the intensive cultivation of cotton and corn. The cotton planters' hatred of grass provides a particularly vivid illustration of the way planters waged "a petite war"—as one contemporary described it—against the soil in a misguided and self-defeating attempt to protect their investment in cotton.[42]

While the cotton was still immature, grass and other weeds could choke its growth, and planters like Torbert had to battle hard to save their cotton from the encroaching grass every spring—an annual ritual that caused a great deal of consternation. On May 23, 1856, for instance, Torbert noted in his journal, "I don't think I ever Saw More young grass Come up in My life." His fears mounted over the next month and a half. On May 27 he complained, "Oh the grass, I must Stay Clost to the hands a while and try to Keep the grass under if it Should rain and a few days wet I would have a bad road to travel with the grass." His fears lingered throughout June. In the middle of the month he reported, "Oh, the Grass My Crop I am afraid will be badly injured with the grass." By July 1 panic had set in: "I never

Saw grass grow as fast in My Life tis So large I can Scarcely plow it with a Shovel." It was not until July 9 that Torbert was able to note with some satisfaction that "at last the grass begins to die."[43] Planters generally had their field hands run plows up and down the furrows in a labor-intensive effort to kill the grass. Plowing the same furrows again and again opened the soil to even more extensive erosion. Worse, as was the case for Torbert in 1856, the practice was largely unsuccessful. His grass problem ended only when the spring rains stopped in early July; the repeated plowings did nothing to solve it.

While the vast majority of planters in Macon County followed similar policies, employing few, if any, conservation measures, some did advocate restraint in clearing new land and caution in cultivating it. The best known of these—indeed, one of the best-known advocates of scientific agriculture in the entire South in the late antebellum era—was Noah B. Cloud, whose farm, La Place, a few miles west of Tuskegee became an experiment station of sorts from which Cloud attempted to persuade the region's planters to develop their plantations more sustainably. Indeed, to the extent that Carver's agricultural vision harkened back to the high-minded husbandry of the nineteenth century, it carried echoes of Cloud's calls for reform.

Reformers such as John Taylor and Edmund Ruffin, along with such "green paternalists" as James Hamilton Couper and James Henry Hammond, are familiar figures to historians of the antebellum South, as are the agricultural interests of many of the leading southerners of the Early Republic—George Washington, James Madison, Patrick Henry, and Thomas Jefferson among others. Overwhelmingly, however, histories of antebellum agricultural reform have focused on the old states along the Atlantic Ocean and have devoted comparatively little ink to agricultural reformers of the Old Southwest.[44]

In part this imbalance reflects the relative interest in agricultural reform in the two regions. The older states had a much longer history of European-style cultivation, experienced soil erosion and exhaustion sooner, and sought solutions for those problems (albeit largely unsuccessfully) well before the forests of the southern frontier had been cleared and put under the plow. Indeed, when agricultural journals began to proliferate in the 1820s, few places in the Old Southwest had been cultivated long enough to warrant much concern over their well-being. In part, however, the imbalance reflects the larger understanding of the root cause of the antebellum reform efforts. In his seminal study of soil exhaustion in the South, Avery

Craven portrayed agricultural reform as the logical outgrowth of the frontier mentality. On the frontier, so the rationale went, waste was the rule. Only after the soils had been exhausted would a more responsible means of cultivation be embraced. Thus, for Craven—who in some ways resurrected the work of Taylor and Ruffin, whom he portrayed as heroes who sought to replace frontier-style waste with enlightened, progressive agricultural practices—soil exhaustion in Maryland and Virginia was not due to "any features that belong to the South alone as a section." Lest readers miss his oblique reference to slave-based plantation agriculture, he added or "its peculiar institutions and characteristics."[45] Craven instead blamed economic calculi in a situation where land was cheaper than labor. Though subsequent scholars would amend Craven's argument (most especially in revising the significance of slavery for southern land use), they have yet to fundamentally challenge it.[46]

Certainly there are solid grounds for embracing such a view, not the least being the fact that the agricultural reformers framed their reforms in just that context. Writing to the noted British agriculturist Arthur Young, for instance, Jefferson explained that Virginians did not practice convertible husbandry based on composting cattle manure and field rotation in the manner of their counterparts in the North and in Europe "because we can buy an acre of new land cheaper than we can manure an old one."[47] But such a focus has minimized the attention historians have devoted to the Old Southwest, which, being "frontier" (at least relative to the states along the Atlantic seaboard), has been assumed to have harbored a less vibrant reform impulse. While historians are well aware of the degree to which southern agricultural reformers advocated contour plowing to minimize erosion, encouraged (without much success) cover crops, founded agricultural and horticultural societies, corresponded with agriculturists in the North and abroad, and decried the exhaustion of agricultural lands, they are considerably less aware of the activities of men such as Cloud and Martin W. Phillips of Mississippi. Indeed, in his environmental history of the American South, Albert Cowdrey asserted that "complaints of planters about soil exhaustion were commonly heard, at least until the late 1840s," when sectional tensions muted them to some degree.[48] Such a narrative leaves little room for Cloud, who did not begin his career as a reformer until the late 1840s.

Born in South Carolina, Cloud was by training a physician, having graduated from Philadelphia's Jefferson Medical College in 1835, but at heart he was a husbandman. He moved to Russell County, Alabama, in 1838 before joining his father in neighboring Macon County five years later. While he was still in Russell County, living on a farm he dubbed Planter's Retreat, he began to undertake agricultural experiments. At about the time he moved to La Place he began publishing his findings, hoping to undermine what he labeled the "kill and cripple, and every way injurious system" of cotton cultivation in the South. His goal was to replace the prevailing cotton culture with "an entirely new and improved system of culture, predicated upon the principle of scientific and enlightened policy."[49]

Cloud overstated the novelty of his "improved system of culture"; he borrowed liberally from the convertible husbandry that agricultural societies in England and the North had long advocated.[50] The sine qua non of this sort of husbandry was livestock penning, and it is thus no surprise that Cloud denounced the South's open-range policy. Though many of the best-known agricultural reformers of the Old South (including Ruffin) downplayed the benefits of penning livestock and compost manuring, Cloud was not the first southerner to advocate convertible agriculture in the region.[51] John Taylor had proposed a program rather similar to Cloud's more than three decades earlier. In a collection of essays titled *Arator*, Taylor echoed English reformers (who, among other things, had sought to justify the enclosure movement) in maintaining that landowners—particularly those with extensive holdings—were better stewards of the land than the general public was under a commons system. Calling into question the region's open-range policy, he advocated the adoption of convertible husbandry with its extensive manuring. But while his essays bolstered the interests of the planter class, Taylor had little use (on a theoretical level, anyway) for slavery, which he considered an inefficient form of agricultural labor.[52] Cloud would disagree with Taylor's view of slavery and instead embrace the notion that only a carefully managed labor force such as that provided by slavery could implement the sort of labor-intensive agricultural regime he espoused. Cloud likewise diverged from other advocates of convertible husbandry in the South, including James Henry Hammond, who advocated keeping and penning livestock but insisted that "more can be made by planting [cotton] largely, than by making manure as a crop."[53] Convinced that "compost manuring, in connection with stock raising and pasturage" was "the true renovator of all agricultural exhaustion," Cloud would make no such compromise.[54]

If Cloud's system was not as novel as he maintained, it was not entirely derivative either. Over the course of the late 1840s and early 1850s he developed and advocated a remarkably strict agricultural program of his own. By the eve of the Civil War, the "Cloud system" had become one of the most talked-about plans for southern agriculture, inasmuch as it laid out a very specific regimen for cotton culture based on extensive compost manuring and deep plowing, which allowed the cotton plant's taproot to take "such hold upon the manure below as to enable the plant to outstrip either grass or weeds." The Cloud system thus solved two problems: it alleviated the erosion brought on by plowing to eliminate grasses and weeds, and it facilitated a more stable slave-based agriculture that did not entail continual expansion west as soils were exhausted.[55]

Cloud had little use for the prevailing method of controlling grass, explaining that repeated plowing weakened cotton plants by cutting their roots. Planters who blamed poor growth on dry spells or rainy weather, he continued, were refusing to admit that their war on grass was self-destructive, that their *grass killing* policy" wrought "disastrous consequences." He likened adding guano to soil treated in such fashion to feeding hogs after knocking out their teeth.[56] Cloud believed that once a cotton plant had begun to grow, there was "no further use for a plough in its subsequent culture." Instead he advocated the use of a "sweep," a scooter plow modified in such a way that it could not "enter the ground deeper than one inch, if so deep." The sweep could be dragged over the ground "so as to kill any grass and weeds that may appear" without threatening the cotton itself.[57]

Other details of Cloud's system included terracing, establishing specific distances between rows (and plants within rows), arranging piles of fertilizer in a particular way prior to plowing, and following a complicated system of crop rotation in which cotton was planted on the same land only once in four years, and then only after the field had been allowed to lie fallow for a year. He believed that only rigid adherence to such details could ensure success, measured in terms of both profitability and improved soil. His own farms, he maintained, had improved as a "result of a *strict and scrupulous adherence to* [the] *system in its management*," and he promised a bushel of his improved seed to anybody who "strictly" followed his plan and did not see at least a fivefold increase in the amount of cotton produced per acre.[58] In essence, Cloud was interested in rationalizing cotton production, comparing, for instance, his "*systematic, economical and philosophic* policy" with the "*inconsistent*, the *reckless* and *grassy* policy of the present practices of the country."[59]

The aim of this rationalization was not to increase the cotton yield aggregately—though he claimed that his system provided "*an infallible insurance for 5000 lbs. of a superior staple per acre*" (a remarkable promise considering that Torbert's farms produced roughly 175 pounds of cotton per acre).[60] Rather, he sought to attain the same production, but on less land through more diligent (and responsible) husbandry. In fact, his system expressly limited the planting of cotton: "The crop of cotton thus planted . . . should not exceed *three to four acres* to the hand."[61] According to Cloud's thinking, then, the exploitative social relations manifest in slavery need not lead to exploitative agricultural practices. On the contrary, slavery was essential to this remarkably labor-intensive plan to "make poor land rich, and rich land richer."[62]

What was possible in theory, however, had little basis in the reality of the Black Belt. Looking around Macon County, Cloud saw "a total absence and disregard of . . . the improvement and protection of the fertility of the soil," and was reminded of Ben Franklin's Poor Richard, who had assured Cloud and his fellow planters "that by constantly taking out of the meal tub and never putting in, we shall soon find the bottom." The typical planter's "acquaintance with this golden truth," Cloud feared, was "theoretic entirely. His exhausted fields and dwarfish, puny cotton, tell tales more positively contradictory and gloomy, than I have room or inclination now to enumerate."[63]

Cloud's peers lavished praise on him, but very few altered their methods of cultivation. Predictably, he grew frustrated at the disjuncture between his reputation—which by the 1850s had grown to the point that noted British agriculturist Robert Russell, on a tour of the South, was willing to walk nearly eight miles to see him—and his inability to persuade farmers to put his plan into practice.[64] He could only conclude that "this beautiful forest must be felled by the ruthless hand of Mr. Carenot, all this maiden and fertile soil must first be exhausted and washed into the branches, gurgling in pure and limpid water . . . and the fields defaced by gullies and poverty grass" before his fellow planters would be willing "to give in to a complete and perfect system of improvement."[65] Considering that he was writing within a tradition that implicitly acknowledged virtue as the actuating principle of a republic and treatment of the soil as a fair barometer of that supposed virtue, this was a serious indictment of his fellow southerners, particularly because it was written amid escalating sectional tensions.[66]

His indictment notwithstanding, Cloud joined a long list of agricultural reformers who earned the praise of their fellow southerners but ultimately failed in their efforts. Cloud would not be the last prophet of agricultural reform in Macon County to find himself praised but not heeded. Carver would offer similar laments, although his proposals were less rigid and he offered them to undermine rather than bolster the plantation system. In time, Carver too would join the ranks of reformers whose efforts wrought more praise than results.

For their part, planters liked the idea of crop diversification because it fit neatly with their growing sense of southern nationalism: self-sufficiency, decreased dependence on the North, and perhaps a chance to stick it to their abolitionist foes (whose cotton mills in the North and England were driven in large measure by slave labor in the Cotton Belt). They flocked to agricultural conventions, subscribed to agricultural papers, and eagerly listened to agriculturists' calls for more rational production. By the eve of the Civil War, for instance, Cloud's paper had a remarkable circulation of some 10,000 (it was rivaled in popularity only by the *Southern Cultivator*, a Georgia periodical).[67] The planters were clearly not unaware of or indifferent to the environmental degradation that attended cotton culture, and they certainly had the wherewithal to make the substantial capital investment fixing the problem would require, but they rejected the critique of southern culture implicit in Cloud's indictment. They saw no need to make serious conservation efforts either to make a profit or to keep their view of themselves as virtuous farmers intact. Thus, as long as growing cotton was profitable—and planters like Torbert certainly found it to be so—they had no intention of altering their means of production.

While southern nationalism blunted the efforts of agricultural reformers to some extent, it did influence the landscape Carver would encounter in Macon County and that of Alabama's Black Belt generally. Many planters were embarrassed by the sorry appearance of their dwellings. Few were made of brick or stone; even fewer could be considered elegant. Most were single-story log buildings with between four and six rooms, and none impressed Frederick Law Olmsted when he passed through Macon County on the Montgomery and West Point Railroad in the early 1850s. He noted a "few dreary villages, and many isolated cotton farms, with comfortless habitation for black and white upon them."[68]

In an address before the Alabama horticultural society in 1851, John Forsyth blamed the general lack of comfort and elegance on a lingering frontier spirit. He had never known, he claimed, a farmer in Alabama "who would not sell out and move for the price of his land." In consequence, the "planter's home is generally a rude ungainly structure, made of logs, rough hewn from the forest." It "is not regarded as a home," he continued, "but only a temporary abiding place." Such an attitude "is a blight on our land. . . . We murder our soil with wasteful culture because there is plenty of fresh land in the West—and," he concluded, echoing a common complaint of antebellum reformers before getting to the heart of his concern, "we live in tents and huts when we might live in rural palaces."[69]

Planters began taking steps to beautify their property and improve their living conditions. As part of their rejection of all things northern, Alabamians embraced a very different sort of landscape design than that recommended by Andrew J. Downing and other northern authorities. Men such as Charles A. Peabody—the horticultural editor of Cloud's paper—advocated a "southern" style of landscape architecture. The result of the campaign to establish a self-consciously southern landscape design led to the re-creation of the environment in Alabama in a thousand different corners, none especially significant in itself, but collectively sufficient to alter the state's environment.

Predictably, the new landscape had little room for grass—a characteristic still evident when Carver arrived in 1896. A visitor to Tuskegee in the first decade of the twentieth century, for instance, was astonished to find that its white cemetery was a "wholly grassless waste of sand, relieved only by clumps of flowering shrubs and scattered trees." Tuskegeans were "very proud" of it, however, and gave it "constant care."[70] While there was room for trees and shrubbery, their longtime association with disease—as late as 1857 the *Southern Cultivator* linked the death of a planter's wife and children to barren mulberry trees growing too near the house—meant that they were cultivated cautiously and sparingly, generally lining the avenue to the house or set in copses to break up open spaces.[71] The most significant changes were in the decorative plants southerners chose to cultivate in their yards and gardens. Prior to the 1850s, such nonnative plants as buckthorn dominated gardens of the Deep South. In the decade before the Civil War, native plants like the magnolias now associated with the region began to replace "exotics" in Macon County and elsewhere in the Black Belt, and there was something of a push to encourage the preservation of old-growth forests. The fact that "Europe, Asia, and Africa had been ransacked for diminutive shrubs to take the place of those great forests" suggested to Peabody, at a minimum, that some planters lacked taste.[72]

But it was southern nationalism's most obvious result that set in motion the events that were primarily responsible for shaping the world Carver encountered in Alabama's Black Belt. The initial jubilation of some in Macon County at Alabama's secession proved short-lived. By the end of 1861, the last year he planted cotton during the Civil War, Torbert's outlook was positively gloomy: "This is the year Commenceing lincoln's wars, and . . . from all appearances we are bound to have harder times than I ever before experienced in My life time."[73] By April 1865 the county had endured two raids by Union cavalry. The reality of the Confederacy's defeat was brought home the following month when Federal troops under Colonel J. B. Moore occupied the county and declared martial law. Whites like Carrie Hunter, a young woman living in Tuskegee, found the loss and occupation "a sickening and humiliating subject."[74]

In 1860 only 2,690 free African Americans lived in the entire Yellowhammer State; at the close of the Civil War more than 18,000 newly freed African Americans called Macon County home.[75] Many would leave in the ensuing years. The 1870 census reported only 12,620 blacks in the county (though some were lost to Lee and Bullock counties in 1867 when county lines were redrawn). For those who stayed, freedom brought both promise and uncertainty. For the first time, the state recognized their marriages. And when the congregations of white churches could not bring themselves to allow their former slaves equal seating and participation, the freedmen established parallel, independent churches that quickly became the chief social centers of the black community.

The aftermath of the Civil War brought uncertainty for the planters as well because it entailed the loss of their slave wealth along with the only social order they had ever known. Fears of black insurrection led to armed patrols. When Congress refused to seat Cullen Battle, a former firebrand and Confederate general elected to represent a district that included Macon County, the county's white residents feared the worst. Their most significant problems, however, were tied to their plantations. Confederate and Union soldiers alike had appropriated much of their livestock, and large-scale theft after the war took most of the rest. Ironically, the planters' fields had never been more vulnerable to livestock, a consequence of the destruction of fences by the Union Army. The most significant problem, however, lay in the fact that the labor system of the county had been thrown into flux.

Over the course of the war, planters' foreign markets had crumbled, their financial institutions had collapsed, and their transportation infrastructure had been devastated. In addition, the loss of wealth in the form of slaves—and in 1859 Torbert was paying more than $1,300 per slave—undermined their ability to get credit. They had kept their land, but as economist and historian Gavin Wright noted, "nineteenth century bankers did not consider real estate to be an acceptable backing for loans," as was evidenced by the fact that "such loans were prohibited by the national bank."[76] Even had such loans been possible, land values had dropped more than 40 percent since 1860, primarily because of the uncertainty surrounding southern agriculture, and planters' collateral worth was concomitantly lower.[77] The failure of the southern banks and the planters' difficulty in acquiring cash loans left them cash poor. Many could not offer freedmen cash wages and had little recourse but to arrange to pay their hands after the harvest.

Given the racial tensions in Macon County, planters were pleasantly surprised in early 1866 when their former slaves proved willing to sign contracts to farm their land. The Civil War had forced agricultural diversification in Alabama's Black Belt, but the planters were eager to see their fields again turn white with the bolls of their beloved cotton—the more so since the pent-up demand for cotton in the wake of the war had driven up its price. Cotton alone held out the possibility of putting cash in their pockets and allowing them to settle their debts. Macon County resident William Varner provides an example of what having cotton could do. He had managed to produce and acquire from his peers some 760 bales of cotton over the course of the war, and his close connections with some northern bankers enabled him to sell them for better than $130,000 after its end. Varner, however, was clearly an exception. James Torbert's experience was more typical. He hired six freedmen, along with three of their children, to tend his fields in 1866 in return for room and board, 25 percent of the corn, and 20 percent of the cotton. Unfortunately for Torbert, his experiment failed and he lost "by the operation about $1,400 counting provisions." The next year Torbert made a small profit by hiring five freedmen, a white man, and his own son for cash.[78]

Socially, it was no small struggle for planters to accept their sudden legal equality with the freedmen. The fact that the planters had gone from holding virtually all the political power of the region to holding almost none added to their woes. The numerical preponderance of African Americans forced white conservatives not disfranchised by Congress to lobby for black votes. For its part, the county's black community, which had mobilized politically by 1867, predictably disregarded whites' claims that they had always been and would continue to be the freedmen's best friends and staunchest supporters. Led by James Alston, a former slave of Cullen Battle, black voters in the county went to the polls that year to support the call for a new state constitution, and the following year to ratify it. Planters were mortified when former slaves, including Alston, were elected to the state legislature that year.

African American political power in the county proved ephemeral. By the summer of 1870 white Democrats had begun to reestablish their authority. It began when a band of unidentified men fired into Alston's house on a June night. Alston and his wife escaped with relatively minor injuries, but Alston was forced to leave the county—by way of a ten-day detour through its swamps to avoid his white pursuers. Over the ensuing months, white conservatives patrolled the county's roads, black churches were burned, and two local scalawags were hanged in effigy in Tuskegee's town square. White Democrats discounted evidence implicating whites in the burning of the churches and the assault on Alston and blamed the violence and racial tension on the black community.[79]

Though Republicans managed to retain power in the county through the 1872 election, "Redemption" came to Alabama with the inauguration of Democrat George Smith Houston in 1874; it came to Macon County the same year. More than anyone else, a local circuit court judge named James E. Cobb was responsible for the reestablishment of white rule in the county. Cobb's position as a judge gave him the power to do things the ballot could not in a county where African Americans constituted better than 70 percent of the population. The county's black state representatives were arrested—one for adultery, the other for grand larceny—and tried in Cobb's courtroom. Both were convicted and sentenced to chain gangs (a source of state-funded labor for local plantations). Cobb further ruled that a Republican judge had not fixed sufficient bond to hold his office and appealed to Governor Houston to name a replacement; of course, the newly elected governor chose a Democrat. With hostile judges in place, African Americans could only expect the legal system to work against their interests.[80]

Perhaps more important, by the mid-1870s planters had largely settled on a labor system that suited their needs—one that trapped most of the county's African Americans in a circular system of debt peonage. Like Torbert, the planters had initially tried to hire groups of unrelated workers. Because the laborers were working for a fixed share of a crop, however, they had every incentive to leave the work to others and still collect an equal portion. Such a system left planters with two significant problems: an inefficient labor force and resentment on the part of those who did the work. A wage labor system was impractical for any number of reasons, lack of cash being a good place to start. Given the nature of cotton production, planters needed a reliable labor force at certain times of the year, especially for the harvest, when a single heavy rain could ruin all of the cotton on the boll. Planters simply could not risk having to scramble for labor because their hands quit at the wrong time. Likewise, the former slaves, especially those with families to support, did not want to rely on seasonal wages that would either leave them unemployed most of the year or force them into migrant labor. The end result was sharecropping and crop liens.[81]

In return for the use of the land, and often seed, mules, and farm equipment, the sharecropper agreed to give a certain percentage of his crop—usually between 25 and 50 percent, depending on whether or not seed and equipment had been advanced to him—to the landowner. Theoretically, a diligent sharecropper could in time become a cash tenant, and eventually a yeomen farmer. The catch came in the fact that tenants often lacked the capital to feed and clothe their families prior to the harvest and were thus compelled to ask merchants to advance them the credit to do so in exchange for a lien on their share of the cotton crop. The merchants frequently charged exorbitant interest rates, and they, along with the property owners—and in Macon County there was a good deal of overlap between merchants and planters—had priority over tenants in collecting any money earned from the profits. The result for the sharecroppers—an overwhelming majority of whom were black in Macon County and elsewhere in Alabama's Black Belt—was a system in which the interest from debts in bad years more than negated the profits of the good years.[82]

Consequently, by the mid-1870s most African Americans in Macon County found themselves perpetually in debt and obligated to ask whites to advance them many of the essentials of day-to-day life. No credit-rating system or "credit number" existed in the late nineteenth century; credit markets were profoundly local, and the only way poor farmers could get credit was to stay in the same area, return to the same creditors, and make good on their bills. Not surprisingly, considering the racial mores of Macon

County's white leaders, African Americans who refused to treat whites deferentially or who insisted on becoming independent had difficulty securing advances. Unable to extract themselves from the endless cycle of debt, by the mid-1870s African Americans were forced to concede white control.

Macon County's African Americans thus found themselves in a peculiar place, socially and economically. In many ways black tenants could operate relatively independently. They could live with their families and benefit from the labor of their wives and children, and they had the freedom to change creditors, albeit within a highly circumscribed system. "Planters can never tell which of their tenants will be with them the following year, but of one thing they can be fairly certain—that they will not leave the county," sociologist Charles Johnson later noted of Macon County tenants. The local nature of the credit market all but ensured that in time the tenants would "rotate, of their own choice, back to the point of beginning."[83] Tenants were free to fish, hunt, and gather firewood on the property they worked, but they had to plant cotton to satisfy their creditors. As of the late nineteenth century, they were still free to vote, but if they wanted credit, they had to acknowledge white authority.

The emergence of sharecropping did more than help planters establish a cheap and reliable labor base. As Gavin Wright and others have argued, it entailed a shift in how planters thought of themselves: they were now landlords rather than "laborlords."[84] In Macon and other Black Belt counties, planters sought to protect their property through passing stock laws. Fencing in crops was an expensive, time-consuming, labor-intensive process, and the planters no longer had slaves whom they could compel to do it. Furthermore, most planters had significantly curbed their livestock production in the wake of the Civil War as a result of widespread theft and saw no reason, as one frustrated planter noted, why "all the negroes and whites *who own no land*" should be allowed to profit from theirs.[85] Because planters often doubled as merchants in the Black Belt, there was an economic motive to close the range as well: advancing credit for foodstuffs was more profitable than allowing tenants to raise their own. Indeed, historian Grady McWhiney went so far as to assert that "one reason why cotton became so popular with postbellum landowners and merchants alike was because the tenants could not eat it."[86] In short, free-range livestock undermined the very dependency the planters, as landlords, sought to reinforce. By 1880 thirty-three of Alabama's sixty-six counties had passed stock laws; Macon County and the rest of the Black Belt counties were among them.[87]

The closing of the range did reinforce black dependency in Macon County, but its impact was probably most felt by independent white farmers. Inasmuch as it undercut perhaps the chief means by which yeomen farmers could subsist in bad years, an already small margin of error was made smaller, and many had to abandon their farms. Over the course of the 1870s the total population of the county fell. For all practical purposes, the loss was due to white migration; in fact, the number of African Americans rose in the county in the same decade. In 1879 alone, nearly 175 parcels of land, the majority of which were between 80 and 160 acres, were put up for auction on tax sales. The taxes generally amounted to less than ten dollars, an indication of how narrow the margin between success and failure had been for independent farmers, and of how vital an open range had been to their livelihood.[88]

Now firmly back in control of Macon County, the planters had reasons to reach out to the black community in the 1870s. They were not unaware of the threat a large-scale migration posed to their plantations and region, and they still held long-cherished, if ill-conceived, notions of beneficent paternalism. And as a pragmatic stimulus, African Americans still had the vote. Consequently, the planters began extending goodwill offerings to the black community, and out of these overtures came the establishment of Tuskegee Institute in 1881.

The county's African American community had first suggested such a school in a letter to the *Macon Mail* in 1878; the next summer a more detailed letter followed. The county representatives to the state legislature, on behalf of the white community, approached Lewis Adams, a leader in the black community, about sponsoring the idea in 1880. In part this may have been an election-year ploy to secure black votes, but the representatives had already been elected in 1878, and voter fraud—not altogether unheard of in the county—would likely have secured their reelection. The white community's willingness to establish a black school probably had more to do with keeping African Americans in the county than with winning elections. (The exoduster movement to Kansas the previous year had attracted a good deal of national attention and caused consternation across the South.) Doubtless, pride in the fact that the county had long been a center of education—home to four of the state's twelve colleges in the 1850s—played a role as well.[89] Whatever the immediate reasons were for founding Tuskegee Institute, its establishment reflected a not-so-subtle transformation in the attitude of white conservatives toward the black community. That white authorities recognized the need to take blacks' demands seriously is evident in the fact that some of the men who had threatened James Alston in 1870, including prominent merchant and banker George W. Campbell, became members of the school's board of trustees.[90]

On behalf of the trustees, Campbell wrote General Samuel C. Armstrong, the white founder of Hampton Institute, requesting the name of a white man who might head the school. Armstrong knew of no white man who would be interested and qualified for the job but eagerly recommended a former pupil and good friend, Booker T. Washington. Campbell, with whom Washington would form a close relationship, and the rest of the board accepted Armstrong's recommendation and hired Washington as the school's principal. The institute opened on July 4, 1881, despite fears in some quarters that it "might result in bringing about trouble between the races." Its thirty students met in "a rather dilapidated shanty near the coloured Methodist church, . . . with the church itself as a sort of assembly room."[91]

Whites' fears that the new school would upset race relations proved unfounded. The twenty-five-year-old Washington cultivated a close relationship with Tuskegee's white community, facilitated by Washington's belief that the solution to the "race problem" rested in black economic progress rather than political agitation for social and political equality. Even so, his first years were frustrating ones. "I do not deny that I was frequently tempted, during the early years of my work," he later wrote in *My Larger Education*, "to join in the general denunciation of the evils and injustices that I saw about me. But when I thought the matter over, I saw that such a course would accomplish no good, and that it would do a great deal of harm."[92] Given the racial realities in Macon County and the plantation regions of the South generally, Washington was probably correct in his assessment that political agitation for social equality would result in more harm than good, though following his ascent to fame, many educated blacks in urban areas and the North came to see his "tactical retreat" as a "surrender." As Edward Ayers astutely pointed out, however, the debate over the relative merits of Washington's "solution" after he burst on the national scene with his 1895 Atlanta Exposition address "were arguments among blacks over the best response to an impossible and deteriorating situation."[93]

Washington did qualify his willingness to accept segregation. "In all things that are purely social," he had conceded in the Atlanta address, "we can be as separate as the fingers, yet one as the hand in all things essential to mutual progress."[94] Mutual progress, however, hinged on economic cooperation. Consequently, as Ayers observed, Washington "encouraged boycotts because such resistance fell into the economic rather than political realm." Thus, he lent his support to a boycott of Atlanta streetcars in 1894, using "the leverage of blacks as paying customers to win their fair rights in the marketplace."[95]

Washington's abandonment of public demands for African American political and social equality mollified fears that his school would threaten the status quo in the county because it put the onus for resolving the "race problem" squarely on African Americans. Indeed, in Tuskegee's early years, local whites aided in fundraising and proved willing to sell land to the institute. The first major acquisition—an abandoned plantation purchased three months after the school opened—was made possible by a personal loan to Washington from the treasurer of Hampton Institute, General J. F. B. Marshall. This purchase allowed the school to move to a more permanent location and facilitated student enrollment, which had roughly doubled in its first three months. By the 1890s the school would own some 1,500 acres and enroll more than 1,000 students.[96]

Given Washington's philosophy, it is not surprising that Tuskegee modeled its coursework after Hampton's, which had a largely "industrial" curriculum. A primary goal of Tuskegee was "to send every graduate out feeling and knowing that labour is dignified and beautiful."[97] Consequently, Washington insisted that the students work: tilling fields for their food, making bricks with which they could construct buildings, and aiding in the general upkeep and maintenance of the grounds. In fact, everything at the school was to be built and maintained by the students themselves, overseen (and aided) by a steadily growing faculty. The school was to stand as a monument to what African Americans were capable of accomplishing, and by the turn of the century it served that purpose, impressing national and international dignitaries who made the otherwise unlikely trek to Macon County for the express purpose of seeing Washington's school.

If the school was a monument, it was also an island, and the orderliness of the campus did not spill over into the surrounding communities. Washington asserted in *Up from Slavery* that he had "found relations between the two races pleasant" when he first arrived in Macon County, a claim belied on the very next page when he recalled being told by members of the black community that they chose candidates in elections by finding out who the whites supported, then voting "'xactly de other way."[98] But he was most struck by the conditions African American tenants faced in the countryside. Whole families were sleeping in one-room cabins without windows and eating virtually nothing but "fat pork and cornbread." After breakfast, they "would, as a general thing, proceed to the cotton-field." "Their one object," Washington discovered, "seemed to be to plant nothing but cotton; and in many cases cotton was planted up to the very door of the cabin." With "few exceptions . . . the crops were mortgaged."[99]

The conditions of the plantation districts surrounding the institute did not differ markedly from conditions elsewhere in the Black Belt. Dominated by black tenants who had every incentive to plant as much cotton as they could and virtually no incentive to care for soil they did not own and from which they could be removed at the whim of a landlord, the region's environment suffered even more than it had during the antebellum years. King Cotton was triumphant as never before, and the deleterious effects of his reign could not go unnoticed. In an 1884 report on Alabama's cotton production, Dr. Eugene Allen Smith, a geology professor at the University of Alabama, lamented the diminishing fertility of the Black Belt: "Where the blacks are in excess of the whites are originally the most fertile lands of the state," he began. "The natural advantages of the soils are, however, more than counterbalanced by the bad system prevailing in such sections." Leaving no doubt as to which system he had in mind, he continued, "viz., large farms rented out in patches to laborers who are too poor and too much in debt to . . . have any interest in keeping up the fertility of the soil."[100]

Indicative of the fact that the efforts of Noah Cloud and other antebellum reformers had been largely forgotten, E. C. Betts, the state's first commissioner of agriculture, asserted that the need to restore nutrients to the soil "is a subject . . . wholly new to our people."[101] In contrast to Smith, however, he accounted for the sorry condition of the Black Belt counties by pointing to their black laborers, whom he insisted were "wholly unqualified" for "the position of independent tenants" and consequently, "almost invariably fail." The problem was aggravated by the fact that whites there tended to "congregate in towns . . . leaving the lands for the most part to the exclusive possession of negroes, thereby relieving them from the moral restraint of the presence of the superior race, as well as from their industrial supervision and control."[102]

In the immediate aftermath of the Civil War, some scientific agriculturists advocated policies similar to Noah Cloud's. The *Rural Alabamian* published a letter that suggested "turning under green crops" and gathering "pond muck or swamp muck . . . for composting purposes." The journal's editor, C. C. Langdon, argued that the best way to restore the "comparatively worn out" land was through "the easiest process imaginable, to wit: *deep plowing, thorough pulveration of the soil, and heavy manuring.*" Even so, he believed that the growing availability of "preparations known as commercial or concentrated fertilizers" portended the dawn of an era in which the earth would "yield its abundance regularly, continuously and with unwavering certainty."[103] But by the 1880s agriculturists were focusing on two solutions: diversification and the use of chemically compounded commercial fertilizer.

Diversification failed to gain much traction. If anything, farmers heeded pleas to grow something other than cotton less than they had in the years preceding the Civil War. To be sure, some agriculturists had hailed the "overthrow" of the "system of labor [slavery] which brought the all-cotton policy into existence."[104] Any hopes they may have harbored for a more diverse agricultural economy, however, had been quickly dashed. As early as 1872, the *Rural Alabamian* had expressed alarm at the rapid proliferation of cotton and pleaded with the state's farmers to produce "all the necessaries of life," before growing "*all you can of cotton.*"[105] The emergence of sharecropping and tenancy had increased cotton production, which both lowered prices on the cotton market and further denuded the environment. By the early 1880s two-thirds of the cultivated land in Macon County was in cotton, a marked contrast to the antebellum years when more land was in other crops aggregately than was in cotton.[106]

On the other hand, Alabama's planters and farmers eagerly embraced agriculturists' pleas for the use of commercial fertilizers. Like farmers in the rest of the nation, those from the Yellowhammer State turned to chemically compounded fertilizers in record numbers. In 1869, 126 factories manufactured fertilizer; by 1889 that number had leapt to 390, employing, on average, nearly half again as many workers as they had in 1869 and marking a growth in the total capital investment in the industry from $4.5 million to $40 million.[107] In 1880 Alabama farmers were spending $2 million a year on commercial fertilizers; six years later the state's agriculture commissioner was pleased to report that fertilizer use was "rapidly spreading."[108] Speaking before the state agricultural convention in February 1888, Dr. N. T. Lupton argued that commercial fertilizers were at the very center of "scientific" farming, insisting that the "manufacture of scientifically prepared fertilizers and their application to the soil is the best means of estimating the progress a country is making in agriculture." As the state chemist, it was Lupton's job to analyze fertilizer samples submitted by planters and farmers. If Lupton found that a fertilizer failed "to come up to the guarantee placed upon it by the manufacturer and dealer," the purchaser did not have to pay for it.[109] In fact, the proliferation of commercial fertilizers had played no small role in the establishment of the state's Department of Agriculture in 1883. Not only was the department responsible for regulating fertilizers, it was charged with "promoting their extension and use."[110]

To be sure, some agriculturists did advocate the use of organic fertilizers. Eugene Smith, in the 1883 *Geological Survey of Alabama*, for example, recommended composting plant debris with Alabama minerals such as lignite, "quick lime," and "calcareous and gypseous marls." He likewise lamented wasted night soil, which was either "accumulated in receptacles" or, worse, channeled into sewers and streams "through which the fertility of our land is . . . drained into the ocean." The holding receptacles for night soil, he claimed, "are in reality so many Guano Islands, whose benefits we can realize with only a nominal cost of transportation." But even Smith argued that failure to use chemical fertilizers indicated the lack of "systematic efforts at the maintenance of the fertility of the soils in Alabama."[111] Thus, if agriculturists' promotion of commercial fertilizer did not preclude their advocating organic fertilizers, the latter certainly received much less attention. Few agriculturists emphasized soil building, or for that matter any notion of "paying back" to the soil. More commercial fertilizer was applied each year, but Alabama's soil continued to degrade rather than improve.

As fertilizer use rose, fertilizer distributors appeared in Macon County. The Macon County Oil Company, which owned six cotton ginneries that collected seeds to be pressed for oil, also operated a fertilizer mixing plant.[112] Even so, the application of commercial fertilizers for cotton production in Macon County and the rest of the Alabama's Black Belt did not match that elsewhere in the state. Eugene Smith noted in 1883 "that in the great cotton-producing areas of Alabama the use of commercial fertilizers in cotton planting is comparatively unknown."[113] The use of commercial fertilizers in Black Belt counties might better be understood, however, as having reached something akin to a saturation point. Not only did landlords believe that their black tenants were incapable of properly applying the fertilizer, they had little incentive to help their tenants produce a banner crop for the market and thereby perhaps escape their crippling dependency. While advancing tenants the credit to purchase fertilizer could reinforce their dependency by adding to their debt, Macon County landlords saw no reason to advance the funds for large amounts of fertilizer—certainly not the amounts recommended by agronomists and the fertilizer companies.

Content to be back in power, the planters largely ignored both the long-term effects of failing to nourish their soil and the complaints of agriculturists. It was the planters Betts had in mind when, in the state's first *Report of the Commissioner of Agriculture*, he argued that "the time is come when we may cease to bewail the condition of the farmer. . . . They live well, take care of their families, and I think are less in debt . . . than they have been for the last twenty years."[114] The formation of the Farmers' Alliance the following year and its subsequent transformation into the Populist Party confirm that Betts' finger was on the pulse of the state's planters, not its independent farmers.

In contrast to the Alabama Grange (whose first chapter had been organized in Tuskegee), neither the Alliance nor the Populists had much influence in Macon County. In large measure this was because African Americans, who did most of the actual farming in the county, were never afforded status as equals either by Alliance members or by the Populists. Further, because white unity against a black majority was paramount in the political calculi of county leaders, when the need arose, the Democrats resurrected the tactics of voter fraud and intimidation they had used during the 1870s and defeated the Populists, removing them from the equation. In Macon County, James E. Cobb, the judge who had helped purge the county of "black rule," was elected to Congress in 1884 in a district that included six predominantly white counties and four Black Belt counties. In 1892 and 1894 he staved off Populist challenges, losing the white counties but winning even bigger in the Black Belt ones. After the 1894 election, the Populist candidate charged Cobb with voter fraud. The charge was subsequently substantiated, and Cobb was removed from office. The Populist victory, however, was short-lived as Democrats regained the seat in 1896.[115] In Macon County, then, the rise of the Alliance and the Populist Party meant little to black farmers.

Indeed, Betts' contention that farmers were in better financial shape than they had been for twenty years was even less applicable to Macon County's African Americans than it was to the state's white yeomen farmers. By the close of the 1890s only 157 African Americans owned their own farms in Macon County, which had nearly 19,000 black residents.[116] For the most part, these black landowners employed every means within their power to be self-sufficient: they had larger families (to provide more labor);

their children married later (and so labored longer for the family); and they sought to limit their borrowing so as not to get drawn back into the slough of debt peonage.[117]

At the time of Carver's arrival, most of Macon County's African Americans were tenants of various sorts; many were sharecroppers. Most lived in crowded, dilapidated cabins with their families on parceled-out plots of land. The cabins were grouped into roughly fifty small farming communities, which were connected to each other by roads winding along the county's ridges—a nod to the many streams that still regularly flooded—and by footpaths through its fields and forests, the very same paths first navigated by slaves prior to the Civil War.[118] Blacks' landholdings were either on the hilly land in the county's north or the sandy soils that lay to the south of the Black Belt soils. The best soils belonged to whites.

The founding of Tuskegee notwithstanding, few educational opportunities existed for African Americans in the county; consequently, illiteracy rates were high. The courts were wholly on the side of white landlords, and all the political momentum in the state indicated that African Americans could expect only a further contraction of their rights. By the late 1890s Jim Crow laws were sweeping the South. In 1901, Carver's fifth year in the state, Alabama would convene a new constitutional convention that disfranchised virtually all of the state's black population. Following its ratification, only sixty-five black voters remained in Macon County where more than two thousand had voted during Reconstruction.[119]

Although there had been no lynchings in Macon County since the establishment of Tuskegee Institute, there remained a good deal of racial distrust and resentment. Vulnerable to fraud, perpetually in debt, and politically powerless, black tenants had little incentive to labor diligently. As they did not own the land and were not tied to it, they had no reason to take good care of it. Whites, in turn, saw what they were conditioned to expect when they looked at black tenants: laziness and negligence. As in other plantation communities across the South, the logic of racial animosity became circular and self-perpetuating. Black tenants "are careless," W. E. B. DuBois explained, "because they have not found that it pays to be careful; they are improvident because the improvident ones of their acquaintance get on about as well as the provident." But most of all, DuBois continued, "they cannot see why they should take unusual pains to make the white man's land better. . . . On the other hand," he concluded, "the white land-owner . . . shows his Northern visitor the scarred and wretched land; the ruined mansions, the worn-out soil and mortgaged acres, and says, This is Negro freedom!"[120]

This was the Macon County that Carver saw when he arrived in 1896. It was a far cry from Iowa. Outside Tuskegee Institute's walls, Carver found himself surrounded by "devastated forests, ruined estates, and a thoroughly discouraged people, many just eking out a miserable sort of existence from the furrowed and guttered hillsides and neglected valleys called farms."[121] He was optimistic, however, that he could help remake it.

CHAPTER 4

In a Strange Land and among
a Strange People

After spending virtually all of his life in the Midwest, it is no surprise that in Alabama's Black Belt Carver found himself "in a strange land and among a strange people."[1] The landscape itself was very different from the ones he had previously known. In place of "the golden wheat fields and tall green corn of Iowa" were "acres of cotton, nothing but cotton . . . stunted cattle [and] boney mules."[2] In contrast to Iowa, where fertile loess soils supported profitable farms, much of Macon County, Carver ruefully noted, had soil that amounted to "practically a pile of sand and clay, making a yield far below the cost of production." Those who worked it received as a reward "another mortgage . . . as an unpleasant reminder of the year's hard labor."[3]

The climate differed markedly as well, to his great delight in the spring of 1897, when he wrote to Louis Pammel's wife that "the weather is simply superb, and as for flowers I never saw anything like it."[4] Three months later his enthusiasm had waned considerably. "The weather [has been] extremely hot," he complained in June, well before the suffocating heat and humidity of his first Alabama summer truly settled in.[5] Although Carver was no stranger to severe storms, he had never seen such frequent heavy rains. The rains worsened the condition of the exhausted soil, which when opened to the wind and rain—as it was virtually all year under the prevalent system of cotton culture—eroded exponentially faster than natural processes could replace it.[6] The scarred and denuded landscape was an affront to Carver's appreciation of all things beautiful. "Where the land is rolling (and most of it is)," Carver lamented, "it washes badly . . . leaving great ditches, gutters, and bald places."[7]

Macon County was as different from Iowa socially as it was ecologically. Though Carver had certainly encountered racism in the predominantly white states of Missouri, Kansas, and Iowa, he had just received a warm sendoff from his white classmates and professors. Few African Americans in Macon County had been befriended by whites the way Carver had been by a succession of individuals and families, from the Carvers and Milhollands to his professors and fellow students at the IAC. Those friendships, along with his advanced degree, had confirmed for him the wisdom of Booker T. Washington's philosophy of self-help and interracial cooperation, but they had left him unprepared to encounter the more virulent racism African Americans faced in the plantation districts of the Deep South. In virtually every way, as Carver wrote Pammel, the Black Belt of Alabama was "indeed a new world."[8]

In time Carver would make his share of friends among the white population of Macon County. In fact, he and Washington occasionally visited with prominent white families in their houses and even sat with them on their front porches, a remarkable concession on the part of whites given the racial mores of the day. Even early on, Carver was protected to some degree because of his connection with Tuskegee. Nonetheless, the specter of racial violence in the county was quite real. One black youth, for instance, was killed as a trespasser when he insisted on seeing his sister while she was working on a white family's property. When he refused to leave the premises, the owner shot him. The boy's family was left with no hope of justice: "'Twas his fault I reckon," the victim's father later told sociologist Charles S. Johnson. "The man said, 'Stay 'way.'"[9]

The reputations of Washington and Tuskegee certainly helped Carver in neighboring counties, but they did not ensure his safety. Carver discovered this firsthand in Montgomery County in 1902 when he was nearly lynched after local whites objected to his presence in a party escorting a white female photographer documenting black schools in the South. The experience, Carver wrote Washington, was "the most frightful . . . of my life . . . and for one day and night it was a serious question indeed as to whether I would return to Tuskegee alive or not as the people were thoroughly bent on bloodshed."[10]

The ecological and social differences he encountered in Alabama would play a definitive role in shaping Carver's environmental vision. To be sure, he arrived with a profound affinity for the natural world, long experience as an amateur naturalist, and particular religious leanings, to say nothing of his thorough training at the IAC. But a genuinely distinctive environmental vision emerged only as he applied those things to the denuded and racialized agroecosystems of Macon County. If the attitudes and training he brought with him to Tuskegee provided the substance of his environmental thought, Macon County was the forge in which it was shaped and sharpened. But his vision took shape within another context as well: Tuskegee Institute itself. Indeed, there is no question that the biggest shock initially came when the warm welcome and support he expected from his peers at the institute failed to materialize. While Carver saw himself as Ivanhoe, his fellow faculty members more often regarded him as Waverley. He was surprised when they failed to see him as a heroic martyr who had sacrificed a promising art career for the good of his race, and viewed him instead as a presumptuous outsider. Virtually all of the institute's faculty had been educated at "Negro" institutions; indeed, many of them had been trained at Washington's alma mater, Hampton Institute. The fact that Carver hailed from a "white" college (and from the Midwest, not the South) marked him as different, perhaps even suspect. For that matter, his advanced degree did as well. This seems never to have occurred to Carver, and his subsequent behavior confirmed their distrust.

Though the IAC, like all institutions of higher education, occasionally had to scramble for funding, Carver's experience had not prepared him for the dearth of funds and equipment he faced at Tuskegee. That he expected the school to see the necessity of properly outfitting him was evident in a letter he penned to the "Messrs. of the Finance Committee" a little more than a month into his tenure at Tuskegee. "You doubtless know that I came here solely for the benefit of my people, no other motive in view," he began. "At present I have no rooms even to unpack my goods. I beg of you to give me these, and suitable ones also, not for my sake alone but for the sake of education." Though he professed confidence that they saw "clearly [his] situation, and [would] act as soon as possible," that was not to be.[11]

Requesting additional rooms to unpack his botanical and mycological specimens at a time when most single faculty members shared rooms came across as arrogant to his coworkers. Certainly there was more than a touch of hubris in the letter to the finance committee: "I do not expect to teach many years," he informed the committee, "but will quit as soon as I can trust my work to others, and engage in my brush work, which will be of great honor to our people. . . . While I am with you please fix me up so that I may be of as much service to you as possible."[12]

Gary Kremer noted that it "is probably true that Carver had no intellectual or creative peer at Tuskegee, but acting as though he knew it"—whether by design or not—"created tension between himself and his coworkers."[13] Carver's eccentricities—collecting weeds to eat from the surrounding fields when he did not care for the fare the cafeteria was serving, paying little attention to his clothing (sometimes making his own, crocheting things like ties), and always wearing a flower in his lapel—further dampened the reception he received from his peers, who by and large never warmed to him, although he always had some supporters among them.[14] Even after he became the school's most celebrated face, Carver remained something of an outsider at the institute. It is telling that one of his close friends at Tuskegee, Harry O. Abbott, refused to give his correspondence with Carver to the institute's archives after Carver's death because he believed the school had treated Carver badly. (They went instead to the Carver National Monument in Diamond, Missouri.)

Carver occasionally voiced his frustration at the lack of cooperation shown him by many of his fellow faculty members, but most of his frustrations were more tangible. To begin with, as Kremer observed—exaggerating but little—Booker T. Washington measured the worth of Tuskegee faculty "by the degree to which they were willing to overtax and inconvenience themselves for the Tuskegee cause."[15] In this regard, Carver had ample opportunity to impress the school's principal.

Carver's first charge was to develop an efficient agricultural department. But his duties did not end there. In its aim of providing a prominent example of what African Americans could accomplish, Tuskegee sought to be entirely self-sufficient; indeed, it aimed to produce a surplus to sell as a way of contributing to the school's expanding financial obligations. Thus, as the director of the agricultural department, Carver oversaw all of the farming done by students and a few staff on both the 700-acre home farm on which the campus buildings were situated and the 800-acre Marshall Farm three miles from the campus. Shortly after his arrival, the acreage he was to oversee increased from 1,500 to 2,300 total acres—a charge that amounted to a full-time job in addition to his teaching and administrative obligations, to say nothing of his experiment station work.

Outside of his brief time as a homesteader, Carver had had no experience in practical farm management, and he no doubt found himself in over his head. In some ways it is remarkable that the farm ran as smoothly as it did. Washington, however, invariably thought it could be more productive, better looking, and less expensive. In time the principal became convinced that Carver was "wanting . . . in ability" when it came "to the matter of practical farm managing which will secure definite, practical, financial results."[16]

But Washington did not reduce Carver's teaching responsibilities to enable him to better tackle the farm. In Carver's first decade at the institute, teaching six different classes a semester was not unusual.[17] To these duties were added those of the school's experiment station: analyzing soil and fertilizer samples, testing the purity of campus wells, serving as the school's unofficial veterinarian, operating a weather reporting station, and, as Linda McMurry noted, "carrying out such miscellaneous chores as 'looking into the matter of reckless driving on campus.'"[18]

Further, because the horticulture department fell under his charge as well, he (along with the school's superintendent, John H. Washington, brother of Booker T.) was also responsible for maintaining and improving the school grounds—which included overseeing the repair of fences, wagons, and the various agricultural outbuildings.[19] Booker T. Washington was particularly demanding in this area. He enjoined Carver to "make such regulations as will result in [the farm buildings] being regularly and systematically whitewashed and kept in an attractive condition," asked him to prohibit students "from working in their undershirts" in the fields, prodded him to clean up "waste wood" in fields, and insisted that "noticeable" weeds be pulled.[20]

Tuskegee had to be more than functional and efficient. When well-heeled northern philanthropists and local supporters toured the campus, as they often did, Washington demanded that the Tuskegee campus and fields look idyllic and that the students appear happy and industrious. Given these demands, it is not surprising that Carver occasionally grumbled when additional responsibilities were placed on his shoulders. A 1907 memo captures one such complaint: "Mr. Carver protests against the additional work which has been given him and asks to be relieved of the responsibility of experimental feeding." Fittingly, Washington's response, scrawled underneath the typed memo reads, "Cannot do as requested."[21]

Complicating matters for Carver was the fact that he received very little material support from Tuskegee in his attempt to undertake the many tasks confronting him. The storage space for his botanical and mycological specimens that he had requested from Washington in his acceptance letter and from the finance committee shortly after his arrival, for instance, never satisfactorily materialized. The Tuskegee administration viewed housing such a collection as impractical because it did not directly enhance Carver's teaching or the profitability of the farm and its capacity to feed the students and faculty. Consequently, after two decades of waiting and numerous letters lamenting insect and water damage caused by improper storage, he shipped the collection back to Pammel at Iowa State.[22]

Carver was expected to keep the expenses of his department to a minimum and scrambled to find ways to do so. On at least one occasion he accepted cattle that had been culled from the herds of the Alabama Polytechnic Institute at Auburn.[23] In the summer of 1898 he complained about the school's lack of tools but told Washington that he would "draw some of them and see if the [school's] blacksmith can make them for us."[24] And he tried to find alternative uses for the equipment the school did furnish. In 1907, for example, he wrote Pammel to ask if "a chicken incubator could be used for bacteriological experiments."[25]

The lack of funding necessarily limited his activities, of course. Most obviously, it limited his ability to carry out much in the way of conventional scientific work. He continued to collect mycological specimens, an endeavor that required little financial support and which, in fact, he could undertake in the course of his daily activities when he happened to notice unusual fungi.[26] He kept abreast of the literature and occasionally joined other scientists at meetings. But in contrast to his situation in Ames, there was little in the way of laboratory work that he was sufficiently equipped to carry out. Indeed, this dearth of funding hampered even the practical (as opposed to theoretical) aspects of his work. His efforts to publish bulletins, for instance, were tied to the experiment station's funding but had to be approved by the school's council. In a letter in the summer of 1898, he complained to Washington that "Bulletin No. 2 has been ready for press for some time" but had yet to be printed. Thirteen years later, Tuskegee's treasurer wrote to inform Carver that he could not "O.K. the order for the printing of Bulletin No. 20, for the reason that there is not sufficient [money] to the credit of the Experiment Station to cover the cost of the

Bulletin." The one hundred dollars allocated for publishing bulletins that year had been used for an earlier printing.[27]

Though in time the limited funding would prove a blessing of sorts in shaping his environmental vision, it inconvenienced Carver in myriad ways. From having an unheated office that made his work uncomfortable in the winter to having to explain to the teachers under him in the department how they could make "fuller use . . . of the material found on the school grounds" when they moaned about the lack of teaching materials, always having to make do with less made his already difficult task more arduous.[28]

Initially, Carver also found himself surrounded by incompetent assistants—and arguably of the worst kind, as many were disdainful of Carver's "book farming." In time Carver would win many of them over (and replace some of the others with students and graduates he had trained), but his first few years proved difficult in this regard. Arguably his greatest such troubles came during his first two summers in Alabama.

In the summer of 1897, "irresponsible students" charged with the care of the institute's livestock cost Tuskegee one horse, two cows, "a multiplicity of pigs, and a number of calves." Fine dairy cows had been wrongly culled and slaughtered for beef; others had been woefully neglected at the Marshall Farm. The blame was laid at Carver's feet because he was the director of agriculture. He suggested that the dairy cows all be kept on one farm, preferably the home farm, and informed Washington that "the dairy herd will always be just as it has been as long as we bend all of our energies to build it up for 9 mo. And demoralize it 3." Irritated that he was held to account for the mistakes of others, he reminded his boss that he was working with the smallest and least experienced staff "of any station in the U.S. . . . It is impossible," he concluded, "for me to do this work without men and means."[29]

The following summer two separate incidents required Carver to proffer further explanations to Washington and the school's administrative council. The first took place in early August, when Charles W. Greene, the man who had organized Tuskegee's first agricultural classes, and who (though he answered to Carver) was responsible for overseeing the day-to-day cultivation of the institute's farms, accidentally killed thirty-two sheep. Greene had consulted with Carver about dipping the school's sheep in a chemical concoction to treat the "scab" that had infected a number of them. Carver had given him some information about making the dip but had understood that Greene would not dip the animals until Carver joined him that afternoon. Greene went ahead without Carver, however, using a dip that "was 4 times too strong." By the time the sheep began to behave abnormally, it was too late to save them.[30] "It is impossible for me to run around after them [his assistants]," Carver wrote to Washington after penning a letter to the school's treasurer explaining the matter. "My office desk is just full of unanswered letters and other matter because I have been doing more or less of this." Adding a not-too-subtle plea for Washington to intervene, he expressed his wish that "there was some way to impress upon them the necessity of consultation."[31]

A week later he had to inform the council that one of his assistants had left a pasture gate open, allowing "quite a number" of cattle to escape. This might not have been too terrible, except that the cattle had wandered into to a field where they consumed some poisonous plants. One animal died before it could be herded back into the pasture. Though the rest of the cattle were still alive, they "were all affected ... and it is only a matter of time when they will go."[32] Once again the blame was his.

Despite Carver's frustrations with his manifold duties, inadequate resources, and incompetent help, it was undoubtedly the micromanaging and competitive nature of Tuskegee's bureaucracy that most annoyed him. The fact that Washington was often away from the campus either speaking or fundraising meant that he had to delegate a considerable amount of authority. He insisted that he be apprised of everything, however, and he established a bureaucratic framework that required approval for every expense. This could transform seemingly pedestrian tasks into large projects requiring department heads to justify for a second time plans that had already been approved. A case in point: in the spring of 1902 a number of gates were delivered to the school, but without hinges. John H. Washington was forced to go before the finance committee to secure approval to buy hinges because there was no petty cash fund from which he could withdraw money sufficient to procure them on his own.[33]

The intensive oversight irritated Carver, who had little taste for the time-consuming administrative aspects of his job. Aware that individual initiative was seldom rewarded at the institute, he scribbled a note to Washington in September 1899 requesting approval to sell some poor dairy cows for beef in order to generate the funds to buy "a real *good dairy* animal." The fact that he had to ask permission to initiate such projects—especially when he would be held accountable for the improvement or decline of the dairy herd—clearly frustrated him. In the same letter he requested advance approval to plant a peach orchard; he wanted Washington's blessing up front in "order that I may not be hindered with my plans as I have frequently been heretofore."[34]

Two years later Washington prodded Carver to give more personal attention "to the condition of the peach orchard. I am very anxious," he warned Carver, "that nothing be lost to the school in connection with the putting out of the peach trees."[35] Carver claimed that he was too busy to devote personal attention to the trees, but that all was well. Washington need not have worried. Carver was quite capable of overseeing the establishment of the orchard, and in fact, thousands of peach trees thrived.[36] Even so, Washington continued to urge Carver to increase his personal oversight of it. "I am in thorough sympathy . . . as to the needs of my personal supervision," Carver replied, going on to note that either his teaching or the farm "must suffer for a while" because one person could not effectively oversee both.[37]

The administration's intrusive management contributed to endemic infighting between and within departments at the institute. No one wanted to endure the censure of the school's council or of Washington himself, and Tuskegee's exacting standards left little room for grace. In 1899, for example, Carver was reprimanded by the principal after John Washington reported that Carver was "tardy at the Directors and Division Instructors meeting Dec. 6th." Carver, who had "publicly announced" the reason for his late arrival at the meeting "and [had] asked Mr. J. H. W. to have the kindness to excuse me," was understandably irritated. "I respect your wishes above any other duty," he wrote Washington, but "I was detained by *you in your office*."[38]

Indeed, some of the bitterest conflicts took place between Carver and John Washington. Because their duties overlapped in maintaining the school grounds, their bickering tended to be territorial in nature. In September 1897, for instance, Carver wrote the principal to complain, "Mr. J. H. does not seem to think it is his place to look after the coal, wood, etc. This seems to me," he continued, "as if this is overstepping my possibilities. . . . This is precisely the point I spoken [*sic*] to you about before accepting the place."[39] That is not to say that their overlapping duties never bred cooperation; on occasion they did. In March 1902 the superintendent proposed that he and Carver pool their assistants to regrade a portion of Tuskegee's campus. He suggested that Carver refuse to let "the Finance Committee rest until they have made some arrangement to supply you with a great number more students than you now have." His motives in hinting at the need for cooperation were not especially altruistic, however, as he noted that having more students would enable Carver "to take up the work connected with the farms, . . . grounds, fences and the yards and get things in better shape."[40]

Departmental competition grew naturally out of such disputes. Carver, of course, believed that the agricultural department got short shrift, complaining in 1902, "I have felt ever since I have been here that we do not give enough attention . . . to the Agricultural department." Still surrounded by assistants and "instructors [who] with but few exceptions are exceedingly deficient," he thought this neglect was most evident "in the way of instructors, etc." But on balance, Carver was annoyed that his department had to compete for resources at all. Recognizing that Washington thought every department should find a way to do more with less, Carver acknowledged in 1898 that his department "will never get everything just as we would like it, but," he added, "until our Depts can cooperate better we will always be just as we are[—]one section save and the other let spoil."[41]

The fact that Washington was often away from Tuskegee made the infighting even more bitter. Teachers and department heads could throw stones at each other from a distance, leaving the principal no alternative but to assume that they were accurately representing the facts in their communiqués and respond accordingly. Understandably, receiving a letter of censure from Washington rankled Carver when he was convinced that he had done no wrong. "Hereafter," he replied to Washington after he received one such letter in his first year at the institute, "if persons will make complaints directly to me with reference to . . . anything connected with my Dept. I will do the best I can."[42] Less than a year later, Carver bemoaned the fact that other faculty members continued to go over his head to the principal: "Mr. Washington I wish you could be here more than you are and look into matters yourself, and not take people's word for it. I know some things would surprise you."[43] There was little Carver could do about the situation, and he certainly was not unwilling to take matters to the principal himself, though he often did try to solve problems through other means.[44]

The bureaucratic framework that facilitated this kind of infighting served to reinforce the hostility many of Carver's peers felt for him. Carver bleated loudly in January 1902 when John Washington, with the council's blessing, began to "compel [students] at the dairy to do things which we say in the classroom [are] wrong." Though he was willing "to cary out the school's wishes to the letter," he wanted it noted that his work had "been hamperd and renderd unsatisfactory the entire school year from similar reasons." In fact, he lamented to Washington, "from causes which I am wholy unable to decipher, I feel I do not get the cooperation of the council." Many "times no attention is paid to my wishes, and things passed over my head which work contrariwise to my efforts to cary out the schools wishes."[45]

Carver's complaint was not without basis. His lack of allies on the school's governing council led to almost incessant petty disagreements. In 1902, for instance, the council refused to commend a former student of Carver's who had organized a farmers' conference in his home community. In rejecting Carver's request, the council maintained that Carver's instruction (which the student was passing on to his neighbors) did not necessarily reflect "the policy of the institution." Carver found this assault on his former student—and by inference on his own teaching—"wholly unfair and out of order."[46]

The most significant of his spats with Tuskegee's administration dragged on for several years and centered on the poultry yard. It had been established in 1899, in part as one of the many projects Carver undertook early on to improve the institute's farms, and in part to facilitate an agricultural education program for girls at the school.[47] By the end of that year, Carver had established the poultry house and expressed his hope to the principal that an "artificial pool" might be built for ducks and geese, though he was aware that funding for the yard would be limited.[48]

Washington's complaints about the poultry yard began almost immediately, but it was the arrival of George R. Bridgeforth in 1902 that pushed the matter into the heart of the most contentious issue Carver would deal with in all his years at Tuskegee. Carver had first heard of Bridgeforth in 1900, when he received a letter from him seeking a position at Tuskegee. "I am going to learn more about him," Carver wrote Washington, "although I am sure he is not the man we want to take charge of the barn and stock." As a graduate of the Massachusetts Agricultural College in Amherst, Bridgeforth might have become an ally, but the two men clashed from the beginning.[49] Indeed, if Carver cherished any hope that the addition of another scientific agriculturist would lighten his burden or provide a kindred spirit with whom he could commiserate, he was sorely disappointed. Bridgeforth became Carver's nemesis in the department and his severest critic. To make matters worse for Carver, he quickly gained Washington's trust, and his ear.

At Bridgeforth's urging, the institute appointed a special committee to investigate the poultry yard in 1904. The committee concluded that the yard was in dismal condition and suggested that Carver had deliberately falsified his reports on it to hide that fact. Carver objected to being "branded as a liar" and all but dared Washington to accept his resignation "if your committee feel that I have willfully lied."[50] Indeed, he seriously flirted with the idea of leaving Tuskegee for Puerto Rico, but his friend and former mentor from the IAC, James Wilson, advised against it: "They cannot spare you yet," he admonished Carver.[51]

Although Washington did not accept Carver's resignation, he appointed a new committee (again at Bridgeforth's urging) to look into the matter of reorganizing the agricultural department in such a way as to remove the poultry yard from Carver's charge. The committee's report amounted to a rather sweeping indictment of Carver's efforts—not only with regard to the poultry yard—in concluding that a reorganization of the entire agricultural department was in order. Carver could remain head of agricultural research and instruction, while Bridgeforth or John Washington should take charge of agricultural industry. Despite his desire to focus on teaching and his frustration at his many duties, Carver's pride would not allow him to surrender any portion of the department—at least on someone else's terms. His new title, he wrote Washington, would be "too far a drop downward." The indignity of the proposal led him to tender his resignation yet again—"as soon," he added, pointing to his sacrificial commitment to the school, "as I can get the herbarium and cabinets labeled and in a place where they will be of highest service to the school." It was his hope that the collection might stand as "one of the monuments to my seven and one half years labor at Tuskegee."[52]

In a parting jab, he pointed out "grievous and damaging errors in the committee's report" that unjustly maligned his work. Where the committee had censured his museum exhibit for having no native birds, for example, Carver noted that in "a casual way I counted 40 this morning that are native to our state."[53] Of his rebuttals, this was perhaps the most salient. Even if the committee is given the benefit of the doubt and excused for this particular mistake on the grounds of ignorance—rather than "deliberate falsification" on their own part—it reinforces the fact that many at Tuskegee saw Carver as an outsider and assumed that the birds (like Carver) were "foreign."

Ultimately, Carver suggested to Washington that he was willing to accept the new role if he could have "an advisory relationship" to the head of the agricultural industries department. That solution would both mollify his ego and allow him to shed some of his least rewarding duties. But he continued to object to the committee's proposal that "industrial classes and theory be separated." This, he argued, "should not be considered for a moment but rather that which will connect them more closely together." The "theory as taught in the classroom" needed to be "consistently carried out in . . . field operations" to an even greater extent than it already was.[54] He offered a counterproposal: the agricultural department should be divided into a "training farm in connection with the Exp. Station where all of the proffessional agricultural students shall be trained," which he would oversee, and a "farm for economic production operated mainly by hired labor and night students," which he would gladly let Bridgeforth run.[55]

Washington decided to take no action in 1904, in part because the Tuskegee council was none too pleased with Bridgeforth's teaching—his predilection to keep his classes late, for example, upset the schedules of other teachers.[56] But he would not let Carver fire Bridgeforth.[57] Consequently, things returned to the status quo antebellum, as it were. In 1908 the conflict between Bridgeforth and Carver again erupted, and again the poultry yard was at its heart; this time the issue was the facility's relatively low production of birds. Carver's hope for an "artificial pool" had come to naught, and he had to explain to the council that "the chief reason why there are not more ducks in the poultry yard is that there is not a sufficient amount of water, as all water has to be hauled" there.[58]

The legitimacy of Carver's excuses notwithstanding, Washington had tired of them, and he decided to turn the agricultural department over to Bridgeforth. Implementing the change took a couple of years, but by 1910 Carver, who had been spending less time than ever in the classroom as the demand for his services as a speaker increasingly kept him away from Tuskegee, found himself with a new title: director of the Department of Research and the Experiment Station. Bridgeforth took charge of the agricultural department proper. In his new position Carver would supervise the experiment station; the issuing of bulletins; bacteriological work; the analysis of water, milk, and foodstuffs for the school; a yet-to-be-built laboratory; and, ironically, the poultry yard. He would also give public lectures and teach "if he desires."[59]

The transition was not a smooth one. The same sorts of problems continued to plague the poultry yard, for instance. "I must call your attention again to the importance of keeping the poultry yard in better looking condition," Washington wrote Carver in May 1911. When Carver took actions to improve the yard's appearance, however, he got a note from John Washington complaining, "It does seem that you have a great excess of labor employed in the poultry yard."[60] There was no winning. More significant, Carver came to discover that his Department of Research was for all practical purposes a myth.

By 1911 Carver was complaining "that the new department is not going to get the sympathy or support of the school," adding, "I have become a mere figurehead."[61] Not "a single piece of apparatus [had been] purchased" for his bacteriological work, and there had been no progress toward the completion of a laboratory. Worse, the initial agreement Carver had accepted in dividing the department—a decision he described as forcing him "to sever my connection with a work that 15 years of my life's blood had gone into, pioneer years in which no one wanted it"—was "modified to the extent that [he] must still teach classes," and those under Bridgeforth's supervision.[62] When Bridgeforth tried to flaunt his new authority over him, Carver complained loudly. Although Washington informed Carver that the institute could not "pursue a policy which permits you or anyone else to argue at length every order that is given, and to lay down the conditions upon which you will" comply, he worked out a suitable solution, more or less forbidding Bridgeforth to interfere in Carver's teaching.[63]

While bureaucratic battles of this sort occupied much of Carver's day-to-day life and understandably led him to look for affirmation outside the school—the sort of affirmation that came with his being heralded as "the world's greatest chemist" in the wake of his emergence as the Peanut Man in the 1920s—his life at Tuskegee was not entirely bleak. In November 1897, for example, he witnessed the dedication of the Slater-Armstrong Agricultural Building on the institute's campus. Named in honor of John F. Slater, a northern philanthropist, and Samuel Chapman Armstrong, the founder of Booker T. Washington's alma mater, the building's dedication was attended by Alabama governor Joseph F. Johnston, Alabama commissioner of agriculture Isaac F. Culver, and U.S. secretary of agriculture (and Carver's good friend and former mentor) James Wilson.[64] Indeed, its dedication was reported nationally.

The *San Francisco Report*, for example, attempted a "clever" racial quip in reporting the building's dedication: "Another attempt to develop in the colored man a taste for other farm products than the festive watermelon was inaugurated when the negro agricultural college was formally dedicated."

Most of the articles mentioned Carver as well—usually noting that he had been "a favorite pupil of Professor Wilson, now Secretary of Agriculture."[65] Four years later, two wings were added to the building, one for a laboratory and the other for a "museum" in which Carver could arrange various displays for the benefit of his students and the institute's frequent visitors. Considering his lack of material resources elsewhere at Tuskegee, the building was, Carver told the Association of American Agricultural Colleges and Experiment Stations in 1902, "well-appointed . . . and quite adequate to our needs."[66]

Personal successes came as well for Carver, many of them small but nonetheless rewarding, the more so because they hushed his critics and provided manifest evidence of his capabilities. Prior to his arrival, for instance, Tuskegee had tried without much luck to raise wheat, but by the early 1900s Carver had managed to make a success of it at the experiment station.[67] Similarly, the number of hogs increased rapidly under Carver's direction despite his often inept helpers and at least one outbreak of hog cholera. In 1899 Carver could boast that the institute had added a hundred pigs to its fold during the previous year.[68] Milk production likewise increased, and the orchard Carver persuaded Washington to let him plant in 1901 grew from a few acres to an even hundred—with some 20,000 peach trees—in a little more than a decade.[69]

The evolution of Carver's environmental and agricultural thinking contributed both to his institutional coups and to his ongoing bickering with the administration. His decision to eschew commercial fertilizers, for instance, gave ammunition to those who saw Carver as an impractical eccentric; everyone knew that the application of chemically compounded fertilizers was one of the hallmarks of scientific agriculture. At the same time, however, he could point to the sometimes spectacular results he was getting as the soil of the experiment station was rebuilt physically as well as chemically.

An understanding of how Carver's conservation work evolved over the course of his years at Tuskegee, however, begins with the campaign he waged on behalf of impoverished black farmers. In this, he was convinced, lay his calling; he had gone first to the IAC for training and then to Tuskegee to bring the gospel of scientific agriculture to his people. Indeed, the heart of Carver's campaign came to rest in his firmly held belief that black farmers in the South (and for that matter southerners generally) failed to apprehend the richness of the natural world around them. "It is a source of regret," Carver lamented, "that we do not recognize and appreciate what Nature has so lavishly provided for us."[70] For those who had eyes to see, he believed, the Great Creator had provided everything that any of his children needed to live, indeed to prosper, in the abundance of the natural environment itself. "Few, if any," Carver asserted in an article aimed at encouraging local farmers to attend the annual Macon County Fair, "realize the wealth within our county and the ease with which we can, not only live, but accumulate much above a living."[71]

Thus, Carver's appreciation of nature, along with his understanding of the foundational principles of ecology, convinced him that black farmers could find succor from the political and economic vicissitudes they endured by turning to the natural world. "You know full well," he wrote the Milhollands in 1905, "that we see in ... things just about what we are looking for."[72] His oblique reference to the absurdity of the racism that surrounded him aside, he intended to show the impoverished tenant farmers of Macon County and the Cotton Belt exactly what to look for in the natural world. If he could open their eyes to that, he could show them how to win their economic independence—and free themselves from the worst of the injustices they endured on account of their race.

Although many of its foundational pieces were in place when he arrived at Tuskegee, Carver's environmental vision did not remain static. It emerged over time, shaped both by his increasing realization of the depth and severity of the problems faced by black farmers in the region and by his increasing familiarity with the natural environments of Macon County and the South. To be sure, his eagerness to seek God in the natural world might have marked him as vaguely different from many of his fellow agriculturists. But when Carver began his tenure at the institute, he undertook his campaign in much the same way any other scientific agriculturist trained at a premier land-grant institution might have done. A genuinely distinctive environmental and agricultural vision emerged only as he came to realize that the conventional currents of scientific agriculture—which emphasized increased production, new (and often expensive) technologies, and the application of commercial chemical fertilizers—made little sense for the poverty-stricken farmers he wanted to help. When it did emerge, however, that vision was remarkably farseeing, emphasizing ecological ideas to a greater extent than virtually any other endeavor in the nascent conservation movement of the Progressive Era.

George Washington Carver before gaining fame as the Peanut Man. Note the characteristic lapel flower. Tuskegee University Archives.

Booker T. Washington, ca. 1900.
Tuskegee University Archives.

Louis Hermann
Pammel, Carver's
graduate adviser at
the Iowa Agricultural
College, collecting
botanical specimens.
Iowa State University
Archives.

Carver (front row, center) with the faculty of the Tuskegee agricultural department. Charles W. Green, sporting a bowtie and glasses, is in the front row, second from left; George Bridgeforth is at the far right of the front row. Tuskegee University Archives.

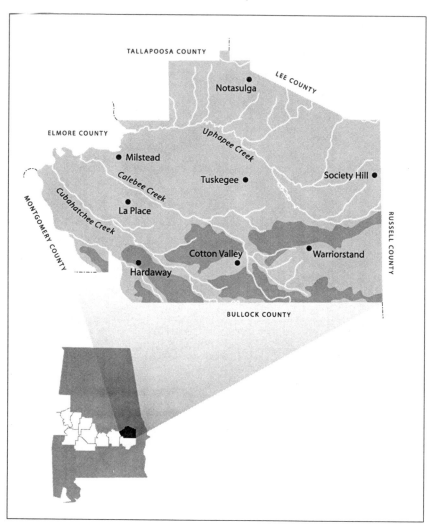

Map of Macon County, Alabama. The easternmost county of Alabama's Black Belt (inset), Macon County was the testing ground for Carver's campaign on behalf of impoverished black farmers. Shaded areas indicate Black Belt soils. After Soil Survey of Macon County, General Soil Map, USDA/NRCS (1998), modified by Kelly Schonour and Mark Hersey.

GET READY

FOR THE

Farmers' Picnic

WHICH WILL BE HELD AT

Mt. Pleasant Church, One Mile South of Mathews, Saturday, July 15th, 1905.

A GRAND SUBJECT FOR DEBATE.

"IS IT OUR DUTY TO EDUCATE OUR CHILDREN?"

This subject will be discussed by some of our ablest people, among whom are, Prof. John A. Wilson, of Montgomery, Ala.; Rev. Shepherd Scott, of Mamie, Ala.; Prof. Augustus Elmore, of Mathews, Ala.; Prof. Geo. W. Carver, of Tuskegee, Ala.; Mr. William Hinson, of Cecil, Ala.

ALL ARE INVITED TO ATTEND.

Prof. Geo. W. Carver is one of the best educated men in our colored race. If your soil don't produce crops well bring some with you and he will tell you the reason why. Some of your fruit trees are failing to bear as they should, break off a small branch and bring it with you, and you will be told the cause. Any question on any kind of plant or any kind of soil you are at liberty to ask him; he is the man to answer.

Don't miss this Grand Picnic. Come and be with us, and feast on the many delicacies we are going to have. Bring tables if desired. Flying Jennies, Watermelon Wagons, etc. Taxes on Tables 25c., Flying Jennies $3.00, Watermelon wagons 15c.

FRANK HINSON, President

ARTHUR BURKE, Secretary.

Advertisement for "Farmers' Picnic," 1905, prominently featuring Carver's pending appearance. Tuskegee University Archives.

Bulletin 6, *How to Build Up Worn Out Soils* (April 1905). Tuskegee University Archives.

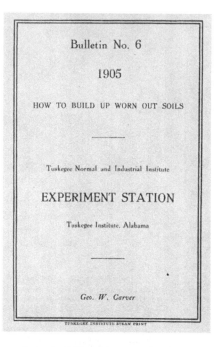

Bulletin No. 6

1905

HOW TO BUILD UP WORN OUT SOILS

Tuskegee Normal and Industrial Institute

EXPERIMENT STATION

Tuskegee Institute, Alabama

Geo. W. Carver

TUSKEGEE INSTITUTE STEAM PRINT

Carver teaching at Tuskegee. The cotton plants on the table in front of him are typical of the examples that invariably accompanied his lectures. Tuskegee University Archives.

Carver and students at the Tuskegee Agricultural Experiment Station.
Tuskegee University Archives.

African American woman in front of a tenant cabin near Tuskegee, ca. 1900.
Tuskegee University Archives.

The Jesup wagon at work. Tuskegee University Archives.

Carver with Henry A. Wallace. Tuskegee University Archives.

Carver examining a *Yucca gloriosa* four decades after his painting of a yucca plant won honorable mention at the 1893 Chicago World's Fair. Tuskegee University Archives.

An elderly Carver collecting botanical specimens, vasculum in hand.
Tuskegee University Archives.

CHAPTER 5

Teaching the Beauties of Nature

Carver's campaign to help "his people" began in the classroom, where he sought to train not only good farmers but agricultural emissaries who would take his gospel of scientific agriculture to black communities throughout the region. Risking the displeasure of Washington and lending credence to his critics' complaints, Carver initially privileged his work with students over that of the institute's farms. Convinced that one or the other "must suffer," as Carver had explained to Washington in 1901, he believed that teaching had to remain paramount for the sake of his campaign. Since "we must send out students who are to represent us," he wrote, "it [is] exceedingly important that they receive their proper training."[1]

Carver's teaching method reflected his training in ecology in that he taught all of his varied subjects in terms of relationships. "Our modes of reasoning," he told the students of Homer College in Jackson, Tennessee, in the summer of 1908, "should be from the known to the nearest unknown."[2] Thus, he would take a plant, a fungus, an animal, or a mineral and explain how the creator had arranged the natural forces that produced it, and how it in turn contributed to the larger environment to which it belonged.

Carver did not think "it wise ... to follow strictly the old Lineal or in fact any of the more modern forms of classification" in discussing biological topics. Indeed, he drafted his own "textbook," titled first "Botany Made Easy" and later expanded to the slightly more pretentious "Suggested Outlines for the Study of Economic Plant Life for Use in Common Schools, High Schools and Academies." In the introduction to the former, Carver noted that he "preferred to adopt the group method instead [of traditional forms of classification in teaching botany], bearing in mind that the chief object of the study of botany is to know plants, their functions, and their relationships to each other." Leaving out some of the more technical terminology made the subject "more attractive to the student," but his aim in doing so was not purely a pragmatic expedient to deal with the rural students (rather than aspiring scientists) Tuskegee tended to attract. On the contrary, he believed that by using the "group method" students could "acquire a larger knowledge and better discipline by clustering at the very beginning [their] activities around a few fundamental facts and letting them radiate therefrom."[3]

Carver's emphasis on relationships allowed him to link any number of fields that might ordinarily be taught separately: biology, chemistry, agriculture, meteorology, botany, mycology, geology, entomology, even art and literature. Education, to Carver, properly consisted of understanding such relationships.[4] He was perhaps overstating the point when he told an audience on one occasion, "I don't lecture"; but his classes did have a very different feel from those of his fellow instructors.[5] As one contemporary noted, his teaching style enabled him to introduce "the great fundamentals of botany, without the pupil realizing that he is involved in science."[6] This sort of teaching style was not universally admired at Tuskegee. "There is criticism among teachers and students to the effect that in your teaching you do not pursue a regular, logical and systematic course, that you jump about from one subject to another without regard to the course of study laid down in the catalogue," Washington admonished Carver on one occasion.[7] On balance, however, Washington admired Carver's teaching. He asked Carver to lead seminars for his fellow faculty members on how they might improve their teaching and maintained that he knew of "few people anywhere who have greater ability to inspire and instruct."[8]

Studying the natural world opened opportunities to convey more than just scientific lessons. "The study of Nature is both entertaining and instructive," Carver wrote in *The Guide to Nature*, "and is the only true method that leads up to a clear understanding of the great natural principles which surround every branch of business in which we may engage." Moreover, he continued, "it encourages personal investigation, stimulates originality, [and] awakens higher and nobler ideas."[9] Clearly the natural world was not a mere backdrop to his conception of agricultural education.

As his reference to "higher and nobler ideas" suggests, Carver extended the connections he emphasized in his agricultural classes to spiritual things as well. For him, God was immanent in nature, and the natural world was thus the place to begin looking for truth, both scientific and spiritual. Carver frequently employed scripture to substantiate this claim, often quoting Job 12:7–8: "But ask now the beasts and they shall teach thee; and the fowls of the air, and they shall tell thee. Or speak to the earth and it shall teach thee; and the fishes of the sea shall declare unto thee."[10] In the light of such a conviction, it is not surprising that he was more likely than not to use an illustration collected from the natural world—be it a sweet potato, a rock, a soil sample, an insect, or a weed—rather than one in a book. Nor is it surprising that he did not confine his teaching to the classroom, but took his students to the experiment station, the farms, and the woods and fields of the campus.

These outdoor forays had a more practical component as well: they familiarized the students with the natural environment they encountered every day—an environment, Carver argued, "rich in native, imported, common, and uncommon plants." This familiarity facilitated his emphasis on relationships by providing an opportunity for students to draw connections on their own. When studying "domestic and foreign geography," for instance, students would "naturally want to know why we should go [abroad] for pine when the whole South abounds in almost innumerable varieties." By teaching them to sort out familiar plants and identify their manifold uses, he was training them to do the same elsewhere, which is to say wherever it was they went after leaving Tuskegee—a skill that was essential if his campaign was to succeed.[11]

This sort of hands-on learning was related to the trend popular throughout the country at the turn of the century, though especially applied to rural, elementary school–age children, of integrating nature study into the formal education of students. Predictably, Carver was an ardent supporter of the nature study movement, which sought to unite the scientific study of nature with an aesthetic and spiritual sympathy for it. In fact, Carver's connection with Wilson and Pammel, along with the cultural significance of Tuskegee, made him a national figure in the movement, albeit a relatively minor one. Indeed, for a time Carver would serve on the board of the movement's national journal, *Nature-Study Review*.[12]

During his first year at Tuskegee, Carver asked Washington to lend the institute's support to the cause of nature study. The approach would not be overly theoretical, he explained, addressing one obvious objection the eminently practical Washington might have. There was no need to crowd "the child's mind with long unmeaning Latin names or any technical science." On the contrary, teachers need only "lead [their students] out carefully and wisely into the great storehouse of wisdom that nature has so abundantly placed all about [them]." Laying out an argument he knew would resonate with the school's principal, who regularly dealt with white planters wary of losing their laborers, he added that the incorporation of nature study into the institute's curriculum could "be the very means of ridding a large number of the false impression, that schools and colleges are for the purpose of educating away from, rather than educating to the farm."[13]

An avid gardener and supporter of the middle-class values that underlay the movement, Washington proffered his blessing, and Carver established a Bureau of Nature Study for Schools and Hints and Suggestions to Farmers at the institute that attempted to popularize the movement, and from which he (and other Tuskegee faculty) published pamphlets of various kinds. Through these publications, along with occasional experiment station bulletins aimed at public school teachers, he attempted to "induce public schools to include Nature Study in their work, especially as it bears upon practical agriculture," and offered suggestions as to how educators might go about doing so.[14]

Even "the wee tots, the kindergarteners are none too small" to be introduced to nature study, Carver insisted.[15] He recommended that the course shift to "general agriculture" for students after the sixth grade, but this was a distinction without a difference—at least in terms of the teaching methods instructors ought to apply.[16] Regardless of the course's title, every lecture was to "be more or less illustrated by natural objects and real things, interspersed here and there by delightful excursions to the woods, fields, orchards, gardens, and experiment stations." And every student should "be urged to familiarize himself with the common things about him."[17]

"If properly taught," Carver argued, "the practical Nature Study method cannot fail to both entertain and instruct."[18] He had no doubt of the efficacy of the method. "I dare say there is not a rational mind, be it old or young, that will not become interested in the story of a grain of corn," he contended, "showing how it must be fed from nature's storehouse until strong enough to reach out, grasp and assimilate food for itself; following it through youth, maturity and old age."[19] Nature study, even in elementary school, also introduced the relationships that bound all living things together. After all, he reasoned, a "real bug found eating on the child's cabbage plant in his own little garden will be taken up with a vengeance in the composition class," and a student "would much prefer to spell the real, living radish in the garden than the lifeless radish in the book."[20] In the end, he believed, "there is nothing better to interest the young mind than nature."[21]

Knowing that most teachers at rural black schools had little agricultural or scientific education, Carver recommended a number of books to remedy their deficiencies. Among these were Liberty Hyde Bailey's *Lessons with Plants*, Emmett S. Goff's *Principles of Plant Culture*, Charles Darwin's *Origin of Species*, and Pammel's *Flower Ecology*.[22] He explained how to compost manure ("Too much stress cannot be laid upon this important item"), how to construct a hotbed for a winter garden (that was the time black children were most likely to be in school), and a number of similar practical matters with which he could not assume the teachers were familiar. The fact that he had to do so highlights a potential irony in his passionate advocacy of the movement. Indeed, the idea of teaching the children of impoverished black tenants—children who were expected to become the next generation of agricultural laborers in the region—to unite an aesthetic and spiritual appreciation of nature with a scientific understanding of the natural world under the banner of agriculture seems an unpromising endeavor. But for Carver, who sought to inculcate a mode of thinking rather than a set of agricultural methods among the African American tenants of the region, it offered a reasonable way to lay a foundation for the sort of agricultural reform he espoused.

Circumstantial evidence indicates that at least for a time Carver's efforts to this end were rewarded. Many of his students found jobs as teachers and integrated nature study methods into their courses; some wrote him to tell him so and to seek advice on matters such as school gardens. Similarly, Carver wrote that the purpose of one of his leaflets was "to set forth . . . the success of our . . . labor in proving the value of practical Nature lessons in the public schools of our section." And in bulletin 18, *Nature Study and Gardening for Rural Schools*, he noted that a previous publication on nature study had been very well received, rapidly exhausting the 1,500 copies initially printed—a success "far beyond the most sanguine hopes of its promoters."[23]

In fact, people throughout the nation wanted copies of Carver's bulletins on the subject. In 1911, for instance, C. A. Prosser, the deputy commissioner of the Massachusetts State Board of Education, answered a letter about agricultural education by recommending Carver's bulletins on the subject. The "very best bulletins on the subject concerning which you made inquiry," Prosser wrote, "are issued by Tuskegee Institute. . . . I think you can secure these by writing Mr. George Carver, Director, Agricultural Education, Tuskegee Post Office."[24] It is thus clear that Carver merited a place of some prominence in one of the most significant impulses of the Progressive conservation movement. It is nevertheless difficult to judge just how effectively nature study was integrated into black schools in Macon County. Given the enormity of the problems facing their students, its impact was probably uneven at best.[25]

Though males constituted the majority of students in Carver's classes, he led a push to open agricultural education at the institute to women as well. This was essential to his campaign because most black women who lived on farms were compelled to work, both in the home and, during the busiest seasons, in the fields. Maximizing women's contributions to the family economy could facilitate a family's rise from the near debt-peonage of tenancy to the relative independence of yeomanry, and a substantial portion of Carver's campaign was aimed directly at them.

Thus, in 1899 Carver wrote to Washington expressing his hope that he could "open the dairy to young women next if we can give them nothing more," though clearly he desired that more be offered, mentioning poultry raising as another suitable field for women.[26] Washington immediately agreed with Carver. By the time he published *Up from Slavery* in 1903, he could boast that the institute trained "a number of girls in agriculture each year. These girls are taught gardening, fruit-growing, dairying, bee-culture, and poultry-raising."[27] That same year, the *Montgomery Advertiser* asserted that "Tuskegee Institute is perhaps the first institution in America to give training in agriculture to girls," mistakenly dating the initiative's beginnings to Carver's arrival at the institute in 1896.[28] Identifying its origins with Carver, however, was the right sentiment, even if the paper had the wrong date.

Although female faculty members generally instructed the young women, Carver took a good deal of pride in the program. This "recent introduction," he told the Association of American Agricultural Colleges and Experiment Stations at its annual meeting in 1902, "has been three years with success." And his position as director of agriculture enabled him to shape their coursework to a considerable degree—even as he developed the more conventional agriculture curriculum.

When Carver arrived, the institute had been offering agriculture courses for three years. Organized by Charles W. Greene, the "course in agriculture" provided a rudimentary introduction to scientific agriculture, but since none of the Tuskegee faculty had been trained in the field, it was necessarily an uneven one. In his first year Carver tried to regularize the coursework, replicating, so far as possible, the IAC's program. He offered courses in entomology, horticulture, practical agriculture, botany, dairying, bacteriology, vegetable physiology and pathology, animal nutrition, principles of heredity, and agricultural chemistry.[29] The following year he added a course in nature study that included animal and human physiology, botany, geology, zoology, and meteorology; and to the standard agricultural curriculum he added courses in market gardening and livestock.

By the turn of the century, with further additions such as stock breeding and apiculture, the department was well established and the annual catalog could boast (perhaps a shade ironically given the criticism leveled at Carver by the administration) that "none of the work of the Tuskegee Normal and Industrial Institute has proven more successful than the work done in the Agricultural Department and that under the supervision of the Agricultural Experiment Station."[30] Agricultural students at Tuskegee acquainted themselves "with the simple problems of farm life," analyzed soil (beginning, significantly, with its physical rather than chemical properties), and were "required to demonstrate [their] ability by putting into practice the lessons learned in the classroom."[31]

Like most of his contemporaries, Carver emphasized the dignity of farming, persuading his pupils that they "should not be ashamed of [their] occupation" and that the image of a farmer as a man "with manners awkward, uncouth and ludicrous, and . . . of very limited intelligence" was inaccurate. Quite the opposite, Carver insisted. It "is all too erroneous and false to say or think that it requires little or no intelligence to be a farmer. On the contrary it requires the highest intelligence." Without the application of his intellect, a farmer would have little success dealing with "all the wonderful and powerful and puzzling forces of nature."[32] Though the words are Carver's, they might well have come from Uncle Henry or almost any other agricultural reformer. "What American agriculture needs more than anything else is that it become intellectualized," Emmett S. Goff and D. D. Mayne argued in *The First Principles of Agriculture* (1904). Carver, along with the Wallaces, Goff, Mayne, and most of the early agronomists, believed that "agriculture needed to be made the purpose and object of mental, as well as physical, effort."[33]

Indeed, much of what Carver taught in the classroom and demonstrated in the fields was fairly conventional—the proper techniques of good farming, Justus von Liebig's "Four Laws," analysis of fertilizers, and the appropriate depth to plow under particular conditions, to name a few. He defined agriculture "as the *cultivation* or the *manipulation* of the soil in *such* a *way* as to bring about the *greatest possible yield* of *products useful* to man with the *least injury* to *the soil* and at the *least expense*."[34] Later agronomists would be content to end the sentence after "man"—much to the chagrin of Wendell Berry and other environmentalists—but Carver's definition was hardly a controversial one at the time. Contemporary agricultural textbooks offered remarkably similar definitions.[35]

Carver's teaching probably resembled that of his contemporaries in less flattering ways as well. He doubtless proffered the same scientific theories as his peers, many of which now seem very outdated. During his days in Ames, for instance, scientists had little idea how hail was formed. One textbook from the period suggested that perhaps "electricity has something to do with it" and noted that "in some parts of Europe, hail storms have been rendered much less frequent by the use of lightning rods."[36] And Professor Budd had fallen in line with the majority of late nineteenth-century scientists in teaching Carver that "properly distributed groves [of trees] do increase rainfall"—Carver had listed it as a "law" in his notebook—and there is no reason to believe that Carver did not pass on the same "fact" to his students during his first years at Tuskegee.[37]

Although most of Carver's fellow agriculturists would have agreed with his assertion that the "science and practice of agriculture are intimate and inseparable companions," few succeeded to the extent Carver did in joining the theory with the reality.[38] In large measure this proved true because Carver lacked the labor-saving equipment available to most of his peers and had little choice but to turn his theoretical knowledge to practical ends. Even so, his refusal to divorce the theoretical from the practical won praise from many of the institute's visitors. A newspaper reporter from the Baltimore-based *Afro-American*, for instance, left Tuskegee with the impression that "scientific agriculture and practical agriculture [had] come to be synonymous terms at Tuskegee, and it is much to this resourceful expert's [Carver's] credit that this is true."[39]

Carver's instruction—even apart from his unusual pedagogical style—was less conventional in other ways. Pammel had interested him in the nascent conservation movement, and Carver's notes touched on the pressing conservation issues of the day.[40] Indeed, he was very cognizant of those issues. Several former advisers at Ames with whom he corresponded became influential in the movement. As secretary of agriculture under William McKinley, Theodore Roosevelt, and William Howard Taft, for instance, James Wilson oversaw Gifford Pinchot's Forest Service, though he essentially gave the latter "*carte blanche* in devising a forest policy," and he kept his former pupil apprised of his activities.[41] "I have been out west, looking at the condition of our national forests," Wilson wrote Carver in 1908. "The more I inquire, the worse I find them." Surveying the damage deforestation had wrought in terms of erosion and increased runoff had left him "more and more impressed with the necessity of taking care of our watersheds."[42]

The incorporation of contemporary conservation issues was hardly the only unconventional thing about Carver's lectures. In agricultural fields Carver saw "the beauties of nature" and the wonder of the working landscape, and he sought to convey that message to his students.[43] Carver resisted the national trend of specialization and compartmentalization of agricultural science a trend Wendell Berry would later deride as a move away from the "liberal" education land-grant schools were chartered to provide, to "practical" education, to "specialized" education.[44] Carver's emphasis on identifying relationships all but ensured that his teaching would include the sorts of connections whose disappearance from agricultural science would later trouble Berry.

Teachers often talk of cultivating a desire to learn and of sparking their students' critical thinking skills; by all indications, Carver actually did so. He demanded a lot from his students, telling them to disdain the word "about," for instance, because science demanded exactness.[45] For that matter, he cared little what the students "thought" about a particular subject. "Students invariably want to discuss the topic, rather than give you a direct answer," he wrote in a nature study pamphlet. "This is not permissible . . . unless their thoughts are based upon facts." Indeed, he continued, "there is nothing to be deplored more in the class-room than to hear a number of pupils pretending to recite, and constantly telling you what they think with reference to matters that the intellectual world has recognized as fact decades ago."[46]

Despite the demands Carver placed on his students, he was a popular teacher, and his passion for the subjects he taught inspired them. Thomas M. Campbell, who in 1906 became the USDA's first black demonstration agent, had entered Tuskegee convinced that he "would never work on the farm, nor live in the country again." But after "coming in contact with men who linked the theory and practice of farming together [an allusion to Carver, after whom he named a son], I soon became convinced that I had missed a great deal that country life afforded."[47]

Furthermore, Carver genuinely cared about his students, and that fact was not lost on them. One student scribbled a long missive to Carver thanking him for taking an interest in the students. "I suppose you are busy as a bee you always are," he wrote, "and yet you always have time to say a kind word to a fellow or give him some good advice or food for thought. How nice it would be," he concluded, drawing a distinction between his experience with Carver and other Tuskegee faculty, "if more of the teachers and instructors were that way."[48] Another student likewise wrote Carver to express his thanks for the "kindness and generous attention" Carver had shown him. "I know I shall never be able to pay you and thank you for the interest you took in me."[49]

Carver offered more than advice to his students. He regularly asked Washington to issue commendations to his best students, as he did with Thomas Campbell in 1902 after he and another student had assembled "the skeleton of a hog for the museum."[50] On occasion he intervened financially, once asking Washington to waive the bill of a hospitalized student. It "is very embarrassing for him to be in this disabled condition and have these bills presented to him," Carver informed the principal, "without anything with which to pay them."[51]

His support continued after the students had left Tuskegee. In 1914, for instance, Carver encouraged a former student turned local schoolteacher by enabling him to serve as a "collector" for Pammel—a genuine scientific occupation, albeit an unpaid one.[52] A fair number of his students corresponded with him long after they left the institute. Often these letters reflect a considerable degree of comfort and familiarity, and they speak to the warmth and depth of the relationships he forged with his students. Many of the letters are addressed to "My dear Dad," "Dear Prof. 'Dady,'" "My dear 'Father' Prof. Carver," and similar titles reflecting the parental role he had taken on for his academic charges.[53] One former student informed Carver that his wife had attended one of Carver's lectures and had come away "more than pleased with her 'father-in-law' and no longer [wondering] where the spring is whence your sons drank agricultural waters."[54] His "sons" and "daughters" kept him apprised of how they were doing, notified him of their current whereabouts and activities and of marriages and births, and asked him for letters of reference—which became increasingly valuable as his fame grew. Others sought personal loans, in which he apparently obliged them, or invited him to visit.[55] Those who became teachers requested his bulletins, and many asked him to pray for them.[56]

Carver's classroom presence began to diminish following his "promotion" to head of Tuskegee's Department of Research and the Experiment Station. During Washington's lifetime Carver was never fully exempted from classroom work, but following Washington's death in 1915, Robert Russa Moton, the institute's second principal and an admirer of Carver, recognized what Carver's growing fame meant to the school. Consequently, he essentially gave him a free hand—Carver could teach or not as he saw fit—bringing his regular teaching duties to a close.

Assessing the success of this prong of Carver's campaign to help poverty-stricken farmers is difficult for a number of reasons. It is clear that student enrollment in the agricultural department was never very high. Most of the young black students who enrolled in Tuskegee dreamed of escaping their parents' farms, not of returning to them, and so pursued the industrial curriculum. On first arriving at Tuskegee, for instance, Thomas Campbell told the registrar that he had no interest in farming. "He then asked me," Campbell related, "if I would like to take agriculture. I said I thought I would like that very well.... Imagine my surprise when I learned that agriculture was farming." Perhaps more telling, at institutional assemblies where Washington would ask the students enrolled in agriculture to stand, Campbell confessed that he "was among those who did not like to stand and did not do so until I had overcome some of my prejudices against country life."[57] The same prejudice existed in some quarters of Tuskegee's faculty, and teachers in other departments often punished misbehavior by "sentencing" students to work on the school's farm.

As of May 1902, twenty-one students had graduated from the agricultural department, and two-thirds of them were either farming or teaching. "This, after all," Carver wrote Washington, "is not so bad—although I wish it were much higher and I shall endeavor to make it so."[58] He attempted to boost enrollment by various means. To begin with, he suggested that the course of study for agricultural students be made more pleasant. Although the students were required to work on the farm, they "had not so much as a few boards put up to protect them from a storm should one come up," Carver lamented. And despite having to be up earlier and stay up later than other students, the agriculture students were "too frequently given no tangible consideration." "More effort," he insisted, "should be made to make conditions . . . comfortable" for them.[59]

Carver's best efforts to increase enrollment, along with those of Washington, Bridgeforth, and others, however, saw little success. Bridgeforth promised Washington in 1907 that "we shall not be satisfied until we have 350–400 students here taking agriculture as a trade." It was an optimistic vision considering that only 76 of Tuskegee's more than 1,000 students were enrolled in the agriculture curriculum that year.[60] But the department's enrollment might not be the best measure of Carver's success in this prong of his campaign.

Many of Carver's students followed his suggestions when they returned to their parents' farms or began operating their own. One student wrote Carver in February 1905 to inform him that he had returned to Texas to help his parents by employing the practices he had learned at Tuskegee. This "is my porpos [purpose] down there to help my parents out and make life happy for them if I can," he scrawled. Already, he had improved their garden, preserved better than one thousand pounds of meat, and planted a number of fruit trees.[61] Another wrote to tell Carver that he was operating a forty-acre farm in North Carolina and was diversifying as best he could, having already put seven acres in wheat and begun raising hogs.[62] Yet another had taken Carver's antipathy for waste to heart and boasted to his former teacher that from "the savings of grease from my kitchen I have made one hundred and sixty pounds of soap." He had also started vegetable and flower gardens and was selling daisies by the dozen for twenty-five cents.[63] Still another thanked Carver for his encouragement and informed him that he was employing what he had learned at Tuskegee "against the will of every farmer" in his community, and was getting spectacular results.[64]

Not all of Carver's students were as successful in implementing their training. A former student living in Virginia, for instance, boasted to Carver in 1918 that he had "been composting manure, dirt, and leaves just like the one [compost pile] you have." However, he added, "I can hardly persuade my father not to buy any of the high price fertilizer."[65] More ominous, perhaps, the father of one of Carver's students wrote him from Oklahoma to ask that his son be excused from classes to help on the family's farm. "But you tell him that he must be careful about '*showing*' me, how to raise more apples, cotton, corn, and sweet potatoes," he implored Carver. His son said that Carver had "learned him lots of things, even to making mules and Horses Bring whole litters of Colts," the father continued, ". . . tell him if he tries to work these things off on me, I might beat him to death before his momma could get to me to pull me off."[66] Even so, the attempts made by his students to employ his suggestions could certainly be considered a victory of sorts for his campaign.

Similarly, many of Carver's students took up positions as teachers in various capacities, working for the USDA or in rural schools across the South. In 1902 Carver listed the occupations of some of his department's graduates, noting that some were farming or teaching locally, a handful held positions in the agricultural corporations that were then beginning to emerge, and two were agricultural "missionaries" in Africa.[67] Indeed, during the years Carver was at the school, no institution trained more influential black agriculturists than Tuskegee.[68] Former students such as Thomas Campbell, for example, became influential nationally; others wound up at larger black institutions such as Voorhees, Utica, Manassas, and Biddle (in South Carolina, Mississippi, Virginia, and North Carolina, respectively).[69] Most of Carver's students who ended up in the field of education, however, worked at small, ill-funded, irregularly attended rural schools. Some stayed in Macon County, teaching in Shorter, Notasulga, and other small communities. The Notasulga school was open only four months a year, for each of which Carver's student received a salary of $25 in 1914. "I have to run a little farm to help surport [*sic*] my family," he wrote to Carver, but he was optimistic that "we Negro teachers will get a better salary in the near future."[70] Others taught elsewhere in Alabama. A former student living in Tuscaloosa wrote Carver in 1911 to inform him of plans to add a cooking course to the school's curriculum just "as soon as I get the necessary utensils."[71] Another, teaching in the hamlet of Cottage Grove in Coosa County, asked Carver to identify some beans and sought medical advice for a student whose foot had been "burned very badly."[72] Similar letters came from elsewhere in the nation. From Manhattan, Kansas, and Victoria, Texas, former students requested bulletins, and from the Tullahassee Mission in Oklahoma a proud student boasted that she had integrated school gardens and nature study into the coursework.[73]

Other students became leaders in their communities and tried to pass on what they had learned at Tuskegee. Some arranged lectures for their local communities; others, like the student Tuskegee's council failed to commend in 1902, organized local farmers' conferences and requested that Carver forward as many bulletins and pamphlets as possible.[74] One former student reported to Carver in a playful letter from May 1911, "Bad disease is breaking out in this community, and it is all laid on me. . . . This disease," he continued, "is 'Self Reliance.' I have been working hard to make these people depend more on themselves, and I am certainly seeing the fruits of my labor."[75] Surely, little victories like these indicate that Carver's hope of training agricultural apostles who could carry his message throughout the South met with at least a measure of success.

Moreover, not everyone Carver taught at the institute was officially enrolled as a student there. He established monthly Farmers' Institutes—a concept born at the IAC—to reach local farmers.[76] On November 11, 1897, a little more than a year after Carver's arrival, Tuskegee hosted its first Farmers' Institute meeting.[77] Thereafter, once a month Tuskegee offered local farmers practical—often hands-on—lessons in subjects such as "when and how cotton land should be prepared," "gardening for profit," "how women can best help their husbands," "the proper terracing for farmlands," and "how to recognize and destroy destructive insects."[78]

A typical meeting, held in May 1901, opened with scripture reading, hymns, and prayer. After the preliminaries, three professors (Carver was not one of them on this occasion) provided instructions on what to plant that month and two other practical issues: poultry raising and "the egg—its value." These addresses were followed by an open forum in which the farmers could raise questions for the instructors to address and offer suggestions to each other. On this occasion there was no visit to the experiment station, but such a tour would not have been unusual. Once in a while Carver even distributed seeds to the attendees.[79]

Predictably, attendance varied by season. During the planting season in 1904, for example, Carver reported to Washington that thirty-five farmers, including six women, had attended the most recent Farmers' Institute meeting, which had "closed with a visit to the Experiment Station where we spent quite . . . half an hour."[80] After farmers had laid their cotton by in July, however, the attendance leaped to ninety-one farmers, not counting their wives. "This shows," Carver wrote Washington, "that the school is gradually reaching the people." In mid-August, a few weeks before picking would begin, the Farmers' Institute held a summer barbecue at which Carver was sure "there were two hundred farmers and their wives present"—so many, in fact, that the meeting had to be moved from the agricultural building to the chapel.[81]

Toward the close of 1903 Carver suggested expanding Tuskegee's efforts to reach local farmers by holding a series of lectures for them during the winter months, when farm duties were relatively light. Institute officials agreed, and in January 1904 a six-week "Short Course in Agriculture" was launched. The first year eleven students enrolled in the course, which started at 10 a.m. and ended at 3 p.m., giving local farmers enough time to get to the institute and return home each day. The following year the course was shortened to four weeks, and enrollment rose to seventeen. The ensuing year saw the final reduction in course length, to two weeks, and enrollment jumped sharply to sixty-two men and eight women. In large measure that jump might be attributed to the fact that Tuskegee began giving wage "work to a number of those who wished it," which enabled those who lived farther from the school to attend the course. Although the institute charged no tuition for the two-week course, the money helped offset the travel and food expenses farmers necessarily incurred being away from their farms.[82]

Thus, by 1906 Carver could note, "Three years experience with the Short Course in Agriculture has enabled us to gather together such things and plan a course of study intensely practical and indispensable to the ambitious farmer." Carver and Bridgeforth served as the primary instructors and offered classes in "farming"—which included the mechanics of soil preparation; the cultivation of cotton, corn, and potatoes; and the uses of manures and fertilizers—as well as livestock, dairying, poultry raising, and fruit growing. At the end of the course, the attendees received awards, including a five-dollar prize to the person who made "the greatest progress in all subjects."[83] The institute's efforts were rewarded the following year when 490 farmers enrolled in the course; by 1912 enrollment exceeded 1,500.[84]

Together with the Farmers' Institute, the Short Course in Agriculture enabled Carver to teach a fair number of farmers who never formally enrolled in Tuskegee. And to these he added more in 1908 when the institute began hosting four-day summer schools in various communities in Macon County for those who could not travel to Tuskegee for the short course.[85] Six-week summer courses for teachers taught the same sorts of practical lessons Carver incorporated into his nature study bulletins. Though the attendance was relatively low at these courses, between thirty and fifty on average, enrollees were subsequently able to convey Carver's teachings to a reasonably wide audience.[86]

The teachers came away as impressed with Carver's pedagogy and ecological worldview as with the agricultural techniques and remedies he presented to them. "I often think of the Summer School, of both the profit and pleasure I derived from it," one student wrote to Carver. "Especially do I recall the pleasant walks and talks with you." Another noted, "I have been traveling all summer in rural districts, and I confess I saw nature as never before. I was able to tell farmers many things of interest after studying agriculture under you six weeks." Lest there be any doubt that he was carrying Carver's message, he added, "I am also teaching them to protect the life of the toad. I never saw anything in him but an ugly creature until you spoke of him in class."[87] Carver's teaching thus reached, either directly or indirectly, a sizable number of impoverished black farmers, and the lives of some of them no doubt materially improved as a result.

As influential as his classes at the institute were, however, Carver probably influenced more people through his public appearances, which constituted the second avenue through which he sought to open the eyes of poor black farmers to the possibilities presented by an environment he believed they took for granted. Perhaps the best known of these were his regular appearances at the institute's annual Negro Farmers' Conference. The first such conference, held on February 23, 1892, predated Carver's arrival at Tuskegee. On that day, about four hundred African American men, most of them farmers (only twenty-three of whom owned their own homes), attended the event and discussed their problems in open forums.

The resulting resolutions adopted at the close of the conference were a mixed bag. One amounted to wishful thinking: "To abolish and do away with the mortgage system just as rapidly as possible"; and one (anticipating a portion of Carver's message) acknowledged the necessity of increased economic independence by admitting the need to "raise our own food supplies . . . at home rather than go in debt for them at stores." The bulk of the remaining resolutions might have been written by middle-class whites, and included doing away with drinking, gambling, "and disgracing ourselves in many other ways"; hiring only "moral men" as pastors; and making sure women behaved demurely (speaking "in a quiet tone of voice" in public and never wearing "their hair wrapped in strings").[88]

The conference's success in attracting black farmers convinced Washington to make it an annual event, and other black institutions—including his alma mater beginning in 1897—followed suit. "Out of this central Negro Conference at Tuskegee," Washington boasted in *Up from Slavery*, "have grown numerous state and local conferences which are doing the same kind of work."[89] Historian Allen Jones pointed out that "hundreds of local conferences—more than 150 in 1899 alone—appeared in rural areas all over Alabama and throughout the South."[90] Delegates from each of these conferences sent representatives to the annual Tuskegee Negro Conference, which by the end of the decade had been joined to a "Negro Workers' Conference," the latter geared toward "officers and teachers who are engaged in educational work . . . in the South."[91]

By the end of 1897 the conference had grown so large (and so important to Tuskegee) that Washington appointed a full-time conference organizer. By 1901 Tuskegee had arranged for special discount fares on rail lines. And in 1903 the institute issued a pamphlet titled *Local Negro Conferences, How to Organize and Conduct Them*, which included a "Planting Calendar" prepared by Carver and a promise that Tuskegee would forward his experiment station bulletins to each local conference.[92]

Conference activities increased and attendance doubled following Carver's arrival in 1896, although he does not deserve sole credit for the increased popularity.[93] Certainly, Washington seized on the annual Farmers' Conference as a chance to thrust his school into the national limelight each year and provide something of a show for the northern philanthropists who poured money into the school, and he promoted it assiduously. Likewise, Tuskegee was a social center for African Americans from Macon and surrounding counties. When, in the first decade of the twentieth century, Ned Cobb, a black farmer from neighboring Tallapoosa County, was courting the woman who would become his wife, she asked him to take her to Tuskegee's commencement. "People from every whichaway come that day to Tuskegee Normal School, colored school, commencement," Cobb recalled. "Crowd so thick you couldn't squeeze between em."[94] Other events, including the Farmers' Conference, had a certain social aspect as well.

Much of the credit for the conference's increased attendance can be attributed to Carver, however, for two principal reasons. First, his experiment station showed conference guests a concrete example of what could be done with relatively little capital and provided an incentive to adhere to the suggestions of conference speakers like himself. The second, and perhaps more important, reason was Carver's friendship with James Wilson. Through his connection with Wilson, Carver was able to procure seeds from the USDA that could be distributed to conference attendees, giving them greater means to achieve such annual resolutions as diversifying their crops. In time, Carver also distributed hybrid seeds developed under his direction at the experiment station.[95]

Carver's participation in the annual conference represented only a small fraction of his public appearances. He also arranged displays and spoke at the Farmers' Institute's annual fair. First held in the autumn of 1898, the fair grew out of the Farmers' Institute meetings Carver had played a primary role in establishing. More or less conventional in featuring agricultural exhibits, demonstrations, and talks, the annual event's attendance grew from a few hundred to thousands within a decade or so. By 1910 the concept of an African American county fair had spread from Tuskegee and proliferated throughout the South.[96] (Ironically, the Farmers' Institute fair was combined with the white county fair into a single Macon County Fair after 1911.)[97] And Carver's public appearances in Macon County were far outstripped by his engagements beyond its borders.

Even before the end of his first decade at Tuskegee, Carver's public lectures had won him invitations to speak at various functions throughout Alabama and the South. In 1903, for instance, state officials invited him to display an exhibit before the state legislature in Montgomery, and in 1908 he spoke before a gathering of the Farmers' Progressive Union attended by Alabama's commissioner of agriculture.[98] Invitations to speak before white audiences were comparatively rare in Carver's early years at Tuskegee, however. Most of his public presentations were before groups that had grown out of the various farmers' conferences spawned by the Tuskegee Conference and at county and state fairs on their "Negro Day." He also regularly spoke at other black institutions and at teachers' association meetings, attempting to persuade educators to increase their focus on agriculture and to integrate nature study into their curricula.[99]

Regardless of the audience, however, promoters of the gatherings generally advertised his appearance as a main attraction and invited farmers to bring soil and plant samples for him to analyze. "If your soil don't produce crops well bring some with you and he will tell you the reason why," proclaimed one advertisement for Carver in 1905. "Any question on any kind of plant or any kind of animal you are at liberty to ask him; he is the man to answer." Utica Institute, a black institution in Mississippi, similarly advertised that Carver would "be on the grounds throughout the conference." He "will be glad to meet and talk with as many of the farmers as possible, and give them advice on all problems confronting them." The flyer encouraged farmers to "bring along samples of soil, diseased plants, insect enemies and anything about which they wish to ask questions and get information."[100]

Occasionally, advertisements would indicate that Carver was not only going to lecture, but also intended to organize a local farmers' conference, as his duties at Tuskegee called for him to do. After returning from a lecture in Social Circle, Georgia, for instance, Carver reported that he had lectured to "five or six hundred people on Agriculture" and had organized a local conference, making "clear that they should be considered part of the Tuskegee Negro Conference work and that delegates should be sent to the meeting here in February."[101] His work did not end once a conference had been established; he kept in touch afterward, sending bulletins and answering various questions.[102] Chiefly, however, his aim was to teach farmers "How to Build Up Worn Out Soils and Make the Farm Pay," as one advertisement noted in 1903.[103]

At a typical conference, held in 1899 at Hampton Institute in Virginia, Carver acknowledged the bleak financial situation facing African American farmers in the South. The "average southern farm has little more to offer than about thirty-seven percent of a cotton crop selling at four and half cents a pound and costing five and six to produce," he noted, but added, "we have a perfect foundation for an ideal country [including] natural advantages of which we may justly feel proud." To be sure, the "exhaustive system of cultivation" practiced in the South, "the destruction of [its] forests, the rapid and almost constant decomposition of organic matter [due to its mild climate that facilitated decomposition year-round], and [its] great number of noxious insects and fungi" made salvaging the region's agriculture more difficult. In fact, he argued, farming in the South required "more brains" than it did in "the North, East, or West."

His insistence that farmers' failure to apply their minds was holding them back was a common theme of Progressive Era proponents of agricultural reform. But the particular way Carver believed farmers ought to apply their intellect was unique. He rooted the problems facing poor farmers in their ignorance of ecological relationships, the fact that they knew "nothing about the mutual relationship of the animal, mineral and vegetables kingdoms, and how utterly impossible it is for one to exist in a highly organized state without the other." This sort of ecological thinking was paramount in Carver's agricultural thought generally, and it undergirded his campaign on behalf of impoverished tenant farmers. On this occasion as on others, of course, Carver offered some "practical" suggestions, in this case how to increase, "both in quantity and quality, all of our farm animals."[104]

Although it certainly was not uncommon for him to enjoin farmers to raise whatever livestock they could, the particulars of Carver's lectures varied. Sometimes conference organizers requested that he speak on one topic or another, and his "practical" suggestions often dealt with the advisability of cultivating some specific plant, or with crop rotation, manuring, or, later, the boll weevil. When invited to speak expressly for a conference's "Ladies' Day," as he often was, he would give cooking demonstrations and bring his "fancy work."[105] He stayed for days at some conferences and barely long enough to lecture at others, but at most he spent "the recesses . . . deluged with questions from this and that farmer."[106]

Regardless of the venue, Carver consistently advocated building up the soil via manuring and crop rotation; emphasized the importance of comprehending "the mutual relationship of the animal, mineral and vegetables kingdoms"; and insisted that farmers could satisfy many of their needs and wants by eschewing waste and finding uses for things they either overlooked or neglected. The Tougaloo College paper began its report of Carver's appearance there by noting that his lectures were "really an appeal to Southern Colored people . . . to open their eyes."[107]

Carver invariably illustrated his lectures with examples, much as he did in the classroom. "When I was a boy," he told an audience at Voorhees Normal and Industrial School, "I was greatly insulted when they told me I did not know beans. I got mad at once. . . . Madness is nearly always the result of ignorance." Segueing into a discussion of cowpeas, which conveniently he had brought with him, he informed the crowd that an "acre of well grown pea vines would bring $30.00 worth of nitrogen alone, free of charge to the farmer, if he would only grow them and turn under the whole crop."[108] On other occasions he would use a sweet potato, peanuts, or, as was usually the case at fairs, an entire exhibit—of canned and dried fruits and vegetables, of peanut or cowpea products, or any of a number of others he put together over the years.

His down-to-earth illustrations, impressive knowledge of all things agricultural, unassuming demeanor, and clever wit made him an enormously popular speaker. Following a 1902 address in Augusta, Georgia, the conference organizers fawned over his presentation. "It is a privilege seldom enjoyed to hear a man talk who *knows* what he is talking about," they gushed, "and at the same time possesses that facility of language, which enables him to clothe scientific and technical information in garb so simple a child may understand." Indeed, they continued, "we do not hesitate to say that [his *three hour* lecture] was the most valuable exposition of farming methods ever given in Augusta."[109]

Such lavish praise was not confined to black Americans. After hearing Carver speak at the Tuskegee Negro Farmers' Conference, University of Georgia chancellor Walter Barnard Hill reportedly remarked, "That was the best lecture on agriculture to which it has ever been my privilege to listen." Carver had "not only shown himself a master of the subject," Hill continued, he was "possessed of pedagogical ability to impart it clearly and forcibly to others—a combination which is possessed by only five or six men in the entire country."[110] For a white southerner to place a black man in such exclusive company was high praise indeed, and it is hardly surprising that many subsequent advertisements for Carver's lectures carried Hill's endorsement. Thus, it was not without reason that a 1918 biographical sketch of Carver noted that he was considered "the drawing card" at farmers' conferences, and that "his name attached to a placard or bulletin announcing a proposed farmers conference will draw a larger number of interested individuals—both white and black—than the name of any other speaker who can be secured."[111]

As Carver's reputation waxed, he attracted increased attention from the press. In the midst of the debate that preceded the passage of the Pure Food and Drug Act in 1906, for instance, *Collier's Weekly* ran an article that centered on one of his lectures. Very much a Progressive, Carver had organized his talk to give "one illustration of the reign of fraud in commerce." "You wonder why your cattle are not satisfied with the food, why they fail to yield the milk and butter which you have a right to expect?" he asked his audience rhetorically. Laying out seven samples of bran, some of which had been adulterated by nearly 50 percent with sawdust and ground corncobs, he concluded dramatically, "Here is your reason."[112]

The following year both Boston-based *Alexander's* magazine and *Colored American* magazine ran pieces on Carver. *Alexander's* was impressed by Carver's exhibit of some three hundred jars of "cotton, corn, and [preserved] vegetables of every kind known to Alabama soil," as well as with his "skillful and efficient" management of the school's agricultural department, a description that doubtless earned a few chuckles around the campus. *Colored American* was impressed with Carver's ability to tease out metaphors—in particular his likening of the denuded southern soils to a sick person. "It is, perhaps, not generally known that soils run down and become sick, a good deal like animals," the article noted; hence the need to "build them up" much like a person recovering from an illness. But like virtually all the sketches of Carver from his first decades at Tuskegee, both were most impressed with his affinity for the natural world—an affinity evident even in the brief encounters his public appearances allowed. The metaphors Carver drew in his talks, the *Colored American* article noted, were "a little too picturesque for science. But Mr. Carver," it continued, "is not merely a scientist, he is also something of a poet and a lover of nature for her own sake." Indeed, Carver had developed "an intimate personal acquaintance" with the soils he worked. *Alexander's* likewise found Carver to be not only "a lover of the beautiful" but so in tune with nature that he could "see beauty in the rapidly decaying bark of a tree as well as in the rose so perfectly developed under his scientific hand."[113]

By 1908 Carver's reputation had grown to the point that the Agassiz Association solicited his endorsement, which was carried in the October issue of its journal, *The Guide to Nature*. That was also the year Harry H. Johnston came to Tuskegee. A British officer, explorer, and amateur botanist who had played a significant role in the conquest of Rhodesia, Johnston had developed a genuine interest in African culture. Historian Jack Temple Kirby noted that Johnston wrote of Africa with "learning and admiration" and, as his experiences there altered his racial views, unusual sympathy for Africans. By 1908 he had become interested in tracking the effects of what would later be known as the African diaspora in the Western Hemisphere. Securing the invitation of Teddy Roosevelt—who admitted that America's treatment of African Americans left a good bit to be desired, even if "at Johannesburg and Kimberly [in South Africa] the Negroes [were] certainly treated worse"—Johnston took his study to the United States. Predictably, Johnston visited Tuskegee, where Washington made certain that he met

Carver, whom the principal considered "the most thoroughly scientific man of the negro race with whom I am acquainted."[114]

Johnston was impressed with Carver as well and devoted a paragraph of his book, *The Negro in the New World* (1910), to him. "He is as regards complexion and features, an absolute Negro," Johnston began, "but in the cut of his clothes, the accent of his speech, the soundness of his science, he might be the Professor of Botany not at Tuskegee, but at Oxford or Cambridge." In fact, Johnston asserted, "any European botanist of distinction, after ten minutes' conversation with the man, instinctively would deal with him 'de puissance en puissance.'"[115]

This sort of juxtaposition of Carver's "unmixed" ancestry and his scientific prowess became the signature mark of subsequent accounts of him. Perhaps this is not surprising. The contrast between what contemporary whites expected of African Americans and Carver's obvious intelligence and ability could be used to dramatic effect. It had the unfortunate result, however, of diverting attention from Carver's purpose in going to Tuskegee. In the ensuing years, including those following his death, this emphasis on Carver's being a *black* scientist was so overwhelming that virtually all of the attention devoted to him revolved around his relative merits as a scientist and a racial symbol.

Inasmuch as it drew attention to Carver, however, this juxtaposition also contributed to his growing reputation, which by the end of his first decade at Tuskegee was clearly on the rise. By 1906 the state commissioner of agriculture was writing Booker T. Washington to beg "Dr. Carver's" presence at various county fairs.[116] In part, Carver was popular among southern whites as well as blacks because of his association with the "safe" ideologies of Washington and Tuskegee. Ironically, his growing popularity also made his position reasonably secure at Tuskegee, where, next to Washington, his was the most recognizable face and name. Had the principal wanted to accept Carver's resignation on those occasions when Carver tendered it, he might have had trouble doing so because it would have been something of a publicity blunder.

Although he was frequently annoyed with Carver, however, Washington genuinely respected him. Recognizing that praise heaped on Carver redounded to Tuskegee's benefit, he publicly lauded him in *My Larger Education* (1911), a book that played an important role in Carver's growing reputation because it had a wide readership and amounted to his first lengthy biographical sketch. The book was published, not coincidentally, shortly after Washington had placed Carver in charge of the largely mythical Department of Research and the Experiment Station, and the sketch was to some extent meant to soothe the ego of the institute's sensitive scientist. "Although Professor Carver impresses every one who meets him with the extent of his knowledge in the matter of plant life," Washington wrote, establishing a motif that most subsequent biographers would follow, "he is quite the most modest man I have ever met." Claiming to recall a time when he had "asked Professor Carver . . . how it was, since he was so timid, that he managed to have made the acquaintance of so many of the best white as well as colored people in our part of the country," Washington found in Carver the embodiment of a moral lesson: "He said as soon as people found out that he knew something about plants that was valuable he discovered that they were willing and eager to talk to him." Thus, the sketch was also intended to serve as evidence for Washington's contention that "the best means which the negro has for destroying race prejudice is to make himself useful and, if possible, an indispensable member of the community in which he lives." He could not think, he professed, "of a better illustration of this than . . . Professor Carver."[117]

By 1911, then, Carver was the subject of a mythology of sorts, albeit one that would not really blossom until the 1920s. The Carver myth emphasized Carver's success in overcoming the hindrances placed before African Americans, his scientific ability, and his humility, and accounts of his career were wont to focus on the sacrifices he had made to aid "his people." *Technical World* magazine, for instance, ran an article titled "Gave Up Art Career for His Race" in 1912. While the article exaggerated Carver's humility and sacrifice, it was not entirely off-base in pointing out that his "experiments and instruction at Tuskegee Institute have been invariably with common things—with just such things as the farmers, housewives and school teachers in Alabama have to deal with every day."[118]

Carver's work at the experiment station had not "invariably" been done "with common things," but by 1912 that had essentially become the case. For by then the economic, social, and political realities facing impoverished black farmers in Alabama's Cotton Belt and elsewhere in the South had forced Carver to alter his campaign. The brand of scientific agriculture in which he had been trained at the IAC proved to be of little use to such farmers until it was sufficiently modified to put the application of its principles within their reach. This transformation of Carver's conception of scientific agriculture is most clearly seen through his work at the experiment station and the publications that grew out of his research there, which together came to constitute the third prong of his campaign, one that dovetailed neatly with his teaching at Tuskegee and his public lectures.

CHAPTER 6

Hints and Suggestions to Farmers

It is perhaps extraordinary that Tuskegee had an experiment station to begin with because it was not a land-grant college when Carver took over the agricultural department in 1896. In 1871, nine years after the passage of the original Morrill Act, Alabama set aside some of the Morrill funds to establish two land-grant colleges, one for whites that opened in Auburn in 1872, and one for blacks that opened a few years later in Huntsville. In 1883 the legislature established an experiment station in Auburn for the purpose of making "cotton production less expensive and less time consuming" so that farmers could turn their "attention to the production of other crops." The emphasis was on the former rather than the latter, however; indeed, the nod to diversification was a perfunctory one. Cotton production was paramount.[1]

The same bill that established the experiment station at Auburn provided for its funding by requiring all commercial fertilizers sold in the state to carry a guarantee tag and setting apart one-third of the funds generated from the sale of these tags. It is not a coincidence that Auburn's station and the Alabama Department of Agriculture were established the same year. The latter was responsible for regulating commercial fertilizers and "promoting their extension and use," while the former was charged with testing fertilizer samples. The fact that the station's funding was tied to sales of commercial fertilizers gave it every financial incentive—had any been needed given the milieu of the time—to promote those fertilizers. It was an incentive that would remain in place for nearly twenty-five years.[2]

In 1890 Congress passed the Second Morrill Act, which included the provision that "no money shall be paid out under this act to any State or Territory for the support and maintenance of a college where a distinction of race and color is made in the admission of students." Congress deferred to the South's segregationist policies, however, when it allowed that "the establishment and maintenance of such colleges separately for white and colored students shall be held in compliance with the provisions of this act" so long as funds for them were "equitably divided." The ambiguity of the last phrase all but quashed the possibility of equality, but it did provide some funding for a black school to establish an experiment station of its own.[3]

Initially, the money from the Second Morrill Act went exclusively to the black land-grant school at Huntsville, and likely would have continued to do so had Washington not become a national celebrity following his Atlanta Exposition address in 1895. He and William H. Councill, the head of the black A&M college in Huntsville, had competed for state funding before, and throughout 1896 and into 1897 both men lobbied the legislature to establish a branch experiment station at their respective schools. Washington made sure that a number of legislators met his new agriculturist, fresh from the IAC, but in the end it was Washington's newfound political influence rather than Carver's charisma and scientific training that decided the matter. In February 1897, four months after Carver's arrival, Governor Joseph F. Johnston signed into law an act providing for a "Branch Agricultural Experiment Station and Agricultural School for the colored race" at Tuskegee. Washington had won despite the fact that Tuskegee was not a land-grant institution, and thus was an unlikely site for a station (a technicality the state rectified in 1899 when it gave the institute 25,000 acres to be sold or leased for revenue).[4]

In theory, the Tuskegee station was a satellite of the experiment station at the Alabama Polytechnic Institute in Auburn. The Alabama commissioner of agriculture, the president of the API, and the director of its experiment station all sat on the Tuskegee station's "board of control." In practice, the reputations of Washington and Tuskegee minimized white oversight, and Carver could pursue any projects he could persuade the school's principal and council to allow. Even so, Carver could not escape some duties. Part of his obligation to "advance the interest of scientific agriculture," for instance, required him "to cause such chemical analysis to be made as are deemed necessary . . . under the supervision of the Commissioner of Agriculture"; in other words, to test commercial fertilizers.[5]

The ten acres initially set aside for the experiment station looked much like the rundown land the county's tenant farmers were working. Former plantation land, the station field had once "been planted by the wasteful methods of the tenant system, year after year."[6] Predominantly a sandy loam that eroded easily, much of the topsoil had been carried away by a stream that cut across the property. Carver only half-jokingly quipped that the soil was so badly eroded that "we could throw an ox into a ditch and . . . have to look down to see it."[7] The land's forest past was evident in the stumps that covered the entire site. Indeed, as Carver noted, the plot "had but little to characterize it other than its extreme poorness, both as to physical and chemical requirements."[8]

Carver began his work at the station in the spring of 1897. He filled the gullies and ditches with "pine tops, hay, bark, old cotton stalks, leaves, etc., in fact, rubbish of any kind that would decay and ultimately make soil," throwing "an occasional load of earth" on top as was necessary to "give it more weight and firmness." With student help, he removed "upwards of one hundred stumps," terraced the land's hilly portions, and cordoned off the station into one-tenth-acre plots. By 1905, when nine additional acres were added to the station for "certain experiments in cotton growing," Carver could report that the "injurious washing has been almost completely overcome." The *Tuskegee Student* reported that the station attracted "the attention of everybody who passes the field."[9]

In the first bulletin issued by the Tuskegee Agricultural Experiment Station, Carver noted that the "object and aims of our Station are essentially the same as those of nearly or quite all of the other stations."[10] He tested fertilizers and planted legumes of various sorts along with myriad vegetables, and, of course, cotton. At the season's end the crops he had raised at the station were either consumed by Tuskegee students or sold in nearby markets.[11] Though he worked with some plants from the beginning—cowpeas and sweet potatoes, to name two—the particular projects he pursued each year varied according to his interests. In the early 1900s, for instance, Carver kept silkworm colonies on some three hundred mulberry trees at the suggestion of James Wilson, who provided Carver with the caterpillars, but his efforts proved nearly as unsuccessful as those of the Georgia colony in the eighteenth century.[12] In 1903 Carver began working with Spanish peanuts, the plant with which future generations would most associate him and which he continued to study long after his experimental plot work at the station came to a close.

Carver's work at the station looked conventional in other regards as well. He analyzed "samples of water, milk, foodstuffs and soil sent to the Institute" and investigated agricultural fraud of various kinds. He advised the public, for instance, to avoid the so-called wonder berry, which he had tested and "found to be absolutely worthless either as a fruit or vegetable."[13] He recommended particular varieties of crops for the institute's farms, exchanged specimens and bulletins with other agricultural stations, and carried on a number of cross-breeding experiments, developing among other things his own hybrid cotton.[14] Requests for bulletins and farming advice came nearly daily. From time to time, Carver would receive unusual requests. On one occasion, for instance, he had to inform an optimistic farmer that he had "failed to find any gold at all in either the fine powder or the rock" the man had sent him. For the most part, however, people wanted remedies for vermin and pests, information on planting and harvesting a particular crop, and suggestions for dealing with problems related to one crop or another.[15]

Carver's early work was not entirely conventional, however. His appreciation for the natural world and his understanding of ecology's fundamental principles made his efforts distinctive in some ways from the very beginning. His first bulletin, for instance, promoted the use of acorns as a food for livestock. His conviction that waste was anathema—a conviction instilled during his days on the Carvers' farm, nurtured by years of poverty and want, and confirmed by his studies under Pammel at the IAC—led him to lament the fact that the "great quantity of acorns produced in our oak forests" had "been hitherto practically a waste product."[16] In contrast to most of his fellow agronomists, Carver was unafraid to look backward for inspiration. Since the advent of fence laws had restricted the movements of free-range livestock, Carver maintained, "the feeding values of this natural product [had been], in great measure, lost sight of." Not only were acorns free to impoverished black farmers, they provided an overlooked economic justification to preserve the forests from the axes of timber companies. "We hope the days are not far distant," Carver noted, "when the destruction of our valuable oak forests will cease."[17] Carver's disdain for waste and his ardent belief that nature produced none led him to turn his attention to other neglected resources as well. In 1902, for example, he asserted that the South's "crab grass is a much better hay than the timothy which we are constantly shipping in," as were the region's "Johnson grass" and "marsh grasses," the latter of which made "good hay if cut before they became too coarse and woody."[18]

Carver was not alone in thinking that the solution to the problems that afflicted rural America lay in "a mighty campaign of education."[19] He was part and parcel of the agrarian impulse of the conservation movement of the time. Men such as Liberty Hyde Bailey and Kenyon L. Butterfield would doubtless have agreed with Carver's assertion that "it is therefore doubly necessary that we know something of the soil and its relations to animal and vegetable life in order [to] get the very best returns from the capital and labor invested."[20] And Bailey, with whom Carver shared a religious reverence for the natural world, would have agreed with Carver's injunction, "Let us become familiar with the commonest things about us." Even so, Carver's emphasis in his bulletins on ecological relationships was relatively unique. He sought to equip farmers first and foremost by convincing them that the "highest attainments in agriculture [could] be reached only when" they clearly understood those relationships. Rural restoration could begin only when farmers recognized that their "plants were real, living things, and that sunshine, air, food, and drink, were as necessary for their lives as for that of the animal."[21] Over time the distinctiveness of Carver's vision would grow more marked as agricultural science grew increasingly production oriented and Carver grew increasingly aware of the realities facing black farmers, but the seed of these differences was evident at the beginning.

With that caveat in mind, Carver's agricultural views were fairly conventional when he began his career at Tuskegee. Seaman A. Knapp, the founder of the USDA's county agent system, captured the prevailing agricultural wisdom of the late nineteenth and early twentieth centuries in his "Ten Commandments" of scientific agriculture: cultivate deeply; use the best seed available; space rows appropriately; till intensively during the growing period; use legumes, barnyard manure, farm refuse, and commercial fertilizers to enrich the soil; rotate crops; use the most up-to-date technology (which he described as "more horse power and better implements"); raise livestock; be self-sufficient (i.e., raise enough food for the farm family and livestock); and keep good records.[22]

To a large degree, Carver espoused these commandments in his bulletins, lectures, and classes. He consistently advocated cultivating the soil to a depth of eight to nine inches, though if it had "been plowed shallow for a number of years," he recommended approaching that depth gradually, two inches at a time.[23] He enjoined farmers to be selective in the seed they used—to hand sort it if need be. He had little to say about the appropriate spacing of rows, at least until the boll weevil arrived on the scene, but there is no evidence to suggest he was anything other than orthodox here. Likewise, he recommended shallow cultivation (no more than two and a half inches because cotton's roots spread laterally and could easily be cut by careless plowing) during the growing season to keep the weeds down and to act as a dust mulch; crop rotation, including winter cover crops, though the last was difficult given cotton's early planting and relatively late harvest; and he tried to persuade farmers to increase the quantity and quality of their livestock.

But Carver revised some of Knapp's commandments. Keeping good records was not an option for many black farmers given the high illiteracy rate among Alabama's black communities at the turn of the century.[24] More significant, perhaps, even literate African Americans had little choice but to accept the records of their white creditors. Those who failed to do so risked eviction, harassment, and racial violence. Thus, the political and social realities of the Cotton Belt rendered the last of Knapp's commandments immaterial, and Carver, despite supporting a campaign to stamp out illiteracy in Alabama, devoted virtually no attention to it.[25] Three others—use the most modern farm implements; be self-sufficient; and use legumes, barnyard manure, farm refuse, and commercial fertilizers—merit further explanation.

Initially, Carver embraced Knapp's commandment to utilize only the best farm equipment. Almost immediately after his arrival in Tuskegee he asked for a two-horse plow—a rather shocking extravagance that exacerbated tensions between him and his peers, but which was granted nonetheless.[26] He likewise used a top-notch harrow (to break up the large clods thrust up by the plow), a "four-toothed cultivator," and "a diamond scooter [plow]" to till the soil while the plants were growing.[27] By the early 1900s, however, Carver had realized that most black farmers simply could not afford modern farm implements, and he stopped endorsing them in his publications, even as other stations promoted them. Knapp, for instance, increasingly enjoined farmers to "use more modern machinery, better horses, more mules, [and] better implements."[28] Carver never denied that "labor saving machinery can be used to advantage," but "desiring to bring it [his work] more closely in touch with the one-horse farmer," he "made it [his] practice to do things ... under conditions similar to those of the farmer."[29]

Financial exigencies played a role in this decision as well. Federal funding for the station was funneled through the state, which predictably allocated the vast majority of the funds to the experiment station at Auburn. Had it not been for Washington's connection with prominent philanthropists and Carver's connection with James Wilson, things might have been even worse for the Tuskegee station, which at its inception received one-tenth the annual funding allocated its counterpart at Auburn and by 1912 received but one-fiftieth.[30] Despite donations from Wilson and others, the institute's station was forced to make do with very little. By the time Carver published the station's sixth bulletin in April 1905—titled *How to Build Up Worn Out Soils*—he could rightly assert, "The Tuskegee station has ... [kept] in mind the poor tenant farmer with a one-horse equipment; so therefore, every operation performed has been within his reach."[31] Thus, by the end of his first decade in Tuskegee, Carver had begun spurning technological solutions. There was no need to buy an expensive manure spreader, for example. One of Carver's assistants insisted that a farmer using only his wagon and "two or three willing boys" would find that "a load of manure soon finds itself spread upon the places needed."[32] And to the degree that Carver continued to reject technology as an unquestioned good in agriculture, he found himself increasingly out of touch with the main currents of agricultural science with each passing decade.[33]

Carver also modified Knapp's commandment to make the farm self-sufficient. Of course he agreed with the principle; his entire campaign was aimed at achieving it. In contrast with the staple crops of the Midwest—corn and wheat—however, cotton is not edible. What is more, tenant farmers had little control over what they planted; that decision rested with their landlord. Consequently, Carver had to be more creative than most of his peers to find ways to enable black farmers to become self-sufficient in terms of subsistence. At times he appealed directly to the landlords, arguing that permitting tenants to grow their own food would increase their efficiency, and thus the landlord's profits. "A sick, worried, rest-broken person cannot do his best," Carver reasoned. "From a purely economic point of view," allowing tenants to cultivate large gardens and raise livestock, and generally to find ways to allow them to diversify the standard salt pork and cornbread diet on which most subsisted was a worthwhile venture.[34]

When such appeals failed, as they almost invariably did, Carver approached the problem in several other ways. To begin with, he encouraged black farmers to grow as much of their own subsistence as possible given their circumstances. So long as they took empty wagons to town and returned with them full of supplies, Carver argued in a passage that might well have appeared in the pages of *Wallace's Farmer*, tenant farmers would remain "the very embodiment of pessimism, and imagine that all sorts of cliques, clans, and plans [were] being originated to militate against them."[35] By 1902 (the year in which he was nearly lynched in Montgomery County), however, Carver was beginning to understand that "cliques, clans, and plans" were indeed organized against African Americans.

This realization shifted the direction of Carver's experiment station work. Increasingly, he turned his research at the station to finding alternative uses for three relatively minor southern crops—sweet potatoes, cowpeas, and peanuts—that could not only contribute to the regeneration of southern soils but could be both consumed and marketed as well. In 1903 Carver published a bulletin on cowpeas, which he insisted were "absolutely indispensable in a wise crop rotation, and in the rational feeding of both man and beast."[36] The bulletin incorporated twenty-five recipes for dishes that could be made from the vegetable. This was the first of many of his bulletins to include recipes, and it pointed to a new direction in his campaign. From 1903 on, housewives were one of Carver's principal target audiences, and most of his publications were aimed as much at them as at their husbands in the fields. After all, he maintained, it "is just as important for the housewife to know how to use . . . farm products wholesomely and economically as it is to produce them."[37]

Carver's antipathy for waste was as evident in his instructions for food preparation as it was in his advice to farmers. "As a rule we are wasteful; we do not know how to save," Carver began a bulletin directed toward "the thoughtful housewife," titled *Three Delicious Meals Every Day for the Farmer*. "Ignorance in the kitchen is one of the worst curses that ever afflicted humanity, and is directly or indirectly responsible for more deaths than all the armies combined."[38] Ever the progressive, he not only lamented the fact that "a poor selection of food" contributed to "the loathsome and dreaded disease known as Pellagra," but complained that "bad combinations of food" left people "unnourished" and "unduly stimulated; and as a result often lead to strong drink, bad morals, and bad manners."[39] His moralizing aside, Carver thought it absurd that southern farmers were among "the most poorly fed of all classes of individuals" when "choice vegetables of some kind can be had every day in the year" from gardens in the South.[40]

Not all of Carver's recipes would win the endorsement of nutritionists today. "Bacon Puffs," for instance, were essentially bacon fritters "made from the very fat portion of the bacon . . . dipped into a thick pancake batter, and fried."[41] But his advice was for the most part sound, and his recipes were considerably healthier than the standard fare of most black farmer families. It was his hope "that every housewife and all those in charge of the preparation of foods would see to it that some kind of green, leafy vegetable is served everyday." If they did, the region's black communities would enjoy "greater vitality, clearer thinking and," revealing once again his Progressive bent, "a greater determination to be a worthwhile somebody in life."[42] More to the point, the recipes he provided were for fruits and vegetables readily accessible to poor farmers, if not on their farms proper then in the woods surrounding them. In keeping with his conviction that nature produced no waste, he instructed farmers "to recognize and appreciate what Nature has so lavishly provided for us" in the form of neglected and overlooked foodstuffs.[43]

"Nature endows or blesses each state or section with an indigenous flora and fauna best suited to that particular soil and climatic conditions," Carver wrote in a 1907 bulletin. Macon County had been blessed "in the quantity, variety and quality of its wild plums." In fact, "many hundred bushels" of them went "to waste every year." The purpose of the bulletin, aptly titled *Saving the Wild Plum Crop*, was "to set forth in a practical way a number of recipes by which every housewife may be successful in the saving of this splendid article of food."[44] Plums were just one such food source. A Carver leaflet titled *Some Choice Wild Vegetables that Make Fine Foods* described both culinary and medicinal uses for common weeds Macon County farmers encountered every day. "Nature has provided us with an almost innumerable variety of wild vegetables," he insisted, "which serve not only as food, but as medicine."[45]

A 1918 article carried in the *Montgomery Advertiser* clarified his esteem for "so-called weeds." "Nature has been so lavish in its wealth of native food stuffs for both man and beast that we could not only live but thrive if all of our cultivated plants were destroyed," he asserted.[46] Believing people saw "in things just about what [they were] looking for," he urged tenant farmers to stop seeing weeds and start seeing food.[47] Entire meals were there for the taking. "A good plate of dandelion greens … or … wild onions, seasoned and fried," Carver maintained, made "a dinner quite inexpensive but very appetizing" with the addition of "an egg or two" or a baked potato.[48] Likewise, those who believed that they could not afford to keep livestock failed to see the possibilities of grasses "regarded generally" as "noxious weeds."[49]

Both weeds and conventional garden fruits and vegetables had to be preserved once they had been collected, and Carver provided instructions for that as well. "Every year it is painfully apparent," Carver noted in a 1912 experiment station circular, "that fully two-thirds of our fruits and vegetables go to waste." With "a little effort in the direction of canning, preserving and drying," he continued, fruits and vegetables harvested in the summer and fall could "be converted into nutritious and palatable dainties, sufficient to last throughout the winter and spring months."[50] The bulletin went on to offer instructions for preserving twenty-two fruits and vegetables, primarily by canning.

By World War I, however, the cost of sugar and jars put canning beyond the reach of most black farmers, and Carver realized that he needed to find "some other method within reach of the humblest citizen."[51] His emphasis shifted to drying fruits and vegetables, and he published bulletins explaining how it could be done and how to deal with the attendant problems, such as keeping insects away. He took a mainstream message during World War I, then—food conservation—and amended it so that those with meager means could embrace it, not necessarily for the country's benefit but for their own.

Although he appropriated a mainstream message, his solution differed markedly from those his fellow agronomists offered—the more so as it was not merely a wartime expedient but reflected a significant philosophical difference. "Many of the old ways of saving food we must rediscover," Carver wrote in 1918. "This so-called reversion will spell progress." Acutely aware of how out-of-step with the era's zeitgeist he was—not only in his manner of preserving food but in his reluctance to advocate technological solutions to poor farmers' problems—Carver added that "the word *reversion* may need, however, to be camouflaged" to accomplish its ends.[52] In a very real sense, then, Carver was looking backward to the high-minded husbandry of the sort espoused by Noah B. Cloud and other farmer-reformers in the mid-nineteenth century. Carver was not entirely backward-looking, of course; in fact, he was at the vanguard of agricultural research as it regarded alternative uses for agricultural products. But his vision had clearly and decidedly drifted away from that of mainstream agricultural science by the second decade of the twentieth century.

Perhaps nowhere was this shift more evident than in the way he tweaked Knapp's commandment to use legumes, barnyard manure, farm refuse, and commercial fertilizers. In contrast to most of his peers in agricultural science, Carver gradually deemphasized the use of chemically compounded commercial fertilizers and instead admonished impoverished black farmers to turn to organic alternatives. This transition took time; he had been taught at the IAC to rely on organic fertilizers only under special circumstances. Professor Budd, for instance, had instructed him to apply chemical fertilizers during a vineyard's first five years, but that after that, "nothing better than Barnyard Manure," supplemented with "veg. mould or humus," was needed for "the fruit to ripen perfectly."[53] There were other exceptions as well, but as a rule, Carver's training reflected late nineteenth-century agronomy's veneration of commercial fertilizers, and his work at the IAC's experiment station had confirmed their benefits.

Given his training, the fact that the funding for Alabama's experiment stations was tied to fertilizer sales, and the oversight of the Tuskegee station by the director of the Auburn station and the state commissioner of agriculture, it is not surprising that Carver began experimenting with commercial fertilizers immediately after breaking ground for the station in 1897. A fertilizer company from New York, he informed Washington, "very kindly donated to the school a large amount of fertilizers [roughly 1,000 pounds] to be used in an experiment," including acid phosphate, muriate of potash, nitrate of soda, sulfate of potash, and lime. A different individual donated an additional 224 pounds of potash.[54] Using the donated fertilizer, Carver began experiments with sweet potatoes and cotton, and two of his first three bulletins offered the results of those experiments.

The bulletins included a close description of how and when to use fertilizers; the bulletin on cotton even included a description (they had "the same general appearance as common table salt") as if he suspected local tenant farmers used little fertilizer because it was so unfamiliar to them. Neither bulletin advocated the use of organic fertilizers. On the contrary, Carver sang the praises of chemical fertilizers. "The nitrogen, potash or phosphoric acid they contain is just as valuable for plant food as the same substances in farmyard manure," he wrote. Indeed, the "chemical manures are much stronger than the farmyard manure" per volume and weight, and so, he implied, were at least as valuable.[55] Cotton would grow best if fertilized with a "complete" fertilizer—a blend of nitrogen, potash, and phosphates. Sweet potatoes required little nitrogen, but "potash and phosphates [were] indispensable to the highest development of the potato." Macon County's "average upland soils" were acidic, in contrast to the alkaline Black Belt soils of the county, and would "be benefited by a light dressing of lime—say 200 pounds to the acre."[56]

Charts showing the "Yield of Plots per Acre" supported his conclusions and demonstrated that the fertilizer worked quite well, albeit with the caveat that more was not always better; high fertilizer costs on some plots led to a net loss. Even so, the application of the fertilizer led to manifold increases in both production and profitability. The cotton produced on the unfertilized plots netted a loss of $10.40 per acre; clearly the soil lacked the necessary nutrients to grow the region's staple crop profitably without a change of one sort or another.[57] For sweet potatoes, the plot with no fertilizer saw a profit, but of only $2 per acre, while the application of $36 worth of fertilizer "reckoned per acre" (the cost Carver presented as the most successful) led to a profit of $121. A fertilizer expenditure of $36 per acre, however, translated to a $720 outlay for a twenty-acre, "one-horse" farm—substantially more than any landlord would consider advancing a tenant.[58] Even a more modest use of fertilizer—say $6 or $7 worth per acre—could cost more than a tenant was likely to make in a year.

By the early 1900s Carver had grown increasingly aware of this quandary facing black tenants and of the fact that the region's eroded and exhausted soils needed physical rebuilding every bit as much as additional nutrients. In a September 1902 report to Dr. A. C. True, the director of agricultural experiment stations for the USDA, Carver mentioned his commercial fertilizer experiments first, but by then he was already shifting his attention to alternative methods of fertilization. The most obvious source was barnyard manure, which he believed to be "of the greatest value, as it added the much needed humus (vegetable matter)." Along "with the chemical," he added, "the physical condition of the soil is most important." Unfortunately, tenant farmers had few animals to supply the manure. In a farmers' leaflet from this time, Carver used the recommendations of the Auburn station for the amounts of fertilizer to be added to a cotton crop, but with a qualification: "In leaving out barnyard manure we do not fail to recognize, nor do we under-rate its value." However, since "in cotton planting almost none is used . . . it is not included. This will continue to be so," he lamented, "until the number of farm animals is greatly increased and more attention is given by the farmers to the proper saving of this, the most valuable of all fertil-izers."[59] In short, he ran up against the problem that had plagued advocates of convertible agriculture from the beginning: cattle, a barn, labor, and—if farmers hoped to reap its benefits over the long term—land cost money. Only the wealthy could afford convertible agriculture, and its practice in the nineteenth century had, to quote historian Steven Stoll, "created a country-side of exclusion."[60] Carver's central hurdle in this regard was thus to find a way to bring the benefits of convertible husbandry to the black tenants he most sought to help without incurring the inherent costs.

Over the course of the first decade of the twentieth century, Carver would gradually develop what he believed to be a viable solution, but in 1902, when Tuskegee's agricultural department issued a leaflet that echoed Noah B. Cloud in advocating penning animals at night; lining their stalls with "sawdust, leaves, leaf mould, straw, etc."; and then composting the bed-ding, the solution was only beginning to make itself clear to him. Of course, there were obvious possibilities for soil improvement. He consistently rec-ommended planting legumes for their nitrogen-fixing value, for instance. A soil's "deficiency in nitrogen can be made up almost wholly," he noted, "by . . . keeping the legumes, or pod-bearing plants, growing upon the soil as much as possible." In particular he advocated "the common cow pea," for its food value as much as its soil-building properties.[61] He likewise advo-cated green manuring, and saw the benefits of that in the steadily improv-ing soil of the station. But it was compost manuring that finally emerged as Carver's solution to the physical and chemical deficiencies of the Cot-ton Belt's soils. Indeed, in 1902 Carver informed his colleagues at the an-nual convention of the Association of American Agricultural Colleges and Experiment Stations that while he was testing conventional commercial fertilizers at Tuskegee, he had also begun working with "swamp muck, for-est leaves, pine straw, etc."—all of which were readily available to even the poorest of the region's farmers.[62]

Carver was far from the first agriculturist to see the possibilities of com-post manuring. On the contrary, the tradition stretched back hundreds of years. Johannes Coler's *Oeconomia*, for example, a German agricultural trea-tise published in several volumes between 1592 and 1606, recommended the application of pond muck to fields when animal manure was not available. In fact, as historians Verena Winiwarter and Richard Hoffman pointed out, pond muck played an important role in "the cycling of nutrients be-tween fields and ponds in pre-modern Europe."[63] But the use of composted muck (and other organic debris) remained a secondary option, like green manuring or mineral manuring (especially marling), that could be part of a comprehensive effort to maintain and improve a soil's fertility but not the central pillar on which that effort rested. Animal manures—especially cattle and horse manure—remained the most widely advocated source of fertilizers well into the nineteenth century.

Coler and other early agriculturists understood the benefits of manuring through practical experience (whether their own or that of farmers they observed). Given the close connections between livestock and farms, it is no surprise that the benefits of animal manure had attracted widespread attention. Over the course of Carver's career, however, that once essential connection between animals and farming began to dissipate. By the time of his death in 1943, tractors were well on their way to replacing horses, mules, and oxen, and agricultural scientists' dual emphasis on efficiency and production had set in motion the process of farm consolidation and laid the foundation for an agribusiness model that would push livestock off farms and into feedlots. In any event, the impoverished tenants Carver most sought to aid could not hope to rely on animal manure—certainly not when a single well-cared-for cow generated enough manure for only two acres over the course of a year.[64] The context for Carver's embrace of compost manuring thus differed from that of his predecessors. Furthermore, he approached the subject from a somewhat different perspective, one rooted both in debates that had grown out of nineteenth-century agricultural science and in a cultural milieu in which the application of chemically compounded fertilizers was adjudged to be a reliable indicator of progressive cultivation.

The scientific context for Carver's adoption of compost fertilizing began to take shape in 1813, when Sir Humphry Davy published *Elements of Agricultural Chemistry*, a landmark work that offered a scientific rationale for the practices farmers had long employed. Davy's collection of essays included one chapter on soils and two on manuring (one on "manures of vegetable and animal Origin" and another on those "of mineral Origin, or fossil Manures"), and, perhaps most important, explained how to measure and evaluate a soil's composition.[65] Although Albrecht Thaer and others had made and were making similar arguments, Davy's book in effect laid a scientific foundation for what would be known as the humus theory, which emphasized the importance of organic matter in the soil. It held sway until the 1840s, when Justus von Liebig argued that all of the benefits of organic matter in the soil were indirect, and that plants lived on a finite number of inorganic nutrients: principally nitrogen, phosphorus, and potassium.[66] This might seem a fine distinction, since the best way to get those nutrients into the soil at the time was to build up its humus, Liebig's postulations about plants securing nitrogen from the air notwithstanding.

Liebig's theory attracted critics almost immediately, and a wide-ranging debate ensued that spurred agriculturists to more rigorous experimentation and a greater emphasis on chemical precision. To be sure, both formulations were simplistic by contemporary standards. But American agriculturists wrestled with the implications of each, blending the ideas of Davy and Liebig in sometimes incongruous ways, until over the course of the late nineteenth century Liebig's view gradually came to hold sway. And as it did, his vision that a "time will come when fields will be manured with a solution . . . prepared in chemical manufactories" proved prescient rather than fantastic.[67] By 1894, so complete was Liebig's triumph that noted chemist Francis Preston Venable could assert that "the old erroneous ideas as to plant nourishment [the humus theory] received their death-blow at the hands of Liebig."[68]

The continued expansion in the use of commercial fertilizers at the turn of the century offers evidence enough that Venable's assertion reflected the conventional understanding of the time. But he might have overstated the matter, at least relative to agricultural chemistry. It would be more accurate to speak of the cooptation of the humus theory than of its death, for while soil scientists had embraced Liebig's reductionist thinking, they had not abandoned the humus theory altogether. On the contrary, they undertook an effort to try to identify a chemical makeup for humus. Soil microbiologist Selman A. Waksman took the effort to task in 1926, pointing out the seemingly obvious detail that the chemical composition of humus depends on the matter that is decaying, the microorganisms aiding that decomposition, and the ecological factors influencing the process. Thus, humus has no single chemical composition, but myriad, essentially infinite, possibilities.[69]

Furthermore, while agriculturists emphasized the importance of soil chemistry (and the benefits of inorganic inputs), they were not unaware that soil has a physical structure. They understood that the inorganic, mineral element of the soil (the decayed rock) gives the soil its essential body—be it sand, clay, or loam—and that humus, made of decaying organic matter, adds nutrients to the soil. They agreed that friable soil facilitates the absorption of plant nutrients, and that friability can be improved by building up a soil's humus. And they recognized that humus-rich soil has an improved capacity to hold water, helps protect the plant from temperature fluctuations, and creates a friendlier environment for the sorts of micro-organisms that break down the soil particles and render the chemicals in the soil useful to plants.[70]

Knowing these things and embracing them as the hallmarks of progressive cultivation, however, proved to be two distinct animals entirely. As a result of the increasing emphasis on soil chemistry over the late nineteenth century, a subtle shift appeared in the conventional understanding of soil exhaustion. As Steven Stoll pointed out, eighteenth- and early nineteenth-century agriculturists saw exhaustion in "any noticed deterioration in fertility or the volume of tilth."[71] By the early twentieth century, except in the case of badly eroded land, exhaustion essentially reflected only fertility. After all, it is difficult to speak of an exhausted land that can still produce a profitable crop, even if commercial chemical inputs are needed to facilitate it. Carver's vision, then, would harken back to that earlier definition; in an era in which soil building was an afterthought, Carver would become a soil builder.

Although Carver continued to experiment with commercial fertilizers, these were almost always blended with swamp muck or some other compost.[72] By 1904 he had set aside three acres of the experiment station for the exclusive use of organic fertilizers. Carver never entirely rejected chemical fertilizers and continued his experiments with them at the station.[73] In providing instructions to teachers for setting up a children's garden, for instance, he advised that organic fertilizer would "be sufficient," though if the teacher desired, it might be "supplemented" with particular amounts of chemical fertilizers.[74] Chemically compounded fertilizers were always to be a supplement, however, never a crutch, and no farmer should rely on them.

Carver bemoaned the fact that "many thousands of dollars are being spent every year here in the South for fertilizers that profit the user very little, while Nature's choicest fertilizer is going to waste."[75] For poor black farmers, however, that terrible waste could be a boon: "the very kind of fertilizer soils are most deficient in" was theirs for the taking at a cost of only labor. A walk through the woods was a walk through a "natural fertilizer factory," which, in its decaying leaves, "trees, grasses, and debris of many kinds," produced "countless tons of the finest kind of manure, rich in potash, phosphates, nitrogen, and humus."[76] Even if impoverished tenants lacked access to sufficient barnyard manure, their efforts in collecting and composting "leaves and muck" would be repaid "many times in the increased yield of crops" despite "the almost unbelievably small amount of actual cash outlay required to do it."[77]

Although he embraced compost fertilizing as a practical expedient, Carver's recognition of ecological relationships confirmed his conviction that chemical fertilizers offered limited benefits because their application implied that nature was in some way deficient and needed something it could not produce. Later in his life he would add other objections, expressing growing concerns over the nutritional implications of overreliance on commercial fertilizers and the potential hazards agricultural chemicals posed to human bodies, but these were not concerns during his first decades at Tuskegee. Indeed, he was as free as any of his contemporaries at the turn of the century in applying Paris Green (an extremely toxic copper arsenic compound) and Bordeaux mixture (copper sulfate and hydrated lime) as an insecticide and fungicide, respectively.[78] If the application of his ecological thinking was thus not always consistent, it nevertheless undergirded his repeated calls for farmers to "appreciate the immense amount of plant food in many things that are now allowed to go to waste."[79]

Collecting enough leaves, muck, and other organic debris to effectively fertilize a farm required a minimum of equipment but an enormous expenditure of labor. Consequently, Carver sought to persuade farmers to alter some of their seasonal activities. In November they should "let every spare moment be put in the woods raking up leaves or in the swamps piling up muck."[80] In December, instead of "'piddling' around, waiting for spring to come so they can begin farming," they should "haul and spread upon the land and plow under large quantities of leaves and straw of all kinds that will rot quickly, or compost the same for applying later."[81] In February, shortly before cotton season began, they should be "hauling out leaves, rich earth from the woods, and muck from the rich swamps."[82] And after the cotton had been laid by in July, he begged them to "put in every spare moment in raking it up, hauling it out, permanently enriching their soil, greatly increasing their crops of all kinds, and reducing their bill for commercial fertilizers to the minimum."[83]

While the Sisyphean experience of impoverished black tenant farmers in the region helped foment Carver's commitment to organic fertilizers, his endorsement of them signaled a larger shift in his agricultural thinking. In a letter Carver penned to Washington in January 1911, he noted that there were "hundreds of tons of the finest kind of manure, which consists of decayed leaves, dead animals, decayed night soils, animal manures that have washed from the hillsides, etc., etc." available on Tuskegee's campus. "It is a source of the keenest regret," he wrote, that the school was neglecting "the acme of manures" and applying instead large quantities of commercial fertilizer on its farms. "We should look to the permanent building up of our soils. We know that commercial fertilizers will stimulate and for a while produce good results . . . but by and by a collapse will come, as the soil will be reduced to practically clay and sand." The "crying need of nearly every foot of land we have in cultivation is vegetable matter (humus)," he added, "and every possible means at our command should be exercised to supply this end." Consequently, he asked the principal to give him the additional manpower he needed to rake up the manure from the hillsides and bottoms, suggested that night soil be collected to supplement this manure, recommended that the institute's animals be penned at night to facilitate the collection of their manure, and proposed that Tuskegee expand its composting. "With the increased number of animals we are getting and the non-expansion of our cultivated lands," he reasoned, "the expenditure for commercial fertilizers should grow less every year." Recognizing that Washington still needed convincing, he added that he intended to "carry out a number of experiments" at the station "to prove its value."[84]

A year later Carver suggested to the institute's council "that the expenses for the school could be reduced greatly by diminishing the amount of commercial fertilizer used." Carver referred them to some of the experiments he had carried out to prove the value of compost manuring, citing "his recent report that he raised two bales of cotton on [one and a half] acres of land . . . using a compost of leaves, muck and barnyard manure." His request "that his name be not used in the matter" signifies more than a recognition of his unpopularity at the school.[85] The use of chemical fertilizers had become an integral part of conventional agricultural science by 1910; agricultural colleges, state departments of agriculture, the USDA, and virtually every other agricultural authority in the nation endorsed the practice. The significance of Carver's request lies in his self-conscious rejection of a central tenet of mainstream agronomy. Suggesting that agriculture be practiced with a decidedly limited application of chemical fertilizers entailed risking his reputation as a practical scientist in the eyes of his critics at the school.

Carver's mention of the "crying need" for humus reflected his concern for the physical makeup of the soil.[86] And if Carver was not entirely alone among his peers in believing that the physical structure of the soil mattered, few were as consistent or emphatic in declaring that "a soil may be poor chemically, physically, or both, and . . . the physical poverty is of just as much importance as the chemical poverty."[87] Carver became even more adamant about that point as the years passed. In 1936, for instance, he insisted that "the first and absolutely the most important thing for every farmer to learn is that the physical condition of the soil is of greater importance than the chemical."[88]

Carver's adamancy was tied to his conviction that caring for the soil carried profound moral implications. Taking a subtle jab at the Jim Crow institutions of the South, Carver began an article titled "Being Kind to the Soil" by asserting that "unkindness to anything means an injustice done to that thing." Though it was generally understood in personal relationships, the principle applied "with equal force to the soil." A farmer "whose soil produces less every year is unkind to it in some way; that is, he is not doing by it what he should."[89] If farmers looked after their soil as they should, even the poorest soils could be "made to yield abundantly."[90] The faint hints of what Aldo Leopold would later eloquently put forward as a "land ethic" notwithstanding, Carver was thus of one mind with Liberty Hyde Bailey in insisting that an "ideal agriculture maintains itself" and enriches the land.[91] High yields and rich profits alone did not a good farmer make.

But soil building, even aided by compost fertilizing, is a painstakingly slow process, and Carver was well aware that African American farmers could not put their lives on hold until the region's soils had been revitalized. Consequently, he issued bulletins offering practical advice on how to take advantage of the natural resources at hand on a day-to-day basis. As Gary Kremer astutely noted, "the phrase 'waste not, want not,' was more than a trite aphorism [for Carver]; it was a philosophical foundation for creative inquiry." [92] And it was one he enjoined farmers to adopt.

Publishing leaflets with such titles as *Are We Starving in the Midst of Plenty? If So Why?*, he encouraged farmers to see the unsuspected munificence of the natural world around them. He invoked the Bible, using verses such as Proverbs 13:23: "Much food is in the tillage [fallow ground] of the poor; but there is that is destroyed for want of judgment," before informing them of edible wild fruits and vegetables, the feeding value of potato and pea vines for livestock, or the neglected fertilizers rotting in the swamps and forests of Macon County. Within the tomato vines most farmers cast aside lay a dye for fabrics. In old corn shucks there were rugs. From discarded grease they could make soap. Watermelon rinds could be pickled and eaten; and acorns and other foods "that Nature provides for us free of charge" presented a plausible solution to what many considered "an unsurmountable problem" facing would-be livestock owners.[93] "We are richer than we think we are," he told black farmers.[94] The region's forests offered "light wood from fat pine trees . . . as well as good dry wood" that could be gathered and sold. For that matter, the forests offered wood from which farmers could fashion fence palings, shingles, baskets, rugs, tool handles, "rustic chairs, settees, tables, etc." that they could use in their own homes or sell in town. Walnut, pecan, beechnut, and hickory trees dropped nuts that could either be consumed or made into "delicious candies and nut cakes, which always find a ready sale when attractively put upon the market."[95]

The natural world offered much more than bare subsistence. Not only did some of the "finest wild plums in the world" grow wild in Macon County, its "woods and fields abound[ed] in the most charming flowers, that furnish[ed] never ending delight to the lovers of the beautiful."[96] What was true of Macon County was true of the rest of the South. "I venture that every able bodied hard working person [could] live . . . comfortably, educate his family, and even have a few of the luxuries around him if he only knew how."[97]

While "inspecting a herd of very fine cows belonging to a wealthy white citizen" in 1902, the *Tuskegee Student* reported, Carver "noticed a clay which attracted his attention."[98] Over the course of the next several years he experimented with clays taken from the soils around him, manufacturing paints and dyes from their extracts. In 1911 he published a bulletin detailing his discoveries, noting that it was "designed primarily to aid the farmer in tidying up his premises, both in and outside," making "his surroundings more healthful, more cheerful, and more beautiful." And the work could be done at virtually no cost because nature had provided everything needed "in her rich deposits of clay."[99]

The nature walks he took early each morning inspired him to proffer a bulletin titled *Some Ornamental Plants of Macon County, Ala.*, in which he lamented that "we do not recognize and appreciate what Nature has so lavishly provided for us." He described where to find and how to care for wild trees, shrubs, vines, ferns, grasses, and flowers. Mountain laurel, for instance, was "plentiful along the banks of Euphorbia Creek, Red Creek, and a number of small streams," while another plant could be "found in rich bottoms west of Chehaw." "Rare beauty and fragrance" were available free of charge to those who eschewed waste and appreciated nature.[100]

Thus, Carver advocated a way of thinking as much as a set of farm practices. "These are only a few of the many ways of becoming thrifty and self-supporting," Carver concluded a bulletin titled *How to Make and Save Money on the Farm*. "Begin at once to put some of them into effect; others I am sure will suggest themselves to you."[101] As farmers and housewives became aware of how the creator had arranged the "mutual relationship of the animal, mineral and vegetable kingdoms," they could not help but recognize ways to make use of materials they had previously discarded or overlooked. "The thrifty wide awake farmer will think of many other things to do and ways to do them," Carver insisted after giving advice on "making the farm comfortable," and his wife "will readily see . . . how she can make many delicious and nutritious things not even mentioned" in his circulars on preserving fruits and vegetables.[102]

This emphasis on learning to think in a different way grew naturally from Carver's educational philosophy, most especially from his conviction that the study of nature "encourages personal investigation, stimulates original-ity, [and] awakens higher and nobler ideas." The lessons he imparted to his students at Tuskegee were the very same ones he tried to teach the farmers of Macon County and the South generally. When he suggested that the solution to the myriad problems facing southern farmers lay in "a mighty campaign of education," he was not referring to classes about fertilizers and the newest farm implements, or even to crop rotation, seed selection, or dust mulches; he meant to "lead the masses to be students of Nature."[103] As they learned to appreciate the interdependence of the elements of the natural world, farmers could decipher on their own the best techniques to conserve the soil and the best tools for their particular interests.

Such a belief was more than unconventional. Endeavoring to facilitate the subsistence of farmers outside the market economy flew in the face of more than a century's worth of economic and political thinking. To be sure, a strong strand of American thought embodied by Thomas Jefferson extolled the virtues of the independent yeoman farmer. But that farmer was always assumed to be operating within and for a market economy, not principally on a subsistence level. Indeed, the celebrated divide between Alexander Hamilton and Thomas Jefferson was in many ways a matter of emphasis. Hamilton believed that industrial development would necessar-ily improve agriculture by creating "in some instances a new, and securing in all, a more certain and steady demand for the surplus produce of the soil," the latter (a surplus) being a given of good farming.[104] For Jefferson and his fellow agrarians, as historian Benjamin R. Cohen astutely noted, "factories were more properly the end product of agricultural origins, not an opposing principle."[105] Put another way, Hamilton and other arch-federalists embraced policies that saw improved agriculture as a by-product of industry and thus favored the latter; agrarians like Jefferson embraced policies that would make industrial development a by-product of agriculture. Neither federalists nor republicans, that is, saw industry and agriculture as irreconcilable.

As early as 1767, the Scottish political economist James Steuart argued that reciprocal obligations held societies together, and that subsistence farmers, who had few such obligations, had no permanent place in a civilized society.[106] The founding fathers had confirmed this, reasoning that a social contract of the sort embodied in the Constitution necessitated mutual obligations as much as individual rights. According to such a rationale, subsistence farmers represented a vestigial remnant of a Hobbesian past. By the 1860s Isaac Newton, the nation's first commissioner of agriculture, could assert that a "surplus of agriculture not only allows the farmer to accumulate wealth and pay his debts, but also does the same for the nation."[107] Thus, the nation's well-being depended on farmers producing a surplus. Viewed from this vantage point, Carver's efforts to persuade black farmers to take advantage of what the natural world provided free of charge could be seen not only as backward looking, but as subversive.

Not all agrarians were interested in cultivating national markets. Probably the best known of those who were not were the supporters of the short-lived back to nature movement, which was rooted in a curious blend of Malthusian, religious, and nativist concerns; agrarian ideology; and utopian thinking, and urged urbanites to return to rural areas and cultivate small farms using up-to-date scientific principles.[108] Most agrarians, however, agreed that farmers' participation in the nation's expanding agricultural markets would ultimately benefit them. In this respect, those agriculturists belonging to the agrarian wing of the Progressive Era push for agricultural reform found themselves in lockstep with those whose concern for country life was limited to streamlining and increasing agricultural production.

Carver's concern for impoverished black farmers forced him to consider national and international markets, but it also pushed him to find ways for those farmers to become self-sufficient in order to extricate themselves from the vagaries of the cotton market. Reflecting his hope that expanding agricultural markets held at least some promise for black farmers, Carver held that "he who puts such a product upon the market as it demands, controls that market, regardless of color." But he also believed that increasing production without making "consumption . . . commensurate with it" amounted to "a bad case of agricultural economics."[109] Thus, Carver's rationale allowed him to consider a farmer who had learned to subsist on the munificence of nature to be progressive whether or not he raised any cotton at all. Carver saw little sense in impoverished black tenant farmers becoming efficient agriculturists in an increasingly interdependent industrial age if their increased productivity did not redound to their benefit, and so he sought to show them how to decrease their reliance on mass-manufactured goods as a means of becoming economically independent.

Not all of Carver's suggestions for becoming economically independent were unorthodox. He argued, for instance, that livestock had "a most important place in the economy of the farm."[110] Since there was "an intimate and inseparable relationship existing between the fertility of the soil and the stock kept on the farm," he recommended that every farmer keep a milk cow. To be sure, he was less emphatic about this than were many of his contemporaries, knowing that cattle were beyond the means of most black farmers in Alabama's Black Belt; indeed, he devoted comparatively little attention to cattle in his campaign.[111] Hogs, however, were "great scavengers, converting into meat much of the waste from the kitchen, farm, garden, dairy, orchard, etc.," to say nothing of the abundance of acorns and other nuts in Macon County, and so could be fed "more cheaply . . . than any other animal."[112] Even better, they did not require much in the way of shelter: A simple lean-to "covered with boards, shingles, straw, grass or anything that is the cheapest and easiest to obtain" was "quite sufficient." These factors, along with their prolific reproductive capabilities, made hogs ideal livestock for impoverished farmers.[113] Alabama's climate did not favor swine production, however, inasmuch as hogs were at their ideal weight for slaughter before the weather was cold enough to do so without risking significant spoilage. Carver addressed this issue in another bulletin, albeit one that was never published, on the "pickling and curing of meat in hot weather," borrowing advice from a USDA bulletin.

Spoilage was not a significant problem for poultry because an entire bird could be eaten quickly, and Carver enjoined farmers to begin raising fowl. In 1912 there were "5,186,536 fowl of all kinds and ages" on the 20,685,427 acres of the state's 223,200 farms, or roughly one chicken, goose, or duck to every 4 acres of improved farmland in the state—a shamefully low number, according to Carver.[114] Predictably, his experience with Tuskegee's poultry yard tempered his enthusiasm. "Of all the get-rich-quick schemes," he admonished his readers, "there is probably none more productive of delusion than that of poultry raising on paper. And yet," he continued, taking an oblique shot at his Tuskegee critics, "with proper facilities and applied intelligence . . . handsome returns can be had from poultry."[115]

In encouraging farmers to raise livestock and keep vegetable gardens, Carver was doing much the same thing that agriculturists at Auburn's station and other extension services throughout the nation were doing. For that matter, Carver's publications often resembled those of other stations in tone as well as substance. Agricultural reform in the late nineteenth and early twentieth centuries was very much a Progressive endeavor and carried with it the middle-class condescension that marked the movement. In some cases this condescension might simply have reflected an excessive emphasis on clarity, as when Carver repeated the necessity of "thoroughly" cleaning jars and cans in an article on preserving fruits and vegetables carried by the *Montgomery Advertiser*.[116]

More often, however, the condescension was tied to moral issues. In a leaflet titled *Some Ways to Save Money on the Farm*, Carver provided a list of annual expenses given him by a man who believed that it reflected his "actual necessities." The list, which included tobacco and whiskey, totaled $666—not likely a coincidence. Carver informed his readers that tobacco and whiskey could "be dispensed with altogether," as they were "not only absolutely useless, but ruinous to both body and soul."[117] Similarly, a pamphlet issued by Tuskegee's Bureau of Nature Study and Hints and Suggestions to Farmers that pleaded with farmers to spend "every minute you can putting trash in the compost heap" included a warning that while the "old folks are lying down at night sleeping . . . the boys and girls are out looking for their own fun, going . . . to some 'frolic.' There in many cases, they find the devil in his full glory."[118]

The often hortatory tone in which he conveyed his message notwithstanding, Carver generally espoused practicable, environmentally sound ideas. Even the poorest farmers could build up soil humus by compost manuring and plowing the remnants of harvested crops back into the land. In theory, at least, they could rotate nitrogen-fixing legumes such as peanuts and cowpeas with cotton and corn. Likewise, maintaining vegetable gardens, raising livestock (whether chickens, hogs, or cows), plowing crosswise to hills rather than straight up and down them, and gathering some of the "many hundred bushels of [wild] plums that go to waste every year" seem both economically practical and ecologically sound.

The chief shortcoming of his experiment station work and the publications that grew out of it lay in the fact that although Carver deliberately wrote in a simple language with "but few technical terms," widespread illiteracy among black farmers ensured that relatively few would read his publications.[119] That is not to say there was no market for Carver's bulletins. Eager readers snatched up the two thousand to five thousand copies printed for each issue, and many copies certainly wound up in the hands of literate black farmers. But many of them also wound up in the hands of white planters, academics, and journalists. Well aware of the educational shortcomings facing African American farmers in the South, Carver developed an extension program for his department to meet their needs.[120]

Booker T. Washington had traveled the countryside surrounding Tuskegee well before Carver's arrival, ostensibly to recruit students but also to learn what he could about their needs and the needs of their families.[121] As was the case with much of what he did, Washington's motives were mixed. On the one hand, he did want to make the courses offered at Tuskegee relevant to the community's needs and to improve the material conditions of rural African Americans, especially those in Macon County. Under his direction the institute provided black-controlled banking services to local farmers, purchased their garden vegetables, loaned stud animals to help improve their livestock, and even purchased land with the intent of selling it cheaply to black farmers.[122] On the other hand, Washington was deeply concerned that Tuskegee's "next-door neighbors . . . presented an unsightly spectacle in many respects," and he feared that the squalor in which impoverished black farmers generally lived reflected badly both on the race and on his school.[123] Thus he put excessive emphasis on superficial, external improvements. When in 1914 he took what would be his last tour of rural Macon County, "he insisted that the houses along the roads traveled by the 'Washington Party' be whitewashed, the yards cleaned, and fences repaired in advance of their coming."[124] When sociologist Charles S. Johnson saw some of those cabins two decades later, he observed poignantly, "That was the last coating they had had."[125] Whatever his motives, Washington encouraged his teachers to make similar excursions into surrounding rural communities, and for roughly a decade after his arrival at the institute, Carver did so.

"In those early years," his former student Thomas Campbell recalled, "it was Dr. Carver's custom, in addition to his regular work, to put a few tools and demonstration exhibits in a buggy and set out . . . on Saturday afternoons, to visit rural areas near Tuskegee. There, during the weekends, he would give practical demonstrations, both varied and seasonal."[126] Like those who succeeded him as Tuskegee's agricultural emissaries, Carver targeted Sunday church services as well and added his gospel of scientific agriculture to the sermon preached that day. In addition to bringing tools and exhibits for the farmers, he brought his fancy work for their wives, teaching them, for instance, how to transform used feed sacks into "attractive . . . chair backs and . . . table covers" by applying vegetable dyes and embroidering them.[127]

The organization in 1901 of the Bureau of Nature Study and Hints and Suggestions to Farmers marked the first attempt to institutionalize extension work within the institute's agricultural department. Carver asked northern philanthropists to donate "small traveling libraries," especially "books on nature study and agriculture." For ten dollars a donor could "provide a traveling library for Tuskegee"; one dollar would "supply a book."[128] Under Carver's direction, faculty affiliated with the bureau began taking "special pains to visit many of the districts."[129] Some "member of the station staff," he informed the Association of American Agricultural Colleges and Experiment Stations, "is out among them [Macon County's communities] more or less every week, in their local conferences, churches, etc."[130] It is thus no surprise, as Carver wrote Dr. A. C. True of the USDA in 1902, that the area "within a radius of twenty miles"—that is, Macon County—felt the greatest impact of his work.[131] The easternmost county of Alabama's Black Belt was the testing ground for Carver's campaign; if it could succeed there, it could succeed throughout the South. Consequently, though most of his bulletins dealt specifically with Macon County, he frequently noted that "what is true of Macon County is true of the adjoining counties, and is more or less true of the entire South."[132]

Carver's success in the countryside inspired Washington to find money for "a more appropriate wagon for this purpose," and in 1904 he suggested to Carver that he initiate a more formal agricultural outreach program.[133] Washington's suggestion was part of a much larger effort on his part to extend the influence of Tuskegee. A year later, for instance, Clinton Calloway, a subordinate of Carver's who helped head up the Bureau of Nature Study and ostensibly oversaw the agricultural department's extension efforts, would initiate a plan to create a genuinely workable public school system for the county's black children.[134] His efforts culminated in the construction of forty-six one-room schoolhouses—essentially one for every community in the county—that served as the models for the so-called Rosenwald Schools that would proliferate throughout the South in subsequent years.[135] For that matter, Tuskegee had already sent three graduates to Togo, in German West Africa, to establish an experimental farm with the aim of improving the quantity and quality of the cotton produced there.[136]

Carver's immediate concerns were more local, but he believed the idea to be "most excellent," and so submitted a proposal, complete with a sketch, for a wagon outfitted with all sorts of demonstration exhibits and equipment.[137] Washington found a willing philanthropist in Morris K. Jesup, who had helped sponsor the agricultural department's startup, and in the spring of 1906 the institute formally commissioned the Jesup Agricultural Wagon under the charge of George Bridgeforth.[138] Though its range was limited (twelve miles was considered a long trip), the Jesup Wagon facilitated extension work by enabling staff members to carry out "countryside demonstrations of the implements and techniques developed at Carver's agricultural experiment station and elsewhere."[139]

The countryside into which Bridgeforth rode was a diverse one in many regards. Washington noted "very striking differences in the character of the population in the different parts of the county" in a 1912 article, explaining that when "the colored people first began to get hold of the land, they settled . . . upon the light soil and cheap lands in the northern half of the county." Indeed, the majority of the 157 black farmers who worked their own land at the turn of the century lived on the thin soils of Macon County's uplands. The popular pejorative "hillside darkeys" reflected the topography of the county's northern section.[140] Although pockets of black homeowners lived elsewhere in the county, virtually no African Americans owned land in the plantation belt that stretched across its center and included the Black Belt soils south of the fall line.

Better than 80 percent of the county's overwhelmingly black population lived in small communities. Some of these had pedestrian names: Shorter, Milstead, Godwyn, Hannon, Armstrong, Hardaway, and Downs; a handful, including Bethlehem and Damascus, had adopted biblical ones. The names of others were more evocative, speaking to the racial atmosphere of the time (Sambo), a mysterious past (New Rising Star, Little Texas, Red Gap), or geography (Cotton Valley, Big Swamp, and Creek Stand). Altogether some fifty such communities dotted the county. The footpaths slaves had once slipped down to visit friends and family remained. "It is a part of the character of this community, it would seem," Charles Johnson wrote, "to be bound together over a wide area by crooked little footpaths which serve as the threads of neighborliness."[141] In the long tradition of rural communities, the members of these rural hamlets depended on each other when assistance was needed, sharing equipment, pooling labor, and supporting one another in times of need.[142]

Segregation was the rule, but in the day-to-day lives of those rural communities an informal, convoluted, and constantly evolving racial etiquette proved more significant. African Americans could not dance with, eat with, or marry whites. Once children were old enough to recognize racial distinctions, playing with peers of the other race was proscribed. African Americans were expected to address their white counterparts as "Mr.," "Miss," or "Mrs.," but were not extended the same courtesy in return. Macon County was more "liberal" than some in its racial policies, however, as African Americans could sometimes drink with whites, could shake hands with and touch them without causing resentment, could sit together in public parks, and on occasion could worship with whites.[143]

An informal segregation of sorts existed spatially as well. Whites tended to live and congregate in the larger towns such as Tuskegee and Notasulga, and were more likely to be found along the rutted, sandy-clay roads that connected those towns with one another and with Montgomery to the west and Atlanta to the east. In part this physical separation of the races gave the communities a sense of security. One tenant farmer in New Rising Star noted that in "this settlement there ain't no white folks. You won't find a white family between here and Red Gap—that's up the road six or seven miles—so we don't have no trouble."[144]

Despite having relatively limited encounters with whites on a daily basis, most black farmers—close to 95 percent in 1900—were tenants who cultivated land belonging to white landlords. As in most of the Cotton Belt, tenant turnover was high because, as Charles Johnson observed, moving was their "one outstanding means of asserting freedom."[145] Few other ways of expressing their disapproval were available to them—at least prior to World War I. One Macon County tenant reasoned, "You know when you get where you can't behave yourself you better move. You got to be loyal, 'cause this is a white man's country." Another put it more succinctly: "You can't do nothing with white folks agin you."[146]

Most of the county's settlements were socially conservative; pastors wielded a disproportionate influence. Johnson found that "any form of life-activity which does not involve obvious and direct manual labor may be said to be under suspicion and disapproval." Though "frolics" drew particular condemnation, many communities forbade card playing, and some banned baseball as well. Such activities were commonplace nonetheless. In his best-known novel, *Ollie Miss*, Harlem Renaissance writer and Macon County native George Wylie Henderson captured the flow of a typical week: "From sun to sun, from Monday morning to Saturday noon!" the black farmers and their families worked. But "Saturday afternoons they went to ball games and picnics. Saturday nights they went to frolics. And on Sundays there was church. They couldn't sweat and sin the week long for nothing."[147]

The soil they worked varied widely. Carver, whose daily walks and unending search for floral and mycological specimens took him up and down the county's roads and footpaths, conducted a soil survey of the county. Slightly more than a quarter of the county's soil—including that in the immediate vicinity of Tuskegee—he classified as "Mulatto, or Orangeburg Sandy Loam." "Where the land is rolling (and most of it is)," he noted, this type of soil "washes badly, and constant care must be exercised to keep it from literally sloughing away and leaving great ditches, gutters, and bald places." It was nevertheless a reasonably responsive soil. Between Calebee and Cubahatchie creeks in the west-central and southwestern parts of the county, "extending from La Place to Cotton Valley" and constituting a little less than 20 percent of the county's soil, was a Black Belt soil that Carver classified as "Orangeburg Clay." It yielded "remarkably well," but its high clay content made this soil trickier to till when it was excessively wet or dry.

"Norfolk Coarse Sand" covered roughly 11 percent of the county. Because it was too porous to hold sufficient water unless it was built up by compost manuring or the season was "unusually favorable," the soil held little promise for farmers. To the north it blended with the dominant soil of the county's northern upland, "Norfolk Gravelly Loam"—the soil on which most of Macon County's black yeomen scraped out a living. Though it was better than "Norfolk Coarse Sand" for cultivation, the gravelly loam was not as good as either the "Orangeburg Sandy Loam" or the "Orangeburg Clay." Three other soils dominated the southern portion of the county. The one Carver called "Luftkin Clay" is more commonly known as Alabama's "red clay." It was responsive but poorly drained and very difficult to work. The second was another coarse sandy soil that washed badly, and the third was another sandy loam similar to the soil surrounding Tuskegee.[148]

Four other types, amounting collectively to about 10 percent of the county's soils (and including "true" Black Belt soil, the most fertile of all those in the area), occurred in isolated pockets. Settlement patterns, of course, reflected the soils. The plantations, which had the largest populations, occupied the better soils; few people lived in areas with the poorest soils; and African Americans were most likely to own land in areas where a living could be made, but on relatively poor soil.[149]

These were the soils from which the tenant farmers of the county's communities worked to wring a living, "their plows singing beneath the sandy loam," to borrow a phrase from *Ollie Miss*. Like farmers elsewhere in the nation, their lives followed the seasons. The latest killing frost Carver documented in his first seventeen years in Alabama came on March 11; on average, Macon County saw 251 frost-free days.[150] Thus, by the end of March the plowing was finished and the cotton was in the ground. Shallow cultivation and chopping followed, reaching their peak in mid-to-late June. "Cotton weather," Henderson wrote of the month. "Short hot nights and long hot days. Field hands had to work cotton fast." With the arrival of "the sweet scent of the cotton blossoms" in July, the crop was laid by. "Plowing and hoeing ceased . . . and field hands took their ease. Watermelons were ripe; late July days were long and lazy."[151] But then came the picking, which could stretch into December. In many cases the winter meant a move to another plantation with the faint hope that things might be better. Though farmers raised corn, sweet potatoes, peanuts, and sugarcane as well, Macon County was mainly cotton country.

This was the world into which Bridgeforth, still answering to Carver, took the Jesup Wagon in the summer of 1906. The experience was frustrating for him. He traveled some sixty miles and gave forty-six demonstrations in his first week, but reached a total of only 158 people because most were still busy in the cotton fields. "I could have reached more [black farmers] by staying around the stores and cross roads," he noted in his report for the week of June 5–9, but "I . . . find that the people that are around the station and stores as a rule are worthless." Worse, he believed that the wagon was "not equiped [*sic*] so as to render the most practical service." Carver, who by 1906 was eschewing technological solutions, had not outfitted it with the up-to-date implements Bridgeforth viewed as practical: "We need plows, planters, cultivators and labor saving machinery," he complained.[152] But when he approached Carver to ask him for more money for equipment, Carver complained of limited funds. He did tell Bridgeforth that if he could cut expenses from another area (such as repairs), he could spend the difference on equipment.[153]

It is no surprise that Bridgeforth found "the colored people doing better on the thin uplands than on the bottomlands." Near Notasulga, in the northern part of the county, he found "a thrifty settlement of colored, that owns several hundred acres of land. Most all the men," he added, "have at some time come to the Farmers Institute and Short Course." He discovered another pocket of black homeowners on the mediocre soils of the southeastern corner of the county near Creek Stand; altogether they owned more than a thousand acres.[154]

In the plantation sections, however, he found primarily sharecroppers and tenants. In Big Swamp, which he visited the week of July 16–23, he found "no landowners at all." The "status of the negro farmers in this settlement is deplorable," he reported. Large "plantations with renters and sharecroppers" were "the order and rule." Worse, there seemed "to be no friendly relation between the landlord and the laborer." In fact, "a few whites" invariably attended Bridgeforth's demonstrations in the area to confirm that he was not fostering discontent among the tenants. The running joke in the community, he was told, was that "the white man [sits] in the store blaming the negro [while] the negro [sits] in the shade blaming the white man." Indeed, he lamented, the institute seemed "to have affected this settlement but little in any way."[155]

He found similar conditions in other plantation districts. Near Cotton Valley, for instance, he encountered a graduate of Tuskegee's agricultural department who was "helping his father pay for the only farm in this section controlled by colored." In the vicinity of Little Texas, "Mr. Varner, Mr. Tolbert, and Mr. Glass own all the land and we had better say own the negroes too." Bridgeforth's demonstrations did not, for the most part, win over the tenants. In fact, landowners took "more interest of an inteligent [*sic*] nature in the demonstrations" than did tenants.[156]

By the end of July Bridgeforth could report that he "had covered the county very thoroughly" and planned to "start over it a second time." As the cotton had been laid by, he had considerably larger audiences this time around. During the week of August 6–12, for instance, he reached 758 people, nearly five times the number he had met in a typical week earlier in the summer. The second tour was cut short, however, when school went back into session.

All told, the Jesup Wagon had reached some 4,708 people, 572 of whom were white, and had gone through the county one and a quarter times before Bridgeforth's efforts ended on August 25. The Jesup Wagon would have a far greater effect than the discouraged Bridgeforth could have anticipated. In November 1906 the federal government adopted (though did not actually fund) the wagon concept as part of Seaman A. Knapp's pioneering efforts to institutionalize local agricultural advisers within the USDA.

Knapp had been persuaded to leave the IAC in 1885 by Kansas banker Jabez B. Watkins to head a speculative project in rice farming. His efforts had helped transform Louisiana into the leading rice-producing state by the end of the decade. In the 1890s Knapp's prominence in the rice industry and his friendship with James Wilson enabled him to travel to Asia on official trips to examine new rice varieties. It was not until 1902, however, when he was appointed the USDA's special agent for the promotion of agriculture in the South, that he began to lay the foundation for what would become the cooperative extension system.

In his work in that capacity Knapp discovered that farmers distrusted government demonstration farms because they were operated by salaried farm managers whose financial security was not contingent on the success or failure of the crops.[157] As a way to persuade them to listen, in 1903 he convinced a private citizen in Terrell, Texas, to launch an experimental farm on seventy acres of his own land. The project was a success, and Knapp came away from Terrell convinced that the government's role in advocating scientific agriculture should be as invisible as possible.

When the Mexican boll weevil exploded on the scene in the summer of 1903, the yield per acre of Texas cotton farms dropped roughly 50 percent. The precipitous drop instigated something of a panic—the "boll weevil emergency"—and by January 1904 James Wilson had laid out a comprehensive plan for the USDA to combat the insect. It was Knapp's job to ensure that cotton planters everywhere in the South learned about the "latest results as to methods of meeting the present emergency."[158] Congress allocated $250,000 for the entire plan, and Knapp's share of that sum steadily increased as he commissioned agricultural agents under seasonal contracts to advise cotton farmers.[159] This money, however, could be spent only in states in which the boll weevil was present, which at that point excluded Alabama.

Knapp circumvented the rule by turning to the General Education Board, a charitable trust organized in 1902 to promote education in the South with a pledge of $1 million from John D. Rockefeller. Beginning in 1906 the board provided funds for Knapp to take his campaign to cotton-growing states in which the boll weevil posed no immediate threat. As the boll weevil moved eastward, the government took over the funding and the general Education Board shifted the money to a new region farther east. This funding enabled Knapp to assign agents to a single county and pay them an annual salary.[160]

This is what Knapp was doing when he visited Tuskegee in the summer of 1906.[161] Favorably impressed by the Jesup Wagon, and aware that black farmers produced the bulk of the region's cotton, Knapp recommended that the USDA adopt the idea. Carver's friendship with Wilson may have facilitated the process, but considering Washington's stature it likely would have happened anyway. With the federal government providing a symbolic dollar every year for its support, the Jesup Wagon was formally commissioned as a USDA project on November 12, 1906. The actual funding came from the General Education Board.[162]

The wagon was placed under the charge of Thomas Campbell, whom both Carver and Bridgeforth had recommended for the job.[163] With Campbell's appointment as a "collaborator in the [USDA's] Bureau of Plant Industry," Carver's trips into the countryside surrounding Tuskegee essentially came to a close. In a letter to Wilson in August 1904 (written during the first fight over the institute's poultry house), Carver had noted that while he could "do very much better financially [elsewhere] . . . and also not have such hard work," he would not think of trusting the job to others until he "got Tuskegee's work on a firm and solid basis." After 1906, with the demand for his services as a speaker rapidly increasing, he more or less entrusted the extension work to others, although he retained at least nominal oversight of the wagon for the remainder of the decade.[164]

As Carver withdrew, the brand of scientific agriculture Tuskegee's agricultural emissaries carried gradually became more conventional. In part this was a practical expedient. As Campbell discovered, southern whites were suspicious of African American expertise of almost any kind, and his perceived legitimacy hinged in large measure on looking the part of an authentic agriculturist. Thus, he added a good deal of modern equipment to the wagon, including a crate "for the purpose of carrying the best breeds of livestock," an Oliver Chilled "two-horse steel-beam plow," as well as dairy tools such as a cream separator and a milk tester, though he was well aware that much of this "equipment was greatly out of proportion to the agricultural status of the people."[165] Campbell's public reports claimed that he was advocating the use of "improved implements such as may be used on any up-to-date farm," along with "the judicious use of commercial fertilizers," and showing farmers how to "make more produce on a smaller number of acres of land at less expense."[166]

Other factors played a role in the Tuskegee extension workers' gradual abandonment of Carver's vision as well. The institute's extension agents understandably drifted toward those most likely to implement their suggestions. Campbell, for instance, sought out "the most prosperous and leading farmers" because they were more receptive.[167] For that matter, though Campbell had been one of Carver's best students, Carver's agricultural vision was only beginning to coalesce when he trained Campbell. He was, for example, just beginning his experiments with compost fertilizer. By the time Carver had adjusted his conception of scientific agriculture, he found the demands on his time as a speaker increasing and his classroom presence diminishing apace.

Most significant with regard to the institute's extension work, however, was the passage of the Smith-Lever Act in 1914, which institutionalized the cooperative extension program initiated by Knapp and required Alabama's African American extension agents to answer to the authorities at Auburn rather than Tuskegee.[168] The autonomy of black agents decreased considerably as a result. *The Functions and Duties of the County Agent*, a publication put out by the Alabama extension service, noted that "the negro agent is assistant agent to the white and works only with his own people."[169] The message of black agricultural agents thus increasingly resembled that of their white counterparts. In fact, by the 1920s the message of Tuskegee's annual Negro Conference was indistinguishable from that of Auburn's extension agents. "Up-to-date farming methods and farm machinery aid in farm improvements," began one declaration endorsed by the thirty-fifth

annual Tuskegee Farmers' Conference in January 1926. "To-day is not yesterday and the methods of yesterday will not suffice to-day"—a far cry from
Carver's assertion less than a decade earlier that "so-called reversion will
spell progress." By 1930, in the midst of the Great Depression, the conference was encouraging black farmers to buy "richer land, better commercial
fertilizer, [and] better varieties of crops and breeds of animals," and to embrace "modern methods, and [the] adequate use of machinery."[170]

Although the message of Tuskegee's agricultural emissaries drifted away
from his own vision, Carver contributed to the extension program when
asked to do so. During World War I, for instance, he provided a leaflet
on drying tomatoes, distilled material from his bulletins into a "Farmers'
Conference Women's Pamphlet," supplied planting calendars to county
agents, exhibited dried fruits and vegetables at the Negro Conference, and
contributed information "on school grounds, gardens and demonstration
plots" to an extension department publication titled *The Negro Rural School
and Its Relation to the Community*.[171] In doing so he did not compromise
his own message. In the extension department publication, for instance, he
advocated that teachers use "hardy native flowers" to decorate the school's
grounds, argued that school gardens taught students the "nearness of nature
and Nature's God," and recommended that basic tools and organic fertilizer
be used. Similarly, when a demonstration agent asked Carver for advice in
1926, he was told to "collect the leaves, muck, farmyard manures, etc., and
actually make some compost, spread it," though he added an implicit criticism of the school's extension department when he admonished the man
to "be very, very sure that you actually help do the work yourself and not
simply stand off, give orders and criticize."[172]

Prior to the assassination of Archduke Franz Ferdinand in June 1914,
however, Carver could not have anticipated that the message of Tuskegee's
agriculturists would drift so far from his own. On the eve of the First World
War, he had every reason to believe that he had fashioned a plausible solution to many of the problems facing impoverished black tenant farmers.
Although he was no longer teaching as regularly in Tuskegee's classrooms,
his former students were disseminating his lessons in rural schools and
black institutions throughout the South. His popularity as a lecturer guar-
anteed large audiences at virtually every venue at which he spoke, furnishing him an opportunity to reach far more farmers than he could have done
cloistered away in Tuskegee. His work at the experiment station had produced methods of cultivation and subsistence that required few resources

beyond a willingness to avail oneself of the abundance the Great Creator so lavishly bestowed in nature, and he had publicized those solutions in bulletins, leaflets, and newspapers. Though short-lived, his extension work had been institutionalized and expanded, and prior to 1915 was carrying Carver's message of economic empowerment through environmental awareness—or at least much of it—to illiterate black farmers.

CHAPTER 7

The Peanut Man

The World War I years were the best and worst of times for Carver. In the summer of 1914 he was injured in an automobile accident. "This summer I came near loosing [*sic*] my life, and I am yet unable to see how I could pass through such an ordeal and yet live," he wrote the Milhollands shortly before Christmas that year. A truck in which he had been riding "turned turtle with several of us in it," and he had been "pinned down under the truck, badly bruised and cut up," but with "no broken bones" or other serious injuries.[1] While he was still recovering, the economy of Macon County, which had encouraged him not long before, fell apart as the war in Europe got under way, interrupting the cotton trade.

The economic situation in Macon County and the rest of the Cotton Belt lent an increased urgency to Carver's campaign to better the lives of poor black farmers. Rising fertilizer prices made compost manuring an even more plausible solution for farmers, he argued in a 1916 circular titled *What Shall We Do for Fertilizers Next Year*. Wartime food conservation measures brought the reissue of several of his bulletins on food preservation.[2] He displayed "a huge case full of dried fruits and vegetables, labeled 'Some Ways to Preserve Food,'" at the Tuskegee Farmers' Conference of 1918 to demonstrate a way of "getting food into convenient form for easy transportation to the fighting men" and to show farmers and their wives how to "utilize more and more completely the fruits and vegetables which they have often allowed to go to waste before the great war came upon us."[3] Insofar "as the war in Europe has destroyed the South's cotton market and forced this section to study diversification of crops and the growth of foodstuffs," he argued in February 1915, "it is a blessing."[4]

Like many agriculturists of the day, he hailed the arrival of the boll weevil, which reached the county shortly after the war began, for its potential to undermine the rule of King Cotton. "Most of us are familiar with the fact, and some of us have seen the beautiful monument erected at Enterprise, Alabama," he wrote of the monument to the boll weevil erected there to celebrate the weevil's "beneficent influence" in 1919.[5] Indeed, Carver had been scheduled to deliver a talk at the monument's dedication, but heavy rains had delayed him. Regardless, he was confident that in "all probability, cotton will never be the universal king again, and indeed personally," he added, "I hope it will not."[6]

As his invitation to deliver an address at the dedication of Enterprise's boll weevil monument suggests, Carver's fame continued to grow during World War I. In fact, it grew at an unprecedented rate. In part Carver owed this to an unfortunate event: Washington's death in November 1915. Their petty bureaucratic bickering notwithstanding, the two had forged a deep respect for each other and a reasonably close personal relationship, and Carver grieved the loss of his friend. "I am sure Mr. Washington never knew how much I loved him, and the cause for which he gave his life," Carver wrote in February 1916.[7] Indeed, Carver slipped into something of a depression following Washington's death, one that Linda McMurry suggested was driven principally by guilt as his "bitter exchanges with the principal seemed to haunt him."[8] But if the death of Tuskegee's principal discouraged Carver, it wrought changes at Tuskegee that would redound to Carver's benefit. Not the least of these was the installation of a new principal who placed fewer demands on Carver and almost invariably sided with him (leading, among other things, to Bridgeforth's departure in 1918).[9] Most significant, however, Washington's death left Carver the best-known individual at the most famous black institution in the nation and allowed him to emerge from the considerable shadow Washington had cast.

Carver's research on alternative crops that could be both marketed and consumed resonated with the zeitgeist of the war years and added more luster to his reputation. His work with preserving food attracted particular attention. "Now that the world is realizing the seriousness of our world food shortage," the *Tuskegee Student* boasted in 1918, "it is well that we should get a glimpse of the work being done by a member of our own race . . . Professor George W. Carver."[10] The student paper was not alone in exalting Carver's work; newspapers as far away as Seattle carried pieces on him, and the *Rural New Yorker*, one of the foremost agricultural journals of the day, published a series of articles written by him.[11]

When Carver was summoned to Washington, D.C., in January 1918 to explain the possibilities offered by his sweet-potato flour, African Americans took great pride in the fact that one of their own had been called before Congress as an expert agricultural witness. George F. King, a black publisher, gushed in a letter to Carver, "I feel so proud of you that I simply can't express myself. Several of the big dailies up here carried editorials on your trip to Washington."[12] William Holtzclaw, the president of all-black Utica Institute in Mississippi, was similarly thrilled. He found it "very interesting that those great men of Washington have to come to members of what they call an inferior race to learn how to make flour out of potatoes."[13]

The relevance of Carver's work to wartime conservation measures impressed southern whites as well. In November 1917 the *Montgomery Advertiser* ran an article titled "A Glimpse of the Remarkable Work of George W. Carver, the Negro Scientist." While the article did not hold up Carver as a refutation of Jim Crow policies and "verification that the Negro is capable of reaching the very highest in science," it did recognize him as something of a genius. Apart from an emphasis on his research on clay products, various crops, and weeds, the article focused on Carver's "continuous, never-tiring" work, his disdain for money, his humility, and his willingness to sacrifice his own good for that of society—all things that fit neatly with expectations of African Americans under Jim Crow rules.[14]

Even so, Carver's star was unmistakably on the rise. In fact, Carver's reputation now extended beyond the nation's borders. Scientists from the Philippines and Puerto Rico contacted him for advice, for example, but one of the clearest indications of his growing international reputation came in November 1916 when Britain's Royal Society of Arts, Manufactures and Commerce elected him a member, probably at the recommendation of Harry Johnston, who had sung his praises after visiting Tuskegee a few years earlier.[15]

The increased attention led to an invitation from Thomas Edison in 1916 to visit Menlo Park and talk about Carver's process for deriving a rubber-like compound from sweet potatoes. Reportedly, this meeting led to a substantial offer (the exact amount is guesswork, though it quickly stretched in media reports from five figures to six) to lure Carver away from Tuskegee to Edison's research staff in New Jersey. Although Carver himself probably leaked the news of Edison's offer, he was never very forthcoming about the details, even with his friends. When Mrs. Milholland sent him a sketch of the events as they had been put forth in newspapers, for instance, Carver merely noted that the "item with reference to Mr. Edison will be alright."[16] Edison's acceptance of Carver as a peer and Carver's subsequent rejection of an enormous salary so that he might remain in Alabama and aid his people made great news fodder, of course, and became an integral part of the mythology that surrounded him.

Carver thus emerged from World War I with the recognition he had long sought, particularly in the nation's black community.[17] The president of the Colored Agricultural and Normal University in Langston, Oklahoma, for example, requested a large photo of Carver to hang in his office and confided that "George W. Carver means more to me than [Judson] Lyons or [Blanche K.] Bruce or [John Mercer] Langston."[18] He was not alone in elevating Carver. The black-run *Indianapolis Ledger* asserted in 1918 that "Carver is worth more to us as a race than all the protesting organizations and alliances we could form twix now and Gabriel's last toot."[19] And the *Charleston (S.C.) Messenger* called him "one of the world's geniuses" and "a wonder of the age."[20]

Carver had yet to become a household name, though, and few associated him with peanuts. To be sure, he had increasingly devoted his energies to the peanut during the war years. The fact that it thrived in sandy soils such as those in Macon County and could be harvested after the cotton was laid by in July made it an ideal crop for the region. Its nutritional value, along with the many ways in which it could be prepared, excited Carver even more. In 1916, for instance, well before he became identified with the peanut, he asserted that by "reason of its superior food value the peanut has become almost a universal diet for man.... I do not know of any one vegetable that has such a wide range of food possibilities."[21] Two years later he expressed his confidence that "of all the money crops grown by Southern farmers, perhaps there is none more promising than the peanut, which can be easily and cheaply grown."[22]

Carver said similarly good things about cowpeas. "We think we are safe in the assertion," he wrote in 1917, "that there is no crop grown in the South which possesses so many good qualities and at the same time is so easily grown as the cow-pea."[23] But it had been his work with sweet potatoes that attracted national attention, as his appearance in Washington indicates. As McMurry pointed out, had either the cowpea or "the sweet potato industry ... been as well organized [as the peanut industry] Carver might never have become the Peanut Man."[24]

But, of course, he did. On September 22, 1919, Carver reported to Robert Russa Moton, Washington's successor as Tuskegee's president, that he had "today made a delicious and wholesome milk from peanuts." Walter M. Grubbs, a representative of the Peanut Products Corporation in Birmingham, heard about Carver's discovery and, after writing Carver to confirm it, paid a visit to Tuskegee. Carver made quite an impression on him, and Grubbs left, as McMurry described it, "dazzled by both Carver and his many peanut products" and convinced that "Carver's work would have a great impact on the rapidly growing peanut industry."[25] This visit set in motion the series of events that would transform Carver into an icon.

Carver burst onto the national scene in January 1921 when he appeared before the House Ways and Means Committee as an expert witness at its tariff hearings. Hoping to persuade Congress to protect their industry with a tariff on imported peanuts, the peanut lobby paid Carver's way to the hearing. "What you produce there," an influential man in the peanut industry told Carver, "will be one of the greatest advertisements for the peanut that has ever taken place. It will be an education and will acquaint people with Mr. Peanut more than anything else, as so few congressmen know anything at all about the peanut."[26] His proclamation would prove prophetic, not least of all in its suggestion that Carver's lecture would "acquaint people with 'Mr. Peanut.'" Although the man was alluding to Carver's habit of anthropomorphizing the plants about which he was lecturing, Carver himself became "Mr. Peanut" in the wake of his presentation before Congress, which saw an initially skeptical committee that had allowed him only ten minutes to speak repeatedly extend his time and thank him with applause after he had finished.[27]

The Peanut Man was in many respects a myth. Carver developed virtually no peanut products that were both original and marketable, but he did play an important role in popularizing a relatively unknown product. When in 1916 he published what would become his most famous bulletin, *How to Grow the Peanut and 105 Ways of Preparing It for Human Consumption*, he had felt obliged to include a reminder to "always remove the brown hull from the peanuts even though the recipe does not say so."[28] Little had changed two years later when a public library requested the bulletin. The librarian had heard "nothing about them" as a food except for "the peanuts in Cracker Jack and eating them as nuts, with salt or without," and so wanted his "collection of recipes for using" them.[29] In the end, Carver became so identified with the peanut in the public's mind that he was wrongly credited for discoveries he had not made and to which he did not lay claim, such as peanut butter.

To some extent Carver was swept up in the stream of accolades and tributes that accompanied his relatively sudden emergence as a national celebrity. When public demand for his renowned peanut exhibit remained high, for example, he had little choice but to continue to show it. "I had intended to bring before you another exhibit entirely—one that you had never seen," he told the Tuskegee Farmers' Conference less than a month after his tariff testimony, "but since this one is attracting the attention of the entire country . . . I thought you ought to see" it.[30] Of course, his appearance before Congress and the irony that one of the South's leading scientists was black made far better copy than his campaign on behalf of impoverished black farmers.

Perhaps under such circumstances a mythology was bound to emerge, but Carver was clearly complicit in the mythmaking that attended his increasing prominence. Having labored under relatively thankless conditions at Tuskegee for twenty-five years, he embraced the attention lavished on him by whites and blacks alike, and offered only oblique denials of fabrications or exaggerations of his accomplishments. A favorite tactic was to hide behind false humility, claiming that the praise he was being given was exaggerated by three quarters or joking that he always learned something new about himself when he was introduced as a speaker. When sent a biographical sketch of himself, Carver would deflect attention from inaccuracies by praising the writing: "I became absorbingly interested in the story, forgetting all the time that you are talking about me," he told Pammel, who had written such a sketch.[31] Outright denials of untruths and exaggerations, however, were not forthcoming.[32]

By the mid-1920s Carver was a celebrity on a par with movie stars. Some of his lectures were invitation-only events attended by society types. In 1928, for instance, the Birmingham Chamber of Commerce sent out one thousand invitations "to representative men and women of Birmingham to attend a lecture by a great scientist and chemist, Dr. George W. Carver of Tuskegee." The lecture, of course, "was principally on the peanut, and its by-products."[33] Invitations to speak at white colleges throughout the nation came regularly. Carver's annual report to the institute detailing his activities in 1925 observed that "unusual interest is being manifested in the work along all lines of Agricultural Chemistry and there has been a constant demand in both white and colored institutions for lectures and demonstrations." In fact, Carver continued, he had spoken in Kentucky, North Carolina, Pennsylvania, Indiana, New York, "etc., etc. Some of these tours were arranged by white colleges, universities, and educational bodies and exclusively for them."[34] In January of the same year, Carver wrote his friend Lyman Ward noting "that the greater part of my work is now among white colleges." At all such appearances he viewed himself as an emissary of racial harmony.[35]

Carver was confident, as he wrote a friend in 1930, that his work was "doing much toward breaking down the color barriers and making it easier for the dear young people" of his race.[36] Perhaps predictably, Carver saw himself as something of a martyr for the cause of racial justice. In a letter to the Milhollands he complained, "I do not do anything but entertain crowds of visitors who want to see the laboratory and incidentally look at the strange character." The sacrifice was worth it insofar as his fame undermined the entrenched racist assumptions of the nation, and he added hopefully, "But I believe that it is God's way of teaching the people that some good can come out of Ethiopia."[37] He was not alone in that belief. The NAACP bestowed its highest honor, the Spingarn Medal, on him in 1923, a remarkable decision considering the disjuncture between the ideology of the NAACP's founder, W. E. B. DuBois, and Tuskegee, which was still associated with DuBois's rival, Booker T. Washington.

For his part, Carver was optimistic that racial strife would ultimately disappear because God would tolerate it for only so long: "I believe in the providence of God working in the hearts of men," he professed in 1923, "and that the so-called, Negro problem will be satisfactorily solved in His own good time, and in His own way."[38] Like many of his peers, he rejected the idea of race as a valid category even as he identified with "his people."[39] For Carver, "no question or questions [were] peculiar to the Negro, but simply a problem of humanity."[40] If Americans, black and white, could "just understand that the Golden Rule way of living is the only correct method, and the only Christ-like method," he argued near the end of his life, "this will settle all of our difficulties that bother us."[41]

It would be easy to dismiss such a conviction as naïve, but Carver was neither unaware of the serious threats posed by racism nor above calling it by its name and confronting it when he felt he could do so diplomatically. When a member of the United Peanut Association planned to trademark and market "Pickaninny" peanuts, for example, Carver crafted a diplomatic letter in which he explained that "my people object seriously to their children being called 'Pickaninnies.'. . . 'Pickaninnies' as they are called by some, are merely caricatures."[42] On another occasion, a group of southern whites attempted to persuade him to openly endorse Jim Crow policies, waxing eloquent about the "mutual benefit" such policies had for blacks and whites. He dismissed them with a single sentence: "Gentlemen, what you do speaks so loud, I can't hear what you say."[43] In private Carver could be even more forthright. Writing to a white friend in 1931, for example, he chided Americans for their callous refusal to examine the nature of their own democracy: "We cry Peace, peace. There is no permanent peace where . . . races hate each other."[44]

Carver never embraced the role of black leader, however, and the expectation that he should do so proved to be an unwelcome burden. When in 1939 a white friend sent him an article he had written titled "Race Prejudice" and complained that he was unable to get it published, Carver first complimented him on having written an article that was "very fine and full of truth." But he was not surprised that "a publisher would not want to raise those questions as some of them are yet pretty sore spots in the minds of people filled with prejudice." In fact, he continued, "I feel that an open discussion of the race problem amounts to just about as much as the discussion of war, as we go on fighting just the same."[45] His friend reluctantly agreed "that it was not profitable to bark up one tree too long and . . . that some trees we had better not bark up at all."[46]

Whatever the merits of his role as a reluctant civil rights advocate, Carver's emergence as the Peanut Man distracted him from the original purpose for which he had gone to Tuskegee, and the celebrity status that came with his adoption by the peanut industry—and then by New South boosters—effectively ended his campaign on behalf of impoverished black farmers. Perhaps the most telling evidence of that can be found in his publication of experiment station bulletins. Prior to World War I Carver produced twenty-five bulletins, and during the war years he published an additional twelve. After number 37, *How to Make Sweet Potato Flour, Starch, Sugar, Bread and Mock Cocoanut*, was published in 1918, however, he published only six more during his lifetime. A seventh, co-written with his assistant Austin W. Curtis, was released after his death. Between 1919 and 1935 the experiment station issued a total of three "new" bulletins, all of which were revised editions of earlier publications.

Carver's efforts to raise southern black farmers from the depths of poverty ended at around the same time the reform efforts of the Progressive Era fizzled out. Like many Progressive endeavors, the campaign ended in neither a blaze of glory nor a momentous defeat. It simply faded away. Following Washington's death in 1915, Carver spent almost no time in the classroom. While he continued to lecture off Tuskegee's campus, the subjects he covered were seldom applicable to impoverished farmers. His growing fame and his position as the institute's most recognizable face increased the demands on his time, and though he continued to publish advice to farmers, he did so less consistently. Much of the material carried in newspapers under his name was recycled from his earlier writings. His research interests likewise shifted from the experiment station to his laboratory, where the discoveries for which he received the most acclaim had been generated. His plot work at the station, which had been declining for a number of years, came to a close in 1925. As the message of Tuskegee's extension agents drifted away from Carver's in the wake of the Smith-Lever Act, few vestiges of his early efforts lingered into the 1920s. During the Great Depression Carver came to regret abandoning the campaign and revisited his concern for poor black farmers. By that time, however, his message faced even greater obstacles. New technologies had become necessities in the eyes even of the poorest black tenants, and they could not be produced on farms no matter how independent.

The campaign had profoundly influenced Carver's environmental vision, however, and it reflected his appreciation of the complexity, interdependence, and fragility of creation; his abhorrence of waste; his belief in long-term solutions rather than short-term fixes; and his reverence for the natural world. The end of the campaign did not end that vision, which was manifested in at least some ways in his subsequent research.

Broadening his work beyond agricultural science, Carver took on the identity of a "creative chemist," a term coined by Edwin E. Slosson, a technological utopian who published a book titled *Creative Chemistry* in 1919.[47] "It took but a glance" at Slosson's book, Carver insisted, "to convince even the uninitiated, that it was the work of a master mind."[48] Carver's lavish praise was in some ways ironic. Slosson would later publish an article title "Back to Nature? Never! Forward to the Machine!," an indictment of the back to nature movement in which he maintained that the "conquest of nature, not the imitation of nature, is the whole duty of man," a philosophy strikingly at odds with Carver's. The more so as Slosson maintained that people should not "love nature," but instead should view it as "a treacherous and unsleeping foe, ever to be feared and watched and circumvented."[49] This philosophical divergence notwithstanding, Carver clearly thought highly of *Creative Chemistry*.

Slosson's collection of essays elevated science (and scientists) generally, but stressed its applied rather than theoretical branches, seeking to demonstrate the practical benefits of seemingly theoretical sciences such as chemistry with which most Americans were unfamiliar. He pointed, for instance, to the Haber Bosch process to argue that the application of theoretical research on nitrogen had proven useful in myriad ways, from developing munitions during World War I to increasing agricultural harvests with synthetic fertilizers. In short, the creative application of theoretical science was crucial to the continued welfare of the nation.

Carver's training had not been in chemistry, however, and he did not leave a lasting legacy in the field. Although he heralded the "vast commercial possibilities" of "several hundred Southern products," his forays into the business world failed.[50] His work with clays, for instance, attracted the interest of some paint manufacturers, but their interest (and limited investment) came to naught, and both of the companies that bore his name (though he ran neither of them) met with very little success. A patent medicine dubbed Penol that he developed from creosote and peanuts to treat respiratory illness attracted good press in the mid-1920s and was manufactured for better than a decade. When the Food and Drug Administration questioned its effectiveness in 1937, however, sales slowed and it died a quiet death in the early 1940s.[51]

Much of what Slosson advocated as "creative chemistry" nevertheless fell in line with the kind of work Carver had long been doing: trying to develop marketable products from crops other than cotton. Expanding his conviction that poor farmers' economic salvation lay in finding new uses for overlooked natural resources to the region as a whole, Carver pioneered in the chemurgy movement, which sought to develop industrial products from agricultural resources.

Widespread interest in the agricultural applications of chemistry had actually emerged in the 1920s as the science, which was then coming into its own, continued to foster long-standing connections to agronomy.[52] The atmosphere of the time was unquestionably right for such an emphasis. The agricultural depression and trade tensions that followed the war compounded the interest and provided chemists with every incentive to embrace agriculture. Researchers at land-grant schools like Carver's alma mater and chemical engineers in the laboratories of chemical companies initiated a number of projects that sought to transform agricultural wastes and surpluses to industrial ends.[53]

The publication of two articles in the autumn of 1926 provided an indication that these initially disjointed efforts were beginning to coalesce. In the first, chemist William Hale contended that "farming must become a chemical industry," a notion he would later clarify when he insisted that farmers should cease viewing themselves as producers of traditional crops like corn and instead define their farms (and themselves) by their production of things useful to industry like cellulose and starch. The second, by Wheeler McMillan (the editor of *Farm and Fireside*), suggested that the problem of overproduction might be ameliorated if chemists turned their attention to agricultural surpluses and by-products.[54] By the end of the 1920s a concerted effort was afoot to find alternative uses for established crops, introduce new crops that would both help limit overproduction and carry industrial benefits, and turn agricultural by-products to useful (and profitable) industrial ends.

In many ways the movement represented an extension of work Carver had initially undertaken in his first years at Tuskegee as part of his larger effort to aid the impoverished farmers of Macon County. "Since the origin of this Department in 1896," Carver wrote in his 1940 report for the school's agricultural research and experiment station, "theories for the solution of farm problems based on the diversification of crops, the finding of new uses for farm crops and waste material have been advocated," and "Tuskegee Institute has been a pioneering institute in Farm Chemurgy."[55] President Franklin Roosevelt's secretary of agriculture, Henry A. Wallace (the son of Henry C. Wallace, Carver's professor at Ames), agreed that Carver had been at the vanguard of the movement. In a speech titled "The Genetic Basis of Democracy," Wallace argued that in Carver's "work as a chemist in the South, he correctly sensed the coming interest in the industrial use of the products of the farm—a field of research which our government is now pushing." For Wallace on that day, Carver's prescient anticipation of chemurgy refuted Nazi ideology inasmuch as it clearly demonstrated that "superior ability is not the exclusive possession of any one race or any one class. It may arise anywhere, provided men are given the right opportunities."[56]

Wallace was in some ways a reluctant convert to chemurgy. Under his guidance the USDA was hesitant to embrace the movement, particularly as New Deal agricultural policies were initially aimed at reducing production, a policy that was anathema to most chemurgists. Most of the support for the movement in the 1930s came from industrialists. Arguably the most important of these, at least in terms of lending the movement credibility in the public sphere, was Henry Ford. In the late 1920s Ford organized the Edison Institute (named, of course, for Thomas Edison, who had also thrown his support behind the movement) with the express aim of researching the industrial uses of agricultural products. By the early 1930s those efforts had focused on the possibilities of soybeans, which could be made into a dent-resistant plastic that Ford could incorporate into his cars (a bushel of beans per car). In May 1935 the automobile magnate hosted a conference in Dearborn, Michigan, at which the National Farm Chemurgic Council was organized, formally ushering in the era of "chemurgy."[57]

Ford's interest in chemurgy led him to Carver, whose work along such lines was well known, and in 1937 he invited the Tuskegee scientist to speak at the Dearborn conference. At that event the two men formed a friendship that would last for the balance of Carver's life.[58] But Carver's connections to the movement proper were fairly tenuous. To begin with, most chemurgists were affiliated with large industrial interests and tended to care more about protective tariffs and industrial development than soil conservation. Indeed, to the extent that New Deal agricultural policies favored soil conservation over initiatives like chemurgy, they chided Wallace for adopting policies they considered naïve. Further, the chemurgists as a group (and for the most part individually) had considerably greater resources at their disposal than Carver did, the more so once the USDA reluctantly threw its support behind the movement. Carver could not have remained on chemurgy's cutting edge in the 1930s even had he wanted to do so.

Thus, although he accepted the honorary mantle of "the first and greatest chemurgist," he was hardly in its mainstream.[59] On the contrary, Carver often misconstrued the movement's aims, imagining they fell more in line with his own than in fact they did. Because Carver had devoted his energies to improving the lives of impoverished black farmers, he saw chemurgy as a field in which scientists addressed "a great human problem."[60] His 1936 injunction to "chemicalize the farm" sprang from his abhorrence of waste rather than a desire for profit, let alone an affinity for chemical pesticides and fertilizers. He wanted "waste products of the farm" to be used for making "insulating boards, paints, dyes, industrial alcohol, plastics of various kinds, rugs, mats and cloth from fiber plants, oils, gums and waxes, etc."[61] What was true of his well-known work with the peanut, he had contended in 1928 as the chemurgy movement was coalescing, was no less true of "the sweet potato, . . . velvet bean, soybean, cowpea, pecan, . . . fiber plants, and many, many other problems with which I have worked and am working." The same was "more or less true with every other farm, garden, orchard and miscellaneous product. All we need . . . is to set the creative mind to work."[62]

Most chemurgists tended to have more material aims. In his account of Auburn's experiment station, Norwood Allen Kerr pointed out that agricultural experiment stations throughout the South began to concentrate "their research on encouraging diversification and searching for new uses for traditional crops" only after the bottom fell out of the cotton market in the early 1930s.[63] Elsewhere in the nation, as Russell Lord argued in 1962, "the first thought" of the "farm chemurgic movement . . . was mainly to transmute excesses of edibles, such as wheat, into nonedible goods: paper and plastics, or most particularly rubber and motor fuel, for which there are all but insatiable and endlessly profitable demand."[64]

Production, of course, underlay those "excesses." The movement not only failed to challenge the notion that greater yields should always be a goal— that they were a measure of the efficacy of both scientific agriculture and the individual farmer—overproduction was its very foundation. As farmers continued to increase their production, the excess could be channeled in profitable ways by breaking the crop down chemically and reconstituting it as something such as rubber or ethanol. The sustainability of the methods used to raise the crops that could be "chemicalized" was immaterial to most of Carver's counterparts in the field. Indeed, in 1945 J. I. Rodale, an outspoken midcentury advocate of organic agriculture, would express his fear that for all its "highly ingenious" products, chemurgy threatened to "extend the single-crop technique of land mining with all its attendant evils of soil exhaustion and erosion."[65]

The motives of most chemurgists could thus hardly have been more at odds with Carver's. His desire to chemicalize the farm had grown out of his campaign to help impoverished black farmers who were compelled to plant cotton. In undertaking the kind of research that was eventually dubbed chemurgy, Carver had hoped to find a crop that was as profitable as cotton and yet consumable as a foodstuff. And he had undertaken the project with the same conviction that had been evident even in his first publication at the IAC: "nature does not expend its forces upon waste material, . . . each created thing is an indispensable factor in the great whole, and one in which no other factor will fit exactly as well."[66] Since waste was not a natural phenomenon, agricultural by-products were not waste; they were simply products whose uses remained to be uncovered. Indeed, he had long sought to persuade farmers to think along those lines, whether by making rugs from discarded corn shucks, extracting dyes from tomato stalks, or compost fertilizing.

Given his distaste for commercial fertilizers, it is perhaps not surprising that Carver cared a great deal how farmers raised agricultural products. "To our amazement," he wrote in 1936, "we are learning that a tomato may not be a tomato nutritionally speaking, but only a hull or shadow of the savory, nutritious, palatable vegetable it should be."[67] Although it might look "in every way just like an ordinary tomato," he added in 1942, favorably citing the work of another scientist, a tomato raised with artificial fertilizers might have comparatively few of the nutritional "qualities of a well-grown unfertilized (artificially) tomato." His concern about the application of chemicals of all kinds to food crops continued to grow. Anticipating the kind of argument Rachel Carson would make in *Silent Spring*, he pointed out that chemicals put on fields made their way into the body. Those "who eat watermelons know that if they are not exceedingly careful they remain sick as long as the watermelon season lasts, because of the improper use of nitrate of soda."[68] He astutely informed a farmer from neighboring Tallapoosa County in 1939 who wrote him asking about "the various Arsenic, Black Flag, Rotonone, and other poisonous compounds" that such chemicals would control pests, but they invited farmers down a slippery slope because they "must be continuously applied . . . and when one generation is killed out another one comes very soon afterwards."[69] Few chemurgists shared that concern.

Even so, Carver supported the chemurgy movement for the remainder of his life, and he had cause for optimism as the movement appeared to be flowering in the early 1940s. Most of the synthetic rubber produced in the nation during World War II, for instance, was manufactured from an agricultural product—grain alcohol—from which butadiene could be extracted. As late as 1951, eight years after Carver's death, *Newsweek* could reasonably contend that "the flood of chemurgy seems to be swelling"; but in fact the movement's death knell had very nearly sounded.[70] Many of the nonfood products derived from agricultural "wastes," such as butadiene, could also be derived from petroleum.[71] The proliferation of inexpensive petrochemical products undermined the chemurgy movement, which had more or less collapsed by the mid-1960s, though the National Farm Chemurgic Council lingered until 1977.

The rebirth of the bio-based products industry at the turn of the twenty-first century—including the establishment in the early 1990s of the New Uses Council, the ideological heir to the Chemurgic Council—has highlighted the disconnect between its advocates and those of sustainable agriculture. Most advocates of ecological agriculture are suspicious of the NUC's claim that "a strong global bioeconomy" based in agribusiness can emerge while "achieving environmental sustainability."[72] But these differences were considerably murkier in Carver's lifetime. Thus, the NUC's ranking of Carver among the "visionaries" from whom they have taken their inspiration is, perhaps, a shade misleading. His emphasis on ecological relationships, to say nothing of his desire to establish an independent black yeomanry, set him apart not only from the chemurgists of his day but from their contemporary descendants. As John Ferrell adroitly noted, "Carver may have been the only leading chemurgist that present-day proponents of sustainable agriculture would instantly recognize as a kindred spirit."[73]

If Carver was both a part of and apart from the chemurgy movement, the same might be said of his place in New Deal agriculture generally. The New Deal turned national attention to the problems that had occupied Carver's career at Tuskegee, and some of the solutions put forward by New Deal reformers sounded very much like Carver's; indeed, some historians have rooted the emergence of the sustainable agriculture movement in the ideas of such New Deal administrators as Rexford Tugwell.[74] Ecologists had the ear of agricultural policy makers in a way they never had before; leading figures in the USDA drew the same sorts of connections between land use and poverty as Carver had; and several influential New Deal bureaucrats (men such as Hugh Hammond Bennett, head of the Soil Conservation Service) shared Carver's passion for soil conservation.[75] For that matter, reformers not connected with the New Deal during the Depression—including the so-called Nashville Agrarians, Ralph Borsodi and other cultural critics, and sociologists such as Rupert Vance—expressed serious reservations about the direction American agriculture was taking, and some of those reservations were in line with Carver's. And given his warm relationship with Secretary of Agriculture Wallace, one might expect Carver to have established a significant link with his fellow agricultural reformers in the 1930s.

For a number of reasons, however, the connection between Carver and the New Deal remained superficial. He had little influence on New Deal policy and negligible contact with those whose work he might reasonably be credited with anticipating. Perhaps the most obvious reason for the disjuncture between Carver's vision and that of the Depression Era agrarians was rooted in a fundamental divide over the best course of reform. Educated and trained at a time when rural reformers generally rejected government intervention that went beyond educational aims (the funding of agricultural schools, experiment stations, and extension work), Carver essentially saw agricultural reform as a moral imperative for individual farmers.[76] His instincts in that direction were confirmed during his years at Tuskegee, where his vision for rural uplift fit neatly with Booker T. Washington's vision for racial uplift inasmuch as both centered on self-help, placing the responsibility for improvement on individuals. By way of contrast, most influential New Dealers, as historian Sarah Phillips argued, drew their inspiration from a group that emerged in the 1920s dubbed the New Conservationists by Lewis Mumford, largely to draw distinctions between their vision and those of Carver's ilk. The New Conservationists placed the bulk of the responsibility for rural uplift on the shoulders of the government rather than individuals, advocating regional planning for land and water resources, rural electrification, and industrial decentralization.[77] Even the Nashville Agrarians and other reformers who objected to New Deal policies tended to embrace inherently political solutions, couching their critiques in political (if sometimes nostalgic) terms.[78] Consequently, if New Deal agricultural reformers concurred with Carver that altering land use by introducing conservation measures could secure the financial feasibility of farming, they espoused remarkably different means.

His friendship with Howard Kester, a socialist reformer, organizer of the Southern Tenant Farmers' Union, and outspoken advocate for racial equality, served to underscore Carver's indifference to political avenues of reform. The two men had met in 1924 at a YMCA conference in which Carver participated as part of his larger effort to improve race relations. Impressed with Carver's spirituality, Kester visited Tuskegee the following year, touching off a deep and abiding friendship. While Carver was well aware that Kester's efforts to challenge Jim Crow and unite poor whites and blacks against the larger economic forces that kept both groups oppressed entailed considerable danger—at one point he provided Kester with instructions for making a "suicide potion" from readily available plants should things take a dramatically bad turn—he gave little thought to the undergirding political ideology that motivated his friend.[79] Carver supported Kester both because the activist was his friend and because they shared a vision of the world in which racial and religious divides were immaterial and nature was venerated. Carver cared for the nuances of political ideologies only to the degree that they promised to advance unity or improve the conditions of "suffering humanity." Thus, when Carver volunteered to Kester his belief that communism's influence was likely to grow because it advocated something of a brotherhood, Kester (aware of Carver's naïveté on political matters) felt obliged to explain exactly what communism entailed. He "never heard [Carver] mention the matter again."[80] To be sure, Carver never embraced any political ideology, or any political party, for that matter. His political vision, if he could be said to have had one, was of a utopia in which enlightened individuals lived "the Golden Rule way of life," and that sort of world simply could not be legislated into existence.[81]

A second obvious reason for Carver's limited connection with the main currents of Depression Era agricultural reform stems from the fact that his attention was diverted in manifold directions during the 1930s: traveling to deliver speeches, taking up his role (however reluctantly) as an ambassador of improved race relations, proffering advice to southern industries (especially peanut companies), and generally pursuing a course that he believed would secure his reputation after his death. The aspect of Carver's work that probably attracted the most attention over the course of the 1930s, for instance, was his purported medical advances, especially a peanut-based massage oil he used to treat poliomyelitis patients. (Newspapers sometimes hinted that Carver might at some point massage President Roosevelt, who of course had suffered from polio.)[82] Carver's reputation as "the world's greatest chemist" lent his work in this direction a credibility that it did not otherwise merit. When it became clear that the medical community dismissed his efforts, he maintained that doctors were slighting not only him but work that held genuine promise as well.

While on a tour of the South in the spring of 1939, Roosevelt visited Tuskegee, where a widely circulated photo captured him and Carver shaking hands, but the president was more aware of Carver's work with peanuts and polio patients than with any connection between Carver's agrarian vision and that of himself or his New Deal administrators. (FDR had been influenced by the New Conservationists during the 1920s and had employed many of their recommendations during his time as governor of New York.)[83] The only correspondence between the two men likewise centered on Carver's work with polio and involved Carver sending some of his oil to the president and receiving a kind reply in which Roosevelt informed Carver that he used "peanut oil from time to time" and was "sure that it helps."[84] The mythology that had surrounded Carver in the wake of his rise to fame thus obscured his more significant work almost immediately and transformed him into something of a caricature: a genius of sorts who dabbled in this and that, but above all else performed mysterious experiments with peanuts.

Indeed, this Carver caricature distracted even those who might otherwise have been aware of the substance of Carver's earlier work. Even Henry A. Wallace, whom Carver had generously taken on botanical expeditions when the secretary of agriculture was a child in Ames, missed the import of Carver's work. This is not to say that Wallace did not admire Carver. On the contrary, he often publicly praised Carver, albeit in vague terms focusing on the ways his father's friend had advanced race relations or the depth and sincerity of Carver's religious faith. And the respect was mutual. In a speech delivered at a soil conservation conference hosted by Tuskegee in 1936 at which the secretary of agriculture was also a speaker, Carver reminisced about his days in Iowa, highlighting the significance of Henry C. Wallace's influence on his education and asserting that his former teacher "had prophetic vision, and passed it on to his son."[85] Their mutual respect notwithstanding, Wallace had serious reservations about the deservedness of Carver's reputation as a "creative chemist," noting in some private correspondence that he was "inclined to think that [Carver's] ability as a chemist has been somewhat overrated. I have been to his chem lab at Tuskegee but frankly I doubt if much of practical value came out."[86] In making such an assessment, Wallace conflated "industrial value" with "practical value," and so lumped Carver with men such as Luther Burbank whose reputations, he believed, outstripped their accomplishments. Predictably, then, the chief architect of New Deal agricultural policy was not inclined to seek Carver's advice on matters of national policy. Even for Wallace, Carver was the Peanut Man. Together with Carver's fundamentally different notion of reform, that persona was enough to effectively blunt most connections between Carver and the broader agricultural reform efforts of the 1930s.

CHAPTER 8

Divine Inspiration

Henry A. Wallace's assessment of Carver's place in chemistry proved more or less accurate. There is no question that Carver's legacy as a scientist, especially as an innovative "creative chemist," has been overblown—a phenomenon rooted in the fact that a number of groups had an interest in bolstering his fame. The peanut industry, the Farm Chemurgic Council, and New South advocates all heralded him as a representative of their respective causes. African Americans saw him as evidence of what could be accomplished in spite of Jim Crow and as an example that undermined the very assumptions on which segregation was built. White Americans in the main saw him as an exceptional but well-behaved black man: humble, pious, long-suffering, and nonthreatening. Perhaps his most enduring supporters, however, have come from the nation's evangelical community.

By the middle of the 1920s, a decade that saw the divide between science and religion widen, America's evangelicals had found in Carver a prime example of a well-respected scientist whose faith dovetailed neatly with his scientific endeavors, a man who would not concede that science undermined scriptural authority or Christianity generally. By the end of the decade, religious presses had begun to publish biographies of him and

Christian periodicals carried articles on his accomplishments. Their celebration of him as a "hero of the faith" would continue well beyond Carver's
lifetime.

Although Carver had spoken regularly at churches throughout his career,
he first caught the attention of the wider evangelical community in 1924
when he spoke at the Marble Collegiate Church in New York City. Dis-
playing a number of his products, he downplayed his own role in discovering them and credited God for the inspiration. Because it was a religious
gathering, this was not surprising, but his apparently offhand admission
that "no books ever go into my laboratory" was a frankly startling assertion for a scientist to make. A *New York Times* reporter in attendance was
taken aback by Carver's confessions and wrote a scathing editorial titled
"Men of Science Never Talk That Way." Arguing that "real chemists do not
scorn books out of which they can learn, and . . . do not ascribe their successes, when they have any, to 'Inspiration,'" the reporter maintained that
by giving God credit for his successes, Carver not only discredited his own
science but risked bringing "ridicule on an admirable institution and on the
race for which [his work] has done and still is doing so much."[1]

The implication that he was something of a charlatan and that his work
might actually be undermining the good of both Tuskegee and his race of-
fended Carver. He wrote a lengthy retort to the paper in which he regretted
"exceedingly that such a gross misunderstanding should arise as to what
was meant by 'Divine inspiration.' Inspiration," he argued, "is never at vari-
ance with information; in fact, the more information one has, the greater
will be the inspiration." Pointing to his training in Ames, a list of some
sixty-two scientists who had been his "inspiration and guide for study," and
"the leading scientific publications" that were delivered to him at Tuskegee,
he established his credentials as a "real" scientist. But he distanced himself
from "scientists to whom the world is merely the result of chemical forces
or material electrons," arguing that divine inspiration was not only a valid
concept but a demonstrable one.[2]

Wondering "what value a book would be to the creator if he [were] not
a master of analytical work," Carver contended that "a master analyst needs
no book; he is at liberty to take apart and put together substances . . . to suit
his own particular taste or fancy." Offering an example of how this inspiration could be manifest, he pointed out that on a visit to the ethnic markets
of New York City, he had been "struck with the large number of taros and
yautias" he saw there. "Dozens of things came to me while standing there

looking at them," he continued. Though he knew of "no one who has ever worked with these roots in this way" and of "no book from which he could get this information," he was confident that he would "have no trouble" in extracting the same sorts of products from them that he had from sweet potatoes. "If this is not inspiration and information from a source greater than myself," he concluded, "kindly tell me what it is."[3]

The *New York Times* did not publish the letter, but it circulated among Carver's friends and was picked up by a number of papers throughout the nation that rallied to his defense.[4] "I did feel very badly" about the *New York Times* editorial, Carver wrote his friend Lyman Ward in January 1925, "not that the cynical criticism was directed at me, but rather at the religion of Jesus Christ. Dear Bro. I know that my Redeemer liveth." But he was greatly encouraged by the "dozens of books, papers, periodicals, magazines, personal letters from individuals in all walks of life" that expressed their support for him.[5]

Carver's admission that he was "not interested in science or anything else that leaves God out of it" made him a hero to a Christian culture that by the end of 1925—the year of the Scopes trial—felt increasingly out of step with the larger American culture, perhaps even under attack. Since the evangelical community paid little attention to the nuances of his theology, Carver's professions of faith had the effect of reaffirming fundamentalism in his audiences. After hearing Carver speak on one occasion, for example, a nurse wrote him, explaining that "we have known for a long time that you were a noted scientist, but we did not know how closely you followed the word of God." His faith had "given [them] a renewed faith in the provision that the Lord has made for His children."[6] What mattered to the Christian community was the fact that he was "a scientist who [believed] that science depends on God."[7]

Austin Curtis, Carver's best-known assistant, expressed some misgivings about the motives behind Carver's elevation to the pantheon of America's religious heroes. After complaining about the common misconception that Carver just began "praying and that all of these various products were dumped on a table in front of him," Curtis acknowledged his suspicion that "there were also people who wanted to exploit him on the basis of his firm religious convictions."[8] It is difficult to say whether the distortions of Carver's accomplishments and his understanding of "divine inspiration" emerged from the baser motives ascribed by Curtis or whether they materialized organically and inadvertently. Clearly, however, Christian publications embraced him warmly and played an important role in his rising popularity.

Catholic and Protestant presses alike, during his lifetime and beyond it, produced books and articles about Carver with such titles as *The World's Greatest Chemist*, "The Power of Faith," "He Worked with God," "George Washington Carver: A Catholic Tribute," "Prayers to Peanuts," *The Man Who Asked God Questions*, *God's Ebony Scientist*, and *George Washington Carver: Man of God*.[9] His reputation as a "hero of the faith" has continued into the early twenty-first century as a Christian subculture uncomfortable with a continuing shift in the direction of enlightenment values (such as the separation of church and state and the ascendancy of science) looks to heroes venerated by the secular world as well. Two of the most recent books on Carver emphasize his Christianity: John Perry's *Unshakable Faith: Booker T. Washington and George Washington Carver* (1999) and William J. Federer's *George Washington Carver: His Life and Faith in His Own Words* (2003).[10] Bible colleges in Atlanta and Kansas City bear his name, and the Christian Broadcasting Network has singled him out as evidence that "faith has played a key role in the history of black Americans."[11]

These publications highlight, and often inflate, Carver's scientific accomplishments, which implicitly refute the notion that Christianity is somehow incompatible with science. Remarkably, however, considering his elevation to near sainthood, critical analyses of his religious beliefs are rare. This continued veneration of Carver would by itself merit a deeper examination of his beliefs, but they are important for more than just the sake of curiosity. Indeed, Carver's religious veneration for the natural world proved as essential to his environmental thought as did the principles of ecology and his conviction that waste was anathema; the three were, in fact, inextricable.

In many respects Carver's Christianity was reasonably orthodox, particularly given the ascendancy of the Social Gospel during the time his faith was forged. Writing to a friend in 1927, he confessed that he wanted his students, and young people generally, "to find Jesus, and make him a daily, hourly, and momently part of themselves." Only in Christ could they "get the fullest measure of happiness and success out of life."[12] Some of the students in his Bible class had conversion experiences. One of them wrote Carver in 1918 telling him, "I know I am not the same because I don't feel the same. . . . I find myself growing [stronger in faith] each day."[13] Carver enjoined his students to read the Bible in morning and evening devotions in order that they might be better equipped to "stand on the promises of God their savior."[14]

When Jim Hardwick, a young white man with whom Carver developed a close relationship, was struggling with his faith in 1924, Carver encouraged him: "Don't be alarmed, friend, when doubts creep in. That is Old Satan. Pray, pray, pray." Assuring his "boy" that "I love you and shall continue to do so for the Christ that is in you," he expressed his confidence that in time God would help Hardwick to overcome his doubts. "Thank God, you will," he promised. Four years later Hardwick had apparently emerged from the struggle, but Carver exhorted him to continue in the faith, paraphrasing Proverbs 3:6: "My dear friend, keep your hand in His, acknowledge Him in all of your ways and He will direct your paths."[15]

Carver's faith appears orthodox in other ways as well. In providing the recipe for a dish that was "to be eaten with cream and a little sugar on Christmas morning," for example, he advised that it should be done "constantly praising God for unfolding before our eyes so much of His Glory."[16] In fact, he occasionally reflected some of the less flattering aspects of America's mainstream Protestantism. In a July 1940 interview, for example, Carver suggested that "the war in Europe" was "God's method of purifying the world." In something of a jeremiad, Carver continued, "We are not in a much better condition now than Sodom and Gomorrah were. Now [the world] has to be purged." His interviewer, the president of Simpson College, followed up Carver's comment with a leading question: "Don't you think the defeat of France was not by the armies of Hitler, but by the fact that its people were dissipated in sin? We all know the morals of France." Carver's response indicated tacit agreement: "As ye sow, so shall ye reap."[17]

Carver's faith was considerably less orthodox in other areas, however. Some deviations were comparatively superficial. In leading worship one Sunday in Tuskegee's chapel, for instance, he focused "upon the manner in which God speaks to men through nature" and illustrated his sermon with "various agricultural products which he had in the chapel."[18] Others, of course, were characteristic of the Social Gospel generally. "Watch your life and doctrine closely," the apostle Paul had enjoined his young charge in 1 Timothy 4:16. Social Gospelers as a group tended to emphasize the first of Paul's injunctions rather than the second, and Carver was no exception. Doctrine was of no great consequence to him. What mattered was living a life of service to his fellow man. True Christians were not those whose faith reflected the historical essentials of the faith—the divinity of Christ, the propitiation of sins wrought by Christ's substitutionary death on the Cross, and his resurrection—but rather those "who believe and live the Golden Rule Way of living, which is the Jesus way of life."[19]

Carver extended this Social Gospel principle further than did most of his peers. Although he identified with the Presbyterian church throughout his life, denominational distinctions were of little significance to him. For that matter, the substance of people's faith mattered little so long as they were interested in "getting beyond self" and sought to serve the larger society. Confident that there was more than one way to commune with God, he endorsed a number of rather unorthodox groups: the Theosophical Society, the Unity Farm, the Divine Philosophy Group, the Universal Group of Intuitives, the Rosicrucian Fellowship, and the Baha'i faith. Baha'i, for example, denies the deity of Christ and contends that all religions are essentially equal, lumping Christ, as the founder of Christianity, into a coequal group that includes Zoroaster, Moses, and Mohammed.[20] Few Social Gospelers would have endorsed that creed. Even more remarkable, Carver believed he had "a number of things in common" with a black religious leader known as Father Divine, whose followers believed him to be "God incarnate."[21] Indeed, Carver laid plans with Christian socialist Howard Kester to establish the George Washington Carver Fellowship, which would "unite all kindred spirits, whatever race, religion or nationality, who behold in the universe the most sublime expression of Love, Truth and Beauty, through which the Great Creator eternally speaks concerning the things that He has created."[22]

A similar unorthodoxy is evident in Carver's unflinching veneration of science. Believing science to be "a regarded body of knowledge" rather than a process, he placed scientific truths on a par with scriptural ones; since Christianity and science were both truth, there could be no contradiction between them.[23] Thousands of religious Americans would have agreed with Carver's fundamental assumption while rejecting as unscientific any scientific inquiry that contradicted scripture. Few would have joined Carver in paraphrasing John 8:32 (as he frequently did) as follows: "And you shall know science and science shall set you free, because science is truth." Indeed, the great purpose of people was "to learn things" rather than to glorify God.[24]

These significant unorthodoxies add a shade of irony to the (increasingly conservative) evangelical community's continued veneration of Carver, the more so given the fact that while Carver's faith amplified his popularity, its basis in both science and religion led him to embrace beliefs that were anathema to the fundamentalists who rallied to his cause. Although he believed in the account of creation given in Genesis, he always explained it in such a way as "to show that there was no conflict between science and religion," using both the Bible and geology.[25] He spoke very highly of Darwin's *Origin of Species*, Asa Gray's *Darwiniana*, and evolution generally, although he doubtless agreed with Pammel's contention that evolution explained changes in life rather than its origins. As to the origin of life itself, Pammel maintained that "only God Almighty can answer that question."[26] In short, as Austin Curtis noted, Carver "used his scientific background to give real meaning to the Bible.... When we were talking about the creation of the earth ... [he] was not talking about the calendar as we know it, as what man has made of the 24 hour day." He "was talking in terms of geological years, and he would have fossil remains to display and show."[27]

Curtis' account is consistent with Carver's own. When in February 1907 Carver launched a Bible study group modeled after James Wilson's at the IAC, he began the study in Genesis and "attempted to explain the Creation story in the light of natural and revealed religion and geological truths. Maps, charts plants and geological specimens were used to illustrate the work."[28] Over the years he worked through substantial portions of the Bible, expositing passages in conventional (and sometimes less than conventional) ways. Although Carver encouraged his students to read the Bible twice daily, he also enjoined them "to be bigger than the pulpit," a term he had to clarify to at least one confused minister. "I want them to ... study the great Creator through the things he has created," Carver explained, "as I feel that he talks to us through these things." The "most significant sermons that It [*sic*] has ever been my privilege to learn has [*sic*] been embodied in just that."[29]

Henry A. Wallace observed in 1956 that "few men combined the scientific and religious world so fruitfully as Carver. He never knew where one left off and the other one began."[30] His was a faith in both science and religion; they overlapped in his mind.[31] Thus, while his faith obviously diverged from orthodox Christianity, it was probably true, as Wallace claimed, that "Carver derived more creative nourishment from the Bible than" most of his fellow scientists.[32] Indeed, Carver consistently maintained that "no true lover of Nature can 'behold the lilies of the field' or 'look unto the hills' or study even the microscopic wonders of a stagnant pool of water, and honestly declare himself to be an atheist or an infidel."[33] In fact, he contended, the way to come into "the closest relationship with the Maker and Pre-server of all things" was not via prayer or Bible study, but by studying "the little things in your own door yard, going from the known to the nearest related unknown, for indeed each new truth brings one nearer to God."[34] Easily the most distinctive aspect of Carver's Christianity was his conten-tion that the natural world offered as important a revelation of God as the Bible did. While this smacks of "natural theology," Carver did not limit his understanding of God to what he discerned by applying his reason to the natural world.[35] This veneration of both the Bible and the natural world was the salient characteristic of his faith and the foundation for a religion of nature that went well beyond conventional Christianity.

Carver's appreciation for the natural world invariably impressed those who met him. A reporter for the *Albany (Ga.) Institute News* asserted in 1915 that "no one can spend any time with Prof. Carver in a grove or woods without getting some conception of nature and nature's God."[36] Before Carver became the Peanut Man, journalists were probably more struck by his appreciation of nature than by anything else about him other than his race. In 1916 the *Afro-American's* Horace Slatter wrote about Carver's "abiding and deep love for nature." Indeed, "such a love of Nature as Mr. Carver possesses is not an acquired art." Few were capable of communing "with nature at all times and in all forms." A decade earlier, a writer from *Alexander's* magazine had noted Carver's remarkable ability to "see beauty in the rapidly decaying bark of a tree as well as in the rose so perfectly de-veloped by his own hand."[37]

This emphasis on Carver's appreciation of nature, however, was muted in the mythology that came to surround him as the Peanut Man; if it was not lost entirely, it became something of a trite afterthought—he possessed a "love of nature" not especially distinguishable from that, say, of the av-erage birdwatcher. Of course, those who had spent much time with him continued to emphasize the depths to which his identity was rooted in his appreciation of the natural world. Henry A. Wallace, for instance, noted in 1944, at the dedication of a portrait of Carver at the Smithsonian, that the "outstanding thing about Dr. Carver was his complete and utter sympathy for nature." But on balance, his reverence for nature was afforded only per-functory attention, at least when compared to his Christian faith.[38]

But for Carver, the two were of a piece. "To me," Carver wrote in a 1912 article, "Nature in its varied forms is the little windows through which God permits me to commune with Him, and to see much of His glory, by simply lifting the curtain and looking in." Searching for an appropriate analogy to convey that it was a two-way communication, not just a glimpse of God's glory as manifest in Creation, Carver added yet another analogy. "I love to think of Nature as wireless telegraphs stations though which God speaks to us every day, every hour, and every moment of our lives."[39]

In light of such a belief in the immanence of God in nature, it is hardly surprising that he rose each morning between four and five o'clock and went on a nature walk to commune with the Great Creator. He had begun such walks no later than his years as a student at Ames, and he continued the habit as long as his health permitted. When Rackham Holt was writing his authorized biography during the last years of Carver's life, for instance, he agreed to talk with her only if she joined him on his morning strolls.

Carver's belief in God's immanence in nature shaped his research as well as his religious beliefs. Gary Kremer pointed out that because Carver "believed that nothing existed without [a divinely appointed] purpose," it was his job as a scientist to discover that purpose "and publicize its possible benefits for mankind."[40] He conceived of his research as a dialectical process—a dialogue between him and the plant with which he was working. When he first worked with the peanut, he later told audiences, he began by asking, "Great Creator, what is a peanut? why did you make it?" His conviction that each plant or lump of clay or anything else in the natural world held some bit of metaphysical truth waiting to be uncovered marked his research from his first days at the experiment station through his last days as a figurehead of the chemurgy movement. When he was working with cotton in 1911, he could not help but come away with the impression that there was "no plant more interesting to the casual observer, or . . . more wonderful to the searcher for truth than the cotton plant."[41] He made similar claims about other plants as each revealed new truths about God to him.

This belief spilled over into his teaching. He wanted his students to "see the Great Creator in the smallest and apparently most insignificant things about them. How I long for each one to walk and talk with the Great Creator through the things he has created," he wrote a friend.[42] Assuring his students of "joy unspeakable when you can work and talk with God through the things He has created," he enjoined them: "Look about you. Take hold of the things that are here. Let them talk to you. You learn to talk to them."[43] He was fond of quoting the opening lines of William Cullen Bryant's poem "Thanatopsis" to his students: "To him who in the love of nature holds / Communion with her visible forms, she speaks / A varied language."[44] That language, he insisted, was the very language of God. Pointing to the fresh flower he always wore in the lapel of his coat, he would tell his students, "When you see this flower, you see thy creator."[45]

In Carver's experience, however, few could see God clearly enough in the "small" and "apparently insignificant" things they encountered daily in the natural world to have any sort of meaningful communion. Carver's closest friends tended to be those who shared his ability to see God in nature. "What would we do without those rare characters that make life really worthwhile," he wrote Lyman Ward in 1939, "those who are in touch with the Great Spirit and permit Him to speak to them through the things he has created?"[46] While on a trip out West on which he visited some of the nation's most awe-inspiring natural wonders, Ward wrote Carver to convey his wish that Carver had been able to join him. "The continual wearing away of the rock by the Colorado River is too wonderful for words," he scribbled to his friend. "I should have liked your comment." In reply, Carver expressed his gratitude that his friend could see God's hand in the natural processes that had resulted in "those marvelous manifestations of nature which the Great Creator has so marvelously opened your eyes to see."[47]

Another of Carver's friends reminded him: "Keep your ear near to Nature's heart and she will speak the deep things of God to you."[48] In writing to Jim Hardwick on an occasion when his friend was discouraged, Carver promised better spiritual things to come: "As soon as you begin to read the great and loving God out of all forms of existence he has created, both animate and inanimate, then you will be able to Converse with Him, anywhere, everywhere, and at all times."[49] The essence of Carver's faith was thus his conviction that closeness to God was impossible outside the context of nature. "We get closer to God as we get more and more intimately and understandingly acquainted with the things he has created," he maintained in 1930. "The singing birds, the buzzing bees, the opening flower, and the budding trees, along with other forms of animate and inanimate matter, all have their marvelous creation story to tell each searcher for truth."[50]

To be sure, Carver belonged to a long tradition of Christianity that has seen evidence of the beneficent hand of a creator in the natural world—a remarkably varied tradition that has included groups from Deists to Puritans and is especially pronounced in American history. Cotton Mather, for instance, who is better remembered for his association with the witchcraft scares of the late seventeenth century than for his interest in natural history, marveled at the fact that "every particular part of the plant has its astonishing uses," interpreting such orderliness in nature as prima facie evidence of a glorious God.[51] American naturalists throughout the eighteenth and nineteenth centuries (William Bartram, Charles Willson Peale, Alexander Wilson, and Louis Agassiz, to name some of the more prominent), reached similar conclusions, as did ministers, artists, politicians, essayists, poets, and writers of all stripes. Perhaps the most celebrated of these are the Romantic poets and painters and the Transcendentalists, who were awed by the sublimity of the natural world they encountered and who exerted a substantial influence in many circles in Carver's time. While the immanence of God in nature is hardly the only tradition in American Christianity (and may not even be the most important), it has a distinguished history quite apart from Carver. In fact, many of his peers in agricultural science—perhaps most notably Liberty Hyde Bailey, whose *Holy Earth* represents a classic joining of science and faith—saw God in natural processes and in the world around them.

Thus, in many regards Carver's religious appreciation of the natural world was fairly conventional and fit comfortably both within the context of his times and, to some degree at least, within orthodox Christianity. Writing a friend in 1927, for instance, Carver recounted a spectacular sunset he had witnessed. "It seems as if I have never been conscious of such beauty and sublimity." As the sky changed from "the marvelous rainbow colors to the soft, ethereal 'Rembrantian' browns and the midnight blues of Maxfield Parrish," he could only bring himself to say "aloud, O God, I thank you for such a direct manifestation of Thy goodness, majesty and power."[52] He might have received a hearty "Amen" from any number of quarters. For that matter, when Carver insisted that "a weed is a flower growing in the wrong place," he echoed Ralph Waldo Emerson's definition of a weed as "a plant whose virtues have not been discovered." And in seeing the divine in agricultural landscapes, Carver differed little from Henry David Thoreau, who was more comfortable in his bean field at Concord than in the wilds of Katahdin.[53]

But Carver also saw God where others often did not. Few of his peers looked for God's glory in the "strange and marvellous things in Fungi and other forms of plant life," which he believed "show the majesty and glory of God as ... nothing else does as they are all microscopic forms."[54] In dissolving a mineral specimen on one occasion, he "was reminded of His

[God's] omnipotence, majesty and power" when "a bunch of sea green crystals ... formed and alongside of them a bunch of snow white ones." So complete were God's "omnipotence, majesty and power" that they extended to a seemingly insignificant experiment in a laboratory. Carver did not need to be outdoors to be inspired by the beauty God had built into natural processes. Whether it be the Grand Canyon, a dooryard flower, a fungus visible only under a microscope, or the result of a laboratory experiment, the manifold wonders of nature enabled Carver to commune with God "everywhere, anywhere, and at all times."[55]

Carver's conception of nature exceeded that of his contemporaries in other ways as well. Replying to a question about his prayer life from a Kansas City minister in 1941, Carver confessed that his "prayers seem to be more of an attitude than anything else." His description of them pointed to the continued significance of the natural world in his life. "I ... ask the Great Creator silently daily, and often many times per day to permit me to speak to Him through the three great Kingdoms of the world [animal, mineral, and vegetable]." He asked God's guidance in understanding "their relations to each other, to us, our relations to them and the Great God who made all of us."

Few of his peers prayed for ecological understanding in the way Carver did. If Carver never referred to the entirety of the natural world as "all God's people" as John Muir did, he did place people within—rather than above—the natural world. Many of his contemporaries were struck by the degree to which he did so. The author of an article that appeared in *Chemurgic Digest* a year after his death, for example, recalled a lecture Carver had given in 1939. "What began as a lecture on botany soon developed into a soul-stirring recital of how immediately all of the plants are related to one another." But the author was most impressed by Carver's emphasis on "how the plants and the animals—mankind included—are inextricably interdependent, and of how the whole of Creation is related to its Creator."[56]

If people were part and parcel of the natural world, they were distinctive in that, like God, they could intelligently alter it. The Great Creator had "made man in the likeness of his image to be co-partner with him in creating ... beautiful and useful things." God had not "forgotten" to put a soul into flowers, he explained to a friend in a thank-you note for a gift of some dahlias, "he put it into us, and we expressed it in the development of just such beautiful flowers as you have sent me."[57] On another occasion he offered a friend an example of how those in close communion with the Great Creator could assist him in his work. Expressing his wish that his friend "could share with me the supreme expression of The Great Creator as he speaks to me so vividly through my beautiful Amaryllis . . . that are opening daily in my window in the little den I call my room," Carver pointed out that the flowers were his "own breeding" and demonstrated "what man (in the generic) can do when he allows God to speak through him."[58]

In some ways, this view of people as potential co-creators with God reflects the scientific hubris that shaped the most environmentally destructive century in the planet's history, but Carver was careful to qualify the power he ascribed to people in such a capacity. While the "Great Creator worked through man," enabling him to "produce roses [of] any color we like, any size we wish," people operated "within a certain limit. If we exceed the limit, we would have a monstrosity. God says, 'Thus far shall ye go, and no farther.'"[59] Not only did God circumscribe the limits within which men could alter his creation, he had bestowed on nature capabilities that people did not have. Speaking at a high school in 1937, Carver illustrated his lecture using "the English horse bean." The white bean produces a green shoot, which turns into a plant that produces "highly colored pink, red, etc." flowers, which generate green pods, which house "a pure white bean. Just where we started from," he concluded. "I would like to see some chemist do that."[60]

If anything, the centrality of the natural world grew more pronounced in Carver's worldview as he grew older.[61] When he was in his mid-to-late sixties, Carver recounted a walk across Tuskegee's campus during which "God seemed to burst forth in . . . a startling way. Everything I touched seemed to say, 'O God how wonderful are Thy works. In wisdom Thou hast made them all.'" He was marveling not at a spectacular sunset but at some decaying branches. Contemplating his own mortality, he explained that the "thing we call death in the plant is only a preparation for myriads of actual microscopic plants that could not have existed had those plants not given up their lives as we term it. How wonderful."[62]

By 1940 Carver's health was failing with increasing regularity, and he worried that the end was near. He asked Rackham Holt to hurry her writing so that she could finish his biography "before it had to close with something sordid," a thinly veiled allusion to his death.[63] As he sought to put his accomplishments in perspective—to lay out how he wanted others to interpret his life and significance—an almost mystical reverence for the natural world became evident. When in a 1942 interview about his artwork, for example, he was asked how he had accomplished so much, he responded, "All these years . . . I have been doing one thing. The poet Tennyson was working at the same job," he maintained, quoting one of the poet's mystical verses:

> Flower in the crannied wall,
> I pluck you out of the crannies.
> Hold you here root and all, in my hand.
> Little flower; but if I could understand,
> What you are, root and all, and all in all,
> I should know what man and God is.

Tennyson, Carver explained, "was seeking Truth," and that was what he too had been seeking not only as a scientist but also as an artist.[64]

In an address at a chapel during a visit to Henry Ford later that year, Carver reminded the audience not to be swept up in the day-to-day trivialities that consumed most of their lives. Those who would hear God "must be patient and wait, as were the old prophets. Isaiah and the old prophets always had their ears and eyes open. You know, Isaiah, listening, heard a voice." But in succumbing to the tyranny of the present, people heard "nothing but noise. It comes and goes and that's all of it, just noise. We can't think very well now because there are so many noises of different kinds."[65] The most effective way to combat that noise was to spend time communing with God in nature. "More and more as we come closer and closer in touch with nature and its teachings," he had contended more than a decade earlier, "are we able to see the Divine and correctly interpret the various languages spoken by all forms of nature around us."[66]

However much Carver's religious affinity for nature increased in his later years, his belief that God was immanent and accessible in it had always been an integral part of his thinking. Like Liberty Hyde Bailey, he believed that "man's abuse of the earth was not only economically unsound but morally wrong" because the natural world was God's handiwork and reflected his glory.[67] Thus, farmers were morally obligated to treat the earth kindly, even if doing so redounded to their short-term detriment, because "nature will drive away those who commit sins against it."[68] Obviously, such a belief lent an added significance to the methods Carver endorsed in his campaign on behalf of black farmers. Indeed, his faith confirmed ecology's central tenets, bolstered his conviction that nature produced no waste, and deepened his commitment to discovering new uses for neglected agricultural by-products. In short, it is impossible to comprehend Carver's environmental work apart from his religious reverence for the natural world.

CHAPTER 9

Where the Soil Is Wasted

As Carver's religious devotion to the natural world mounted in his last years, so too did his regret about abandoning the campaign he had initiated following his arrival at Tuskegee. He had come to the Deep South, after all, with the aim of lifting impoverished African American farmers from the slough of tenancy and sharecropping; it was his great purpose, a divinely appointed one. While celebrity had brought its rewards, it had distracted him from that purpose, and so in the twilight of his life he turned his eyes again to the impoverished black farmers of Macon County and the South. Consequently, when he was asked to display his peanut exhibit in 1938, he refused, noting that it was a "technical exhibit [of] no value except to interest the curious, and maybe a very few factory people." It did not "touch the rank and file."[1] His insistence two years later that all of his "operations as nearly as possible are kept within the reach of the individual farthest down" recalled his early efforts to better the lives of Macon County's farmers rather than his laboratory work as "the world's greatest chemist."[2]

Drawing links between land use and poverty, Carver looked around him in the late 1930s and observed, "Wherever the soil is wasted the people are wasted. A poor soil produces only a poor people—poor economically, poor spiritually and intellectually, poor physically."[3] Revisiting the injunctions of his initial campaign, he assured farmers in a 1936 bulletin that "the farmer with one horse, mule, or ox ... with practically no tools and a soil recognized as literally worn out" could and should rebuild his soil. All they need do was take advantage of the "many thousands of tons of the finest fertilizers going to waste all over the state, in the form of decaying leaves of the forest and the rich sediment of the swamp, known as 'muck.'"[4] Compost and green manuring, thorough preparation of the soil, a good garden, crop diversification, and eliminating waste promised to rescue farmers from the bleak conditions of the Depression Era South just as they had in the years prior to the Great War. His attempt to renew his campaign came too late, however, and amounted to too little.

Indeed, Carver's hope that poor black farmers who embraced his peculiar brand of scientific agriculture could become economically independent proved hollow well before he returned to his campaign. In her study of Tuskegee's extension service, Karen Ferguson contended that the unsuccessful efforts of Booker T. Washington and Tuskegee to create "an independent black yeomanry free from the racial and economic exploitation that defined southern agriculture" demonstrate "in vivid relief the perils of playing with the devil."[5] To the extent that Tuskegee's extension service had to win the blessing of white landowners, it was indeed "playing with the devil," but the failure was not complete, as Ferguson claimed.

Before celebrity distracted him from his campaign, Carver had reason for optimism. Encouraging letters came regularly. A former student wrote Carver that she had made "a wonderful success canning and preserving fruits and vegetables by the direction of your little buletine [sic] on such." In fact, "a large number" of people in her town had used her "buletine with the same success," and she hoped he could forward additional copies, along with "anything new you've gotten out to aid housekeepers."[6] Similar letters arrived at the offices of Tuskegee administrators. One to the institute's treasurer, Warren Logan, in 1904 reported that "Prof. Geo. W. Carver's talk here to the farmers, has caused a large percentage of them to try his plans."[7] And a World War I era report on Macon County's rural public schools observed that "school gardens [were] being conducted at most of these schools."[8]

Principally, however, the grounds for optimism came in the increase in homeownership among Macon County's African Americans. Between 1900 and 1910, the number of black farmers in the county who tilled their own soil more than tripled, rising from 157 to 507. Considering the fact that the county was home to roughly 22,000 African Americans, historians might dismiss the increase as inconsequential, but it should not be ignored. In 1900, only 5 percent of the farms operated by African Americans in Macon County were owned by the men who tilled them; by 1910 that number had risen above 13 percent. It was enough to encourage Washington, Carver, and others who believed salvation for African Americans lay principally in the realm of economic empowerment. By 1908, in fact, Washington saw "signs of a grand awakening among the masses of the Negro farming population."[9]

More factors were at work here than Carver's campaign. With the backing of northern philanthropists, for instance, Hampton and Tuskegee institutes jointly organized the Southern Improvement Company in 1901 with the purpose of selling "farms of twenty to eighty acres to blacks on easy terms."[10] That same year the company bought some 4,000 acres in northwestern Macon County, and by 1911 twenty-five families owned their farms outright and thirty more were paying off mortgages.[11]

On the eve of World War I the school launched a similar project, purchasing an additional 1,800 acres on the northwestern edge of the county under the auspices of the Tuskegee Farm and Improvement Company. Aware that his white supporters would frown on any plan intended to get land into the hands of African Americans, Washington "cautioned those who were assisting him" not to let the land's sellers get "an inkling of what we have in mind." The best the company could hope for should that happen was a higher price, and it was as likely that the landowners "might try to back out of their bargain to sell."[12] Together, the two land companies—along with a similar for-profit endeavor launched in 1912—accounted for seventy-eight black-owned farms. Only fifty or so, however, could have been counted in the 1910 census, leaving a still-impressive increase of three hundred black landowners.

In 1912 Washington wrote, "I ought, perhaps, to say that it was not until about ten years ago that Negroes began to buy land to any large extent in this part of the country." Citing the rise in landownership among African Americans in the county, he argued that "it would not be far from the truth to say that the Negro communities in Macon County have made more progress during the last five years than they did during the previous twenty-five." Washington credited the county's relatively good "colored public schools," which attracted "a more enterprising class of Negro farmers" to the county, for this improvement.[13] His assessment notwithstanding, it seems likely that Carver's campaign played a substantial role in the increase in the county's black yeomanry. To be sure, the increase in landownership prior to the First World War suggests that there was some room to climb the agricultural ladder, and offered legitimate grounds for hope.

But a number of factors combined to make the prewar years the high point for African American landownership in the county. To begin with, wartime conditions created an artificial surplus in the United States, causing cotton prices to plummet.[14] By the time prices recovered in 1916 and began a steady rise over the next three years, Macon County's black farmers were not in a position to benefit. In part this was because the government had encouraged cotton farmers to diversify their crops for patriotic reasons. Far more significant, however, was the fact that the high cotton prices—which extended, excepting a brief collapse in 1920, through 1926—coincided with the arrival of the boll weevil.

Historian James Giesen and others have pointed out that the boll weevil's influence in southern agriculture is often overstated. The weevil's effect in any given place was limited in duration. When the insect entered a particular area, it temporarily upset agricultural practices, but farmers adapted relatively quickly and returned their emphasis to cotton culture accordingly. In Alabama, the toughest years were between 1915 and 1923, when the cotton yield dropped by about 27 percent. By the mid-1920s farmers had "learned to cope with the plague."[15] Thus, while in 1912 Alabama had put 3,730,000 acres in cotton, by 1917 the state's cotton acreage had fallen to 1,977,000 acres.[16]

It was Macon County's bad luck that the weevil's arrival coincided with the high cotton prices of World War I and the early 1920s. Credit, be it for food at the grocery or a mortgage for land, was difficult to secure despite the high cotton prices because lenders were unwilling to advance funds to farmers who did not know "how to raise cotton under the boll weevil conditions." As merchants and landlords advanced less money to tenants, opportunities to purchase land decreased as well.[17]

Macon County's farmers had been in unusually dire straits even before the boll weevil appeared. When the cotton price collapsed in 1914, landowners in Alabama's Black Belt had no recourse but to release their tenants. A Department of Labor bulletin noted that in the absence of the "customary advances of provisions to Negro tenants," the USDA and the Red Cross had to distribute food "to the starving negroes."[18] "During this past year," Booker T. Washington wrote in May 1915, "this part of the South . . . has been passing through one of the most trying and difficult experiences it has been called upon to pass through since the Civil War."[19]

The economic turmoil of the period narrowed the already thin margin between success and failure for African American yeomen. A former student teaching in Notasulga wrote Carver in September 1917 requesting a loan "to redeem my home which was sold under a mortgage sale yester[day]. It grieves my wife's soul almost out of her," he pleaded. Few of the county's black residents had friends like Carver to whom they could turn. "The economic condition in Macon County is so upset," Bridgeforth reported in 1916, "that I feel the school should send out a special committee to study" the problems in order to make recommendations that might alleviate some of the suffering. In 1916 Tuskegee's extension service began issuing "certificates of merit" to successful farmers as a means of encouraging them. But as farmers were graded not only on their hard work but on criteria such as their "character as a husband and father," the certificates undoubtedly fostered as much resentment as encouragement.[20] In the event, the school provided almost no material help.

Moreover, the war had created a labor shortage in American industry just as the demand for American manufactures rose. The "unusual state of unrest" created by "the extraordinary wage inducements in the North and West," along with the "coming of the boll weevil," Carver wrote an acquaintance in 1922, "meant, of course, migration in large numbers."[21] Though many African Americans left the southern countryside for southern cities, many more left the region altogether. Between 1910 and 1920 the black population of Chicago increased from 44,103 to 109,458. New York and Philadelphia saw comparable growth, but the migration altered the demographics most sharply in smaller midwestern industrial cities. Cleveland's black population rose from 8,448 to 34,451, and Detroit's rose from 5,741 to 40,838.[22]

Many in Macon County joined the exodus, much to the consternation of the institute and whites in the region. Like Washington, most of the Tuskegee faculty believed that the best hope for African Americans over the long term lay in agriculture. Speakers at the Tuskegee Negro Conference held in January 1917 thus looked for ways to check the migration, assuring blacks that only empty promises awaited them in the North. The rising racial tensions sparked by the migration—tensions that resulted in even more restrictive racial policies in the region—added urgency to their pleas. It was this further restriction of African Americans' civil liberties that the speakers were alluding to when they suggested that the "chief cause of unrest among colored people . . . is a lack of adequate protection under the law."[23] Their pleas had little effect in either the white or black community. The following year, in fact, Macon County whites attempted to institute pass laws.[24] Such tactics gave added impetus to those African Americans inclined to leave, and by 1920 the number of black residents in Macon County had declined nearly 9 percent.[25]

It was not until 1925 that Thomas Campbell could note that the "migration to the North has perceptibly slackened."[26] By that time only 277 African Americans were tilling their own land in the county. If the additional 61 black farmers who held mortgages on their land are included, that number rises to 338 black farm owners total—a marked decline from the better than 500 Washington had boasted of in 1912.[27] Indeed, the last of the more than 50 black holdings of the Southern Improvement Company had been sold in 1919.[28] Whether the 1914 price collapse and the boll weevil had forced the black yeomen to forfeit their land and step down a rung on the proverbial agricultural ladder or they had moved out of the county to cities in the North or elsewhere in the South, the decline was real.

Larger economic factors also played a role in subverting the well-being of black tenants in the old Cotton Belt. While Alabama's cotton farmers were adjusting to the boll weevil in the late 1910s and early 1920s, cotton production on the southern plains and in the Southwest, especially in Texas and Oklahoma, exploded. Texas, which had become the largest cotton-producing state in the nation prior to World War I, nearly doubled its cotton production, putting more than 7 million additional acres in the crop between 1919 and 1926. Oklahoma added almost 2 million acres. By 1930, 70 percent of all Texas farms and 42 percent of Oklahoma's farms were drawing at least 40 percent of their income from cotton. Better capitalized than their counterparts in the South, Oklahoma and Texas farmers mechanized their farms, making production more efficient and thus cheaper, in essence enabling them to outcompete cotton producers in the Deep South.[29]

Texas and Oklahoma were not the only cotton-producing regions with which the South found itself competing. By the 1930s some fifty nations were exporting cotton. Cotton production had boomed in India, Egypt, Brazil, Australia, Japan, China, Russia, and European colonial holdings in Africa in the postwar years. Farmers in the old Cotton Belt also faced increased competition from new textiles. American factories had first produced rayon in 1910, and by the mid-1920s American manufacturers were using some 40 million pounds of the fabric each year.[30] Collectively, those economic factors made the already difficult climb up the agricultural ladder even harder.

In the mid-1920s, 88 percent of Macon County's black farmers were tenants; thus, black homeownership had decreased since 1910 in both numbers and percentage. Conditions improved marginally in the late 1920s, and black homeownership increased accordingly. By 1930, 407 African Americans owned their farms outright and another 66 were partial owners, leaving roughly 85 percent of black farmers working as tenants of one sort or another. The Great Depression predictably diminished landownership again. In 1935 only 371 African Americans worked their own soil in the county while 86 more clung to the tenuous hope that they could keep up with their mortgage payments—this despite the fact that 41 more black families lived in the county than in 1930. If mortgage holders are included, there were 457 black-owned farms in Macon County when Carver returned to his campaign in the mid-1930s, 50 fewer than there had been in 1910.[31]

When sociologist Charles S. Johnson came to Macon County in the early 1930s, virtually all of the 61 black landowners he encountered had purchased their land prior to 1914—but even these owners found "ownership almost as onerous as tenantry."[32] Few of the tenants "had cleared cash incomes since 1921, and many had made nothing since the World War." In 1932, for instance, nearly 90 percent of the tenants either broke even or went further in debt. The total income of the 10 percent who made a profit "ranged from about $70 to $90."[33]

Of the 612 Macon County families Johnson interviewed, only 237 owned work animals, though many did keep small gardens.[34] Often ill tended, these gardens were next to dwellings that differed little from the shanties Carver had first encountered in 1896. If anything, the buildings were even more "worn and sagging."[35] More than half of the families lived in dilapidated one- or two-room cabins. When Johnson asked the wife of a tenant farmer whether her roof leaked, she quipped, "No, it don't leak in here; it jest rains in here and leak outdoors; dis ain't no house; it jest a piece of a house."[36] But if the residents hung onto their sense of humor, their hardships were nonetheless real.

Predictably, Johnson encountered evidence of the black exodus to the North. The county had lost 242 farms between 1920 and 1930, only 7 of which had been run by whites. In the families he surveyed Johnson found a "deficiency of males," especially "among those between the ages of fifteen and forty"—able-bodied men, in short, who could seek wage labor elsewhere.[37] Even more telling was the fact that of the 98 boys he interviewed, only 6 wanted to pursue a career in farming. He judged by their remarks that they ranked farming "below even domestic service and unskilled labor."[38] Likewise, only 3 of 146 girls wanted to stay on a farm; the rest wanted to marry someone who was "going somewhere." Reports of a relaxed racial etiquette from peers who had been to Chicago and other cities in the North reinforced the hope that "going somewhere" was possible.[39]

Johnson's conclusions reflected Carver's experience. Writing to a father concerned about his sons who "seem to dislike farm work and want to go to town to work," Carver advised the man to ask his sons forthrightly "what it [was] that attracted [them] to town." If it was "wholesome," the man should "try to supply it at home," be it "books, better clothes, a little more money, music, not quite so much drudgery."[40] What the farmer could not supply to his sons—and what Carver could not manufacture, despite his many fine suggestions—was a consistently legitimate opportunity for black farmers to advance from tenants to yeomen.

On the whole, it is clear that Carver's efforts met with little success among the poorest black farmers—the sharecroppers and tenants—whose dependence on landlords and other creditors was essentially unaltered by his crusade. As Campbell noted in his account of Tuskegee's extension service in 1936, most African American farmers "throughout the Black Belt of Alabama and [in] other Southern States" continued to live in "squalid, ramshackled cabins," struggling "year after year in cotton fields . . . trying to eke out a miserable existence."[41]

This raises an obvious question: If Carver's advice was environmentally sound, and if it was practical inasmuch as it required few resources beyond a willingness to avail oneself of the abundance the Great Creator so lavishly bestowed in nature, why did his campaign meet with such meager success? Neither the economic tumult that attended World War I and the arrival of the boll weevil nor the shift in Carver's energies that came with his growing celebrity offers an adequate explanation for his campaign's failure. Indeed, had those been the only obstacles, the outcome might have been very different. But the chief obstacles Carver faced in his efforts to restore the vitality of southern soils and help the region's black farmers gain economic independence were deeply rooted in the social, political, and economic structures on which southern agriculture (and society) rested.

Taking Carver's call for crop diversification as an example, the correctness of his assertion that "thoughtful farmers are aware that any one crop system is disastrous to the average farmer and those who are living independently and happily on the farm are those who diversify their crops, or in other words raise some cotton, corn, peas, peanuts, hay, potatoes, sugar cane, [and] garden vegetables" proved immaterial in light of the fact that tenant farmers in general and sharecroppers in particular were obliged to plant what their creditors wanted them to plant.[42] Landlords allowed tenants to diversify only in years when the cotton market was particularly depressed. In good years for the market, landlords expected their tenants to plant cotton as widely as possible.

Added to the farmers' lack of independence were ecological constraints on diversification. Most of the subsistence crops a farmer might grow had to be cultivated in the spring and summer, when farmers were putting almost all of their effort into the cotton crop.[43] Thus, though diversification was not impossible, farmers found it very difficult to grow other crops even when landlords allowed it. Indeed, one of the reasons why Carver began researching peanuts was because they could be harvested in late July, after the cotton had been laid by, and if replanted immediately could produce a second crop after the bulk of the cotton was in.

Certainly, Carver and Tuskegee's subsequent agricultural emissaries were aware that tenants were obligated to plant what their landlords required. In 1916, in fact, the Tuskegee Negro Conference adopted a resolution "respectfully [requesting] of the planters to urge upon Negro tenants to grow crops other than cotton, to have gardens, . . . and to raise their food supplies at home."[44] And in 1912 Washington publicized the names of some "good" landlords who were amenable to Tuskegee's program.[45] Carver acknowledged the issue outright in one experiment station bulletin, noting that the "renter and those who must be advanced have a much more complex problem to solve. They must cooperate with the landlord, and get him to assist in providing ways and means by which they [Carver's suggestions] can be carried out."[46] The "respectful requests" of Tuskegee's extension agents notwithstanding, that assistance was seldom forthcoming. White landlords were interested primarily in improving the value of their property and recovering their investments from their tenants. Aiding the black farmers who worked their land was at the bottom of their list of priorities. Ned Cobb, a black farmer from neighboring Tallapoosa County, pointed out, "It wasn't that I was ignorant of what I had to do," but "you had to do what the white man said, livin here in this country. And if you made enough to pay him, that was all he cared for."[47]

Similarly, although it made sense to raise livestock of various sorts, most sharecroppers were not in a position to lay out the initial payment for a well-bred animal. Tuskegee loaned its stud animals to local farmers for breeding purposes, but many African Americans did not own any animals to which they could be bred.[48] Getting a loan for such an animal could be difficult. Securing credit in the South—as in the rest of the nation—was still a local proposition during the Progressive Era, and thus to a large extent was controlled by local politics. Black tenants appealing to white landlords and merchants had to show the proper deference. Since any attempt to become independent of their landlords could be interpreted by their creditors as an effort to transcend "their place," pursuing the means to financial independence could jeopardize credit, and thus make acquiring loans more difficult.[49]

Even when loans could be secured, a crop-lien system in which farmers might pay anywhere from 20 to 100 percent interest on supplies they purchased on credit all but eliminated the possibility of profit for most tenants. Indeed, Alabama's cooperative extension director, P. O. Davis, blamed the state's "iniquitous credit system," for the fact that Alabamians' average incomes were half those of the United States as a whole. African American farmers made only a shade more than half the state average.[50] Davis' lament notwithstanding, the fact that it was "the prevailing [custom]," as Charles Johnson observed, allowed "the merchant or planter [to] exact exorbitant charges without feeling that any injustice [was] being done to the tenant."[51] Pleas for better renting conditions generally fell on deaf ears.[52]

Moreover, 25 percent of Macon County's African American men were illiterate in the 1930s and another 50 percent had fewer than five years of elementary education, and this widespread illiteracy left African Americans open to exploitation in a legal system that relied on written contracts.[53] Cobb's father, for instance, got permission to sell one of his cows, which were under lien, and after selling it gave the money to his landlord in payment of a debt. The landlord, however, "turned around and sued my daddy for sellin mortgaged property." "If my daddy'd had the release in writin," Cobb continued, "maybe he couldn't have been messed up that way." Likewise, one of Cobb's creditors tried to trick him into signing a contract that would have placed a lien not only on the land he was attempting to buy, but also on his mules, cows, hogs, and wagon, which Cobb owned outright.

Only the fact that his wife could read enabled him to escape the trap. "If I'd a signed it," Cobb observed, "I could have lost it all. Just be late payin on the land and they would take everything."[54]

Literacy and homeownership were correlated throughout the Cotton Belt, but even literacy could not protect tenants from corrupt landlords.[55] Given the nature of the cotton economy in the 1930s, even tenants with honest landlords could wind up in debt at the year's end. As the landlord controlled all of the records, however, the tenant had no choice but to take his landlord at his word, honest or not. Failing to accept what the landlord told him about the status of his account might prove counterproductive because it could make him a "credit risk" and jeopardize his family's well-being. "I have notice [sic] in the greater proportion of the cotton states," a man wrote Carver in 1918, that "my race is over scharge [charged] and Their Earnings is taking from them their home. Been no help for it. in minnie [many] part of the country have notice The White is trying to hinder my Race."[56]

Without question the situation provided ample opportunity for cheating and corruption. There was no check on landlords, because they controlled the legal mechanisms that might otherwise have protected the tenants.[57] In fact, tenants often did not know the value of the goods with which they were furnished or the interest rate they were being charged. It made little difference. As one Macon County tenant complained to Johnson, "I don't know 'zactly how much it was he [his former landlord] got for the cotton; but he tole me he got ten, seven, eight, nine cents for some of it." Of course, he continued, "you couldn't do a thing but take his word for it."[58]

The more the tenant depended on advances, the greater the opportunity for exploitation. Sharecroppers thus occupied the most tenuous position in the region, but landlords and merchants could take advantage of cash renters as well. One Macon County tenant, for instance, agreed to pay $100 in rent for a farm on which he and his family raised "4 bales of cotton, 100 bushels of corn, 23 gallons of syrup, 300 pounds of pork, 25 bushels of potatoes." At the end of the season, however, their landlord "closed them out," a term tenants used when their creditors took everything they owned. In this instance the landlord took their mule, wagon, corn, and cotton before informing them that they still owed $53. When they asked for an itemized bill, the landlord responded by increasing their bill to $308.98. This left them with no recourse but to move. "If you move to a place and find out you at the wrong place," another Macon County tenant told Johnson, "the best thing to do is move, isn't it?"[59]

Similar stories abound. Taking the advice of Tuskegee's black extension agents, a family of renters bought two mules, a wagon, and two plows. Using their increased horsepower and new implements, they raised ten bales of cotton, all of which their landlord took, and then presented them with a bill for $623.25. When they could not pay, she took the wagon, the mules, all the hay they had cut, and thirty-seven bushels of corn to boot. Again, there was nothing to do but move on to another, hopefully better, landlord.[60]

Yet another tenant told Johnson that he had "tried keeping books one year," but his landlord "kept worrying me about it, saying his books was the ones he went by anyhow. . . . They got you," he continued, on two counts. First, "you have to carry your cotton to his mill to gin and you better not carry your cotton nowhere else." Second, disputing a landlord's records risked both future credit and immediate violent repercussions. "When the book says so and so you better pay it, too," the man explained, "or they will say, 'So, I'm a liar, eh?' You better take to the bushes too if you dispute him, for he will string you up for that."[61] While Carver recognized that the political and economic systems of the South rendered black tenants vulnerable at every turn, he could find no effective way to address the problems they faced and so could only encourage them to appeal to their landlords for cooperation.

The white power structure initially greeted the message of Carver and Tuskegee's extension agents with suspicion. Writing in the 1930s, Campbell acknowledged that "white landowners and others at first questioned the advisability of having Negro agriculturists come, especially among their tenants, lest something be done to disturb the established plantation relationship."[62] When Thomas Campbell took over the Jesup Wagon, he recalled that "a certain leading White man, merchant and planter" tried to turn him away, telling him, "I don't need you, the U.S. government nor anybody else to tell me how to handle my 'niggers.'" At least on one level, such fears were justified. Karen Ferguson pointed out that any effort "to create an independent yeomanry through landownership and self-sufficiency in a region where white prosperity depended on cotton monoculture and the subjugation of black labor" was decidedly subversive.[63]

In order to spread its message, however, the institute needed the support of both white philanthropists and local planters. Ultimately, this meant that

Carver, Washington, and the institute's extension agents had to at least publicly align themselves with the interests of Tuskegee's white supporters and appeal to the planters' self-professed beneficent paternalism. The reputations of Washington and Tuskegee aided the institute's extension agents in this effort. Even so, support for "Negro Demonstration work" came slowly, really gathering momentum only at the onset of World War I, which coincided with the demise of Carver's influence over the institute's extension programs. Admonitions to tenant farmers to "farm for your landlord just as though the farm belonged to you" ingratiated Tuskegee's agents with the white community, but as Campbell pointed out, led blacks to wonder "if we [the agents] were not paid by the white people to encourage Negroes to do more work for White people."[64] Predictably, the support of whites diminished the agents' credibility among black tenant farmers.

Tenant farmers found it difficult to take seriously the resolutions of a farmers' conference that included an expression of their collective appreciation for "the spirit of friendliness and fairness shown us by the southern-white people in matters of business and in all lines of material development."[65] Indeed, Clinton J. Galloway of Tuskegee's agricultural department aptly noted that "in many places in this neighborhood and county" there existed "a feeling which [was] not friendly to [the] Institution." If it is not certain that Carver himself encountered resistance from the farmers he visited in his first decade at Tuskegee, the institute's extension agents clearly did when they began bringing his ideas to the poor farmers of the county after 1906. Campbell recalled that "the masses of Negroes themselves were none too receptive" to the message carried out from the school.[66] Understandable as the black farmers' suspicion may have been, given the circumstances, it blunted a potentially liberating message.

Even if tenant farmers had proven less suspicious and Tuskegee's agents more true to his suggestions, however, Carver's campaign would have faced substantial hurdles. Theodore Rosengarten pointed out that within black communities of the Deep South, "one could be guilty ... of excessive zeal in the pursuit of the good life and excessive pride in attaining it. Righteousness consisted in not having so much that it hurt to lose it. This notion," he continued, "appears to cater to landlords, merchants, bankers, and furnishing agents by discouraging resistance or ambition on the part of their farmer debtors. But people who lived by it achieved a measure of autonomy."[67] Campbell alluded to this attitude when he acknowledged that the "Negro renter ... is not quickly influenced by the progress which his

Negro land-owning neighbor, living in much better circumstances, is making."[68] Johnson's research in the 1930s confirmed that point. Members of a black family that owned 129 acres it had purchased in 1904 confessed to him that they "had few friends in the community" in which they lived.[69]

Campbell and Johnson were hardly the only contemporary black southerners to recognize this phenomenon. In his classic autobiographical novel, *Black Boy*, Richard Wright described his father as "a creature of the earth" for whom "joy was as unknown . . . as . . . despair," and who "endured, hearty, whole, seemingly indestructible, with no regrets and no hope." And in Macon County, Janey Leonard, who boasted of cooperating with Tuskegee's agents, found herself estranged from her husband, who resented Janey's ambition. Looking back on their divorce, Janey recalled, "When the deacons asked my husband why we parted, he said, 'She's too damned high-minded. She wants too much.'"[70]

There was good reason for this "lay low" attitude. As Rupert Vance pointed out in 1929, a "tenure of twenty years [gave] the renter no more right to remain than a tenure of twenty days."[71] Worse, "to incorporate permanent improvement in land or buildings would . . . be presenting a free gift to the landlord."[72] Johnson was as adamant in condemning the system as Vance. "As matters now stand, the tenant who really works on his place, who labors to restore the soil, who repairs and builds, is merely inviting his landlord to raise his rent." Indeed, if a tenant were to "use all his time and energy in improving the place," he would still "have no recourse if his landlord demanded a higher rent or notified him that he would have to leave the next year." It was no wonder, Johnson insisted, "that the soil is exhausted, buildings not fit for habitation, and the tenants themselves thoroughly inured to habits and attitudes that . . . will keep them impoverished."[73]

In asserting as much, he concurred with the assessment W. E. B. DuBois had made in 1903 that "there are few incentives to make the laborer a better farmer," or, for that matter, for a black farmer to take "unusual pains" to improve the fields of his white landowner. "If [a tenant] is ambitious he moves to town or tries other labor; as a tenant-farmer his outlook is almost hopeless."[74] For their part, Macon County whites saw the indifference of blacks as a sign of "shiftlessness." Scholars studying the region found that whites would often bring up anecdotes "of ludicrous spending" whenever a black tenant got "his hands on money," using such stories "to justify the regular condition of poverty."[75]

For that matter, success, or even its pursuit, could breed jealousy and resentment not only within the African American communities of Alabama's Black Belt but among whites as well. One African American farmer in Macon County had scarcely finished paying off the mortgage on his farm when a white man discovered that he was chopping wood "too close" to his property line. Though the black farmer had not left his farm to cut the wood, the white man advised him to sell the wood and bring the money to a bank in Tuskegee, presumably to be confiscated. Before the farmer could do so, however, his white neighbor showed up with the sheriff, who arrested the farmer for "cutting timber closer to the line without a permit." A judge set his bond at an unreasonable $2,000. "I could stand $1,000," the farmer told Johnson. The man was held in jail for two months, and soon the sheriff began arresting his relatives. The farmer convinced the judge to release his family members but was himself sentenced to ninety additional days of hard labor. Before he had finished his sentence, members of the white community had forced his family off their land and confiscated their cotton. With the county's law enforcement mechanisms and courts against him, there was little he could do but move.[76]

George Bridgeforth had encountered a similar situation in the summer of 1906 when he was making his rounds of Macon County in the Jesup Wagon. "The people on the road to Real Town own but little land," he noted in his report for the week of July 2–9. "It seems many have bought lands in there and have lost them in some mysterious way."[77] In light of such a possibility, it is not surprising that many African American farmers took a fatalistic approach. "I'd be glad if I could git me a comfortable home," one sharecropper informed Johnson, "but folks won't let you have nothing less you mortgage it and when you git it all fixed up they come in and take it."[78] Another tenant confided matter-of-factly, "I ain't got nothin' 'gainst white people, but they won't give Negroes a chance. We ... ought to have a equal chance, but we can't get it here."[79]

In sparking white jealousy and resentment, of course, black success could also raise the specter of white violence. The Ku Klux Klan's march across Tuskegee's campus in 1923 offers testimony enough to that end. In neighboring counties, racial violence was even more pronounced. Ned Cobb recounted the sad tale of a neighbor who raised enough cotton to pay off his debts with plenty left over. The man's landlord had him assaulted and stole his cotton as he was bringing his crop into town to sell. "Beat him up," Cobb recalled. "Poor fellow got out of there after they left enough life in him to leave. Some of em said they cut his secrets off." Cobb poignantly added, "That's the way colored people met their lives in this country, livin on a white person's place."[80]

Such conditions offered little motivation for tenant farmers to embrace the suggestions of either Carver or Tuskegee's extension agents, especially when these involved a good bit of sacrifice. In a 1902 leaflet titled *Buying Homes among the Farmers*, Clinton J. Calloway described what a farmer needed to do to become a landowner. "This means harder work, no . . . showy things of any kind. . . . It will mean for your wife to stay at home and raise chickens, eggs and vegetables." Slipping in an appeal for middle-class morality, Calloway contended that it would also "mean for all to leave off buying tobacco, snuff, whiskey and coffee." Instead, they could "drink the milk and sweeten the hot water with syrup." Tenants would need to raise everything they ate, but should not eat everything they raised. They would "have to do without buying a buggy for a while" and could not "go on excursions" or "to circus shows or ride on 'flying jennies.'" In short, he concluded, "It simply means that every extra cent must go into the FARM."[81] The years of sacrifice and hard labor Calloway's suggestions entailed hardly seemed worthwhile when jealous white neighbors could force them off their property at any time.

To be sure, other factors were at play in the seeming indifference of Macon County's black community. "Respectability," for instance, was not tied to landownership in Macon County as it was in, say, the Midwest, but was found in things such as church membership, "the fact that no one of the family has been in jail," and in adherence to community values.[82] The last of these undermined Carver's campaign inasmuch as communities insisted on "traditional" values and practices regardless of what science said about the matter. The wife of a well-to-do landowner, for example, confessed to Johnson that she felt compelled "to continue using a midwife rather than get talked about" despite the fact that she was "convinced that she lost her last baby through the ignorance and carelessness of the midwife."[83] It is difficult to say which, if any, of Carver's suggestions might have violated such traditions. It is clear, however, that Carver did his best to discourage folk farming methods, arguing that while in "its day the moon idea served a good purpose," it no longer had any value as a planting guide; if farmers fed "the plant right . . . the moon [would] behave."[84] A farmer who spent his days collecting swamp muck might well have risked his family's standing in the community.

And to these obstacles even more might be added. Hunting, for instance, which might add protein to tenant farmers' diets, was increasingly regulated during the early twentieth century. In 1907 Alabama enacted legislation (primarily as a conservation measure) requiring hunters to carry permits. As the white community did not relish the prospect of a heavily armed black population, African Americans were often discouraged from getting such permits. Thus, when Johnson surveyed Macon County in the 1930s, he talked to one tenant who confided, "I had 'chicken' for supper today. I have to call it 'chicken' 'cause it's 'g'inst the law to hunt rabbits now."[85]

Even these combined obstacles rooted in the structure of southern society and agriculture—most of which related to racial rather than economic practices, though disentangling the two is difficult—might not offer a sufficient explanation for the limited success of Carver's campaign. After all, its failure prompts a second question, more difficult to answer but no less relevant in light of rise of ecological agriculture: To what extent was Carver's campaign practical?

Carver's colleagues at Tuskegee certainly had their misgivings about the practical benefits of his agricultural policies. In the midst of a heated exchange in 1912 revolving around the sort of work that ought to be done at the experiment station, Booker T. Washington offered a frank assessment of Carver's strengths and weaknesses. Although he acknowledged Carver's abilities as a teacher and conceded that Carver had "great ability in original research in making experiments with the soil and . . . on untried plants," Carver's "organizational and administrative skills were lacking." Most significant, Carver was "wanting again in ability" when it came "to the matter of practical farm managing which will secure definite, practical, financial results."[86]

Indeed, few of his peers among the institute's faculty thought Carver's research practical.[87] John Washington, for instance, criticized Carver's work with clays, claiming that it was "easy to get up a few samples of things which can never be made practical," by which he meant "industrially marketable." (Marketability, after all, reveals the degree to which people find something useful or desirable.) Defending himself, Carver pointed out that marketability had not been his aim; he had been trying to find ways for farmers to beautify their homes "easily, effectively, and inexpensively."[88]

No one captured the prevalent impression across the campus that Carver was a fine, but impractical, scientist better than Monroe N. Work, a prominent Tuskegee sociologist and administrator who had come to the school in

1908. In a review of two 1943 biographies of Carver, Work contended that "Washington was highly critical of Carver's impracticability. He insisted that Carver raise chickens, hogs, produce crops; in other words furnish results." In his own experience, Work continued, "Carver . . . was unable to produce all the results demanded of him," and, alluding to the fallout from the conflict over the institution's poultry house, noted that Carver was stripped of his position as overseer of practical farming accordingly.[89]

To be sure, Carver's suggestions often raised more eyebrows than cheers at Tuskegee. The farming methods that would enable tenant farmers to reduce their furnishing were not necessarily the same ones that brought the highest returns in the short term. The "application of inferior ready mixed commercial fertilizers" might not increase the fertility the soil, but it did improve the yield of a particular year's crop.[90] Building up soil was a protracted process, but at Tuskegee, both before and after Washington's passing, there was a great deal of pressure to produce tangible results quickly.

Carver's evolving environmental thinking contributed in myriad ways to his incessant conflicts with the institute's council. Even early on, Carver inadvertently cultivated an image as an impractical eccentric. One colleague accused Carver of "going crazy" when he published his first bulletin, which extolled the virtues of acorns as hog feed.[91] And as his vision grew more distinctive, he found himself as out of step with his colleagues at Tuskegee as he did with the main currents of early twentieth-century agronomy. At times, his suggestions proved too much for Tuskegee's administration to humor, as was the case with a bulletin on the birds of Macon County that Tuskegee never sent to press.

If Americans bothered to "seek the cause" of the rising threat insects posed to farmers, Carver maintained, "every farmer and citizen [would] unite in one grand effort, not only to save, but to protect the birds, the greatest insect destroyers known."[92] Carver was hardly alone in supporting this cause. In their textbook *Elementary Principles of Agriculture* (1908), Alexander Ferguson and Lowery Lewis warned that "Beneficial Birds Should not be Killed for food, neither for sport, nor for decoration for hats," and included a list of twenty-one such birds and their food. Similarly, Emmett S. Goff and D. D. Mayne complained in their agricultural textbook that "birds living on insects have greatly decreased in number in the past few years."[93]

The effort to protect songbirds was an early success of the nascent conservation movement, and Carver linked his rationale to those efforts.

"Again we must remember," he noted, "that the woodman's axe and the forest fires have robbed thousands of our feathered songsters of their homes and haunts." Together with the "pernicious peanut-shooter in the hands of the [small] boy, and the more deadly Winchester upon the shoulder of his older brother," this habitat loss had led to an alarming decline in many bird populations. Had the bulletin stopped there, it might well have seen daylight, but Carver spent well over thirty pages laying out detailed descriptions of eighty birds and assessing the economic value of each.[94]

Probably most at issue here was Carver's rather expansive definition of "economic value," which included the "bright plumage and soft, sweet song" of the American goldfinch because it added "much brightness and good cheer to the surroundings." The cardinal ate "weed-seeds" and insects but was more notable "as a great songster." Carver felt "sure that no one can listen to their sweet song or look upon a group of them flitting hither and thither among the rich, dark-green foliage of the pine, cedar, and magnolia without forgetting everything else except their supreme beauty." Unusual "economic" justifications to be sure, the more so considering the era in which he wrote them.[95]

Science and economics were distinctly masculine realms at the time; beauty, as Adam Rome and others have pointed out, was "traditionally the province of women." Consequently, most conservation-minded men argued for reform on purely economic grounds. Opposition to "progress" based on aesthetics was suitable only for middle-class women who were supported by their husbands; they were not the ones who encountered the economic realities of the business world—or so went the logic. Men who embraced reform, especially environmental reform, for noneconomic reasons risked the derision of a society that saw them as "sentimental," and thus effeminate. The American Forestry Association, for instance, initially welcomed women but by 1910 was backpedaling because the women's calls for preservation undermined its pleas for "practical forestry"—which is to say, a forestry organized around more tangible economic concerns.[96]

Carver's seemingly effortless navigation between traditional gender roles doubtless also contributed to the perception across Tuskegee that he was a talented but impractical scientist. On the one hand, science was a decidedly masculine profession at the time; on the other hand, his high voice, fancy work, prowess in the kitchen, and unabashed appreciation of the beauties of nature were categorically feminine. This ability to navigate between gender roles aided his campaign to improve the lives of poor farmers immeasurably because he could assume a role that women later would take up as "home demonstration agents" as well as that of a more traditional agricultural scientist; but it contributed to the perception that he was an impractical eccentric.[97] Some at the school, in fact, considered him effeminate and made him feel the need to defend his masculinity. Tendering his resignation in the wake of his conflicts with Washington and the council over the poultry house, he insisted, was "the only manly thing to do."[98]

Thus, it is hardly surprising that Carver's suggestions alternately confounded and amused his colleagues. There is no record indicating that Carver approached Washington to solicit his support in 1900 when he asked James Wilson for the USDA's backing for a plan to cultivate a small breeding herd of white-tailed deer with the aim of reintroducing the animals as an alternative food source for impoverished black farmers. (Wilson could offer no financial support, though he thought the plan had some genuine promise and recommended that Carver ask Washington to persuade northern patrons "to send down a little herd.")[99] If Carver did approach Washington on this score, it died in the principal's office and at most was quietly joked about behind Carver's back. But many of Carver's other suggestions—diminishing the institute's reliance on commercial fertilizer, using acorns as a feed for the school's livestock, turning the "fine soot . . . from our boilers" into paint—along with the sort of "sentimental" esteem for the natural world evident in his unpublished bulletin on Macon County's birds, confirmed his impracticality in the minds of his critics.[100]

In fact, some of Carver's suggestions appeared questionable, even ridiculous, to those outside Tuskegee as well. In writing an article on a Carver exhibit on alternative food sources during World War I, a reporter from Baltimore poked gentle fun at the Tuskegee scientist's proposals. "It will take time even in the South," the reporter began, "to get accustomed to the sweet potato meal substitute for corn and wheat flour and to relish boiled, fried, stewed and baked peanuts, while at the same time giving up coffee for a substitute made from peas." Noting that a fellow audience member had "remarked, 'they will have us eating acorns after a while,'" the reporter continued, "it looks very much as if Tuskegee were sterring [steering] in that direction."[101] Carver's contention that many common weeds provided not only palatable food but medicine as well must have received a similar response. Much the same thing might be said of his calls to eschew commercial fertilizer, which promised more immediate results than soil building of the sort Carver advocated, and of any number of his other unconventional suggestions.

But as Carver grew increasingly aware that the more conventional currents of scientific agriculture made little sense for the poverty-stricken farmers of the region, he came to see his suggestions as eminently practical. Although Carver's campaign required a substantial effort on the part of the farmer, both in terms of actively seeking to learn about the natural world and in terms of outright physical labor, it did offer ways for farmers to improve their soil, yields, and homes that required virtually no cash outlay. Indeed, where his suggestions were followed, they often wrought the promised benefits. His critics' accusations of his impracticality were in this instance, at least, off base because Carver's campaign represented arguably the most "practical" work the institute carried on to improve the lives of black farmers. The question of its larger practicality, however, hinges on the degree to which Carver had legitimate grounds to believe that his campaign had a reasonable hope of success.

It would be easy to criticize Carver for not providing a more substantive critique of the social, political, and economic factors that undercut his plan and kept the black labor force of Alabama's Black Belt and the rest of the South in thralldom as a perpetually cheap and pliant labor force for white landlords. Such a criticism, however, would not be warranted. Like most of the African American farmers he sought to help, Carver wanted only to be a man free to pursue his own agenda. Even if he had been willing to speak out more forcefully against the region's economic and social institutions, there is no evidence to suggest that doing so would have aided his cause.

And to be fair to him, despite the number of factors working to undermine his efforts, impoverished farmers might have implemented Carver's vision more completely than they did. When Carver admonished black farmers, "Look about you, take hold of the things that are here," his advice was not impractical.[102] Alabama farmers as a whole spent some $20 million for commercial fertilizers in 1937.[103] How much of that tenants purchased is not clear, but even a reasonably successful black farmer like Cobb could have spared himself the annual expense of "guano" by relying on swamp muck, compost, and manure in the manner Carver suggested.

Regardless of whether African American farmers reinforced their dependency on their landlords and contributed to the perpetuation of their cycle of debt by failing to employ Carver's suggestions, Carver's limited success is no surprise. Not only did it challenge the economic and political culture of the South, along with some significant cultural norms of the region's people—both black and white—it flew in the face of powerful trends toward an industrial ideal in agriculture. The era of modern agribusiness was already dawning as Carver waged his campaign, portending the demise of autonomous, self-sufficient farms.[104]

The changes Johnson documented in Macon County during the 1930s mirrored those taking place elsewhere in the state; the plantation system did indeed seem to be teetering precariously. As late as 1910 Alabama had boasted 7,287 plantations; by 1940 their number had declined by 75 percent; only 1,801 plantations—defined as farms operating with wage labor or more than five tenants—remained.[105] This might be construed as an improvement of sorts, except that most black farmers lived in the same debilitating poverty they had lived in when Carver first arrived in the Black Belt in 1896.

In many ways, though, Johnson's description of Macon County in the 1930s does not differ much from Carver's in the 1890s. There were new additions, of course. "Excessively noisy and antiquated" automobiles—"rattle-trap Fords," Johnson called them—could be seen on the county's roads, and the "old blacksmith shop and stable of the early days . . . [had] given way to an automobile repair shop." Even so, Johnson observed, the "houses are the same, only generations older." He was struck, much as Carver had been, by the ubiquitous and "sad evidences of an artless and exhausting culture of cotton." In the fields, many of which were badly eroded, "the Negroes . . . still [hung] on, trying to nurse a living out of the earth." Upon "these two—black man and the earth—the [landlord], growing ever poorer himself," continued to depend "for the mutual preservation of all."[106]

Unlike Carver, however, Johnson recognized that the "approaching final desolation" of the South's plantation culture was at hand.[107] He believed that southern farmers would have to mechanize if they were to have any hope of competing in the post–World War I cotton market, a transformation that would necessarily entail the large-scale displacement of black tenants.[108] He was not alone in thinking so. Another student of the South, Rupert Vance, believed by the mid-1930s that very few alternatives existed to stave off an impending black exodus from the region. The "continued industrialization" of the South was one of them, as it might draw displaced tenants to industrial cities in the South. New Deal programs might be developed to alleviate their poverty and, in improving the lives of impoverished tenants, make them less likely to migrate. Pointing to a field in which Carver was leading the way, he was hopeful that southern farms might generate "raw materials for the chemical industry." Last and most promising of all, he thought that "scientific forestry" might provide opportunities for black employment in the region, albeit in more limited numbers than agriculture. Neither man saw Carver's hope for an independent black yeomanry as even a remote possibility.[109]

The industrialization of southern agriculture was for many a foregone conclusion by the time Carver returned to his campaign. Even in the 1920s a speaker at Tuskegee's Negro Conference had asserted that the South needed to standardize its agricultural products, package them better, and control supply and demand via modern marketing techniques.[110] Henry A. Wallace concurred a decade later when he addressed Tuskegee in September 1936. "The use of machinery in farming is increasing every day. In the long run machines give us more goods and relieve us of . . . drudgery." It was unfortunate, he acknowledged, that "in the absence of social planning, their first effects may hurt people," conceding that by throwing tenants out of work, "machines may make their goal of farm ownership harder than ever to attain."[111] Inasmuch as mechanization was inevitable, however, that was immaterial. Indeed, he joked that a large part of his career was spent "making life safe for corn breeders [a field in which he first earned national recognition] and for machines."[112] Given the nation's focus on increased productivity and economic growth, the gradual disappearance of the yeoman farmer represented, as Wendell Berry later wryly noted, "a kind of justice: it [was] their own fault; they ought to have been more efficient; if they had to get bigger in order to be more efficient, then they ought to have got bigger."[113]

For his part, Carver never admitted that large-scale industrial farms were inevitable. On the contrary, he gave every indication of following his adviser, Louis Pammel, in believing it to be "far better to have a large number of farms successfully run by individual owners than large farms, run by companies and corporations."[114] Carver's conviction notwithstanding, most contemporaries were convinced that what was happening elsewhere in the country in terms of the consolidation of farmland and its industrialization was certain to happen in the South as well. And there is no denying that the path Macon County took was a far cry from the world of small farms Carver had envisioned when he first undertook his campaign.

The New Deal programs had an important effect in Macon County and elsewhere in the Cotton Belt. The conflict between tenant and landlord over government subsidies played out much as it did in other counties. The acreage reductions required to comply with the conditions for the subsidies predictably led to a rise in tenant displacement. Probably the most significant transformation wrought in the county by the New Deal, however, was a result of the Resettlement Administration's submarginal land program. Under the Bankhead Jones Farm Tenant Act (1935), the federal government purchased more than 10,000 acres in the north-central part of the county between 1935 and 1938. The upland soil had never been especially favorable for agriculture—Carver had classified the dominant soil type of the region as Norfolk Gravelly Loam and described it as marked by "droughty and scalding propensities"—and it fit the criteria for submarginal land purchases.[115] Much of it was land on which black farmers had tried to scrape out a living. Dubbed the Tuskegee Land Utilization Project, the area was turned toward nonagricultural purposes: timber production, recreational land, and wildlife sanctuary. In 1959 it would become Tuskegee National Forest.

Apart from presaging the demise of cotton culture in the region, the establishment of the national forest signaled the direction in which the county—and indeed, the Black Belt as a whole—was headed. In the early twenty-first century only 20 percent of the county remains in cropland. After being displaced for a while, cotton once again is the crop of choice, but rising corn prices threaten its position. Seventy-five of the remaining 80 percent of the county is "forested," mostly in super-loblolly pine and other saw- and pole-timbers.[116] Although 11,070 acres of these acres lie in Tuskegee National Forest, most of the 288,800 forested acres in the county are privately owned.

Throughout the state's twelve Black Belt counties, tracks of timber culture (doubling as hunting land) and catfish farms separate herds of cattle and scattered farms. Individuals and, more often, investment firms and timber companies own better than 70 percent of the land in several Black Belt counties—including Macon. For the most part, the owners do not reside in the county and contribute only marginally to the tax base. (Mississippi's and Georgia's taxes on timber companies are two to three times higher than Alabama's.) Outside the larger towns of the region, the population density is only three people per square mile—remarkably comparable to the central plains; more deer live in Alabama's Black Belt today than people. And it remains poor, unbelievably poor by American standards. More than 30 percent of Macon County's residents live below the poverty line. In fact, in the 1980s, when sociologist Paul L. Wall undertook a follow-up project to Johnson's *Shadow of the Plantation*, more than 70 percent of the families he interviewed earned less than $3,000 a year. A surprisingly large percentage of those living in the county, which is more than 80 percent black, did not have indoor plumbing.[117]

Judging Carver's campaign on the basis of the path the county took relative to the world he envisioned it could become, it was a miserable failure. The remarkable thing about Carver's campaign, however, is not that it failed, but rather that he waged it at all. In retrospect, his hope of establishing a permanent and sustainable basis for southern agriculture that rested on diversified, self-sufficient farms appears an unrealistic dream. But a sparsely populated, impoverished Black Belt was not inevitable. It is the result of the rationalization of agriculture along lines quite different from those Carver proposed and white southerners' shortsighted insistence on keeping a cheap and pliable black labor force even when it redounded to their long-term economic detriment. Whether or not Carver developed a genuinely practical way to restore both the soil and the people of Macon County, the environmental thinking that undergirded his attempt was basically sound. In the solutions he proposed can be seen the germ of the push for ecological agriculture that would emerge in the years after his death. Indeed, an examination of his campaign suggests that it is time to reconsider Carver and think of him not just as a scientist, a racial symbol, and the Peanut Man, or even as another agrarian, but as a prophet of sustainable agriculture.

My Work Is That of Conservation

Forty years after he first stepped down from a train in Macon County, Carver looked back over his career—not only his efforts to improve the lot of impoverished black farmers but his work as a "creative chemist"—and declared, "My work is that of conservation." In the immediate context of his declaration, he was addressing "the saving of things that the average person throws away," and he had in mind his life's work, from encouraging farmers to see in forests a natural fertilizer factory and in the clays on which they walked dyes and paints, to finding industrial uses for neglected crops such as soybeans and peanuts. The context of his claim, however, might well be expanded.[1] Indeed, Carver merits serious consideration as a conservationist in the conventional sense of the word, which is to say that he belongs in discussions of early twentieth-century conservation.

The nascent conservation movement was not nearly as narrow as it is often portrayed, and its evolution from its nineteenth-century origins to the modern environmental movement was considerably less linear than is often assumed.[2] To be sure, Carver fits uneasily into the conventional narrative of Progressive Era conservation, in part because of his race, in part because of the region in which he worked, and in part because he was little involved with the seminal organizations of the era. His was in many ways a voice alone, the voice of one calling not in the wilderness—like his more famous contemporaries—but in denuded and depleted fields white with bolls of cotton.

Nevertheless, as Steven Stoll observed, forestry "did not make up the whole of American conservation," even if more attention has been lavished on the forestry, wilderness, and wildlife branches of the movement than on its agricultural aspects.[3] What attention has been given to the connection between agriculture and the movement has very often leaned in the direction of pest control and the reclamation of swamps and arid lands, and has been used to highlight the ironies of the era's conservation ethos.[4] But the conservation movement had a substantial agrarian impulse, represented by Carver and Liberty Hyde Bailey (its most-referenced exemplar) among others.

For such agrarians, conservation meant more than affording protection to raw natural resources that could serve as fodder for an infinitely growing national economy. Conservation meant preserving the soil, the source of food, and the relationship of farmer and farm. Bailey would have given a hearty amen to Carver's contention that farmers needed "to be kind to the soil," and Carver to Bailey's insistence that a farmer in the truest sense of the word left "his part of the earth's surface in more productive condition than when he received it," understood "the powers of the soil and means of conserving them," and "derive[d] pleasure in watching and making things grow."[5] Both believed that farmers needed to do more than feed people.

This agricultural dimension of the conservation movement climaxed with the Country Life Commission, established in 1908 by President Theodore Roosevelt and headed by Bailey. The commission toured twenty-nine agricultural states, including those in the South; but it deliberately avoided dealing with tenant-landlord relations in the region. In fact, to placate southern fears that race would factor into the commission's recommendations, it canceled a stop at Tuskegee, where its members might have visited with Carver and gleaned from him the insights he had gained in the more than ten years of his campaign.[6] Like Carver, the commission was forced to ignore that with which it could not hope to deal.

Carver, no less than Bailey, serves as a reminder that turn-of-the-century agronomy could be relatively "green," even if the field subsequently drifted so far in the direction of efficiency and productivity that by the 1960s and 1970s those impulses had all but been forgotten. The birth of the modern environmental movement in the 1960s and 1970s represented an important challenge to scientific agriculture. The significance of biological interde-pendence in agriculture was not a new concept, however. Progressive Era ecologists had seen agricultural science as a kindred field in which their science might find a useful application. Only as ecologists sought to estab-lish their discipline as a distinct theoretical science and agronomists drifted toward prioritizing production at almost any cost did ecology and scientific agriculture drift apart.[7] Though Carver contributed nothing to the theoreti-cal foundation of ecology, he gave primacy to ecological ideas, and his work offers a case study of those long-lost connections.

For that matter, Carver was hardly the only African American of his generation thinking deeply about the natural world. William J. Edwards, the president of the Snow Hill Institute (an all-black school also located in Alabama's Black Belt), drew connections between land use, racism, and poverty, arguing that soil erosion rather than "Negro domination" posed the gravest threat to the region, the opinion of "the average white man of the South" notwithstanding.[8] W. E. B. DuBois drew similar connections and offered tentative explanations for the perceived indifference of African Americans toward the iconic landscapes being set aside as state and na-tional parks.[9] And Carver's boss at Tuskegee, Booker T. Washington, found in his prized garden the opportunity "to touch nature, not something that is artificial or an imitation but the real thing." Indeed, he claimed to "pity the man or woman who has never learned to enjoy nature and to get strength and inspiration out of it."[10]

Examining the environmental thought of prominent African Americans will inevitably offer new insights into their motivations and philosophies, adding a new layer of complexity to their thinking and proposals. In the case of Washington and DuBois, such an examination may provide a new common ground for men generally portrayed as foils. Historians have only begun to identify and trace the origins of a distinctively African Ameri-can environmental ethic. Perhaps the most difficult work still to be done will be parsing out the connections that comparatively anonymous African Americans—the people Carver most wanted to help—fostered with the environment. Such connections will be variously rooted in a heritage of slavery and tenancy, distinctive religious worldviews, or larger traits shared by cultures born of the African diaspora. Neither Carver's views nor those of Washington, DuBois, or Edwards are exemplary of those connections, but Carver's environmental ethic offers a significant reminder that the his-tory of conservation—even in the Progressive Era—was hardly lily white.

Few people of any race or nationality thought about the environment as fruitfully as Carver did.

The fact that Carver was black and seeking solutions to problems specific to African American farmers muted his influence in the conservation movement, and his subsequent rise to iconic status artificially inflated his influence on southern agriculture even as it obscured his work along conservation lines. He did not "salvage the economy of the South during the early 1900s" as Southwest Airlines' *Spirit* magazine suggested, and if measured by the degree to which he affected political transformations or inspired future generations of environmentalists, he wielded little influence in the larger conservation movement. But his vision for southern agriculture represents a proverbial road not taken, one that might have made all the difference for communities like those in Alabama's Black Belt.

This is not to overlook the failure of Carver's campaign, which reveals much about the limits of conservationist thought—suggesting, for instance, that where it cannot account for gross social and economic inequities, it has little hope of success. That failure also illumines an important regional distinction in the environmental history of early twentieth-century America. While a thirst for economic profit played a tremendously important role in shaping the tenant landscapes of Macon County, it alone was not responsible for their transformation. Efforts to reinforce the existing social order, including the racial hierarchy, proved at least as important a catalyst in the process.

In contrast to much of the South, Alabama's Black Belt had more appealing economic prospects than cotton could offer by the early twentieth century, being well situated for cattle raising as a result of its alkaline soils and prairie remnants. Though a handful of progressive farmers sought to switch from cotton to cattle as early as World War I, cotton was a familiar, albeit fickle, friend—one that required a pliable, economically dependent labor force and offered a convenient justification for maintaining the racial status quo. Indeed, one of the impediments to adopting cattle farms on a large scale was a conviction among the region's whites that "the average Black Belt Negro is decidedly incompetent as a stock farmer." Consequently, their logic went, the "high ratio of Negro to white farmers thus becomes a significant factor limiting the expansion of the cattle industry."[11] Only as the plantation system collapsed during World War II did cattle outstrip cotton in economic, if not cultural, significance. The effort to preserve the racial status quo—no less than that to maximize profit—thus shaped the "devastated forests, ruined estates, . . . furrowed and guttered hillsides and neglected valleys called farms" that Carver sought with little success to rectify.

But to dismiss Carver because his campaign failed is to miss the import of his efforts. After all, the New Dealers failed, too. Even within a context that acknowledges that New Deal programs tended to favor landowning farmers rather than tenants (and whites rather than blacks), the New Dealers' efforts achieved little more than Carver's did, and this despite the backing of the federal government and a slew of programs aimed at enabling farmers to stay on the land. If for a time New Deal agricultural policy was shaped by men who sought to aid the most marginal farmers, ultimately, as Sarah Phillips noted, "the balance of power shifted to those who believed that there were just too many farmers."[12]

Their assessment embraced a clear, if flawed, moral logic. Carver's friend Henry A. Wallace earnestly believed that modernizing agriculture by encouraging hybrid crops and the adoption of the newest technologies would enable American farmers to produce more on less land, and thus simultaneously increase their production and extend their conservation efforts. It seems never to have occurred to him that farmers might not be content with "enough" if more was available for the taking.[13] His naïveté in that regard rivaled (if it did not surpass) Carver's, but it does not render Wallace's efforts to reshape American agriculture irrelevant.

Industrial agriculture has accomplished much of what its supporters said it would. By the 1970s the USDA could boast that 5 percent of Americans produced more food than nearly ten times their number had produced in 1900. Technological change, federal subsidies, and the advent of petrochemicals made that possible, but in doing so created an agricultural industry that has often displayed a callous disregard for the soil, poured pollutants into the environment, and all but closed out family farms. Since the end of Carver's life, America's farm-based population has declined from 30 million to 5 million while the nation's population has doubled.[14]

As critiques of industrial agriculture mounted in the 1970s, environmentalists were dismissed in much the same way Carver was by his peers at Tuskegee: they were deemed impractical, idealistic, sentimental, and vaguely effeminate for refusing to value production over people. But there is evidence to suggest that the agricultural system shaped by the main currents of agricultural science over the past century might prove in the long run impractical itself, not only because its methods may not be sustainable but also because the one-size-fits-all philosophy that undergirds them has proven as capable of generating new problems as it has of solving old ones. When America and the West generally began exporting industrial agriculture to developing nations in the name of economic growth, for example, the results proved profoundly disappointing. Bigger did not prove better in many African countries, and industrialized agriculture created problems as troubling as those it set out to solve. Farmers displaced from rural communities moved to cities where neither jobs nor the communal support networks on which they had previously depended awaited them. This, in turn, exacerbated infrastructural shortcomings, led previously self-sufficient nations to begin importing food, and contributed to the outbreak of epidemic diseases.[15]

Closer to home, in the midst of the race riots of the 1960s, the executive secretary of the National Sharecroppers Fund cited "ample evidence" that many of tenants who were "being pushed off the land to the unwelcoming city slums would prefer to remain" in the South. There, at least, they had "clean air, living space, . . . and a closeness of community which is lacking in the cynicism and despair which greet the farm poor when they give up and migrate to the city."[16] Political equality rang hollow in many areas, including Macon County, where African Americans were elected to positions of authority but oversaw perpetually economically depressed communities with a meager tax base and comparatively few black-run industries. Moreover, the hint of a connection between environmental issues and the civil rights movement contained in the executive secretary's assertion remained only a hint. As the modern environmental movement coalesced in the late 1960s and early 1970s, it fostered few connections with civil rights advocates of any sort, creating issues for the movement that are as yet unresolved, and further obscuring Carver's connection to it.[17]

The publication of British economist Ernst F. Schumacher's *Small Is Beautiful: Economics as if People Mattered* in 1973 reflected the increased rejection in many circles of the simplistic "bigger is better" philosophy undergirding Western agriculture.[18] Schumacher decried the dehumanizing effect of making "efficiency" the paramount economic value and industrial agriculture a religion, and perpetuating environmentally unfriendly interactions with the natural world as it did so.[19] His essays made him a hero of the environmental movement, and out of his writings grew a call for the use of "appropriate technology," which is to say the application of technology appropriate not only to a particular environment but to a particular culture given its circumstances at a particular time. Carver never teased out the implications of such a philosophy, which involves complicated economic calculi and can be applied to industries other than agriculture, and he never thought in the sort of explicitly political terms that undergirded the philosophy. Nevertheless, his campaign on behalf of impoverished sharecroppers anticipated important portions of it.[20]

In many ways Carver would have fit more comfortably into the camp of American agriculture's critics than within the field of agricultural science by the 1970s. When in 1977 Wendell Berry argued that "the best farming requires a farmer—a husbandman, a nurturer," he meant it as a critique of agricultural science. In leveling such a critique, he neglected some of the positive aspects of technological advances in agricultural science—veterinary medicine, to name but one—and rooted his rationale in a mythological, idyllic agrarian past. A "good farmer," he contended, "is a cultural product ... made ... by generations of experience." Carver, who had little use for folk farming methods, would not have concurred with Berry's conclusion that "generations of experience" necessarily made a good farmer, but he might well have written Berry's contention that nurturing the soil is part and parcel of being a good farmer.[21]

As Berry's critique implied, however, notions of nurturing the soil had fallen by the wayside. By the late 1960s American farmers were applying, on average, 260 pounds of chemical fertilizer per acre, and few saw that as a potential problem.[22] Carver's insistence that "the first and absolutely the most important thing for every farmer to learn is that the physical condition of the soil is of greater importance than the chemical" would have seemed ridiculously old-fashioned.[23] His vision of rebuilding the vitality of the soil chemically by rebuilding it physically had put him out of step with mainstream agronomy even in his own time; in postwar America it had, in effect, been eliminated from the field.

Much of what Carver advocated, however, continues to resonate. "Conservation is one of our big problems in this section," he argued of the South in 1940. "You can't tear everything up just to get the dollar out of it without suffering as a result."[24] Surely, this sentiment is as fresh today as it was on the eve of World War II. For that matter, in India, Africa, China, and elsewhere, the early twenty-first century finds rural communities caught between tradition and modernity. Not unlike those in Macon County during Carver's lifetime, farmers in those communities have little protection from the invading forces of modernity and face vast disparities in political power and wealth.[25] The promise of financial windfalls and access to goods and products that might make their lives considerably easier lures farmers into securing loans, which in turn demand increased production for the market. Far too often, however, rural farmers find the promised benefits elusive and the reality of debt all-encumbering, a fate with which the farmers of Macon County could certainly have identified. Carver's campaign hardly offers a clear roadmap for circumventing such issues on a large scale, but his refusal to embrace purely technological solutions seems prescient in light of the spate of cotton farmer suicides in India that marked the turn of the twenty-first century.

Carver's conviction that God had chosen him to lead his people out of the economic dependency of tenancy came to little in a material sense; he never did get to return to his "brush work." But that conviction drove and inspired him. "Your tragic quality," the great poet Robinson Jeffers wrote of Woodrow Wilson, "required the huge delusion of some major purpose to produce it."[26] The same might be said of Carver. The failure of his efforts, however, does not render Carver unworthy of attention any more than his exaltation by various interests to serve divergent ends makes him a fraud. David Danbom argued that the Progressives as a whole "failed and failed badly, but the magnitude of their failure matched the nobility of their effort."[27] Surely, no less should be said of Carver.

Mart Stewart has asked historians to imagine what modern environmentalism would have looked like if John Muir "had developed more than a passing infatuation with the landscapes" of the South, if they had valued "nature pastoralized" rather than the wilderness of the West. He suggests that people might have figured into the landscapes, that agriculture rather than wilderness might have been paramount in the movement, and that people would have realized sooner "that landscapes are always riven by what we used to call 'race'"—all things that Carver's work accounted for.[28] As environmental historians increasingly turn their attention to the South, they may discover that if Carver did not influence the environmental movement in the way that men such as Muir or Pinchot did, he anticipated more clearly some of the directions in which it would move. They might also find that his life's work is no less relevant than those of his contemporaries with more celebrated conservation legacies.

NOTES

Prologue

1. George Washington Carver, "A Few Hints to Southern Farmers," *The Southern Workman and Hampton School Record* (September 1899).

2. Joseph J. Ellis, *American Sphinx: The Character of Thomas Jefferson* (New York: Vintage Books, 1998).

3. See *Saturday Night Live*, season 10, episode 9 (December 15, 1984); *Seinfeld*, season 3, episode 10, "The Stranded" (1991); *American Dad*, season 2, episode 13, "Black Mystery Month"; Stevie Wonder, "Same Old Story," on *Stevie Wonder's Journey through the Secret Life of Plants* (1979).

4. See, for instance, *Modern Marvels: George Washington Carver Tech*, History Channel, 2005.

5. This is just one example. In June 2005 the *Kansas City Star* ran an article in which Lewis W. Diuguid used Carver to attack Missouri governor Matt Blunt for allowing a Confederate flag to fly at the Confederate Memorial State Historic Site, insisting that "Blunt needs to see this beautiful history of a black man [Carver] saving America." See "Lewis W. Diuguid, "Let's Remember Our Heroes," *Kansas City Star*, June 17, 2005, B9.

6. Perhaps the best example of this is Barry Mackintosh, "George Washington Carver: The Making of a Myth," *Journal of Southern History* 42 (November 1976): 507–28.

7. Linda O. McMurry, *George Washington Carver: Scientist and Symbol* (New York: Oxford University Press, 1981); Gary Kremer, *George Washington Carver: In His Own Words* (Columbia: University of Missouri Press, 1987).

8. See David Donald, "An Ambitious Figure," *New Republic*, October 28, 1981, 36.

9. McMurry pointed this out, but Donald and others overlooked the point.

10. On Carver's opportunity to pursue a PhD, see George Washington Carver (henceforth GWC) to Booker T. Washington (henceforth BTW), May 30, 1898, box 4, George Washington Carver Papers, Tuskegee University Archives, Tuskegee, Alabama (henceforth, GWCP, TUA); and GWC to BTW, July 9, 1900, GWCP, TUA, box 4, folder 5. Linda McMurry has made a similar argument in Linda O. McMurry, "A Vision of the Future?: George Washington Carver's Approach to Technology and Nature," unpublished paper. I am indebted to her for sharing this paper with me. Note: The Tuskegee University Archives, including the George Washington Carver Papers, have recently been reorganized under the guidance of Dan Chandler. This document and all others from the archives are cited as they were found under the old system.

11. McMurry, *George Washington Carver*, 311.

12. Peter Duncan Burchard, *George Washington Carver: For His Time and Ours: Special History Study—Natural History Related to George Washington Carver National Monument, Diamond, Missouri* (National Park Service, 2005).

13. The prevalence of the Hetch Hetchy controversy is evident in its incorporation into traditional textbook narratives. James Oakes et al., *Of the People* (2010), for example, devotes three paragraphs to the conservation movement in the text, but includes a two-page inset on the fight over the Hetch Hetchy Valley, ultimately concluding that "the battle for the valley gave birth to a modern environmental movement" (716). See James Oakes, Michael McGerr, Jan Ellen Lewis, Nick Cullather, and Jeanne Boydston, *Of the People: A History of the United States* (New York: Oxford University Press, 2010), 714–16. The classic (and hugely influential) work in terms of framing the nascent conservation movement in such terms is Samuel P. Hays, *Conservation and the Gospel of Efficiency: The Progressive Conservation Movement, 1890–1920* (1959; reprint New York: Atheneum, 1975).

14. Quoted in Edna D. Bullock, *Agricultural Credit* (New York: H. H. Wilson, 1915), 34.

15. GWC to A. C. True, September 16, 1902; George Washington Carver, *Possibilities of the Sweet Potato in Macon County, TAES* Bulletin 17 (March 1910), 5.

Chapter 1. Were It Not for His Dusky Skin

1. Rackham Holt, who completed Carver's "authorized" biography in consultation with him shortly before his death, devoted 117 pages—more than a third of her book—to his pre-Tuskegee years. See Rackham Holt, *George Washington Carver: An American Biography* (Garden City, N.Y.: Doubleday, 1943). The best account of Carver's early years is in McMurry, *George Washington Carver*, 3–45.

2. Gary R. Kremer, *In His Own Words*, 20, 22. For Carver providing 1864 as the year of his birth, see the two "authorized" biographies of Carver: Raleigh H. Merritt, *From Captivity to Fame, or, The Life of George Washington Carver* (Boston: Meador, 1929); and Holt, *George Washington Carver*. Following the National Park Service Study that concluded that Carver was born in 1860, Holt amended her book accordingly.

3. Anna Coxe Toogood, *Historic Resource Study and Administrative History, George Washington Carver National Monument, Diamond, Missouri* (Denver, 1973), 6.

4. Quoted in ibid., 18.

5. See ibid., 2–21, for an in-depth discussion of the controversy over Carver's birth date.

6. Ibid., 19.

7. McMurry, *George Washington Carver*, 10.

8. See "Moses Carver and His Family," folder 622, Archives of the George

Washington Carver National Monument, Diamond, Missouri (henceforth GWCNM).

9. For the census figures on Moses Carver's livestock and produce from 1850–80, see Toogood, *Historic Resource Study*, 49.

10. The slave schedule for Newton County is available online at http://freepages.history.rootsweb.ancestry.com/~cappscreek/1860slave.html, accessed July 1, 2010.

11. Jim was listed as a mulatto in the census records, and consequently had a white father. George, by contrast, was always listed as a "negro." See Kremer, *In His Own Words*, 20.

12. On slavery in Newton County and Marion Township, see Toogood, *Historic Resource Study*, 27; and http://freepages.history.rootsweb.ancestry.com/~cappscreek/1860slave.html, accessed July 1, 2010.

13. McMurry, *George Washington Carver*, 10–11.

14. In the 1920s and 1930s, authors bent on treating Carver as the subject of a great American epic placed an undue emphasis on this event. Perhaps the best example is Frank H. Leavell, "The Boy Who Was Traded for a Horse," *Baptist Student* (November 1938).

15. Quoted in Kremer, *In His Own Words*, 20.

16. McMurry, *George Washington Carver*, 7.

17. For more on the history of the high-minded husbandry of the antebellum era, see Steven Stoll, *Larding the Lean Earth: Soil and Society in Nineteenth-Century America* (New York: Hill and Wang, 2002).

18. For further evidence of Moses Carver's antipathy for waste, see McMurry, *George Washington Carver*, 9.

19. Ibid., 13.

20. Ibid.

21. Toogood, *Historic Resource Study*, 32, 37; Kremer, *In His Own Words*, 20.

22. Kremer, *In His Own Words*, 23.

23. Ibid., 20.

24. GWC to My Dear Mrs. Goodwin, January 25, 1929, folder 1391, GWCNM.

25. See Toogood, *Historic Resource Study*, 25. For more on the establishment of school segregation in Missouri, see Paul C. Nagel, *Missouri: A History* (Lawrence: University Press of Kansas, 1988), 93–94.

26. See Toogood, *Historic Resource Study*, 26.

27. GWC to My Dear Mrs. Goodwin, January 25, 1929.

28. For a similar list, see McMurry, *George Washington Carver*, 20–21.

29. Ibid., 20.

30. Ibid., 20–21.

31. Kremer, *In His Own Words*, 21.

32. Ibid., 21.

33. Quoted in Nell Irvin Painter, *Exodusters: Black Migration to Kansas after Reconstruction* (1976; reprint New York: W. W. Norton, 1992), 159.

34. See Territorial Kansas Online, at http://www.territorialkansasonline.org/ ~imlskto/cgi-bin/index.php?SCREEN=immigration&option=more, accessed August 19, 2010; McMurry, *George Washington Carver*, 21.

35. "Negro Immigrants in Kansas," *New York Times*, April 21, 1876.

36. For more on Nicodemus and the exoduster movement generally, see Painter, *Exodusters*.

37. "Tremendous Tragedy: A Mad Mob Drags the Demon Down to Death, Howard the Hound, Ends His Earthly Career, and Meets Retribution on a Lamp Post," *Fort Scott Daily Monitor*, March 27, 1879. For an exaggerated account of the incident, see Holt, *George Washington Carver*, 32. For more on the event, see "Burning in City 86 Years Ago Worst Crime in Town's History," *Fort Scott Tribune*, March 27, 1965; McMurry, *George Washington Carver*, 22; and Matt Dodge, "George Washington Carver: Kansas Homesteader," *True West* 31 (April 1984): 24.

38. Quoted in McMurry, *George Washington Carver*, 23.

39. Quoted in ibid., 22. He actually used this phrase in reference to the work he found in Fort Scott, though it is equally applicable elsewhere.

40. Basil Miller, *George Washington Carver: God's Ebony Scientist*, 2nd ed. (Grand Rapids, Mich.: Zondervan, 1943), 39. Miller was an avowedly religious author, writing for a religious press. He also wrote hagiographical biographies of Martin Luther, George Muller, David Livingstone, Charles G. Finney, John Wesley, and Praying Hyde to name just a few.

41. See Toogood, *Historic Resource Study*, 44; McMurry, *George Washington Carver*, 23.

42. Kremer, *In His Own Words*, 24.

43. In Rackham Holt's account, Carver was exploited in this real-estate deal. McMurry merely noted that he bought the property for $100 in January and sold it for $500 in November. A 500 percent profit in ten months' time hardly sounds especially exploitative, but Carver might still have been forced to sell. See Holt, *George Washington Carver*, 40–41; and McMurry, *George Washington Carver*, 24.

44. "'I'll Find My Breakfast All Right,' Said Carver," *Better Way*, September 9, 1943, folder 168, GWCNM.

45. When "proving up" on his land in Ness County, Carver claimed that he had previously been a farmer in Doniphan County. "Testimony of Claimant," Examiner Records, WaKeeney Kansas, September 12, 1889, box 101, GWCP, TUA.

46. See *Handbook of Ness County Kansas* (Chicago: C. S. Burch, 1887).

47. The *Ness City Times* reported on Thursday, December 30, 1886, "It is now assured that all will be completed to Ness City by Saturday Night."

48. Daniel D. Holt, ed., *County History Project* (Topeka: Kansas State Historical Society, 1987), 159. Beelerville was not formally platted until March 1887. See *Handbook of Ness County Kansas*.

49. See "Testimony of Claimant."

50. O. L. Lennen (1942), quoted in "Testimony of Claimant." For more on the soddy, see Dodge, "George Washington Carver: Kansas Homesteader," 26.

51. For more on the phenomenon of tree planting in Kansas, see Brian Allen Drake, "Waving 'A Bough of Challenge': Forestry on the Kansas Grasslands, 1868–1915," *Great Plains Quarterly* 23 (winter 2003): 19 34.

52. McMurry, *George Washington Carver*, 26; see also "Testimony of Claimant."

53. "Testimony of Claimant."

54. Quoted in Dodge, "George Washington Carver: Kansas Homesteader," 26.

55. See "The Blizzards of 1886–1888," *Buffalo News*, January 19, 2004.

56. McMurry, *George Washington Carver*, 26.

57. "Testimony of Claimant."

58. *Ness County News*, March 31, 1888.

59. McMurry, *George Washington Carver*, 26.

60. See, for instance, "Ness Pioneer Woman Recalls Early Days," *Ness City News*, July 13, 1961.

61. *Walnut Valley Sentinel*, May 12, 1888; "Witness Testimonies," Examiner Records, WaKeeney, Kans. 9431, September 12, 1889, box 101, GWCP, TUA.

62. Kremer, *In His Own Words*, 21.

63. McMurry, *George Washington Carver*, 27; "10.50 received from G. A. Borthwick *Receiver* . . . to pay Interest on G. W. Carver Loan Due Dec 22, 1893," box 101, GWCP, TUA.

64. GWC to Mrs. Milholland, August 16, 1918, folder 1469, GWCNM. See Mildred Hoskins Wood, *A Star in Winterset's Crown* (Winterset, Iowa, 1988), 3, on Carver's affiliation with the Winterset Baptist Church.

65. Probably the most familiar relic of the Social Gospel era is Charles M. Sheldon, *In His Steps* (1897; reprint, Chicago: Advance, 1898), a novel written with the intent of "hastening" the coming of "the Master's kingdom on earth" (preface) that traces the events in the life of a minister who decides to approach each decision by asking "What would Jesus do?" For more background on the Social Gospel movement, see William G. McLoughlin, *The Meaning of Henry Ward Beecher; an Essay on the Shifting Values of Mid-Victorian America, 1840–1870* (New York: Knopf, 1970); and Ann Douglas, *The Feminization of American Culture* (New York: Anchor Press/Doubleday, 1988).

66. GWC to Dr. Milholland, March 8, 1928, folder 1462, GWCNM.

67. GWC to Mrs. Closson, March 25, 1935, folder 1417, GWCNM. The Bible speaks of children "rising up" to call their parents blessed; see for instance, Proverbs 31:28.

68. GWC to Mrs. Milholland, August 16, 1918.

69. Ibid.

70. Holt, *George Washington Carver*, 63.

71. McMurry, *George Washington Carver*, 28.

72. "President Gross's Interview with Doctor Carver at Tuskegee," July 17, 1940, Simpson College Archives, Indianola, Iowa.

73. Interview with Pauline Tyler Townsend regarding Carver at Simpson, November 9, 1957, transcribed June 1988, Simpson College Archives, Indianola, Iowa, 4.

74. GWC to Mrs. Milholland, n.d. (1890), folder 1484, GWCNM.

75. Quoted in McMurry, *George Washington Carver*, 28.

76. "Statement of Credits," Mrs. Bernadino Carpenter, Registrar, to Mr. A. W. Curtis, October 18, 1938, Simpson College Archives, Indianola, Iowa. Many accounts of Carver reference his "fine tenor voice"; over the years a myth arose that he had been accepted to the Boston Conservatory of Music. See, for example, Dodge, "George Washington Carver: Kansas Homsteader," 27; see also interview with Pauline Tyler Townsend, 24.

77. Toogood, *Historic Resource Study*, 44; "Mrs. Flummer Remembers Dr. Carver at Indianola," *Des Moines Bystander*, June 21, 1943.

78. McMurry, *George Washington Carver*, 30; "Simpson College in the Nineties," Simpson College Archives, Indianola, Iowa, 8–9.

79. GWC to Mr. and Mrs. Milholland, August 6, 1891, folder 1480, GWCNM.

80. See GWC to My Beloved friend Dr. Gross, July 20, 1940; and GWC to Gross, October 23, 1940, Simpson College Archives, Indianola, Iowa.

Chapter 2. The Earnest Student of Nature

1. Quoted in Joseph Cannon Bailey, *Seaman A. Knapp: Schoolmaster of American Agriculture* (New York: Arno Press and the New York Times, 1971), 80.

2. See Louis Hermann Pammel (henceforth LHP), "Dr. Charles Edwin Bessey," in *Prominent Men I Have Met* (Ames: Powers Press, n.d.), 6, box 22, folder 1, Louis Hermann Pammel Papers (henceforth LHP Papers), Iowa State University Archives, Ames, Iowa (henceforth ISU Archives). For more on Bessey's role in shaping the nascent field of ecology, see Donald Worster, *Nature's Economy: A History of Ecological Ideas*, 2nd ed. (New York: Cambridge University Press, 1994), 205–20; and Ronald C. Tobey, *Saving the Prairies: The Life Cycle of the Founding School of American Plant Ecology, 1895–1955* (Berkeley: University of California Press, 1981).

3. For more on this movement, see Philip J. Pauly, *Biologists and the Promise of American Life: From Meriwether Lewis to Alfred Kinsey* (Princeton: Princeton University Press, 2000); and Philip J. Pauly, *Fruits and Plains: The Horticultural Transformation of America* (Cambridge: Harvard University Press, 2007).

4. See Pauly, *Fruits and Plains*, 125. Some authors give Budd more credit for his

efforts than Pauly; see, for instance, "Joseph Lancaster Budd," *Journal of Heredity* 22 (1931): 66.

5. Bailey, *Seaman A. Knapp*, 96.

6. Ibid., 96–98. For a sketch of the fight over this bill, see Alan I. Marcus, *Agricultural Science and the Quest for Legitimacy: Farmers, Agricultural Colleges, and Experiment Stations, 1870–1890* (Ames: Iowa State University Press, 1985), 171–220.

7. Marcus, *Agricultural Science and the Quest for Legitimacy*, 220.

8. Bailey, *Seaman A. Knapp*, 103.

9. See Pammel, "Dr. Charles Edwin Bessey," 7; Andrew D. Rodgers, *American Botany, 1873–1892: Decades of Transition* (Princeton: Princeton University Press, 1944), 228.

10. Quoted in Richard S. Kirkendall, *Uncle Henry: A Documentary Profile of the First Henry Wallace* (Ames: Iowa State University Press, 1993), 81.

11. Wallace was not opposed to the Alliance per se, but was convinced that reform could be achieved using conventional channels within the political system as it existed. For more on this divide in the Iowa Alliance and Wallace's role in it, see Jeffrey Ostler, *Prairie Populism: The Fate of Agrarian Radicalism in Kansas, Nebraska, and Iowa, 1880–1892* (Lawrence: University Press of Kansas, 1993), 120–48, 203 fn. 52.

12. Quoted in Kirkendall, *Uncle Henry*, 82.

13. Louis Hermann Pammel, "William Miller Beardshear," in *Prominent Men I Have Met*, 7–8, LHP Papers, ISU Archives.

14. LHP to Prof. L. B. Schmidt, May 18, 1922, LHP Papers, box 1, folder 14, ISU Archives.

15. Fred W. Lorch, "George Washington Carver's Iowa Education," 15, Simpson College Archives, Indianola, Iowa. This piece is replete with errors, and it is difficult to know how much credence to give to Lorch's contention that Budd smoothed the admission process for Carver.

16. LHP to Schmidt, May 18, 1922.

17. See GWC to LHP, May 5, 1922; LHP to GWC, May 18, 1922; and GWC to LHP, May 22, 1922, box 4, folder 14a, LHP Papers, ISU Archives.

18. GWC to Dr. and Mrs. Milholland, August 6, 1891.

19. "Simpson College in the Nineties," 11.

20. For one football player's reminiscences of Carver's duties in this position, see Burt German, "I Knew George Washington Carver," *Alumnus* (May 1955), 8–9, ISU Archives. Carver "had almost a magic touch in those long fingers," German recalled (8).

21. GWC to LHP, May 5, 1922.

22. For more on his activities, see McMurry, *George Washington Carver*, 33–37.

23. Holt, *George Washington Carver*, 86–88; McMurry, *George Washington Carver*, 38; GWC to LHP, June 11, 1921, box 4, folder 14, ISU Archives. McMurry

credited the students with buying him the suit, but in the letter to Pammel, Carver expressly credited Pammel for the purchase: "I really wanted you to see the suit of clothes, hat, gloves, underwear, you helped fool me downtown and bought for me, preparatory to going to Cedar Rapids for the Art exhibit with some of my pictures."

24. GWC to LHP, May 5, 1922.

25. See George W. Carver, "Plants as Modified by Man," BSA thesis (1894), GWC Files, box 2, folder 11, ISU Archives. Pauline Tyler Townsend, a friend of Carver's at Simpson, recalled in a 1957 interview that Budd had "told him to write his thesis on the cactus." His thesis was actually somewhat larger in scope, but he did publish an article titled "Grafting the Cacti" a year before he graduated. See interview with Pauline Tyler Townsend, 19. For reference to Budd's overseeing the orchard, see Bailey, *Seaman A. Knapp*, 87.

26. Donald Winters, *Henry Cantwell Wallace as Secretary of Agriculture, 1921–1924* (Urbana: University of Illinois Press, 1970), 15.

27. GWC to LHP, May 5, 1922.

28. George Washington Carver, "Coming Events Cast Their Shadows Before," box 65, folder 4, GWCP, TUA.

29. Henry A. Wallace, "The Genetic Basis of Democracy," in *Democracy Reborn: Selected from Public Papers*, ed. and intro. Russell Lord (New York: Da Capo Press, 1973), 154; Henry A. Wallace, "The Uniqueness of George Washington Carver," delivered at the dedication of the Carver Science Hall at Simpson College, October 5, 1956, Simpson College Archives, Indianola, Iowa.

30. Russell Lord, *The Wallaces of Iowa (Boston: Houghton Mifflin, 1947),* 124–25. See Wallace, "The Genetic Basis of Democracy," 154–55.

31. Henry C. Wallace, *Our Debt and Duty to the Farmer* (New York: Century, 1925), 196, 194. For a fuller discussion of the book (which was written in support of the McNary-Haugen Bill), see Winters, *Henry Cantwell Wallace*, 247–88.

32. George Washington Carver, "What Chemurgy Means to My People," *Farm Chemurgic Journal* 1 (September 1937): 2.

33. Wallace, *Our Debt and Duty to the Farmer*, 18–19.

34. Henry Wallace, "'Good Farming, Clear Thinking, Right Living,'—an exposition of the motto of *Wallace's Farmer* published Feb 18, 1916," College of Agriculture, Department of Food and Technology, box 1, ISU Archives.

35. For details of the accusations against Harry Wallace, see A. C. Tupper, *Iowa's Humiliation: Pseudo-science Played Out at Ames* (Osage, Iowa, 1894); and Tom O'Donnell, "Political, Publishing Hero—and Fired from ISU," *Iowa State Daily*, January 22, 1982, box 1, College of Agriculture, Department of Food and Technology Files, ISU Archives.

36. For reference to his support for enclosure, see "'Tama Jim' Wilson: A Sketch of the Life of Traer's Greatest Citizen," *Traer Star-Clipper*, September 3, 1920.

37. James W. Wilson to LHP, December 15, 1925, box 1, folder 1, James Wilson Papers, ISU Archives.

38. "A Sketch of the Life of Traer's Greatest Citizen."

39. For more biographical detail on Wilson, see Earley Vernon Wilcox, *Tama Jim* (Boston: Stratford, 1930), 1–27. Wilcox's book is a hagiographical account (done in collaboration with Wilson's daughter, Flora), but no one has written a documented biography of the man, despite his impressive résumé and obvious importance in the expansion of the USDA.

40. Quoted in Holt, *George Washington Carver*, 96.

41. GWC to the Milhollands, August 6, 1891.

42. James Wilson to GWC, February 1, 1911, James Wilson Private Book no. 13, from December 4, 1906, to July 3rd, 1911, James Wilson Papers, box 4, folder 3, ISU Archives.

43. Quoted in Wilcox, *Tama Jim*, 46–47.

44. Quoted in ibid., 51.

45. GWC to BTW, April 12, 1896; GWC to BTW, May 16, 1896, box 4, GWCP, TUA.

46. GWC to LHP, April 29, 1918, box 4, LHP Papers, ISU Archives. For similar professions by Carver, see Louis H. Pammel, "Conversation with Prof. G. W. Carver at Tuskegee, Alabama, February 11, 1924," box 4, LHP Papers, ISU Archives; and GWC to LHP, June 18, 1921, LHP Papers, box 4, ISU Archives.

47. Marjorie Conley Pohl, "Louis H. Pammel: Pioneer Botanist, a Biography," *Proceedings of the Iowa Academy of Science* 92 (January 1985): 3.

48. Quoted in ibid., 5.

49. L. H. Pammel, "On the Structure of the Testa of Several Leguminous Seeds," *Bulletin of the Torrey Botanical Club* 13 (February 1886): 17–24.

50. Rodgers, *American Botany*, 225–28; Pohl, "Louis H. Pammel," 8.

51. Pohl, "Louis H. Pammel," 9.

52. According to Pohl, "Pammel wrote about seven hundred papers and miscellaneous publications, in addition to ten books." Many of these were related to his "second career" as a conservationist, and hence were not scientific. For a list, see Pohl, "Louis H. Pammel," 40–50.

53. GWC to My esteemed friend, Miss V. Pammel, March 17, 1935, box 4, LHP Papers, ISU Archives.

54. In his 1903 textbook, Pammel referred to Darwin as "the greatest naturalist of the last century." See Louis Herman Pammel, *Ecology* (Carroll, Iowa: J. B. Hungerford, 1903), v.

55. Rodgers, *American Botany*, 2, 318–19.

56. Cited in Pammel, *Ecology*, 217. Darwin had recommended that gardeners plant seed raised in different localities in alternating rows to foster cross-fertilization.

57. Worster, *Nature's Economy*, 192.

58. The accounts of ecology's origins draw heavily from sketches written by early scientists in the field. Paul B. Sears, a student of Henry Cowles at the University of Chicago and unquestionably one of the early twentieth century's most important ecologists, produced probably the most cited of these accounts, and most subsequent accounts have followed his. See Paul B. Sears, "Some Notes on the Ecology of Ecologists," *Scientific Monthly* 83 (July 1956): 22–27.

59. Worster, *Nature's Economy*, 198.

60. Pammel, *Ecology*, preface.

61. Walter P. Taylor, "What Is Ecology and What Good Is It?," *Ecology* 17 (July 1936): 333.

62. Sears, "Notes on the Ecology of Ecologists," 22.

63. See Victor E. Shelford, "The Organization of the Ecological Society of America, 1914–1919," *Ecology* 19 (January 1938): 164–65.

64. Sears, "Notes on the Ecology of Ecologists," 24. In the preface to *Ecology*, Pammel claimed that a decade had passed since *Flower Ecology* was published, which would place the publication of the book in 1893, the same year as the first gathering of ecologists at the Madison Botanical Congress. WorldCat gives the publication date as 1890, which is unlikely for a number of reasons, including the fact that Pammel cited experiments from the early 1890s. See Louis H. Pammel, *Flower Ecology* (Carroll, Iowa: J. B. Hungerford, n.d.).

65. See Worster, *Nature's Economy*, 205–12.

66. Pammel, *Ecology*, 288.

67. Ibid., 332–39, 289; Louis Herman Pammel, *The Weed Flora of Iowa*, Iowa Geological Survey Bulletin (Des Moines: Iowa Geological Survey, 1913), 687.

68. For more on this concern with invasive species, see Pauly, *Biologists and the Promise of American Life*, 71–92.

69. Louis H. Pammel, "Some Economic Phases of Botany," *Science*, January 7, 1921, 4–15.

70. Liberty Hyde Bailey, "Coxey's Army and the Russian Thistle: An Essay on the Philosophy of Weediness," in Bailey, *The Survival of the Unlike*, 2nd ed. (New York: Macmillan, 1897), 201.

71. Pammel, "Some Economic Phases of Botany," 13.

72. Although historians have yet to pay much attention to the early connections between agriculture and ecology, scholars have offered a number of thoughtful analyses of ecology's origins. For more on the early history of ecology, see Tobey, *Saving the Prairies*; Robert McIntosh, *The Background of Ecology: Concept and Theory* (New York: Cambridge University Press, 1985); Sharon E. Kingsland, *The Evolution of American Ecology, 1890–2000* (Baltimore: Johns Hopkins University Press, 2005); Frank Benjamin Golley, *A History of the Ecosystem Concept in Ecology: More than the Sum of the Parts* (New Haven: Yale University Press, 1993); Joel B. Hagen, *An Entangled Bank: The Origins of Ecosystem Ecology* (New Brunswick:

Rutgers University Press, 1992); Gregg Mitman, *The State of Nature: Ecology, Community, and American Social Thought, 1900–1950* (Chicago: University of Chicago Press, 1992).

73. Pammel, *Ecology*, 53.

74. Louis Herman Pammel, "Training Modern Botanists," *Alumnus* (May 1914).

75. Barrington Moore, "The Scope of Ecology," *Ecology* 1 (January 1920): 4.

76. For more on the connections between ecology and agronomy during the Progressive Era, see Mark D. Hersey, "'What We Need Is a Crop Ecologist': The Co evolution of Ecology and Agronomy in Progressive Era America," *Agricultural History* 85 (summer 2011): forthcoming.

77. See Sears, "Ecology of Ecologists," 22; Taylor, "What Is Ecology?," 335. Easily the most influential scientist in this regard, however, was Aldo Leopold, whose *Sand County Almanac* is canonical among environmentalists today.

78. Pammel, *Ecology*, 52.

79. Louis Hermann Pammel, "The Preservation of Natural History Spots in Iowa," box 38, folder 2, LHP Papers, ISU Archives.

80. "Proceedings: Meetings of the Ecological Society of America at Toronto Meeting of December 28, 1921," *Ecology* 3 (April 1922): 170–71.

81. George Washington Carver, "A Few Hints to Southern Farmers," *Southern Workman and Hampton School Record* (September 1899).

82. See Pohl, "Louis H. Pammel," 11; Louis Hermann Pammel, "Dr. Asa Gray," in *Prominent Men I Have Met* (Ames, Iowa: Powers Press, n.d.), 27, box 22, LHP Papers, ISU Archives.

83. GWC to Mrs. Milholland, March 5, 1934, folder 1470, GWCNM Archives.

84. Eugene Cittadino, "Ecology and American Social Thought, Abstract," http://www.nd.edu/~ccolthco/abstracts_cittadino.htm, accessed July 1, 2010. The classic account of the connections between the development of ecology and American social thought is Mitman, *The State of Nature*.

85. Transcript of George W. Carver, GWC Papers, ISU Archives.

86. Geo. W. Carver, "Grafting the Cacti," *Report of the Iowa State Horticultural Society for the Year 1893*, box 2, folder 10, GWC Papers, ISU Archives. "On motion," the report added, "Mr. Carver was made an honorary member" (259).

87. Carver, "Plants as Modified by Man," BSA thesis, 1894, box 2, folder 11, GWC Papers, ISU Archives.

88. Ibid., 2–3.

89. Commencement of the Iowa State Agricultural College, Tuesday, November 13, 1894," folder 110, GWCNM Archives; Charles D. Reed, "George Washington Carver, Mystic Scientist," *Annals of Iowa: An Historical Quarterly* 24 (January 1943): 248–53. His friends from Simpson "sent him a handsome bouquet as a token of remembrance." See *Simpsonian* (December 1894).

90. Carver to My dear friends, October 15, 1894, folder 1432, GWCNM Archives.

91. "Census Record for the Family of Eliza Owens," GWC Papers, box 1, folder 4, ISU Archives.

92. *The Bomb* (1896), 55.

93. "Dr. Pammel's Letter," *Ames Daily Tribune,* July 9, 1928.

94. Ibid.; LHP to Mrs. L. D. McCullough, November 3, 1928, LHP Papers, ISU Archives.

95. Louis Hermann Pammel and George W. Carver, *Treatment of Currants and Cherries to Prevent Spot Diseases,* Iowa Agricultural Experiment Station Bulletin 30 (1895); Louis Hermann Pammel and George W. Carver, "Fungus Diseases of Plants at Ames, Iowa, 1895," *Proceedings of the Iowa Academy of Science* 3 (1895): 140–48.

96. George W. Carver, *Best Ferns for the North and Northwest,* Iowa Agricultural Experiment Station Bulletin 27 (1895), GWC Papers, box 2, folder 10, ISU Archives.

97. George W. Carver, *Our Window Gardens,* Iowa Agricultural Experiment Station Bulletin 32 (1896), GWC Papers, box 2, folder 10, ISU Archives.

98. *Report of the Iowa State Horticultural Society for the Year 1895* 30 (Des Moines: F. R. Conway, State Printer), 147.

99. *Forty-second Annual Report of the Board of Directors of the Iowa State Agricultural Society for the Year 1895* (Des Moines: F. R. Conway, State Printer, 1896), 239; *Report of the Iowa State Horticultural Society for the Year 1895,* 63.

100. Quoted in Holt, *George Washington Carver,* 95–97.

101. GWC to BTW, April 3, 1896, box 4, GWCP, TUA.

102. GWC to BTW, April 5, 1896, box 4, GWCP, TUA.

103. GWC to BTW, April 12, 1896, box 4, GWCP, TUA.

104. BTW to GWC, April 17, 1896, box 4, GWCP, TUA.

105. GWC to BTW, April 21, 1896, box 4, GWCP, TUA.

106. GWC to BTW, May 16, 1896, box 4, GWCP, TUA.

107. *Iowa Agricultural College Student,* October 6, 1896, 5.

108. "A Card of Thanks," *Iowa Agricultural College Student,* October 27, 1896, 7.

Chapter 3. The Ruthless Hand of Mr. Carenot

1. For more on the Creeks, see Steven C. Hahn, *The Invention of the Creek Nation, 1670–1763* (Lincoln: University of Nebraska Press, 2004); John R. Swanton, *Early History of the Creek Indians and Their Neighbors* (1922; reprint, Gainesville: University Press of Florida, 1998); Marvin T. Smith, *Archaeology of Aboriginal Culture Change in the Interior Southeast; Depopulation during the Early Historic Period* (Gainesville: University Presses of Florida, 1987); Robbie Ethridge, *Creek Country: The Creek Indians and Their World* (Chapel Hill: University of North Carolina Press, 2003); and Robbie Etheridge and Charles Hudson, eds., *The Transformation of the Southeastern Indians, 1540–1760* (Oxford: University Press of Mississippi, 2002).

2. Quote is from William Bartram, *Travels and Other Writings* (New York: Library of America, 1996), 323–25.

3. Ethridge, *Creek Country*, 36.

4. H. Thomas Foster II, ed., *The Collected Work of Benjamin Hawkins* (Tuscaloosa: University of Alabama Press, 2003), 37–38.

5. See, for example, Captain Basil Hall, *Travels in North America in the Years 1827 and 1828* (Edinburgh: Cadell, 1830), 3:249.

6. Foster, ed., *The Collected Works of Benjamin Hawkins*, 33s–34s.

7. For more on canebrakes in the antebellum South generally, see Mart A. Stewart, "From King Cane to King Cotton: Razing Cane in the Old South," *Environmental History* 12 (January 2007): 59–79.

8. Bartram, *Travels*, 55.

9. The geological and ecological literature on the Black Belt is voluminous. For a small sampling, see Jim Lacefield, *Lost Worlds in Alabama's Rocks: A Guide to the State's Ancient Life and Landscape* (Paleo-Alabama Project, 2000); A. S. Jones and E. G. Patton, "Forest, 'Prairie,' and Soils in the Black Belt of Sumter County, Alabama," *Ecology* 47 (January 1966): 75–80; M. R. Harper, "The Limestone Prairies of Wilcox County, Alabama," *Ecology* 1 (July 1920): 198–203; M. R. Harper, "A Botanical and Geological Trip on the Warrior and Tombigbee Rivers in the Coastal Plain of Alabama," *Bulletin of the Torrey Botanical Club* 37 (1910): 107–26; J. A. Barone and J. G. Hill, "Herbaceous Flora of the Blackland Prairie Remnants in Mississippi and Western Alabama," *Castanea* 72 (December 2007): 167–71; J. A. Barone, "Historical Presence and Distribution of Prairies in the Black Belt of Mississippi and Alabama," *Castanea* 70 (September 2005): 170–83; W. W. McGuire, "On the Prairies of Alabama," *American Journal of Science and Arts* 26 (July 1834): 93–98.

10. Bartram, *Travels*, 324–25.

11. Ibid., 324.

12. Philip Henry Gosse, *Letters from Alabama, Chiefly Relating to Natural History* (Tuscaloosa: University of Alabama Press, 1993), 75.

13. John Leighly, ed., *Land and Life: A Selection from the Writings of Carl Ortwin Sauer* (Berkeley: University of California Press, 1963), 144.

14. George Washington Carver, "A Few Hints to Southern Farmers," *Southern Workman and Hampton School Record* (September 1899).

15. See Ethridge, *Creek Country*, 154–55.

16. J. Leitch Wright Jr., *Creeks and Seminoles: The Destruction and Regeneration of the Muscogolge People* (Lincoln: University of Nebraska Press, 1986), 42. For a further discussion of the impact of the Yamasee War, see Ethridge, *Creek Country*, 24–25; Hahn, *Invention of the Creek Nation*, 81–83; and Shepard Krech III, *The Ecological Indian: Myth and History* (New York: W. W. Norton, 1999), 157.

17. See Krech, *The Ecological Indian*, 171.

18. Ethridge, *Creek Country*, 13.

19. For more on the Treaty of Indian Springs and the Treaty of Washington (1826), see R. Douglas Hurt, *The Indian Frontier, 1763–1846* (Albuquerque: University of New Mexico Press, 2002), 145–48.

20. For a complete listing of the towns and their populations in 1836, see Elizabeth Hughes Yamaguchi, "Macon County, Alabama: Its Land and Its People from Pre-history to 1870" (master's thesis, Auburn University, 1981), 216 fn. 13. The estimate of six thousand Creeks living in the county comes from T. S. Woodward, an early settler of Macon County who was employed by the Bureau of Indian Affairs in the 1830s. See Woodward to Governor Clement C. Clay, February 18, 1836, in *American State Papers: Documents, Legislative and Executive of the Congress of the United States for the First and Second Sessions of the Twenty-fourth Congress: Military Affairs* 6 (Washington: Gale and Seaton, 1861), 697–98.

21. Yamaguchi, "Macon County," 50, 206 fn. 31, 343.

22. Charles Hudson, *The Southeastern Indians* (Knoxville: University of Tennessee Press, 1976), 460.

23. *Montgomery Advertiser*, May 17, 1836.

24. See Una Pope-Hennessy, ed., *The Aristocratic Journey: Being the Outspoken Letters of Mrs. Basil Hall, Written during a Fourteen Months' Sojourn in America, 1827–28* (New York: G. P. Putnam's Sons, 1931), 243; Basil Hall, *Travels in North America in the Years 1827 and 1828*, 2:276; and George W. Featherstonaugh, *Excursion through the Slave States, from Washington on the Potomac, to the Frontier of Mexico; with Sketches of Popular Manners and Geological Notices* (New York: Harper, 1844), 152. On Europeans' awe for the richness of America's resources, see Harriet Martineau, *Society in America* (London: Saunders and Otley, 1837), 1:214–17.

25. H. M. King, "Historical Sketches of Macon County," *Alabama Historical Quarterly* 18 (1956): 209; Yamaguchi, "Macon County," 64.

26. See Yamaguchi, "Macon County," 226 fn. 35, 67. Not all of that acreage was in Macon County.

27. Ibid., 65, 219 fn. 16, 226 fn. 35.

28. The debate was announced in the *Macon Republican* on November 22, 1849, cited in Yamaguchi, "Macon County," 267 fn. 37.

29. Yamaguchi, "Macon County," 258 fn. 33.

30. Ibid., 321 table 8. Yamaguchi transcribed statistics for the county from the 1850 census.

31. Ibid., 321 table 8, 323 table 10.

32. Ibid., 324 table 11.

33. Weymouth T. Jordan, *Rebels in the Making: Planters' Conventions and Southern Propaganda* (Tuscaloosa, Ala.: Confederate Publishing, 1958), 19. Jordan actually applied this to all southerners but drew his evidence almost exclusively from Alabama sources. For a discussion of crop diversification in antebellum Alabama,

see Weymouth T. Jordan, *Antebellum Alabama: Town and Country* (Tallahassee: Florida State University Press, 1957), 9–15.

34. Hiram Fuller, *Belle Britain on Tour, at Newport and Here and There* (New York, 1858), 112, quoted in Jordan, *Antebellum Alabama*, 21.

35. James M. Torbert, "James M. Torbert's Journal for 1856," *Alabama Historical Quarterly* 18 (1956): 219, 225, 229, 230.

36. Ibid., 236. All Torbert quotes are verbatim. As they are replete with grammatical and spelling errors, using "*sic*" would make them too difficult to follow.

37. Ibid., 279–80.

38. James M. Torbert, "James M. Torbert's Journal for 1857–1874," *Alabama Historical Quarterly* 22 (1960): 47–48, 37, 43, 54–55.

39. Johnson, *Shadow of the Plantation*, 13.

40. Albert E. Cowdrey, *This Land, This South: An Environmental History* (Lexington: University Press of Kentucky, 1983), 76.

41. In his classic work *Breaking the Land*, Pete Daniel asserts that "until the 1880s [cotton] seeds were discarded, except for enough to plant the next year." This was not the case in Macon County. James Torbert, for instance, noted in March 1859, "I am Manureing all My Corn this year with Cotton Seed." To be certain, I'm not sure how experimental Torbert's use of cottonseed was. Because the Civil War interrupted his cotton production three years later, there is no clear record as to whether or not he continued to use it. See Pete Daniel, *Breaking the Land: The Transformation of Cotton, Tobacco, and Rice Cultures since 1880* (Urbana: University of Illinois Press, 1985), 52.

42. Noah B. Cloud, "Chapter II: Dr. N. B. Cloud's Improved System of Cotton Culture," in *The Cotton Planter's Manual: Being a Compilation of Facts from the Best Authorities on the Culture of Cotton; Its Natural History, Chemical Analysis, Trade and Consumption; and Embracing a History of Cotton and the Cotton Gin*, by J. A. Turner (New York: C. M. Saxton, 1857), 53.

43. Torbert, "Tobert's Journal for 1856," 245–55.

44. For a representative, though hardly exhaustive, literature on antebellum southern agriculture, see Avery O. Craven, *Soil Exhaustion as a Factor in the Agricultural History of Virginia and Maryland, 1606–1860* (University of Illinois Press, 1925; reprint, Columbia: University of South Carolina Press, 2006); Lynn Nelson, *Pharsalia: An Environmental Biography of a Southern Plantation, 1780–1880* (Athens: University of Georgia Press, 2007); Edmund Ruffin, *Nature's Management: Writings on Landscape and Reform, 1822–1859*, edited by Jack Temple Kirby (Athens: University of Georgia Press, 2000); Mart A. Stewart, *"What Nature Suffers to Groe": Life, Labor, and Landscape on the Georgia Coast, 1680–1920* (Athens: University of Georgia Press, 1996); Benjamin R. Cohen, *Notes from the Ground: Science, Soil, and Society in the American Countryside* (New Haven: Yale University Press, 2009); and Lewis C. Gray, *History of Agriculture in the Southern United*

States to 1860, 2 vols. (Washington, D.C.: Carnegie Institution, 1933). This is not to say, of course, that the Old Southwest has been completely ignored, though it attracted considerably more attention in the mid-twentieth century than it has in recent decades. See, for instance, John Hebron Moore, *Agriculture in Antebellum Mississippi* (1958; reprint, Columbia: University of South Carolina Press, 2010); and the works of Weymouth T. Jordan, who focused a good deal of attention on Cloud; also Weymouth T. Jordan, "Noah B. Cloud's Activities on Behalf of Southern Agriculture," *Agricultural History* 25 (April 1951): 53–58.

45. Craven, *Soil Exhaustion as a Factor in the Agricultural History of Virginia and Maryland*, 164.

46. Mart Stewart made this point in Stewart, "From King Cane to King Cotton," 60–61.

47. Quoted in Craven, *Soil Exhaustion as a Factor in the Agricultural History of Virginia and Maryland*, 34.

48. Cowdrey, *This Land, This South*, 76.

49. Quoted in Jordan, *Antebellum Alabama*, 110.

50. The most complete account of this sort of high-minded husbandry in North America is Stoll, *Larding the Lean Earth*; also see Cohen, *Notes from the Ground*.

51. See Stoll, *Larding the Lean Earth*, 153; and Ruffin, *Nature's Management*, xix–xx, 47–99.

52. See John Taylor (of Caroline County, Virginia), *Arator: Being a Series of Agricultural Essays, Practical and Political: in Sixty one Numbers*, 3rd ed. (Baltimore: J. Robinson for John M. Carter, 1817). For more on Taylor, see Craven, *Soil Exhaustion as a Factor in the Agricultural History of Virginia and Maryland*, 99–103; and Nelson, *Pharsalia*, 75–80.

53. Quoted in Stoll, *Larding the Lean Earth*, 125.

54. Cloud, "Cloud's Improved System," 56.

55. Ibid., 53 (italics here and in all other excerpts from Cloud are his).

56. Ibid., 69–70.

57. Ibid., 55–56.

58. Ibid., 65.

59. Ibid., 60.

60. Ibid., 54.

61. Ibid., 55.

62. Ibid., 76.

63. Ibid., 63–64.

64. Robert Russell, *North America: Its Agriculture and Climate, containing observations on the agriculture and climate of Canada, the United States, and the Island of Cuba* (Edinburgh: Adam and Charles Black, 1857), 297.

65. Cloud, "Cloud's Improved System," 73–74.

66. For more on the connection between the treatment of soil and the virtue of

those who worked it, see Stoll, *Larding the Lean Earth*, 31–41; and Cohen, *Notes from the Ground*, 1–48.

67. See Weymouth T. Jordan, "Noah B. Cloud and the *American Cotton Planter*," *Agricultural History* 31 (October 1957): 44. Cloud had launched the paper in 1853. It merged with the Georgia-based *Soil of the South* in 1857 to form the *American Cotton Planter and Soil of the South*.

68. Frederick Law Olmsted, *Journeys and Explorations in the Cotton Kingdom of America* (1861), 274.

69. Quoted in James C. Bonner, "Plantation Architecture of the Lower South on the Eve of the Civil War," *Journal of Southern History* 11 (August 1945): 374.

70. See Clifton Johnson, *Highways and Byways of the South* (New York: Macmillan, 1904), 88–89.

71. Bonner, "Plantation Architecture," 383–84, 386.

72. See ibid., 385–86, 385 fn. 52.

73. Torbert, "Torbert's Journal for 1857–1874," 56–57.

74. Quoted in Yamaguchi, "Macon County," 142.

75. Lucille Griffith, *Alabama: A Documentary History to 1900*, rev. and enl. (Tuscaloosa: University of Alabama Press, 1972), 418.

76. Gavin Wright, *Old South, New South: Revolutions in the Southern Economy since the Civil War* (New York: Basic Books, 1986), 89.

77. David Danbom, *Born in the Country: A History of Rural America* (Baltimore: Johns Hopkins University Press, 1995), 116.

78. Yamaguchi, "Macon County," 157–58; Torbert, "Torbert's Journal for 1856," 63.

79. An account of the assault on Alston (and of the process of "Redemption" in Macon County) can be found in Robert J. Norrell, *Reaping the Whirlwind: The Civil Rights Movement in Tuskegee* (New York: Alfred A. Knopf, 1985), 3–11. He drew much of his evidence from testimony that various members of the county gave before Congress in 1872. See U.S. Senate Reports, no. 22, *Testimony Taken by the Joint Select Committee to Inquire into the Conditions of Affairs in the Late Insurrectionary States, Alabama*, 42nd Cong., 2nd Sess., vol. 9 (Washington: Government Printing Office, 1872), 1016–1112.

80. Griffith, *Alabama: A Documentary History*, 490. See also Norrell, *Reaping the Whirlwind*, 10–11, 19–20, 36.

81. For a discussion of the emergence of sharecropping, see Wright, *Old South, New South*, and *Political Economy of the Cotton South* (New York: W. W. Norton, 1978).

82. See Wright, *Old South, New South*, 102.

83. Johnson, *Shadow of the Plantation*, 25.

84. For a deeper discussion of this transformation, see Wright, *Old South, New South*.

85. Quoted in King, "The Closing of the Southern Range," 57.

86. McWhiney, "The Revolution in Nineteenth Century Agriculture," in *From Civil War to Civil Rights: Alabama, 1860–1960: An Anthology from the* Alabama Review, ed. Sarah Woolfolk Wiggins (Tuscaloosa: University of Alabama Press, 1987), 128.

87. See King, "The Closing of the Southern Range," 63–64, 67.

88. Yamaguchi, "Macon County," 146; McWhiney, "The Revolution in Nineteenth Century Agriculture."

89. See Yamaguchi, "Macon County," 272 fn. 3.

90. For more on the founding of Tuskegee, see Norrell, *Reaping the Whirlwind*, 11–18; and Booker T. Washington, *Up from Slavery by Booker T. Washington, with Related Documents*, edited with an introduction by W. Fitzhugh Brundage (New York: Bedford/St. Martin's, 2003), 89–94.

91. Washington, *Up from Slavery*, 91, 95.

92. Booker T. Washington, *My Larger Education* (New York: Doubleday, 1911), 63.

93. Edward L. Ayers, *The Promise of the New South: Life after Reconstruction* (New York: Oxford University Press, 1992), 326.

94. I am indebted to Linda McMurry Edwards for insisting that I note Washington's qualification. He is too often portrayed as something akin to a race traitor and as a poor foil to W. E. B. DuBois.

95. Ayers, *Promise of the New South*, 324.

96. See *Tuskegee Normal and Industrial Institute Catalogue, 1896–97* (Tuskegee, Ala.: Normal School Steam Press Print, 1897).

97. Washington, *Up from Slavery*, 190.

98. Ibid., 90.

99. Ibid., 92–94.

100. Eugene Allen Smith, *Report on the Cotton Production of the State of Alabama* (Washington, D.C.: GPO, 1884), 64.

101. *Report of the Commissioner of Agriculture of the State of Alabama, from September 1, 1883, to September 1, 1886* (Montgomery, Ala., 1886), 8. For more on the Grange in Alabama, see William Warren Rogers, "The Alabama State Grange," in *From Civil War to Civil Rights*, ed. Wiggins, 133–44

102. *Report of the Commissioner of Agriculture of the State of Alabama, from September 1, 1883, to September 1, 1886*, 18–19.

103. *Rural Alabamian* (January 1872): 9; *Rural Alabamian* (April 1872): 178; *Rural Alabamian* (November 1872): 515–17, 524 524–25, emphasis his.

104. *Rural Alabamian* (November 1872), 524.

105. Ibid.

106. Eugene Allen Smith, *Geological Survey of Alabama: Report for the Years 1881 and 1882, Embracing an Account of the Agricultural Features of the State* (Montgomery, Ala.: W. D. Brown, 1883), 492.

107. See Alan I. Marcus, "Setting the Standard: Fertilizers, State Chemists, and Early National Commercial Regulation, 1880–1887," *Agricultural History* 61 (winter 1987): 50.

108. *Report of the Commissioner of Agriculture of the State of Alabama, from September 1, 1883, to September 1, 1886*, 8–9.

109. *Addresses of Dr. N. T. Lupton and Dr. Eugene A. Smith Delivered before the State Agricultural Society in Convention at Selma, Ala., Feb. 2d, 1888* (Montgomery, Ala.: W. E. Allred, 1888), 23.

110. *Report of the Commissioner of Agriculture of the State of Alabama, from September 1, 1883, to September 1, 1886*, 10.

111. E. Smith, *Geological Survey of Alabama*, 112–14, 310.

112. Charles S. Aiken, *The Cotton Plantation South since the Civil War* (Baltimore: Johns Hopkins University Press, 1998), 45–46.

113. E. Smith, *Geological Survey of Alabama*, 11.

114. *Report of the Commissioner of Agriculture of the State of Alabama, from September 1, 1883, to September 1, 1886*, 16.

115. See Norrell, *Reaping the Whirlwind*, 19–20.

116. Booker T. Washington, "The Rural Negro Community," *Annals of the American Academy of Political and Social Science* 40 (March 1912): 85.

117. See Edward L. Ayers, *Southern Crossing: A History of the American South, 1877–1906* (New York: Oxford University Press, 1995), 35–36.

118. Washington, "The Rural Negro Community," 85.

119. See Norrell, *Reaping the Whirlwind*, 21.

120. DuBois, *The Souls of Black Folk*, 128.

121. George Washington Carver, "A Gleam upon the Distant Horizon," unpublished typescript (1941), box 65, GWCP, TUA.

Chapter 4. In a Strange Land and among a Strange People

1. George Washington Carver, "A Gleam upon the Distant Horizon."

2. Script for George Washington Carver Broadcast: U.S. Office of Education, October 19, 1941, box 66, GWCP, TUA.

3. George Washington Carver, "What Chemurgy Means to My People," *Farm Chemurgic Journal* (September 1937): 40; George Washington Carver, *The Need of Scientific Agriculture in the South*," Farmer's Leaflet from the Bureau of Nature Study for Schools and Hints and Suggestions for Farmers, no. 7 (April 1902).

4. GWC to Mrs. L. H. Pammel, March 30, 1897, box 14, LHP Papers, ISU Archives.

5. "Agricultural Experiment Station Notes" (1897), box 67, GWCP, TUA.

6. See Steven Stoll, *Larding the Lean Earth*, 16.

7. For some yearly rainfall totals, see George Washington Carver, *A Study of the Soils of Macon County, Alabama and Their Adaptability to Certain Crops*, Tuskegee Agricultural Experiment Station [henceforth TAES] Bulletin 25 (October 1913), 6.

Carver later reported that this soil erosion cost the South an estimated $400 million yearly. See Carver, "What Chemurgy Means to My People," 40.

8. GWC to Mrs. L. H. Pammel, March 30, 1897. Though addressed to Pammel's wife—an indication of Carver's close relationship with the Pammels—Carver expected his former professor to read the letter as well.

9. Johnson, *Shadow of the Plantation*, 191.

10. For Carver's account of the incident, see GWC to BTW, November 28, 1902, box 4, GWCP, TUA.

11. GWC to the Messrs of the Finance Committee, November 27, 1896, box 4, GWCP, TUA.

12. Ibid.

13. Kremer, *In His Own Words*, 60.

14. For more on Carver's "scavenging" for weeds, see transcript of Toby Fishbein interview with Austin W. Curtis in Detroit, Mich., March 3, 1979, box 2, GWC Papers, ISU Archives; and George Washington Carver, *Nature's Garden for Victory and Peace*, TAES Bulletin 43 (March 1942), 331.

15. Kremer, *In His Own Words*, 60.

16. BTW to GWC, February 26, 1911.

17. "Schedule of Classes Taught per Week by G. W. Carver," 1905?, box 4, GWCP, TUA.

18. McMurry, "A Vision for the Future." For Carver's charge to test the water, see BTW to GWC, October 11, 1898, box 4, GWCP, TUA; and GWC to Mr. Thomas, September 20, 1899, box 4, GWCP, TUA.

19. GWC to BTW, April 28, 1899, box 4, folder 4, GWCP, TUA.

20. BTW to GWC, September 8, 1900, box 4, folder 5, GWCP, TUA; BTW to GWC, October 11, 1898, box 4, GWCP, TUA; BTW to GWC, September 28, 1900, box 4, GWCP, TUA.

21. BTW memo, box 7, GWCP, TUA.

22. See LHP to GWC, October 29, 1919, box 14, LHP Papers, ISU Archives.

23. See GWC to BTW, July 19, 1898, box 4, GWCP, TUA; BTW to GWC, April 15, 1901, box 4, GWCP, TUA.

24. GWC to BTW, August 27, 1898, box 4, GWCP, TUA.

25. GWC to LHP, September 18, 1907, box 14, LHP Papers, ISU Archives.

26. For some of his mycological work, see J. B. Ellis and B. M. Everhart, "New Alabama Fungi," *Journal of Mycology* 8 (June 1902): 62–73, which includes a substantial list of fungi "collected in the vicinity of Tuskegee, Alabama by George W. Carver."

27. GWC to BTW, June 21, 1898, box 4, GWCP, TUA; Warren Logan to GWC, January 24, 1911, box 8, GWCP, TUA.

28. GWC to BTW, November 23, 1900, box 4, GWCP, TUA; "Faculty Meeting D. of Ag.," November 1, 1910, box 68, GWCP, TUA.

29. GWC to BTW, May 30, 1898, box 4, GWCP, TUA.

30. GWC to Mr. W. Logan, August 4, 1898, box 4, GWCP, TUA.

31. GWC to BTW, August 4, 1898, box 4, GWCP, TUA.

32. GWC to Mr. Logan, August 11, 1898, box 4, folder 3, GWCP, TUA.

33. John H. Washington [henceforth JHW] to BTW, April 5, 1902, box 68, GWCP, TUA.

34. GWC to BTW, September 7, 1899, box 4, GWCP, TUA.

35. BTW to GWC, May 17, 1901, box 4, GWCP, TUA.

36. See R. E. Malone, *Smudging an Orchard with Native Material in Alabama*, TAES Bulletin 28 (1915).

37. GWC to BTW, July 23, 1901, box 4, GWCP, TUA.

38. BTW to GWC (and GWC's reply), December 23, 1899, box 4, GWCP, TUA, emphasis his.

39. GWC to BTW, September 20, 1897, box 4, GWCP, TUA.

40. JHW to GWC, March 26, 1902, box 4, GWCP, TUA; JHW to GWC March 31, 1902, box 4, GWCP, TUA; and JHW to GWC, March 28, 1902, box 4, GWCP, TUA.

41. GWC to BTW, August 4, 1898.

42. GWC to BTW, September 14, 1897, box 4, GWCP, TUA.

43. GWC to BTW, June 21, 1898, box 4, GWCP, TUA.

44. See, for example, Council Report in the BTW Papers at the Library of Congress—Department of Research, Exp. Sta., 1912, box 68, GWCP, TUA; GWC to BTW, August 4, 1898.

45. GWC to BTW, January 17, 1902, box 4, GWCP, TUA.

46. GWC to BTW, April 25, 1902, box 4, GWCP, TUA.

47. See BTW to GWC, September 29, 1899, box 4, GWCP, TUA.

48. GWC to BTW, n.d. (ca. fall 1899), box 4, GWCP, TUA.

49. GWC to BTW, December 6, 1900, box 4, GWCP, TUA.

50. GWC to BTW, October 14, 1904, in Kremer, *In His Own Words*, 70.

51. GWC to James Wilson, July 23, 1904; and James Wilson to GWC, July 25, 1904, GWCP, TUA (microfilm), roll 2.

52. GWC to BTW, November 8, 1904, in Kremer, *In His Own Words*, 71–72.

53. Ibid., 72.

54. GWC to BTW November 14, 1904, in Kremer, *In His Own Words*, 72–75.

55. Ibid., 75.

56. See R. C. Bruce to GWC, December 28, 1904, box 5, GWCP, TUA.

57. GWC to BTW, December 7, 1904, box 5, GWCP, TUA.

58. BTW Papers (1908), box 68, GWCP, TUA.

59. See GWC to BTW, May 4, 1912, in Kremer, *In His Own Words*, 76.

60. BTW to GWC, May 1, 1911; and JHW to GWC, May 4, 1911, box 8, GWCP, TUA.

61. GWC to BTW, February 21, 1911, box 8, GWCP, TUA.

62. Louis R. Harlan, ed., *The Booker T. Washington Papers*, 14 vols. (Urbana:

University of Illinois Press, 1972–89), 11:312; GWC to BTW, May 4, 1912, in Kremer, *In His Own Words*, 76; BTW to GWC, March 1, 1911, box 8, GWCP, TUA.

63. BTW to GWC, February 26, 1911, box 8, GWCP, TUA; BTW to GWC, March 1, 1911.

64. BTW to Mary Elizabeth Preston Stearns, January 8, 1898, in Harlan, *Booker T. Washington Papers*, 4:360–61.

65. "For the Negro," *San Francisco Report*, November 18, 1897; see also the *Chicago Journal*, November 17, 1897.

66. See George Washington Carver, "The Tuskegee Normal and Industrial Institute and Experiment Station," *Proceedings of the Sixteenth Annual Convention of the Association of American Agricultural Colleges and Experiment Stations*, USDA, Office of Experiment Stations Bulletin 123 (1902). Although Carver expected one wing to house his herbarium and the other the "museum," it did not turn out that way. See GWC to LHP, February 12, 1902, LHP Papers, box 14, ISU Archives; Bennie D. Mayberry, *The Role of Tuskegee University in the Origin, Growth and Development of the Negro Cooperative Extension System, 1881–1990* (Tuskegee, Ala., 1989), 51.

67. See George Washington Carver, *Successful Yields of Small Grains*, TAES Bulletin 8 (January 1906).

68. GWC to BTW, June 5, 1899, box 4, GWCP, TUA; GWC to BTW, May 30, 1898.

69. GWC to BTW, August 6, 1890, box 4, GWCP, TUA; Malone, *Smudging an Orchard*, 4.

70. George Washington Carver, *Some Ornamental Plants of Macon County, Ala.*, TAES Bulletin 16 (October 1909), 5.

71. George Washington Carver, "Twelve Reasons Why Every Person in Macon County Should Attend the Macon County Fair," *Negro Farmer and Messenger* 18 (November 1916).

72. GWC to Mr. and Mrs. Milholland, February 28, 1905, GCWNM Archives; also in Kremer, *In His Own Words*, 152.

Chapter 5. Teaching the Beauties of Nature

1. GWC to BTW, July 23, 1901.

2. "Prof. Geo. W. Carver of Tuskegee Institute Visits Homer College—a Farmers' Conference Organized," *Christian Index* (Jackson, Tenn.: Christian Methodist Episcopal Church Publishing House), July 2, 1908.

3. George Washington Carver, "Botany Made Easy," n.d., box 65, folder 16, GWCP, TUA (emphasis added); George Washington Carver, "Suggested Outlines for the Study of Economic Plant Life for Use in Common Schools, High Schools and Academies," n.d., box 63, GWCP, TUA. For a contemporary scientist's view of the textbook, see Chas. S. Parker to Dr. R. R. Moton, February 12, 1920, box 68, GWCP, TUA.

4. See McMurry, *George Washington Carver*, 93–111; and Linda Elizabeth Ott Hines, "Background to Fame: The Career of George Washington Carver,

1896–1916" (PhD diss., Auburn University, 1976), 100–108. In an essay titled "How to Search for Truth," for example, Carver asserted that children "will study with increased enthusiasm the striking analogy" the life of a butterfly "bears to the human soul." See George Washington Carver, "How to Search for Truth" (1930), in Kremer, *In His Own Words*, 20.

5. George Washington Carver, "Address by Dr. G. W. Carver at Voorhees," 1.

6. Chas. S. Parker to Dr. R. R. Moton, February 12, 1920.

7. BTW to GWC, May 3, 1912; quoted in Barry Mackintosh, "George Washington Carver: The Making of a Myth," *Journal of Southern History* 42 (November 1976): 512–13.

8. McMurry, *George Washington Carver*, 95, 99; BTW to GWC, February 26, 1911.

9. George Washington Carver, "The Love of Nature," *Guide to Nature*, December 19, 1912, box 64, GWCP, TUA.

10. See, for instance, Carver, "How to Search for Truth," in Kremer, *In His Own Words*, 142.

11. Carver, "Botany Made Easy," 1.

12. Maurice A. Bigelow (managing editor of *Nature-Study Review*) to GWC, September 8, 1904, GWCP, TUA (microfilm), reel 2. For more on Carver's connection with Liberty Hyde Bailey, who likely recommended Carver for the board, see Pohl, "Louis H. Pammel," 23; and GWC to LHP, May 1, 1905, box 14, LHP Papers, ISU Archives.

13. GWC to BTW, n.d., partial letter, box 62, GWCP, TUA.

14. George Washington Carver, *Nature Study and Children's Gardens*, Teacher's Leaflet no. 2, Extension Division, Department of Agriculture, Tuskegee Normal and Industrial Institute, Alabama, n.d. See also George Washington Carver, *Nature Study and Gardening for Rural Schools*, TAES Bulletin 18 (June 1910); George Washington Carver, "Progressive Nature Studies," Tuskegee Institute Print (1897).

15. Carver, *Nature Study and Gardening for Rural Schools*, 5.

16. George Washington Carver, "Carver's Question box," March 27, 1926, box 64, GWCP, TUA.

17. George Washington Carver, "Agriculture and Nature Study," report submitted to BTW, April 20, 1910, box 65, GWCP, TUA.

18. Carver, *Nature Study and Gardening for Rural Schools*, 3.

19. GWC to BTW, n.d., partial letter.

20. Carver, *Nature Study and Gardening for Rural Schools*, 5.

21. GWC to BTW, n.d., partial letter.

22. See George Washington Carver, *Suggestions for Progressive and Correlative Nature Study*, Teacher's Leaflet no. 1 (1902), 18, box 63, GWCP, TUA.

23. See ibid.; and Carver, *Nature Study and Gardening for Rural Schools*.

24. C. A. Prosser to My dear Mr. Wilkinson (Stillwater, Okla.), March 4, 1911, box 68, GWCP, TUA.

25. For more on the significance of the nature study movement within Progressive conservation, see Kevin C. Armitage, *The Nature Study Movement: The Forgotten Popularizer of America's Conservation Ethic* (Lawrence: University Press of Kansas, 2009).

26. GWC to BTW, June 5, 1899.

27. Washington, *Up from Slavery*, 190.

28. "They Teach Farming at Tuskegee," *Montgomery Advertiser*, January 8, 1903.

29. *Tuskegee Normal and Industrial Institute Catalogue*, 1896–97.

30. *Tuskegee Normal and Industrial Institute Catalogue*, 1897–98; *Tuskegee Normal and Industrial Institute Catalogue*, 1901–2.

31. Carver, "Tuskegee Normal and Industrial Institute and Experiment Station."

32. "Prof. Geo. W. Carver . . . Visits Homer College."

33. Emmett S. Goff and Dexter Dwight Mayne, *First Principles of Agriculture* (New York: American Book Company, 1904), 11–12.

34. GWC, "Class Notes," box 67, folder 7, GWCP, TUA (emphasis his).

35. See, for instance, George B. Emerson, Charles L. Flint, and Charles Anthony Grossman, *Manual of Agriculture for the School, the Farm, and the Fireside by George B. Emerson and Charles L. Flint*, new ed., rev. by Charles A. Grossman (New York: O. Judd, 1890), 1.

36. Ibid., 38–39.

37. George Washington Carver, "Notes on Various Subjects," box 67, GWCP, TUA.

38. George Washington Carver, untitled (1914), box 65, GWCP, TUA.

39. Horace D. Slatter, "Men I Have Known: George W. Carver," *Afro-American* (Baltimore), October 14, 1916.

40. See, for instance, Carver's discussion of "parks" in "Notes on Various Subjects."

41. Wilcox, *Tama Jim*, 70.

42. James Wilson to GWC, September 1, 1908, in Peter Duncan Burchard, *George Washington Carver: For His Time and Ours. Special History Study—Natural History Related to George Washington Carver National Monument, Diamond, Missouri* (National Park Service, 2005), 35. For evidence of the involvement in the conservation movement of some of Carver's other mentors, see Gifford Pinchot, "Appreciation," in Henry C. Wallace, *Our Debt and Duty to the Farmer*, viii–ix; LHP to GWC, December 13, 1926, box 14, LHP Papers, ISU Archives; and Rebecca Conard, "Hot Kitchens in Places of Quiet Beauty: Iowa State Parks and the Transformation of Conservationist Goals," *Annals of Iowa* 51 (summer 1992): 441–79.

43. Slatter, "Men I Have Known."

44. Wendell Berry, *The Unsettling of America: Culture and Agriculture* (1977; reprint, San Francisco: Sierra Club Books, 1986), 147.

45. See Toby Fishbein interview with Austin Curtis, 33.

46. Carver, "Progressive and Correlative Nature Study," 5.

47. Thomas Monroe Campbell, "Cooperative Extension Work in Agriculture and Home Economics, State of Alabama, a Supplement to the Annual Report of the Agricultural Extension Service as Performed by Negroes for the Year Ending Dec. 31, 1919," Thomas Monroe Campbell Papers, TUA.

48. Oscar Parks (Council Bluffs, Iowa) to GWC, July 16, 1917, box 10, GWCP, TUA. Also see "Ki-Yi's Parting Address to Prof. C. [sic] W. Carver," *Tuskegee Botanical News* 1 (February 1915); and Elisha G. Jones (Tuscaloosa, Ala.) to GWC, January 14, 1911, box 8, GWCP, TUA.

49. See Kremer, *In His Own Words*, 85–86.

50. GWC to BTW, April 10, 1902, box 4, GWCP, TUA. See also GWC to BTW, April 25, 1902.

51. GWC to BTW, December 13, 1912, in Kremer, *In His Own Words*, 86.

52. R. Potts to LHP, August 15, 1914, September 12, 1914, and September 19, 1914, LHP Papers, ISU Archives.

53. See, for example, George? (Cornell, N.Y.) to GWC, July 25, 1917, box 10, GWCP, TUA; Penelope Sims (Ridgeway, S.C.) to GWC, July 1, 1918, box 10, GWCP, TUA; and J. H. Ward (Charlotte, N.C.) to GWC, February 16, 1918, box 10, GWCP, TUA.

54. J. H. Ward to GWC, October 10, 1917, box 10, GWCP, TUA.

55. See, for example, Ernest B. Frazier to GWC, December 18 and 26, 1918, box 10, GWCP, TUA. The former enclosed ten dollars to repay an earlier loan; the latter asked for yet another one. See also Wa. McMohan to GWC, July 9 and 15, 1917, box 10, GWCP, TUA—he had "had a misfortune & I lost everything," would Carver send money; and J. A. Taylor (Chicago, Ill.) to GWC, December 10, 1917, box 10, GWCP, TUA. For a request that Carver visit, see Ambrose Calliver (Nashville, Tenn.) to GWC, December 1, 1917, box 10, GWCP, TUA.

56. See, for instance, Charles D. Bonner to GWC, July 19, 1910, box 8, GWCP, TUA. On Carver's relationships with students, see, for example, unnamed student (Knoxville, Tenn.) to GWC, August 8, 1917, box 10, GWCP, TUA; J. L. Campbell (Manhattan, Kans.) to GWC, May 28, 1917, box 10, GWCP, TUA; Ambrose Calliver to GWC, December 1, 1919; "Cricket" (Hartford, Conn.) to GWC, January 26, 1919, box 10, GWCP, TUA.

57. Thomas M. Campbell, *The Movable School Goes to the Negro Farmer* (Tuskegee, Ala.: Tuskegee Institute Press, 1936), 47, 67.

58. GWC to BTW, May 14, 1902, box 4, GWCP, TUA.

59. GWC to BTW, June 4, 1906, box 7, GWCP, TUA.

60. George R. Bridgeforth to BTW, March 3, 1907; and George R. Bridgeforth to BTW, April 15, 1907, box 68, GWCP, TUA.

61. Thos. G. Roberts (Eagle Lake, Tex.) to GWC, February 3, 1905, box 6, GWCP, TUA.

62. Reilly(?)(Elizabeth City, N.C.), to GWC, November 11, 1917, box 10, GWCP, TUA.

63. A. O. Bains (San Antonio, Tex.) to GWC, July 16, 1917, box 10, GWCP, TUA.

64. H. B. Bennett (Stullo, Miss.) to GWC, July 19, 1910, box 8, GWCP, TUA.

65. Ger. D. White to GWC, February 22, 1918, box 10, GWCP, TUA.

66. S. R. Cassius (Meridian, Okla.) to GWC, February 13, 1911, box 8, GWCP, TUA.

67. GWC, "Tuskegee Normal and Industrial Institute and Experiment Station."

68. Allen W. Jones, "Thomas M. Campbell: Black Agricultural Leader of the New South," *Agricultural History* 53 (1979): 42.

69. For examples of Carver's students at such institutions, see J. H. Ward to GWC, October 10, 1917; John W. Goiens to GWC, January 22, 1919; and Geo W. Irwin (Alcorn, Miss.) to GWC, April 19, 1919, box 10, GWCP, TUA.

70. R. Potts to LHP, September 19, 1914, box 1, LHP Papers, ISU Archives. On teachers' pay, see Roy V. Scott, *The Reluctant Farmer: The Rise of Agricultural Extension to 1914* (Urbana: University of Illinois Press, 1970), 223.

71. Elisha G. Jones (Tuscaloosa, Ala.) to GWC, January 14, 1911, box 8, GWCP, TUA.

72. M. L. Moore (Cottage Grove, Ala.) to GWC, August 24, 1917, box 10, GWCP, TUA.

73. See J. L. Campbell (Manhattan, Kans.) to GWC, May 28, 1917; E. N. B. Campbell (Victoria, Tex.) to GWC, September 17, 1910, box 8, GWCP, TUA; and Teresa (Tullahassee Mission, Okla.) to GWC, October 7, 1910, box 8, GWCP, TUA.

74. James Donald (Philadelphia, Miss.) to GWC, July 6, 1910, box 8, GWCP, TUA; GWC to BTW, April 25, 1902.

75. H. B. Bennett to GWC, May 28, 1911, box 8, GWCP, TUA.

76. Scott, *The Reluctant Farmer*, 70, 80.

77. See Allen W. Jones, "The Role of Tuskegee Institute in the Education of Black Farmers," *Journal of Negro History* 60 (April 1975): 258–59.

78. Agenda for Farmer's Institute meeting, Tuesday, April 19, 1904, GWCP, TUA (microfilm), reel 1.

79. See, for example, GWC, "Notice," April 2, 1910, box 65, folder 2, GWCP, TUA.

80. GWC to BTW, March 18, 1904, GWCP, TUA (microfilm), reel 2.

81. GWC to BTW, July 20, 1904, box 5, GWCP, TUA; GWC to BTW, August 16, 1904, GWCP, TUA (microfilm), reel 2. For Washington's response, see BTW to GWC, August 20, 1904, box 5, GWCP, TUA.

82. See Jones, "The Role of Tuskegee," 261; and "Farmers' Short Course in Agriculture" (1906), box 65, folder 2, GWCP, TUA.

83. "Farmers' Short Course in Agriculture."

84. Jones, "Role of Tuskegee," 262; Mayberry, *Role of Tuskegee*, 54–55.

85. "Second Annual Session of Farmers' Summer School," *Tuskegee Messenger*, July 23, 1909.

86. See GWC, "Class Notes"; "Agricultural Experiment Station Notes and Records, 1902–1910," box 67, folder 3, GWCP, TUA. As early as 1898 Carver had suggested to Washington that Tuskegee "do as Cornell College [and] open a school

for teachers in nature Studies." See GWC to BTW, ca. 1898, box 4, folder 3, GWCP, TUA.

87. See G. W. Bell (Middlesboro, Ky.) to GWC, August 9, 1910, box 8, GWCP, TUA; unnamed student (Atlanta, Ga.) to GWC, August 29, 1918, box 10, GWCP, TUA. For similar paeans to Carver's summer school, see P. B. Speer (Atlanta, Ga.) to GWC, June 22, 1910, box 8, GWCP, TUA; and J. B. Bickerstaff (Roanoke, Ala.) to GWC, August 3, 1910, box 8, GWCP, TUA.

88. A copy of the resolutions of the first Tuskegee Negro Farmers' Conference can be found in Campbell, *The Movable School Goes to the Negro Farmer,* 84–86.

89. Washington, *Up from Slavery,* 191.

90. Allen Jones, "Improving Rural Life for Blacks: The Tuskegee Negro Farmers' Conference, 1892–1915," *Agricultural History* 65 (1991): 112.

91. Washington, *Up from Slavery,* 191.

92. Jones, "Improving Rural Life," 113; *Local Negro Conference Guide,* n.d., Extension Files, TUA.

93. Hines, "Background to Fame," 128. Allen Jones, "Improving Rural Life for Blacks," 109.

94. Theodore Rosengarten, *All God's Dangers: The Life of Nate Shaw* (Chicago: University of Chicago Press, 1974), 69.

95. See Carver, "Notice"; and Hines, "Background to Fame," 128.

96. Jones, "Improving Rural Life for Blacks," 260.

97. For a fuller discussion of the county fair and Tuskegee Negro Farmers' Conference, see ibid., 252–61; and Hines, "Background to Fame," 126–34.

98. "Second Anniversary of the Farmers' Progressive Union," GWCP, TUA (microfilm), roll 1.

99. See Carver, "A Few Hints to Southern Farmers," *Southern Workman and Hampton School Record* (September 1899); "The Seventh Annual Negro Farmers' Conference at the Voorhees Industrial School," GWCP, TUA (microfilm), roll 1; "Kentucky State Teachers Association: Louisville, Ky., December 28–30, 1903: Program," GWCP, TUA (microfilm), roll 1; "Program for the Twentieth Annual Session of the Alabama State Teachers Association, 1901," GWCP, TUA (microfilm), roll 1; "Program of the Meeting of the Negro Teachers of the United States, together with those interested in Negro Education at Nashville, Tennessee, August 10, 11 and 12, 1904," GWCP, TUA (microfilm), roll 1.

100. "Get Ready for the Farmers' Picnic," Mt. Pleasant Church, July 15, 1905, GWCP, TUA (microfilm), roll 1; "The Utica Institute's Annual Farmers' Conference," n.d., GWCP, TUA (microfilm), roll 1.

101. "Madison Baptist Association in Social Circle, Georgia, Sept. 22, 1905," GWCP, TUA (microfilm), roll 1; *Tuskegee Student* (September 1905), box 65, GWCP, TUA. For another example, see J. W. Rawson (Industrial Missionary Association of Alabama) to GWC, September 1, 1904, GWCP, TUA (microfilm), roll 2.

102. See, for example, Geo. E. Majitte (St. Paul Normal and Industrial School) to GWC, July 18, 1914, box 10, GWCP, TUA.

103. "Farmers' Convention to Be Held at Clark University, December 17 and 18, 1903," GWCP, TUA (microfilm), roll 1.

104. Carver, "A Few Hints to Southern Farmers."

105. For one such request, see J. W. Cobb (secretary of the Madison County, Ala., Chautauqua) to GWC, April 21, 1919, box 10, GWCP, TUA.

106. "Mississippi Farmers Hold Conference at Utica Institute," *Voice of the People* (Birmingham, Ala.), February 5, 1916.

107. "Professor Carver's Lecture," *Tougaloo News* (Tougaloo College, Tougaloo, Miss.), March 1917, box 99, GWCP, TUA.

108. "Address by Dr. G. W. Carver at Voorhees Normal and Industrial School," February 19, 1919.

109. "Prof. Geo. W. Carver" (1902), box 64, GWCP, TUA.

110. *Tuskegee Student*, March 14, 1908.

111. Biographical sketch included in Jesse O. Thomas (principal, Voorhees Normal and Industrial School) to GWC, April 11, 1911, box 8, GWCP, TUA.

112. *Collier's Weekly*, April 29, 1905, box 99, GWCP, TUA.

113. *Alexander's* (Boston, Mass.) (May 1906), box 99, GWCP, TUA; "A Negro Soil Doctor," *Colored American* 11 (July 1906): 57–59.

114. For more on Johnston and his trip, see Jack Temple Kirby, *Darkness at the Dawning: Race and Reform in the Progressive South* (Philadelphia: J. B. Lippincott, 1972), 108–11; quoted in "Work of Gifted Negro Teacher Is Praised by Dr. Washington," *Christian Science Monitor*, December 26, 1912.

115. Quoted from "Professor Carver's Lecture." This is found in virtually every account of Carver. See, for example, McMurry, *George Washington Carver*, 156.

116. R. R. Poole to BTW, September 12, 1906, box 68, GWCP, TUA.

117. Quoted in "Work of Gifted Negro Teacher Is Praised by Dr. Washington"; McMurry, *George Washington Carver*, 157.

118. "Gave Up Art Career for His Race," *Technical World* 27 (May 1912), box 99, GWCP, TUA.

Chapter 6. Hints and Suggestions to Farmers

1. Norwood Allen Kerr, *A History of the Alabama Agricultural Experiment Station, 1883–1983* (Auburn: Alabama Agricultural Experiment Station, 1985), 5; Mayberry, *The Role of Tuskegee*, 31–32.

2. Kerr, *History of the Alabama Agricultural Experiment Station*, 8–9, 34.

3. See Mayberry, *The Role of Tuskegee*, 32.

4. See ibid., 49, 52–53; and Linda O. Hines, "George W. Carver and the Tuskegee Agricultural Experiment Station," *Agricultural History* 53 (January 1979): 73.

5. George Washington Carver, *Feeding Acorns*, TAES Bulletin 1 (February 1898), 3–4.

6. George Washington Carver, *Fertilizer Experiments on Cotton*, TAES Bulletin 3 (November 1899), 3.

7. George Washington Carver, "What Chemurgy Means to My People," *Farm Chemurgic Journal* 1 (September 1937), box 64, GWCP, TUA.

8. See George Washington Carver, *How to Build Up Worn Out Soils*, TAES Bulletin 6 (April 1905), 4.

9. Ibid., 4–5; "Ag. Exp. Station Notes, 1897"; *Tuskegee Student*, July 29, 1905.

10. Carver, *Feeding Acorns*, 5.

11. See, for example, "Ag. Exp. Station Notes and Records, 1902–1910."

12. See GWC to BTW, ca. 1904, in Burchard, *For His Time and Ours*, 8. For more on his introduction of silkworms and the Spanish peanut, see Hines, "George W. Carver and the Tuskegee Agricultural Experiment Station," 79.

13. George Washington Carver, "The Wonder Berry," 1909, box 65, GWCP, TUA.

14. See, for example, George Washington Carver, "Sweet Potatoes," report to BTW, October 1903, box 65, GWCP, TUA; Alice G. McCloskey (Cornell University) to Clinton J. Calloway, November 25, 1904, box 68, GWCP, TUA; H. A. Surface (professor of zoology at Penn State) to Clinton J. Calloway, November 19, 1904, box 68, GWCP, TUA; N. E. Hanson (vice director of the South Dakota Agricultural Experiment Station in Brookings) to GWC, October 6, 1917, box 10, GWCP, TUA; and George Washington Carver, *Improvement of Cotton*, Farmers' Leaflet 16, Extension Division, Department of Agriculture, n.d., box 63, GWCP, TUA.

15. For other examples, see W. O. Holmes to GWC, n.d., box 61, GWCP, TUA; (Mrs.) C. H. Hill (White) (Topeka, Kan.) to GWC, July 26, 1917, box 10, GWCP, TUA; GWC to Mr. J. T. Ratliff (Tuskegee, Ala.), August 2, 1918, box 10, GWCP, TUA.

16. Carver, *Feeding Acorns*, 6.

17. Ibid., 6, 9.

18. George Washington Carver, *The Forage Crop*, Farmers' Leaflet 9 (September 1902).

19. George Washington Carver, *The Need of Scientific Agriculture in the South*, Farmers' Leaflet 7 (April 1902).

20. GWC to BTW, partial letter, ca. 1897.

21. George Washington Carver, *The Need of Scientific Agriculture in the South*.

22. See Alfred Charles True, *A History of Agricultural Extension Work in the United States, 1785–1923* (New York: Arno Press and the New York Times, 1969), 64.

23. George Washington Carver, "Being Kind to the Soil," *Negro Farmer*, January 31, 1914.

24. See Ayers, *Promise of the New South*, 418–19.

25. For Carver's support of literacy campaigns, see George Washington Carver, *A New and Prolific Variety of Cotton*, TAES Bulletin 26 (1915), 3.

26. See "Agricultural Experiment Station Notes, 1897," box 67, folder 2, GWCP, TUA.

27. George Washington Carver, *Experiments with Sweet Potatoes*, TAES Bulletin 2 (May 1898), 3–5.

28. See Seaman A. Knapp, "How to Make Farming Profitable," *Southern Workman*, n.d., Extension Files, TUA.

29. See George Washington Carver, *Cotton Growing on Sandy Soil*, TAES Bulletin 7 (September 1905), 11; Carver, *How to Build Up Worn Out Soils*; and "Script for Dr. George Washington Carver."

30. For a discussion of the funding of the Tuskegee experiment station, see Hines, "George W. Carver and the Tuskegee Agricultural Experiment Station," 71–83; McMurry, *George Washington Carver*, 73–77.

31. Carver, *How to Build Up Worn Out Soils*, 4.

32. Clinton J. Calloway, *Barnyard Manure*, Farmers' Leaflet 15 (1902).

33. See, for instance, Henry A. Wallace, "Common Aims in Agriculture," *Tuskegee Messenger* (October, November, December 1936). The speech was given at Tuskegee on September 10, 1936; Charles S. Aiken, *The Cotton Plantation South since the Civil War* (Baltimore: Johns Hopkins University Press, 1998), 127.

34. See George Washington Carver, *Three Delicious Meals Every Day for the Farmer*, TAES Bulletin 32 (1916), 5.

35. Carver, *The Need of Scientific Agriculture in the South*.

36. George Washington Carver, *Cow Peas*, TAES Bulletin 5 (November 1903), 3.

37. Carver, "Address at Voorhees," 2.

38. George Washington Carver, "Three Delicious Meals Every Day for the Farmer," *Negro Farmer and Messenger*, February 10, 1917.

39. Ibid., 3, 5.

40. Ibid., 3–4.

41. George Washington Carver, "The Fat of the Land—How the Colored Farmer Can Live on It Twenty-one Times Each Week," *Negro Farmer*, July 31, 1915.

42. George Washington Carver, "Some Choice Wild Vegetables That Can Be Gathered Now," n.d., box 64, GWCP, TUA.

43. George Washington Carver, *Some Ornamental Plants of Macon County, Ala.*, TAES Bulletin 16 (October 1909), 5.

44. George Washington Carver, *Saving the Wild Plum Crop*, TAES Bulletin 12 (June 1907), 3.

45. George Washington Carver and Austin W. Curtis, *Some Choice Wild Vegetables That Make Fine Foods*, Special Leaflet 1, rev., February 1938. Portions of this were later reproduced in a bulletin issued in March 1942. With the nation at war,

Carver seized the opportunity "to render a service much needed at the present time" and so issued a bulletin titled *Nature's Garden for Victory and Peace*.

46. George Washington Carver, "What this Section Holds for Science after the War," *Montgomery Advertiser*, October 27, 1918.

47. GWC to Mr. and Mrs. Milholland, February 28, 1905, GWCNM; also in Kremer, *In His Own Words*, 152.

48. Carver, "Some Choice Wild Vegetables That Can Be Gathered Now."

49. George Washington Carver, "Using So-Called Weeds as Food for Men and Stock," *Montgomery Advertiser*, October 27, 1918.

50. George Washington Carver, *The Canning and Preserving of Fruits and Vegetables in the Home*, Experiment Station Circular (1912), box 63, GWCP, TUA.

51. George Washington Carver, "How to Dry Vegetables and Fruits of the Tree and Vine," *Montgomery Advertiser*, May 27, 1918.

52. "Negro Health Week," *Southern Workman* (April 1918): 169–70.

53. Carver, "Notes on Various Subjects."

54. GWC to BTW, May 20, 1897, box 4, GWCP, TUA.

55. Carver, *Fertilizer Experiments on Cotton*, 3–4, 13; George Washington Carver, *Experiments with Sweet Potatoes*, TAES Bulletin 2 (May 1898), 3–5.

56. Carver, *Fertilizer Experiments on Cotton*, 13; Carver, *Experiments with Sweet Potatoes*, 15.

57. Carver, *Fertilizer Experiments on Cotton*," 8, 15.

58. Carver, *Experiments with Sweet Potatoes*, 13.

59. George Washington Carver, *The Improvement of Cotton*, Farmers' Leaflet 16 (Extension Division, Department of Agriculture), n.d., box 63, GWCP, TUA. Carver frequently cited Auburn's fertilizer recommendations; see, for instance, George Washington Carver, *Cotton Growing for Rural Schools*, TAES Bulletin 20 (June 1911), 10.

60. Stoll, *Larding the Lean Earth*, 91.

61. Calloway, *Barnyard Manure*.

62. Carver, "The Tuskegee Normal and industrial Institute and Experiment Station."

63. See Richard C. Hoffman and Verena Winiwarter, "Making Land and Water Meet: The Cycling of Nutrients between Fields and Ponds in Pre-modern Europe," *Agricultural History* 84 (summer 2010): 352–80.

64. See Stoll, *Larding the Lean Earth*, 51–52.

65. Sir Humphry Davy, *Elements of Agricultural Chemistry in a Course of Lectures for the Board of Agriculture* (New York: Eastburn, Kirk, 1815), 136–82, 239–306.

66. See Justus von Liebig, *Organic Chemistry in Its Applications to Agriculture and Physiology* (London: Taylor and Walton, 1840).

67. Ibid., 187–88.

68. Francis Preston Venable, *A Short History of Chemistry* (1894; reprint, Boston:

D. C. Heath, 1909), 149. For more on the ways American agriculturists sought to make sense of the theories of Davy and Liebig, see Jack Temple Kirby's introduction to Ruffin, *Nature's Management*, xxii–xxv; and Cohen, *Notes from the Ground*, 81–123.

69. See Selman A. Waksman, "The Origin and Nature of the Soil Organic Matter or Soil 'Humus': I. Introductory and Historical," *Soil Science* 22 (1926): 123–62, quoted in Alan I. Marcus, "The Wisdom of the Body Politic: The Changing Nature of Publicly Sponsored American Agricultural Research since the 1830s," *Agricultural History* 62 (spring 1988): 23.

70. For more-or-less typical treatments of Progressive Era soil science, see Liberty Hyde Bailey, ed., *Principles of Agriculture: A Text-Book for Schools and Rural Societies* (New York: Macmillan, 1912), 16–63; and Goff and Mayne, *First Principles of Agriculture*, 44–56.

71. Stoll, *Larding the Lean Earth*, 17.

72. See, for example, Carver, *How to Build Up Worn Out Soils*, 8–11; and Carver, "Question Box for Your Advancement," May 1924, box 64, GWCP, TUA, in which Carver advocated a 10-3-3-4 mixture of organic fertilizer with phosphate, kainit, and nitrate of soda.

73. See, for example, George Washington Carver, *Increasing the Yield of Corn*, TAES Bulletin 15 (June 1909), 6; George Washington Carver, *Possibilities of the Sweet Potato in Macon County, Alabama*, TAES Bulletin 17 (March 1910), 9; George Washington Carver, *How to Grow the Peanut and 105 Ways of Preparing It for Human Consumption*, TAES Bulletin 31 (March 1916), 2; Carver, "Notice"; George Washington Carver, "One of the Most Interesting Farms in Alabama," report submitted to Tuskegee Institute, July 31, 1915, box 65, GWCP, TUA.

74. Carver, "Nature Study and Gardening for Rural Schools," 17.

75. George Washington Carver, *What Shall We Do for Fertilizers Next Year*, Experiment Station Circular, November 1916.

76. Carver, "One of the Most Interesting Farms in Alabama"; Carver, *What Shall We Do for Fertilizers Next Year*.

77. Carver, *What Shall We Do for Fertilizers Next Year*; George Washington Carver, *How to Build Up and Maintain the Virgin Fertility of Our Soil*, TAES Bulletin 42 (October 1936), 10.

78. See George Washington Carver, "Experiments on Insects," report to BTW, n.d., ca. 1909, box 65, GWCP, TUA. See also George Washington Carver, "Experimental Work on Insects and Fungus Diseases," September 10, 1909, box 65, GWCP, TUA. On Paris Green, see http://ptcl.chem.ox.ac.uk/MSDS/CO/copper_acetoarsenite.html, accessed July 1, 2010.

79. George Washington Carver, "Some Fertilizers That Are Now Going to Waste," *Gospel Plea* (Southern Christina Institute Press, Edwards, Miss.), December 8, 1917. See also Carver, *How to Grow the Peanut*, 2.

80. Carver, *What Shall We Do for Fertilizers Next Year.*

81. Carver, "Some Fertilizers That Are Now Going to Waste."

82. Carver, "Helps for the Hard Times."

83. Carver, "One of the Most Interesting Farms in Alabama."

84. See GWC to BTW, January 26, 1911, box 8, GWCP, TUA; GWC to Mr. R. M. Atwell, n.d., ca. 1902, box 62, GWCP, TUA.

85. Council report in the BTW Papers at the Library of Congress—Department of Research, Exp. Sta., 1912.

86. Carver, *How to Build Up and Maintain the Virgin Fertility of Our Soil*, 6.

87. Carver, "Being Kind to the Soil."

88. See Carver, *How to Build Up and Maintain the Virgin Fertility of Our Soil*, 5.

89. Carver, "Being Kind to the Soil."

90. George Washington Carver, "The Productive Power of Our Light Sandy Soils," ca. 1905, report to BTW, box 65, folder 2, GWCP, TUA.

91. Bailey, ed., *Principles of Agriculture*, 2.

92. Kremer, *In His Own Words*, 121.

93. George Washington Carver, "How to Raise Pigs Successfully with Little Money," *Montgomery Advertiser*, December 10, 1916; George Washington Carver, "How to Make the Acorn Crop into Money," *Montgomery Advertiser*, December 23, 1917.

94. George Washington Carver, "Provide Food to Win the World's War," *Journal and Guide* (Montgomery, Ala.), February 2, 1918, box 64, GWCP, TUA.

95. Carver, *How to Live Comfortably This Winter*, Experiment Station Circular (1916), 7–8; Carver, "Helps for the Hard Times."

96. George Washington Carver, "A New Industry for Colored Young Men and Women," *Colored American* 14 (January 1908): 33.

97. George Washington Carver, "Some Ways to Save Money on the Farm," n.d., box 65, GWCP, TUA.

98. *Tuskegee Student*, March 15, 1902.

99. George Washington Carver, *White and Color Washing with Native Clays from Macon County, Alabama*, TAES Bulletin 21 (September 1911), 5.

100. Carver, *Some Ornamental Plants of Macon County, Ala.*, 5, 7, 12.

101. George Washington Carver, *How to Make and Save Money on the Farm*, TAES Bulletin 39 (1927), 16.

102. "Carver Question Box," April 24, 1926; Carver, *The Canning and Preserving of Fruits and Vegetables in the Home.*

103. Carver, "The Need of Scientific Agriculture."

104. Alexander Hamilton, *Report on Manufactures: Communication to the House of Representatives, December 5, 1791*, Senate Document 172, 63rd Cong., 1st Sess. (Washington, D.C.: GPO, 1913), 11. For other connections between agriculture and industry in the report, see pp. 5, 7, 14–16, 34–35.

105. Cohen, *Notes from the Ground*, 29.

106. Steuart devoted a chapter of his multivolume *An Inquiry into the Principles of Political Economy* (1767) to "the Abuse of Agriculture and Population"; Steven Stoll, "A Physics of Society: Industrialism and Political Economy in the Nineteenth Century," paper presented at the annual meeting of the American Society for Environmental History, Houston, Texas, March 17, 2005.

107. Isaac Newton, "Report of the Commissioner of Agriculture for the Year 1862," available online at http://www.jlindquist.com/newton.html, accessed June 27, 1010.

108. For more on the back to nature movement of the Progressive Era specifically, see David E. Shi, *The Simple Life: Plain Living and High Thinking in American Culture*, rev. ed. (1985; reprint, Athens: University of Georgia Press, 2007), especially 175–214; Peter Schmitt, *Back to Nature: The Arcadian Myth in Urban America* (Oxford University Press, 1969; reprint, Baltimore: Johns Hopkins University Press, 1990); Richard White, "Poor Men on Poor Lands: The Back-to-the-Land Movement of the Early Twentieth Century—a Case Study," *Pacific Historical Review* 49 (February 1980): 105–31; Donald J. Pisani, "Reclamation and Social Engineering in the Progressive Era," *Agricultural History* 57 (January 1983): 46–63. See also Josiah Strong, *Our Country: Its Possible Future and Its Present Crisis* (1885; reprint, New York: Baker and Taylor, 1891), which captures the nativist, religious, and Malthusian fears that helped spark the movement.

109. Carver, *The Need of Scientific Agriculture in the South*; Carver, "What Chemurgy Means to My People," 2.

110. GWC to BTW, n.d., ca. 1900, box 61, GWCP, TUA.

111. Carver, "Being Kind to the Soil."

112. Carver, *How to Raise Pigs Successfully with Little Money*; GWC to BTW, n.d., ca. 1900.

113. Carver, *How to Raise Pigs Successfully with Little Money*.

114. George Washington Carver, *Poultry Raising in Macon County, Alabama*, TAES Bulletin 23 (July 1912), 3.

115. Ibid., 3.

116. George Washington Carver, "Canning and Preserving of Fruits and Vegetables in the Home," *Montgomery Advertiser*, n.d., box 64, GWCP, TUA.

117. Carver, "Some Ways to Save Money on the Farm."

118. *The Winter Fun*, Farmers' Leaflet 3 (December 1901), box 63, GWCP, TUA.

119. Carver, *Feeding Acorns*, 4.

120. For evidence of Carver's concern about illiteracy, see *A New and Prolific Variety of Cotton*, 3.

121. Campbell, *The Movable School Goes to the Negro Farmer*, 80.

122. For further discussion of Washington's effort to purchase land with the intent of selling it to black farmers, see Robert E. Zabawa and Sarah T. Warren,

"From Company to Community: Agricultural Community Development in Macon County, Alabama, 1881 to the New Deal," *Agricultural History* (spring 1998): 459–85.

123. Thomas M. Campbell, "The Alabama Movable School," quoted in Mayberry, *The Role of Tuskegee*, 103.

124. Campbell, *The Movable School Goes to the Negro Farmer*, 87–88.

125. Charles S. Johnson, *Shadow of the Plantation*, 13.

126. Campbell, *The Movable School Goes to the Negro Farmer*, 82.

127. Toby Fishbein interview with Austin Curtis, 17.

128. "Education in Agriculture" (November 1904), box 66, GWCP, TUA.

129. GWC to A. C. True, September 16, 1902.

130. Carver, "Tuskegee Normal and Industrial Institute and Experiment Station."

131. GWC to A. C. True, September 16, 1902.

132. Carver, *Possibilities of the Sweet Potato in Macon County, Alabama*, 5; see also George Washington Carver, "Medicinal Roots, Barks and Herbs in Macon County," *Montgomery Advertiser*, November 28, 1918.

133. Mayberry, *The Role of Tuskegee*, 97–98.

134. See USDA Office of Experiment Stations, *Organization Lists of the Agricultural Colleges and Experiment Stations in the United States*, Bulletin 111 (March 1902), 13.

135. See Mary S. Hoffschwelle, *The Rosenwald Schools of the American South* (Gainesville: University Press of Florida, 2006), 24–85.

136. For a thorough and insightful analysis of Tuskegee-Togo connection, see Andrew Zimmerman, *Alabama in Africa: Booker T. Washington, the German Empire, and the Globalization of the New South* (Princeton: Princeton University Press, 2010).

137. GWC to BTW, November 16, 1904, quoted in McMurry, *George Washington Carver*, 125; Campbell, *The Movable School Goes to the Negro Farmer*, 91; "The Jesup Agricultural Wagon," GWCP, TUA (microfilm), reel 47.

138. In its report on the dedication of the Slater-Armstrong Building in 1897, the *San Francisco Report* noted that Morris K. Jesup, William E. Dodge, "and other big men have furnished much financial aid." See "For the Negro," *San Francisco Report*, November 18, 1897.

139. Karen J. Ferguson, "Caught in 'No Man's Land': The Negro Cooperative Demonstration Service and the Ideology of Booker T. Washington, 1900–1918," *Agricultural History* (winter 1998): 36.

140. For an example of the application of this moniker, see, "Gave Up Art Career for His Race."

141. Johnson, *Shadow of the Plantation*, 13.

142. For an example of sharing equipment and pooling labor, see ibid., 118.

143. Charles S. Johnson, *Growing Up in the Black Belt: Negro Youth in the Rural South* (Washington, D.C.: American Council on Education, 1941), 277–78.

144. Ibid., 17.

145. Johnson, *Shadow of the Plantation*, 25.

146. Ibid., 27.

147. George Wylie Henderson, *Ollie Miss* (Chatham, N.J.: Chatham Bookseller, 1935; reissued, 1973), 109.

148. GWC, *A Study of the Soils of Macon County, Alabama and Their Adaptability to Certain Crops*, 6–14. For a comparative soil survey, see Henry J. Wilder and Hugh Hammond Bennett, "Soil Survey of Macon County, Alabama," in *Field Operations of the Bureau of Soils, 1904* (Washington, D.C.: GPO, 1905), 291–315.

149. Carver, *Cotton Growing for Rural Schools.*

150. Carver, *A Study of the Soils of Macon County, Alabama and Their Adaptability to Certain Crops*, 5.

151. Henderson, *Ollie Miss*, 109–10.

152. George R. Bridgeforth, "Report of the Jesup Wagon, June 5–9/1906," Extension Files, TUA.

153. George R. Bridgeforth, "Report of the Jesup Wagon, July 2–9/1906."

154. George R. Bridgeforth, "Report of the Jesup Wagon, June 25–July 2/1906"; George R. Bridgeforth, "Report of the Jesup Wagon, July 2–9/1906"; and George R. Bridgeforth, "Report of the Jesup Wagon, July 30–Aug 6."

155. George R. Bridgeforth, "Report of the Jesup Wagon, July 16–23/1906."

156. George R. Bridgeforth, "Report of the Jesup Wagon, August 6–12/1906"; George R. Bridgeforth, "Report of the Jesup Wagon, July 23–30/1906"; George R. Bridgeforth, "Report of the Jesup Wagon, July 9–15/1906." Tolbert may well have been a misspelling of Torbert; decades after the Civil War, the descendents of influential antebellum planters continued to control much of the land and labor in the county.

157. Bailey, *Seaman A. Knapp*, 137–48.

158. Ibid., 170.

159. Ibid., 169–71.

160. Ibid., 215–19.

161. Knapp was supposed to arrive on May 15 but may actually have come later. See *Tuskegee Student*, May 5, 1906.

162. See Bailey, *Seaman A. Knapp*, 227. Carver may also have played a role in securing funds; see David H. Jackson Jr., *A Chief Lieutenant of the Tuskegee Machine: Charles Banks of Mississippi* (Gainesville: University Press of Florida, 2002), 63.

163. See GRB to BTW, November 7, 1906, Extension Files, TUA.

164. GWC to Wilson, August 5, 1904, box 5, GWCP, TUA; BTW to GWC, November 18, 1910, box 8, GWCP, TUA.

165. Thomas M. Campbell, "Cooperative Extension Work in Agriculture and

Home Economics, State of Alabama, a Supplement to the Annual Report of the Agricultural Extension Service as Performed by Negroes for the Year Ending December 31, 1919," 1, 6, Thomas Monroe Campbell Papers, Tuskegee University Archives; King, *King's Agricultural Digest, 1923*, 9; Campbell, *The Movable School Goes to the Negro Farmer*, 94; Mayberry, *The Role of Tuskegee*, 73.

166. Quoted in Mayberry, *The Role of Tuskegee*, 73.

167. Ibid.

168. See For Booker T. Washington's concerns that the Smith-Lever Act would not redound to the benefit of African Americans, see BTW to Thomas Jesse Jones, November 16, 1914, in Mayberry, *The Role of Tuskegee*, 81; and Russell Lord, *The Agrarian Revival: A Study of Agricultural Extension* (New York: American Association for Adult Education, 1939), 93.

169. *The Functions and Duties of the County Agent. How Our Organization Can Help*, n.d., Alabama Cooperative Extension Service Records, Auburn University Archive.

170. "Galley Proof: Declarations of the Thirty-fifth Annual Tuskegee Farmer's Conference," January 27, 1926, Extension Files, TUA; "Declarations of the Fortieth Annual Tuskegee Negro Conference," December 3, 1930, Extension Files, TUA.

171. See George Washington Carver, "How to Dry Tomatoes," July 30, 1917, box 65, folder 2, GWCP, TUA; GWC to Mrs. (B. T.) Washington, September 16, 1916, box 9, GWCP, TUA; Monroe N. Work to GWC, October 24, 1916, box 9, GWCP, TUA; *The Negro Rural School and Its Relation to the Community* (Tuskegee: Tuskegee Institute Extension Department, 1915), foreword. See also GWC, "Much Good Foodstuff Can Yet Be Saved," n.d., box 65, GWCP, TUA.

172. Carver, *The Negro Rural School and Its Relation to the Community*, 41, 53–55; "Carver's Question Box," April 24, 1926.

Chapter 7. The Peanut Man

1. GWC to "My dear friends" [the Millhollands], December 23, 1914, GWCNM.

2. "Negro Health Week."

3. Carver, "Provide Food to Win the World's War."

4. Carver, "Helps for the Hard Times."

5. Carver, "Some Choice Wild Vegetables That Can Be Gathered Now."

6. "Address by Dr. G. W. Carver at Voorhees Normal and Industrial Institute, Denmark, S.C.," February 19, 1921, box 65, GWCP, TUA.

7. Quoted in Kremer, *In His Own Words*, 78.

8. See McMurry, *George Washington Carver*, 159.

9. For more on the transition from the Washington to Moton administrations at Tuskegee, see McMurry, *George Washington Carver*, 159–71.

10. "Professor George W. Carver and Food Conservation," *Tuskegee Student*, February 9, 1918.

11. See, for instance, [illegible; Seattle Inter-Ocean Barge and Transport Company] to GWC, December 26, 1917 (included a clipping from the *Seattle Times*), box 10, GWCP, TUA; George Washington Carver, "Drying Fruits and Vegetables," *Rural New Yorker*, n.d., box 64, GWCP, TUA.

12. George F. King to GWC, March 6, 1918, box 10, GWCP, TUA.

13. William Holtzclaw to GWC, March 26, 1919, box 10, GWCP, TUA. See "Professor George W. Carver and Food Conservation"; Littell McClung to GWC, February 1, 1918, box 10, GWCP, TUA; GWC to Mrs. Milholland, March 2, 1918, GWCNM.

14. McClung, "A Glimpse of the Remarkable Work of George W. Carver, the Negro Scientist." Littell McClung and Carver were in fact good friends. See Littell McClung to GWC, April 5, 1919, box 10, GWCP, TUA.

15. Vicente Mitre (Manila, Philippine Islands) to GWC, September 30, 1918, box 10, GWCP, TUA; Juan Palop (Utuado, Puerto Rico) to GWC [in Spanish], August 26, 1918, box 10, GWCP, TUA; *Tuskegee Monthly News*, n.d., box 99, GWCP, TUA. For an unconfirmed reference to Carver's election to a similarly prestigious French society, see "Prof. Geo. W. Carver Elected Member of Scientific Societies," *Montgomery Journal*, November 12, 1916.

16. "Professor Carver's Lecture"; Slatter, "Men I Have Known"; George Washington Carver, Some Uplifting Forces at Work in Mississippi," *Rural Messenger*, May 26, 1920; GWC to Mrs. Milholland, October 21, 1918, GWCNM.

17. He received, for instance, a request for a reference letter for a former student from the U.S. Civil Service Commission addressed to "Mr. G. W. Corner" in July 1917; see John A. McIlheny (president of the U.S. Civil Service Commission, Washington, D.C.) to Mr. G. W. Corner, July 1917, box 10, GWCP, TUA.

18. Ferguson to GWC, March 11, 1918, box 10, GWCP, TUA.

19. John W. Goins (NYC) to GWC, August 20, 1918, box 10, GWCP, TUA. After citing the *Ledger*'s praise, Goins added, "The guy who wrote that has *nearly* as good opinion of you as . . . Goins."

20. "The Ninth Annual Farmers Conference and the Third Annual Workers Conference," *Charleston (S. C.) Messenger*, March 1, 1919.

21. George Washington Carver, "105 Ways of Preparing Peanuts for Use on Your Table," *Montgomery Advertiser*, December 24, 1916.

22. Carver, "Provide Food to Win the World's War."

23. George Washington Carver, "How to Use Cowpeas on the Table," *Montgomery Advertiser*, July 22, 1917.

24. McMurry, *George Washington Carver*, 171.

25. Ibid.

26. See King, *King's Agricultural Digest*, 26.

27. For a longer treatment of Carver's testimony before Congress, see McMurry, *George Washington Carver*, 172–74; "Address by Dr. G. W. Carver before the

Committee on Ways and Means—House of Representatives, January 21, 1921," 9, box 65, GWCP, TUA.

28. George Washington Carver, foreword to *How to Grow the Peanut and 105 Ways of Preparing It for Human Consumption*, TAES Bulletin 31 (March 1916). One indication of this bulletin's popularity can be found in the fact that by 1925 it was in its eighth printing.

29. Brookfield Public Library to Tuskegee Institute, February 18, 1918, box 10, GWCP, TUA.

30. "Professor G. W. Carver's Lecture, Farmer's Conference," February 16, 1921, box 65, GWCP, TUA.

31. GWC to LHP, July 15, 1928, box 14, LHP Papers, ISU Archives.

32. A far more complete analysis of Carver's complicity in the mythmaking is in McMurry, *George Washington Carver*.

33. "Macon County Products Exploited," *Tuskegee News*, February 26, 1928.

34. George Washington Carver, "Report of the Tuskegee Institute Experiment Station, 1924–1925," box 65, GWCP, TUA.

35. GWC to Lyman Ward, January 15, 1925, in Kremer, *In His Own Words*, 131.

36. GWC to Dr. M. L. Ross, July 27, 1930, in Kremer, *In His Own Words*, 168.

37. GWC to Mr. Milholland, March 8, 1928, GWCNM.

38. GWC to G. F. Peabody, September 20, 1923, box 13, GWCP, TUA.

39. Linda McMurry has made this argument elsewhere; see Hines, "White Mythology and Black Duality," 134–46; and McMurry, *George Washington Carver*, 204.

40. George Washington Carver, untitled, January 29, 1913.

41. GWC to "My esteemed friend, Rev. Haygood," August 24, 1940, in Kremer, *In His Own Words*, 136.

42. GWC to "Dear Sir," November 29, 1929, in Kremer, *In His Own Words*, 154–55.

43. Toby Fishbein interview with Austin Curtis, 24–25.

44. GWC to Jim Hardwick, partial letters, p. 3, GWCP, TUA, box 62. Carver's correspondence during the war both captures his concern over students whose lives were directly affected by it and puts a more personal face on his racial views, as he sought to encourage former students at a time when racial tensions ran particularly high. For a representative sampling, see William M. Mayers to GWC, July 28, 1917, box 10, GWCP, TUA; William M. Mayers to GWC, July 25, 1918, box 10, GWCP, TUA; Ernest Frazier to GWC, July 15, 1917, box 10, GWCP, TUA; "Willie" to GWC, September 2, 1917, box 10, GWCP, TUA; Walter L. Hutcherson Jr. to GWC, April 7, 1918, box 10, GWCP, TUA; GWC to Mr. and Mrs. Milholland, December 26, 1917, GWCNM; "Rosebud" to GWC, n.d., ca. 1917, box 10, GWCP, TUA; Oscar Parks to GWC, July 16, 1917, box 10, GWCP, TUA; and "Cricket" (Hartford, Conn.) to GWC, January 26, 1919, box 10, GWCP, TUA.

45. GWC to Lyman Ward, October 20, 1939, box 46, GWCP, TUA.

46. Lyman Ward to GWC, October 24, 1939, box 46, GWCP, TUA.

47. Edwin E. Slosson, *Creative Chemistry: Descriptive of Recent Achievements in the Chemical Industry* (New York: Century, 1919).

48. George Washington Carver, "Some Benefits and Possibilities of Creative Chemistry in the South," box 65, folder 6, GWCP, TUA; David J. Rhees, "Justification by Utility" (master's thesis, University of North Carolina, 1979).

49. See Edwin Slosson, "Back to Nature? Never! Forward to the Machine!," *New York Independent*, January 3, 1920, 6, 37.

50. *Milwaukee Journal*, n.d., ca. February 1919, Extension Clippings, 1919, Extension Files, TUA.

51. See Kremer, *In His Own Words*, 143–44, 149.

52. For more on the early connections between chemistry and agriculture, see Cohen, *Notes from the Ground*.

53. For a brief synopsis of the chemurgy movement, see Mark R. Finlay, "Old Efforts at New Uses: A Brief History of Chemurgy and the American Search for Biobased Materials," *Journal of Industrial Ecology* 7, nos. 3–4 (2004): 33–46. For a study of the work being done at Iowa State, see Alan I. Marcus and Erik Lokensgard, "The Chemical Engineers of Iowa State College: Transforming Agricultural Wastes and an Institution, 1920–1940," *Annals of Iowa* 48 (1986): 177–205.

54. Quoted in Finlay, "Old Efforts at New Uses," 35, 37.

55. George Washington Carver, "Report of the Agricultural Research and Experiment Station," March 22, 1940.

56. Henry A. Wallace, "The Genetic Basis of Democracy," *Democracy Reborn: Selected from Public Papers*, edited with an introduction by Russell Lord (New York: Da Capo Press, 1973), 154–55.

57. Finlay, "Old Efforts at New Uses," 38, 36.

58. McMurry, *George Washington Carver*, 232.

59. The title was bestowed on him in a 1939 history of chemurgy. See Christy Borth, *Pioneers of Plenty: The Story of Chemurgy* (New York: Bobbs-Merrill, 1939), 226.

60. GWC to J. Alex Moore, February 3, 1928.

61. GWC to the *Peanut Journal*, Suffolk, Virginia, June 11, 1936, in Burchard, *For His Time and Ours*, 71.

62. GWC to J. Alex Moore, February 3, 1928, in Kremer, *In His Own Words*, 157.

63. Kerr, *History of the Alabama Agricultural Experiment Station, 1883–1983*, 52.

64. Russell Lord, *The Care of the Earth: A History of Husbandry* (New York: Nelson, 1962), 381.

65. Quoted in John S. Ferrell, "George Washington Carver: A Blazer of Trails to a Sustainable Future," in *Land and Power: Sustainable Agriculture and African Americans*, ed. Jeffrey Jordan, Edward Pennick, Walter A. Hill, and Robert Zabawa (Waldorf, Md.: Sustainable Agriculture Research and Education, USDA, 2009), 24.

66. Carver, "Grafting the Cacti."

67. "Dr. Carver Writes Soil Conservation Conference Report," *Montgomery Advertiser*, September 12, 1936.

68. GWC to Frank Camsall [Henry Ford's secretary], November 10, 1942, in Burchard, *For His Time and Ours*, 121–22.

69. GWC to William J. Wheat, July 15, 1939, quoted in Burchard, *For His Time and Ours*, 125.

70. "Chemurgy: A New and More Bountiful Era Emerges from Our Farms and Laboratories," *Newsweek*, December 3, 1951, 82–83.

71. Lord, *The Care of the Earth*, 381.

72. See http://www.newuses.org/about.php, accessed July 1, 2010.

73. Ferrell, "A Blazer of Trails to a Sustainable Future," 23.

74. See Randal S. Beeman and James A. Pritchard, *A Green and Permanent Land: Ecology and Agriculture in the Twentieth Century* (Lawrence: University Press of Kansas, 2001), in which the authors argue that Rexford Tugwell is the most characteristic figure of "the first stages of ecological agriculture" (25).

75. For more on the ways in which ecologists had the ears of policy makers, see Beeman and Pritchard, *A Green and Permanent Land*, 20–63; and Donald Worster, *Dust Bowl: The Southern Plains in the 1930s* (New York: Oxford University Press, 1979). For a concise discussion of Bennett, see Lynn Nelson, *Pharsalia*, 1–12.

76. The Progressive Era reformers themselves were drawing on a long tradition of agricultural reform, which had with few exceptions advocated individual restraint over government intervention. For a fuller discussion of that history, see Stoll, *Larding the Lean Earth*; and Cohen, *Notes from the Ground*.

77. For a more nuanced discussion of the New Conservationists, see Sarah T. Phillips, *This Land, This Nation: Conservation, Rural America, and the New Deal* (New York: Cambridge University Press, 2007), 1–74.

78. For more on the Nashville Agrarians and the New Deal, see Emily S. Bingham and Thomas A. Underwood, eds., *The Southern Agrarians and the New Deal: Essays after* I'll Take My Stand (Charlottesville: University of Virginia Press, 2001); and Jess Gilbert and Steve Brown, "Alternative Land Reform Proposals in the 1930s: The Nashville Agrarians and the Southern Tenant Farmers' Union," *Agricultural History* 55 (October 1981): 351–69.

79. See McMurry, *George Washington Carver*, 217.

80. Quoted in ibid., 281.

81. For more on Carver's politics (or lack thereof), see Linda O. Hines, "White Mythology and Black Duality: George Washington Carver's Response to Racism and the Radical Left," *Journal of Negro History* 62 (April 1977): 134–46; and McMurry, *George Washington Carver*, 210–18, 256–89.

82. Some scholars have questioned whether or not poliomyelitis was actually the cause of Roosevelt's paralysis. See Armond S. Goldman, Elisabeth J.

Schmalstieg, Daniel H. Freeman Jr., Daniel A. Goldman, and Frank C. Schmalstieg Jr., "What Was the Cause of Franklin Delano Roosevelt's Paralytic Illness," *Journal of Medical Biography* 11 (2003): 232–40.

83. See Phillips, *This Land, This Nation*, 59–74.

84. Quoted in McMurry, *George Washington Carver*, 253. For a deeper analysis of Carver's work with polio, see pp. 242–55.

85. George Washington Carver, "Coming Events Cast Their Shadows Before," box 65, folder 4, GWCP, TUA.

86. Henry A. Wallace to Don, June 25, 1965, quoted in McMurry, *George Washington Carver*, 254. For a comparison of this view to his father's, see Henry C. Wallace to Mr. W. O. Saunders, August 8, 1923, GWCP, TUA, Tuskegee, Alabama.

Chapter 8. Divine Inspiration

1. "Men of Science Never Talk That Way," in "Topics of the Times," *New York Times*, November 20, 1924, 22. For McMurry's account of this, see McMurry, *George Washington Carver*, 208–9.

2. GWC to "My dear Sir," November 24, 1924, box 1, GWC Papers, ISU Archives.

3. Ibid.

4. See, for instance, "Carver Reply to Attack by a N.Y. Paper," *Des Moines Register*, January 11, 1925, box 2, GWC Papers, ISU Archives.

5. GWC to Lyman Ward, January 15, 1925, in Kremer, *In His Own Words*, 130–31.

6. Quoted in Burchard, *For His Time and Ours*, 149.

7. "President Gross's interview with Doctor Carver at Tuskegee, July 17, 1940," Simpson College Archives, Indianola, Iowa.

8. Toby Fishbein interview with Austin W. Curtis, 21.

9. Lou Wilkins, *George Washington Carver: The World's Greatest Chemist* (Fort Worth, Tex.: South Western Theological Seminary, 1929); George Matthew Adams, "The Power of Faith," *Think* (February 1943): 18, 28; Marion Lereu, "George Washington Carver: Wizard of Tuskegee Research Laboratory," *Mission Fields at Home* 6 (October 1933): 6–8; Thelma Pearson, "He Worked with God," *St. Joseph Magazine* (St. Benedict, Ore.) (June 1949): 23–24, 38; "Dr. George Washington Carver: A Catholic Tribute," *Interracial Review: A Journal for Christian Democracy* (February 1943): 23–25; J. H. Hunter, "Prayers to Peanuts," *HIS* (March 1943): 20–22; Mary Jeness, *The Man Who Asked God Questions: George Washington Carver* (New York: Friendship Press, 1946); Miller, *God's Ebony Scientist*; Alvin D. Smith, *George Washington Carver: Man of God* (Middleton, Ohio: Perry, 1961).

10. Federer also wrote *Judicial Tyranny* (2005), *Back Fire: A Nation Born for Religious Tolerance No Longer Tolerates Religion* (2005), and *America's God and Country: Encyclopedia of Quotations* (2000).

11. http://www.cbn.com/cbnnews/us/2010/February/George-Washington-Carver-Master-Inventor-Artist/, accessed July 1, 2010.

12. GWC to My beloved friend, Mr. Byrd, March 1, 1927, in Kremer, *In His Own Words*, 134–35.

13. Edmund S. Burke to GWC, August 11, 1918, box 10, GWCP, TUA.

14. "Your sincere boy David (David A. Jackson) to GWC, January 19, 1918, box 10, GWCP, TUA; S. J. Thomas (Chattanooga, Tenn.) to GWC, July 30, 1910, box 8, GWCP, TUA.

15. GWC to Jim Hardwick, July 10, 1924, in Kremer, *In His Own Words*, 138; GWC to My dear, dear friend Mr. Hardwick, March 9, 1928, box 17, GWCP, TUA.

16. Partial letter, 1917, box 10, folder 4, GWCP, TUA.

17. "President Gross's interview with Doctor Carver at Tuskegee, July 17, 1940."

18. *Southern Letter* (Tuskegee Institute), August 1904, box 5, GWCP, TUA.

19. GWC to Mr. Milholland, March 8, 1928.

20. George Washington Carver, "The Bahai Movement," April 4, 1941, box 66, folder 2, GWCP, TUA.

21. McMurry, *George Washington Carver*, 269–70.

22. See Robert F. Martin, *Howard Kester and the Struggle for Social Justice in the South, 1904–1977* (Charlottesville: University Press of Virginia, 1991), 170 fn. 22.

23. Faculty meeting, Department of Agriculture, September 15, 1909, box 65, GWCP, TUA.

24. GWC, "How to Search for Truth," 1930, in Kremer, *In His Own Words*, 142. For an allusion to the Scopes Monkey Trial, see GWC to Mrs. Milholland, March 5, 1934, GWCNM. Also see "People's Recorder, Orangeburg, S.C. Voorhees Annual Negro Farmer's Conference," *Southern Voice* 13 (March 1916).

25. GWC to My dear Rev. Kunzman, March 24, 1925; and GWC to My esteemed friend, Mr. Stevenson, March 17, 1937 in Kremer, *In His Own Words*, 133.

26. See, for instance, George Washington Carver, "A New Industry for Colored Young Men and Women," *Colored American* 14 (January 1908): 33; quoted in Pohl, "Louis H. Pammel," 11.

27. Toby Fishbein interview with Austin Curtis, 20.

28. GWC to BTW, May 28, 1907, box 7, GWCP, TUA. For examples of students influenced by Carver's Bible class, see Jno. Reed (Passaic, N.J.) to GWC, October 12, 1917, box 10, GWCP, TUA; Alphonso Sellers to GWC, September 24, 1917, box 10, GWCP, TUA.

29. GWC to My esteemed friend, Rev. Haygood, August 24, 1940, in Kremer, *In His Own Words*, 136.

30. Henry A. Wallace, "The Uniqueness of George Washington Carver," speech delivered at the dedication of the Carver Science Hall at Simpson College on October 5, 1956, Simpson College Archives. Wallace astutely added that Carver integrated the artistic world into scientific and religious views.

31. On the view that a "satisfying country life" was not only profitable and

educational but "fundamentally religious," see "Thirty-fifth Annual Tuskegee Negro Conference Open Wednesday," *Montgomery Advertiser*, January 28, 1926, 7.

32. See Wallace, "The Uniqueness of George Washington Carver."

33. GWC to My beloved friend, Mr. Byrd, March 1, 1927; George Washington Carver, "The Love of Nature," *Guide to Nature*, December 19, 1912. He recycled this in a 1930 article titled "How to Search for Truth."

34. Carver, "How to Search for Truth."

35. See Wallace, "The Uniqueness of George Washington Carver."

36. "Tenth Annual Bible Conference," *Albany (Ga.) Institute News*, March 1915, box 83, GWCP, TUA.

37. *Alexander's* magazine (Boston, Mass.), May 1906; Slatter, "Men I Have Known."

38. See "Smithsonian Gets Carver Portrait," May 3, 1944, box 102, GWCP, TUA.

39. Carver, "The Love of Nature."

40. Kremer, *In His Own Words*, 102.

41. Carver, *Cotton Growing for Rural Schools*, 5.

42. GWC to My beloved Friend, Mr. Byrd, March 1, 1927, in Kremer, *In His Own Words*, 134–35.

43. Incomplete letter, box 62, GWCP, TUA; "Carver Quotes," box 62, GWCP, TUA.

44. Carver, "Suggested Outlines for the Study of Economic Plant Life for Use in Common Schools, High Schools and Academies."

45. Quoted in Burchard, *For His Time and Ours*, 13.

46. GWC to My beloved friend, Principal Ward, May 4, 1939, box 43, GWCP, TUA.

47. Lyman Ward to GWC, August 18, 1939, box 44, GWCP, TUA; GWC to Lyman Ward, August 21, 1939, box 44, GWCP, TUA.

48. H. C. Lyman to GWC, August 29, 1917, box 10, GWCP, TUA.

49. GWC to Jim Hardwick, July 10, 1924.

50. GWC, "How to Search for Truth."

51. Cotton Mather, *The Christian Philosopher: A Collection of the Best Discoveries in Nature, with Religious Improvements* (London, 1721), quoted in Richard Judd, *The Untilled Garden: Natural History and the Spirit of Conservation in America, 1740–1840* (New York: Cambridge University Press, 2009), 26–27. Though a sidelight to the thrust of his excellent book, Judd makes a compelling argument that the "idea of nature as an ecological system owes much to this way of thinking" (28).

52. GWC to My esteemed Friend Judge McCord, December 13, 1927, in Kremer, *In His Own Words*, 137.

53. Although the quote is often attributed to Carver, it can't be found in any primary document. Nevertheless, Carver offered enough similar assertions that it can be safely maintained that the quote does not distort his take, even if he would have been quick to point out that a flower is only part of a plant while a weed is

an entire plant. Thanks to Peter Burchard for confirming this point. Arguably the classic take on the sublime in American environmental history is found in Roderick Nash, *Wilderness and the American Mind* (New Haven: Yale University Press), especially chapter 3; but see also Judd, *The Untilled Garden*, especially 246–77. For a more literary take, see Rob Wilson, *American Sublime: The Genealogy of a Poetic Genre* (Madison: University of Wisconsin Press, 1991).

54. GWC to James T. Hardwick, December 7, 1930, in Burchard, *For His Time and Ours*, 51–52.

55. GWC to My beloved Friend, Mr. Byrd, March 1, 1927.

56. Christy Borth, "My Last Visit with Dr. Carver," *Chemurgic Digest*, April 29, 1944, III, quoted in John S. Ferrell, *Fruits of Creation: A Look at Global Sustainability as Seen through the Eyes of George Washington Carver* (Wynnewood, Pa.: Christian Society of the Green Cross, 1995), 64.

57. GWC to My dear Mr. Woods, September 7, 1940, in Kremer, *In His Own Words*, 141.

58. GWC to My esteemed Friend, Mr. Zissler, March 1, 1932, in Kremer, *In His Own Words*, 138.

59. Glenn Clark, "In the Upper Room with Dr. Carver, March 18, 1939," quoted in Burchard, *For His Time and Ours*, 106.

60. GWC, "Speech at the Jackson High School Auditorium," April 12, 1937, in Kremer, *In His Own Words*, 72–73.

61. Gary Kremer recognized this in asserting that "Carver's mysticism seemed to increase with his age"; Kremer, *In His Own Words*, 140.

62. GWC to Jim Hardwick, November 29, 1931, in Burchard, *For His Time and Ours*, 52. A very similar letter is available at Tuskegee. See partial letters, box 62, GWCP, TUA.

63. GWC to My dear Mrs. Holt, October 14, 1942, in Kremer, *In His Own Words*, 32–33.

64. Bess B. Walcott, "Meet George Washington Carver: American Artist," *Service* (January 1942).

65. "Address of Dr. George Washington Carver at the Martha-Mary Chapel, Greenfield Village, July 29, 1942," *The Herald*, n.d., quoted in Burchard, *For His Time and Ours*, 99.

66. GWC, "How to Search for Truth."

67. Nash, *Wilderness and the American Mind*, 194.

68. James H. Cobb Jr., "Ford and Carver Point South's Way," *Atlanta Journal*, March 17, 1940, quoted in Ferrell, *Fruits of Creation*, 30.

Chapter 9. Where the Soil Is Wasted

1. GWC to H. G. Ritchie, October 7, 1938, quoted in McMurry, *George Washington Carver*, 313.

2. Quoted in Burchard, *For His Time and Ours*, 15.

3. George Washington Carver, "Top Soil and Civilization," *Montgomery Advertiser*, June 21, 1938.

4. George Washington Carver, *Can Live Stock Be Raised Profitably in Alabama?*, TAES Bulletin 41 (April 1936), 3, 8.

5. Ferguson, "Caught in 'No Man's Land,'" 34.

6. Mary Harris Gilmer (Tuskegee class of 1912) to GWC, May 26, 1918, box 10, GWCP, TUA.

7. Illegible to Warren Logan, ca. 1904, box 250, Warren Logan Correspondence, TUA.

8. Kimuel Huggins, "Report: Rural Public School Agricultural Work for 1918, Macon County, Alabama," Extension Files, TUA.

9. Quoted in Mayberry, *The Role of Tuskegee*, 55.

10. Robert E. Zabawa and Sarah T. Warren, "From Company to Community: Agricultural Community Development in Macon County, Alabama, 1881 to the New Deal," *Agricultural History* (spring 1998): 465.

11. Ibid., 466.

12. Ibid., 467.

13. Booker T. Washington, "The Rural Negro Community," *Annals of the American Academy of Political and Social Science* (March 1912): 85–86.

14. For more on the immediate economic impact of the war on cotton, see Edwin J. Clapp, *Economic Aspects of the War* (New Haven: Yale University Press, 1915).

15. Kerr, *The Alabama Experiment Station*, 51.

16. John Shelton Reed and David Joseph Singal, *Regionalism and the South: Selected Papers of Rupert Vance* (Chapel Hill: University of North Carolina Press, 1982), 98. For more on the boll weevil, see James C. Giesen, "The South's Greatest Enemy: The Cotton Boll Weevil and Southern Society, 1894–1930" (PhD diss., University of Georgia, 2004).

17. "Address by Mrs. C. J. Calloway at Annual Conference, 1917"; Aiken, *The Cotton Plantation South since the Civil War*, 93.

18. Quoted in Rupert B. Vance, *Human Factors in Cotton Culture: A Study in the Social Geography of the American South* (Chapel Hill: University of North Carolina Press, 1929), 137.

19. Booker T. Washington, "The Principal's Report to the Board of Trustees of Tuskegee Institute," May 3, 1915, in Mayberry, *The Role of Tuskegee*, 84–85.

20. George R. Bridgeforth to Robert R. Moton, August 31, 1916, Extension Files, TUA; Alabama Extension Service, "'Certification of Merit Farmer' Score Card," Extension Files, Auburn University Archives; "Win the War by Working Six Days per Week," Extension Files, TUA; Thomas M. Campbell, *The Saturday Service League*, Alabama Polytechnic Institute Extension Service Circular 40 (March 1920), 30–36.

21. GWC to Mr. J. W. McCrarey, May 2, 1922, box 12, GWCP, TUA.

22. Charles S. Johnson, *The Negro in American Civilization: A Study of Negro Life and Race Relations in the Light of Social Research* (New York: Henry Holt, 1930), 17; also see Hahn, *A Nation under Our Feet*, 466.

23. *Buffalo (N.Y.) Courier*, January 19, 1917; and *Cincinnati Enquirer*, February 15, 1917, in Extension File Clippings, 1917, Extension Files, TUA.

24. Linda O. McMurry, *Recorder of the Black Experience: A Biography of Monroe Nathan Work* (Baton Rouge: Louisiana State University Press, 1985), 138.

25. Ferguson, "Caught in 'No Man's Land,'" 51.

26. Untitled, ca. 1925, Thomas Monroe Campbell Papers, TUA.

27. Johnson, *Shadow of the Plantation*, 104.

28. Zabawa and Warren, "From Company to Community," 467.

29. Vance, *Human Factors in Cotton Culture*, 130–33; Reed and Singal, *Selected Papers of Rupert Vance*, 100–101; Charles S. Johnson, Edwin R. Embree, and W. W. Alexander, *The Collapse of Cotton Tenancy: Summary of Field Studies and Statistical Surveys, 1933–1935* (Chapel Hill: University of North Carolina Press, 1935), 40–43; John A. Todd, *The World's Cotton Crops* (London: A. & C. Black, 1915), 90.

30. Johnson et al., *The Collapse of Cotton Tenancy*, 34–37, 44–45.

31. Zabawa and Warren, "From Company to Community," 472.

32. Johnson, *Shadow of the Plantation*, 45, 105–6.

33. Johnson, Embree, and Alexander, *The Collapse of Cotton Tenancy*, 12–13.

34. Johnson, *Shadow of the Plantation*, 118.

35. Ibid., 10.

36. Ibid., 94.

37. Ibid., 10, 16.

38. Johnson, *Growing Up in the Black Belt*, 194.

39. Ibid., 197, 17.

40. "Carver's Question Box," January 17, 1925, box 64, GWCP, TUA.

41. Campbell, *The Movable School Goes to the Negro Farmer*, 80–81, 109–10.

42. Carver, "Being Kind to the Soil."

43. Johnson, Embree, and Alexander, *The Collapse of Cotton Tenancy*, 16.

44. "Declarations of the Twenty-fifth Annual Tuskegee Negro Conference," January 19, 1916, Extension Files, TUA.

45. Washington, "The Rural Negro Community," 87.

46. Carver, "Three Delicious Meals Every Day for the Farmer," 4.

47. Theodore Rosengarten, *All God's Dangers: The Life of Nate Shaw*, 108.

48. See Ferguson, "Caught in 'No Man's Land,'" 49.

49. Wright discussed the credit dilemma more thoroughly in Gavin Wright, *Old South, New South: Revolutions in the Southern Economy since the Civil War* (New York: Basic Books, 1986), 98–102.

50. P. O. Davis, "Southern Agriculture: Past, Present, Future," n.d., Alabama Cooperative Extension Service Records, Auburn University Archives.

51. Johnson, Embree, and Alexander, *The Collapse of Cotton Tenancy*, 30.

52. For an example of such a plea, see "Declarations of the Thirtieth Annual Tuskegee Negro Conference," 1921, Extension Files, TUA.

53. Johnson, *Shadow of the Plantation*, 129–30.

54. Rosengarten, *All God's Dangers*, 28, 266–68.

55. See, for instance, Hahn, *A Nation under Our Feet*, 459.

56. George W. Moore (Alligator, Miss.) to GWC, December 1, 1918, box 10, GWCP, TUA.

57. See Johnson, Embree, and Alexander, *The Collapse of Cotton Tenancy*, 8, 22.

58. Johnson, *Shadow of the Plantation*, 117; see also Johnson Embree, and Alexander, *The Collapse of Cotton Tenancy*, 18.

59. Johnson, *Shadow of the Plantation*, 121–22.

60. Ibid., 121.

61. Ibid., 127–28.

62. Campbell, *The Movable School Goes to the Negro Farmer*, 147.

63. Ferguson, "Caught in 'No Man's Land,'" 48. See Ferguson's excellent article for further discussion of the failure of Tuskegee's extension program. Her contention that the program's intent was at least de facto subversive is applicable to Carver's campaign as well. Also see Thomas Monroe Campbell, "Cooperative Extension Work in Agriculture and Home Economics, State of Alabama, a Supplement to the Annual Report of the Agricultural Extension Service as Performed by Negroes for the year ending Dec. 31, 1919," Thomas Monroe Campbell Papers, TUA.

64. "Declarations of the Twenty-fifth Annual Tuskegee Negro Conference"; Campbell, "Cooperative Extension Work in Agriculture and Home Economics, State of Alabama."

65. Quoted in Allen Jones, "Improving Rural Life," 109.

66. Clinton J. Calloway to Booker T. Washington, October 1, 1913, quoted in Ferguson, "Caught in 'No Man's Land,'" 44. At the time Calloway reported the unfriendly feeling, he was the head of Tuskegee's extension division; Campbell, *The Movable School Goes to the Negro Farmer*, 147.

67. Rosengarten, *All God's Dangers*, xx–xxi.

68. Campbell, *The Movable School Goes to the Negro Farmer*, 117.

69. Johnson, *Shadow of the Plantation*, 88.

70. Richard Wright, *Black Boy (American Hunger)* (New York: Harper Perennial, 1993), 40–41; Rhussus L. Perry, "Janey Gets Her Desires," in *Up before Daylight: Life Histories from the Alabama Writers' Project, 1938–1939*, ed. James Seay Brown Jr., 172–73 (Tuscaloosa: University of Alabama Press, 1982).

71. Rupert Vance, "Cotton Culture and Social Life and Institutions of the South," in Reed and Singal, *Selected Papers of Rupert Vance*, 24.

72. Rupert Vance, "The Old Cotton Belt," in Reed and Singal, *Selected Papers of Rupert Vance*, 88. Clinton J. Calloway, Tuskegee's extension director, estimated that supplies and building materials for a new house would cost $559.82. See Clinton J. Calloway, "The Farm Home," Supplement to Farmers' Leaflet 5.

73. Johnson, Embree, and Alexander, *The Collapse of Cotton Tenancy*, 20–21.

74. W. E. B. DuBois, *The Souls of Black Folk*, edited and with an introduction by David W. Blight and Robert Gooding-Williams (New York: Bedford Books, 1997), 120, 128.

75. Johnson, Embree, and Alexander, *The Collapse of Cotton Tenancy*, 15.

76. Johnson, *Shadow of the Plantation*, 121–23.

77. George R. Bridgeforth, "Report of the Jesup Wagon, July 2–9/1906," Extension Files, TUA.

78. Johnson, *Shadow of the Plantation*, 94.

79. Johnson, *Growing Up in the Black Belt*, 17.

80. Rosengarten, *All God's Dangers*, 484–85.

81. Clinton J. Calloway, *Buying Homes among the Farmers*, Farmers Leaflet 2 (November 1901).

82. Johnson, *Shadow of the Plantation*, 85.

83. Ibid., 88.

84. George Washington Carver, *The Need of Scientific Agriculture in the South*, Farmers' Leaflet 7 (April 1902); "Prof. Geo. W. Carver of Tuskegee Institute Visits Homer College—a Farmers' Conference Organized," *Christian Index* (Jackson, Tenn.: CME Church Publishing House), July 2, 1908.

85. Johnson, *Shadow of the Plantation*, 181.

86. BTW to GWC, February 26, 1911. For background on the clash that led to this assessment, see GWC to BTW, February 18, 1911, box 8, GWCP, TUA; GWC to BTW, January 26, 1911, box 8, GWCP, TUA; GWC to BTW, February 21, 1911; and Mark D. Hersey, "'My Work Is That of Conservation': The Environmental Vision of George Washington Carver" (PhD diss., University of Kansas, 2006, 358–61).

87. See BTW to Thomas Jesse Jones, December 2, 1910, in *The Booker T. Washington Papers*, ed. Louis R. Harlan, vol. 10: *1909–1911* (Urbana: University of Illinois Press, 1981), 496–98.

88. McMurry, *George Washington Carver*, 138. For an example of the institute promoting Carver's work along economic grounds, see "The Latest Contribution to Negro Progress," *Tuskegee Alumni Bulletin* 1 (January–March 1914): 1–2, box 128, GWCP, TUA.

89. Monroe Work, "Review: Biography and Science," *Journal of Negro Education* 13 (winter 1944): 84–85.

90. Frank H. Cardoza, *Relation of Weather and Soil Conditions to the Fruit Industry of Southeastern Alabama*, TAES Bulletin 11 (January 1908).

91. GWC to BTW, May 10, 1898. Carver took particular delight in the fact that Auburn later echoed his claim.

92. George Washington Carver, "Eighty Birds of Macon County, Alabama, and Their Relation to Our Prosperity," Bulletin no. 26 (unpublished, 1914), 1, box 65, GWCP, TUA.

93. Alexander M. Ferguson and Lowery L. Lewis, *Elementary Principles of Agriculture* (Sherman, Tex.: Ferguson, 1908), 181–85; Goff and Mayne, *First Principles of Agriculture*, 143–48.

94. Carver, "Eighty Birds of Macon County, Alabama, and Their Relation to Our Prosperity," 1.

95. Ibid., 18–19, 3, 10.

96. See Adam Rome, "'Political Hermaphrodites': Gender and Environmental Reform in Progressive America," *Environmental History* 11 (July 2006): 440, 449–50.

97. This navigation between gender roles also led to whispers about his sexuality, but there is no convincing evidence that he was gay. It is true that he never married, forged close relationships with young men, volunteered as a "rubber" for the IAC's football team, crocheted, and waxed poetic about "floral beauties." Even so, few of those who knew him well believed he was a homosexual. In the early 1910s, he apparently carried on a serious relationship with a woman—whom Carver's best-known personal assistant and good friend, Austin Curtis, believed to be a fellow faculty member—nearly marrying her. A former summer school student wrote Carver, claiming that his wife "would be just delighted to meet Professor and Mrs. Geo. W. Carver. See?" His wife thought "it would be just grand to meet your other half." The timing of his love interest coincides with some of his darkest days at Tuskegee and offers, perhaps, another reason why he did not leave the school following his reassignment to a largely mythical department. See Toby Fishbein interview with Austin Curtis, 33; P. L. Breaux to GWC, January 9, 1911, box 8, GWCP, TUA. Seven years later, another friend wrote Carver noting that it was "dandy to pose as [Carver's] matrimonial agent." See J. M. Marquess (president of the Colored Agricultural and Normal University, Langston, Okla.) to GWC, September 14, 1918, box 10, GWCP, TUA. For a contrary view on his sexuality see http://www.glbtq.com/social-sciences/carver-gw,4.htm, accessed January 12, 2011.

98. GWC to BTW, October 14, 1904, in Kremer, *In His Own Words*, 70.

99. James Wilson to GWC, October 11, 1900, *James Wilson's Private Book No. 8 from September 8, 1900 to June 17, 1901*, James Wilson Papers, ISU Archives.

100. Quotation from GWC to BTW, June 19, 1911, box 8, GWCP, TUA.

101. "The Old Order Changeth," *Afro-American*, February 9, 1918, box 83, GWCP, TUA.

102. Quotations and photographs of George W. Carver, Simpson College Archives, Indianola, Iowa, 13.

103. P. O. Davis, "The Type of Farming We Need," his "New Year's Message to the South," 1938, Alabama Cooperative Extension Service Records, Auburn University Archives.

104. See Vance, *Human Factors in Cotton Culture*, 270–71.

105. Aiken, *The Cotton Plantation South since the Civil War*, 67.

106. Johnson, *Shadow of the Plantation*, 12, 14; Johnson, Embree, and Alexander, *The Collapse of Cotton Tenancy*, 14.

107. Johnson, *Shadow of the Plantation*, 12.

108. Johnson, Embree, and Alexander, *The Collapse of Cotton Tenancy*, 43.

109. Rupert Vance, "The Old Cotton Belt," 119–21. Although Vance conceded that the yeoman was nearly a thing of the past, he would not admit that it ought to be that way. See Rupert Vance, *Farmers without Land*, Public Affairs Pamphlet 12 (Washington, D.C.: Public Affairs Committee, 1938), 28.

110. "Thirty-fifth Annual Tuskegee Negro Conference Opens Wednesday," *Montgomery Advertiser*, January 28, 1926.

111. Henry A. Wallace, "Common Aims in Agriculture," *Tuskegee Messenger* (October, November, December 1936).

112. Russell Lord, *The Agrarian Revival: A Study of Agricultural Extension* (New York: American Association for Adult Education, 1939), 152.

113. Berry, *The Unsettling of America*, 63.

114. Quoted in Pohl, "Louis H. Pammel: Pioneer Botanist," 22–23.

115. Carver, *A Study of the Soils of Macon County, Alabama and Their Adaptability to Certain Crops*, 11.

116. *Soil Survey of Macon County, Alabama* (Washington, D.C.: USDA, 1998), 108.

117. John Archibald and Jeff Hansen, "Land Is Power and Most Who Wield It Are Outsiders," *Birmingham News*, October 13, 2002, available online at http://www.al.com/specialreport/birminghamnews/?blackbelt.html, accessed July 1, 2010; Paul L. Wall, "Changes in the Black Community," *American Journal of Agricultural Economics* 63 (December 1981): 904; Bill Bryson, *The Lost Continent: Travels in Small-Town America* (New York: Harper Perennial, 1987), 71; "Census: Fewer People Do without Indoor Plumbing," *USA Today*, July 5, 2002, available online at http://www.usatoday.com/news/nation/census/2002-07-05-plumbing.htm, accessed August 30, 2010.

Epilogue

1. George Washington Carver, "A Few Notes on the Demonstration by Dr. G. W. Carver to the Cooking School for Chefs," June 29, 1936, box 65, GWCP, TUA.

2. The relevant historiography is beginning to reflect this multifaceted conception of the environmental movement's origins, even if it has not yet made its way

into classrooms and textbooks. See, for instance, Robert E. Kohler, *All Creatures: Naturalists, Collectors, and Biodiversity* (Princeton: Princeton University Press, 2006); Stoll, *Larding the Lean Earth*; Armitage, *The Nature Study Movement*; Judd, *The Untilled Garden*; and Pauly, *Fruits and Plains*.

3. Stoll, *Larding the Lean Earth*, 183.

4. Environmental history textbooks capture the conventional treatment of such impulses. See Ted Steinberg, *Down to Earth: Nature's Role in American History* (New York: Oxford University Press, 2002), 145–47. Liberty Hyde Bailey, Carver, and others who might better represent the era's agrarian impulse do not appear in the index. Nor do they appear in the index of John Opie's *Nature's Nation: An Environmental History of the United States* (New York: Harcout, Brace, 1998).

5. Carver, "Being Kind to the Soil"; Liberty Hyde Bailey, *The State and the Farmer* (New York: Macmillan, 1908), 59; and Stoll, *Larding the Lean Earth*, 183.

6. Clayton S. Ellsworth, "Theodore Roosevelt's Country Life Commission," *Agricultural History* 34 (October 1960): 162.

7. Barrington Moore, "The Scope of Ecology," *Ecology* 1 (January 1920): 4.

8. See William J. Edwards, *Twenty-five Years in the Black Belt* (1918; reprint, Westport, Conn.: Negro Universities Press, 1970), 86–87.

9. Kimberly Smith has probably explored DuBois's environmental thought— and indeed African American environmental thought—more fully than anyone else to date. See Kimberly Smith, *African American Environmental Thought: Foundations* (Lawrence: University of Kansas Press, 2007).

10. Washington, *Up from Slavery*, 265.

11. J. Sullivan Gibson, "The Alabama Black Belt: Its Geographic Status," *Economic Geography* 17 (January 1941): 22.

12. Phillips, *The Land, This Nation*, 10.

13. See ibid., 240.

14. Beeman and Pritchard, *A Green and Permanent Land*, 5.

15. McMurry, "A Vision of the Future."

16. Aiken, *The Cotton Plantation South since the Civil War*, 347.

17. For a brief discussion of some of these lingering issues, see *To Love the Wind and Rain: African Americans and Environmental History*, ed. Dianne D. Glave and Mark Stoll (Pittsburgh: University of Pittsburgh Press, 2006).

18. *The Times Literary Supplement* ranked *Small Is Beautiful* in 1995 as one of the one hundred most influential books written since World War II. For the 1995 list, see http://www.interleaves.org/~rteeter/grttls.html, accessed July 1, 2010.

19. E. F. Schumacher, *Small Is Beautiful: Economics as if People Mattered* (1973; reprint, New York: Harper Perennial, 1989). As the title suggests, the book is about more than agriculture.

20. McMurry, "A Vision of the Future?"

21. Berry, *The Unsettling of America*, 45. Not everyone would agree that

Berry's thought is rooted in a mythical American past. For a contrary view, see Kimberly K. Smith, *Wendell Berry and the Agrarian Tradition: A Common Grace* (Lawrence: University Press of Kansas, 2003), chap. 5.

22. Berry, *The Unsettling of America*, 62.

23. Carver, *How to Build Up and Maintain the Virgin Fertility of Our Soil*, 5.

24. The same year, Carver argued that as "one rides over our beautiful southern states . . . and sees the evidence of erosion and devastation wrought by the forest fires and the woodman's axe he is at once impressed with the importance of the subject" of conservation writ large. See George Washington Carver, *The Need of Scientific Agriculture in the South*, Farmers' Leaflet 7 (April 1902).

25. Thanks to Donald Worster for helping me make this connection.

26. Robinson Jeffers, *Selected Poems* (New York: Vintage Books, 1965), 36.

27. David Danbom, *The World of Hope: Progressivism and the Struggle for an Ethical Public Life* (Philadelphia: Temple University Press, 1987), 241–42.

28. Mart A. Stewart, "If John Muir Had Been an Agrarian: American Environmental History West and South," *Environment and History* 11 (April 2005), 139–62.

INDEX

Abbott, Harry O., 86
abolitionists, 15, 60, 67. *See also* slavery
Adams, Lewis, 74
Afro American, 107, 186
Agassiz, Louis, 189
Agassiz Association, 120
agribusiness. *See* industrial agriculture
agricultural chemistry, 34, 105, 137–39, 166, 169–70
agricultural reform: in antebellum South, 62–63, 68, 77; Carver and, 1, 48, 49, 67, 103, 175–78; and gender, 212; in Progressive Era, 117–18, 145, 147, 168, 174–75, 267n76; scientific agriculture and, 31–32, 33–34, 155; and southern nationalism, 67, 69
agricultural reformers: in antebellum South, 62–63, 64, 66–67; of the New Deal Era, 174–75; in post-Reconstruction Alabama, 77–79; in the Progressive Era, 133, 276n76; mentioned, 11. *See also* agricultural reform
Agriculture, U.S. Department of. *See* USDA
Alabama Department of Agriculture, 79, 80, 124–25
Alabama Grange, 80
Alabama Polytechnic Institute experiment station (Auburn), 88, 124, 125, 130, 134, 135, 147, 157, 172
Albany Institute News, 186
Alcorn Agricultural and Mechanical College, 45, 46
Alexander's magazine, 120, 186
Alston, James, 71, 75, 243n79
American Forestry Association, 212

Ames, Iowa. *See* Iowa Agricultural College (IAC)
Arkansas Valley Town Company, 17
Armstrong, Samuel C., 75, 96
Association of American Agricultural Colleges and Experiment Stations, 97, 105, 136, 149
Auburn, Ala. *See* Alabama Polytechnic Institute experiment station (Auburn)
Axell, Johan Severin, 36–37

back to nature movement, 145, 169
Bailey, Liberty Hyde, 39, 41, 103, 128, 142, 189, 192, 220, 278n4
Ballinger, Richard, 33
Bankhead Jones Farm Tenant Act (1935), 217
Bartram, William, 50, 51, 52–53, 55, 189
Battle, Cullen, 69, 71
Beal, William J., 36–37
Beardshear, William M., 28, 45
Beeler, John F., 17, 20
Beelerville, Kans., 18, 230n48
Bennett, Hugh Hammond, 174
Bentley, John, 11
Berry, Wendell, 106, 107, 216, 225, 278n21
Bessey, Charles Edwin, 25–26, 27, 36–37, 38
Betts, E. C., 77, 80
Black Belt region, 49, 146, 149, 221; cotton production in, 58–59, 70, 77, 79, 197–98, 202, 217; plantation culture in, 58–60, 67–68, 71–73, 77–78, 154, 215, 222; population density in, 217–18; racial issues in, 80, 81, 84, 198–99, 208, 214, 222–23, 224; slavery in, 58; soils

McMillan, Wheeler, 170

McMurry, Linda O., 230n43, 233n23; on Carver and Washington, 161; on Carver as scientist and symbol, 3, 4, 6; on Carver at Simpson, 21; on Carver at Tuskegee, 87; on Carver childhood, 12; on Carver in Kansas, 19; on Carver the Peanut Man, 164; on Moses Carver, 11

migration, African American, 198–201, 215–16

Milholland, Helen and John, 20–23, 28, 33, 41, 43, 84, 98, 160, 163, 166

Minneapolis, Kans., 16–17

Missouri, 13, 14, 84, 227n5

Montgomery, Ala., 59, 116, 151

Montgomery Advertiser, 55, 104, 132, 147, 162

Montgomery and West Point Railroad, 67

Montgomery County, Ala., 55, 84, 131

Moore, Barrington, 39–40

Moore, J. B., 69

Moore, Richard, 16

Morrill Act, 24, 124–25

Moton, Robert Russa, 109, 164

Mueller, Fritz, 36–37

Mueller, Herman, 36–37

Muir, John, 5, 190, 226

Mumford, Lewis, 175

NAACP, 166

Nashville Agrarians, 174–75

National Farm Chemurgic Council, 171, 174, 179

National Sharecroppers Fund, 224

nature study movement, 101–2, 103–4, 105, 112, 116

Nature-Study Review, 34, 102, 249n12

Nebraska, University of, 27, 38

Neosho, Mo., 11, 13, 14, 16

Ness City Times, 230n47

Ness County, Kans., 17–20, 230n45

Ness County News, 19

New Conservationists, 175, 177

New Deal, 171, 174–75, 177–78, 215–16, 217, 223

Newsweek, 174

Newton, Isaac, 145

Newton County, Mo., 9, 10

New Uses Council, 174

New York Times, 15, 180, 181

Nicodemus, Kans., 15

Olathe, Kans., 16

Olmsted, Frederick Law, 67

open-range policy, 64, 74

organic fertilizer, 79, 139–42, 157–58, 160, 219. *See also* compost manuring

Owens, Eliza, 43–44

Pammel, Louis Hermann, 28, 88, 108, 165, 235n52; cotton rot research by, 35–36; on Darwin, 235n54; and emerging field of ecology, 37–40; and evolutionary science, 41, 185, 235n54; and *Flower Ecology*, 37–38, 103, 236n64; as mentor to Carver, 29, 34–36, 42, 44, 45, 83, 101–2, 107, 216, 233n23, 246n8

Panic of 1893, 38, 39

Paola, Kans., 16

Peabody, Charles A., 68–69

Peale, Charles Willson, 189

peanut industry, 164, 167, 179

Penol, 169

Phillips, Martin W., 63

Pinchot, Gifford, 5, 33, 107, 226

plantation culture: agricultural reform and, 67; after Civil War, 69–71, 73, 262n156; ecological impact of, 60–63; labor system of, 69–70, 71–73; in

94–96, 97, 223; Carver's reminiscence
of time at, 191; establishment of,
74–77; funding and material support
at, 85–86, 88–89, 90; poultry yard
issues at, 95–96, 147, 211, 213; and
race relations, 74–76, 81–82, 84–85,
208, 220; Roosevelt visit to, 177; and
scientific agriculture, 156–57; Wallace
address to, 216; Washington as head
of, 75–76, 211, 221. *See also* Tuskegee
Institute extension service
Tuskegee Institute extension service:
and abandonment of Carver's vision,
156–59, 206; "certificates of merit,"
198; and Jessup Wagon, 149–50,
153–55, 156, 205, 208, 262n162; Karen
Ferguson on, 195, 274n63; population
served by, 149–55; and Smith-Lever
Act, 157–58; and white power
structure, 202–7
Tuskegee Land Utilization Project, 217
Tuskegee National Forest, 217
Tuskegee Negro Farmers' Conference,
117, 119; and African American
migration, 198–99; and Carver's
message, 157–58; and crop diversification, 202; and food conservation,
160–61; and industrial agriculture,
216; peanut exhibit at, 165; success of,
114–16
Tuskegee Student, 126, 143, 162

Union Springs, Ala., 56
United Peanut Association, 167
Uphapee Creek, 50, 51
USDA, 6, 44, 111, 135, 149, 223; and chemical fertilizers, 141; and chemurgy
movement, 171; extension program
of, 25, 128, 155–56; Knapp and, 128,
155–57; Lacey Act and, 38–39; and
New Deal, 171, 174; and Wilson as

agriculture secretary, 33, 96–97, 107,
116, 213, 235n39

Vance, Rupert, 175, 207, 215, 277n109
Varner, William, 70, 154
Venable, Francis Preston, 138
voting rights, 73, 74, 81

Waksman, Selman A., 138
Wall, Paul L., 218
Wallace, Alfred Russell, 35
Wallace, Henry A., 30, 170–71, 177, 179,
185–86, 216, 223, 269n30
Wallace, Henry "Harry" Cantwell,
29–34, 170, 177–78
Wallace, "Uncle" Henry, 27, 29, 31–32,
106, 233n11
Wallace's Farmer, 31, 131
Ward, Lyman, 166, 181, 188
Warming, Eugenius, 36–38
Washington, Booker T.: and African
Americans in Macon County,
196–98; and agricultural training for
women, 104; assessment of Carver
by, 210–11; Atlanta Exposition
address by, 75–76, 125; Carver's hiring
by, 45–48; Carver's relationship
with, 33, 87, 94, 121–22, 161; death of,
109, 161, 168, 211; on nature, 221; and
race relations, 75–77, 84, 175, 244n94;
and Tuskegee Experiment Station,
125–26, 195; and Tuskegee extension
service, 148–50, 202; as Tuskegee
principal, 75–77, 86, 87, 90–91, 92, 96,
148; in *Up from Slavery*, 76–77, 104,
115
Washington, George, 62
Washington, John H., 87, 90, 91–93, 96
Watkins, Andrew and Mariah, 14, 16
Watkins, Jabez B., 155
Watson, J. C., 56

Welch, Adonijah, 26
white-tailed deer, 53–54, 55, 213
Whitney, Eli, 54
Wilson, Alexander, 189
Wilson, James "Tama Jim": as agriculture secretary, 33, 96–97, 107, 116, 155, 213, 235n39; in Congress, 32; at IAC, 27–28, 32, 33–34, 44, 45; as mentor to Carver, 29, 33, 34, 42, 45, 94, 101–2, 130, 185
Winterset, Iowa, 20, 27
women, agricultural education and, 104–5

Woodward, T. S., 56, 240n20
Work, Monroe N., 210–11
World War I: African Americans and, 151, 195, 197, 206, 215–16, 265n44; Carver's message during, 133, 158, 160–62, 213; chemurgy movement after, 169–70; cotton industry and, 197–201, 215
World War II, 7, 30, 174, 222–23, 225
Wright, Richard, 207

Yamasee War (1715), 54
Young, Arthur, 63

ENVIRONMENTAL HISTORY AND THE AMERICAN SOUTH

Lynn A. Nelson
Pharsalia: An Environmental Biography of a Southern Plantation, 1780–1880

Jack E. Davis
An Everglades Providence: Marjory Stoneman Douglas and the Environmental Century

Shepard Krech III
Spirits of the Air: Birds and American Indians in the South

Paul S. Sutter and Christopher J. Manganiello, eds.
Environmental History and the American South: A Reader

Claire Strom
Making Catfish Bait out of Government Boys: The Fight against Cattle Ticks and the Transformation of the Yeoman South

Christine Keiner
The Oyster Question: Scientists, Watermen, and the Maryland Chesapeake Bay since 1880

Mark D. Hersey
My Work Is That of Conservation: An Environmental Biography of George Washington Carver